*Development and Society*

*The Dynamics of Economic Change*

# *Development*

## THE DYNAMICS OF

Edited by *DAVID E. NOVACK* and
*ROBERT LEKACHMAN*

# *and Society*

## ECONOMIC CHANGE

ST MARTIN'S PRESS     NEW YORK

SECOND PRINTING

225540  Econ. Hist

## ACKNOWLEDGMENTS

"The Economics of Development" and "Barriers to Economic Development," from *International Trade and Economic Development* by Jacob Viner, 1953, are reprinted by permission of the Clarendon Press, Oxford.

"Is Economic Growth Desirable?," from *The Theory of Economic Growth* by W. Arthur Lewis, 1955, is reprinted by permission of George Allen & Unwin Ltd and Richard D. Irwin, Inc.

"Four Fallacies about Economic Development" by William Letwin is reprinted by permission from the Summer 1963 issue of *Dædalus,* Journal of the American Academy of Arts and Sciences.

"The Stages of Economic Growth" by W. W. Rostow is reprinted by permission from *The Economic History Review,* August 1959.

"Contemporary Theorizing on Economic Growth" by Henry J. Bruton is reprinted from *Theories of Economic Growth,* Bert F. Hoselitz *et al,* eds., by permission of The Free Press. Copyright 1960 by The Free Press, A Corporation.

"Critical Observations on Some Current Notions in the Theory of Economic Development" by Gottfried Haberler is reprinted by permission from *L'Industria,* No. 2, 1957.

"The Size of the Market and the Inducement to Invest," is reprinted by permission from *Problems of Capital Formation in Underdeveloped Countries* by Ragnar Nurkse, Oxford University Press, Inc., 1953.

"Investment Decisions in Underdeveloped Countries" by Henry G. Aubrey is reprinted by permission from *Capital Formation and Economic Growth,* National Bureau Committee for Economic Research. Copyright 1955 by Princeton University Press.

"Land Reform: Defects in Agrarian Structure and Obstacles to Economic Development" is reprinted by permission of the United Nations (1951.II.B.3).

"Population and Economic Development" by Ansley J. Coale, from *The American Assembly, The Population Dilemma,* © 1963, by The American Assembly, Columbia University, N. Y. Reprinted by permission of Prentice-Hall, Inc. Englewood Cliffs, N. J.

"Population Pressures as a Force for Development" is reprinted by permission of Yale University Press from *The Strategy of Economic Development* by Albert O. Hirschman. Copyright 1958 by Yale University Press, Inc.

"A Sociological Approach to Economic Development" by Bert F. Hoselitz is reprinted by permission from *Atti del Congresso Internazionale di Studio sul Problema delle Aree Arretrate* II, 755-78, Milan: Centro Nazionale di Prevenzione e Difesa Sociale, 1955.

"Personality and Economic Growth," from *The Theory of Social Change* by Everett E. Hogan, 1962, is reprinted by permission of the Center for International Studies, Massachusetts Institute of Technology, and Richard D. Irwin, Inc.

"The Achievement Motive in Economic Growth" by David C. McClelland, "The Social, Economic, and Technological Problems of Rapid Urbanization" by Philip M. Hauser, and "The Social and Psychological Determinants of Savings and Investments in Developing Societies" by Richard D. Lambert, from *Industrialization and Society,* Hoselitz and Moore, eds., 1963, are reprinted by permission of UNESCO.

"Cultural and Personality Factors Affecting Economic Growth" by Ralph Linton and "The Problem of Adapting Societies to New Tasks" by Melville J. Herskovits are reprinted from *The Progress of Underdeveloped Areas,* Bert F. Hoselitz, ed., by permission of The University of Chicago Press. Copyright 1952 by The University of Chicago.

"From the Stone Age to the Twentieth Century," from *New Lives for Old* by Margaret Mead, copyright © 1956 by Margaret Mead, is reprinted by permission of William Morrow and Company, Inc. and Victor Gollancz Ltd.

"The Social Anthropology of Economic Underdevelopment" by J. L. Sadie is reprinted by permission from the *Economic Journal,* June 1960.

"Competing Status Systems" by Melvin M. Tumin is reprinted by permission from *Labor Commitment and Social Change in Developing Areas,* Ulbert E. Moore and Arnold S. Feldman, eds., copyright 1960 by the Social Science Research Council, New York.

"Barriers to Economic Development in Traditional Societies: Malabar, a Case Study" by Thomas W. Shea, Jr., is reprinted by permission from *The Journal of Economic History,* December 1959.

"The Culture of Poverty," from *The Children of Sanchez* by Oscar Lewis, is reprinted by permission of Random House, Inc. © Copyright 1961 by Oscar Lewis.

"Mental Health and Technological Change" from *Cultural Patterns and Technical Change,* Margaret Mead, ed., 1955, is reprinted by permission of UNESCO.

"The Conditions of Economic Integration" by Gunnar Myrdal, from *Na-*

*tional Policy for Economic Welfare at Home and Abroad*, Robert Lekachman, ed., 1955, is reprinted by permission of the Trustees of Columbia University in the City of New York.

"International Economic Development" by P. T. Bauer is reprinted by permission from the *Economic Journal*, March 1959.

"A Political Theory of Foreign Aid" by Hans Morganthau is reprinted from *Why Foreign Aid?*, Robert A. Goldwin, ed., (Chicago: Rand McNally, 1963), © 1963 by the Public Affairs Conference Center, University of Chicago.

"A Humanistic Guide to Foreign Aid" by E. F. Shumacher is reprinted from *Commentary*, November 1961. Copyright 1959 by the American Jewish Committee.

"Why Visiting Economists Fail" by Dudley Seers is reprinted from the *Journal of Political Economy*, August 1962, by permission of the University of Chicago Press.

"The Military in the Political Development of the New States" by Edward Shils, is reprinted by permission from *The Role of the Military in Underdeveloped Countries*, John J. Johnson, ed., Princeton University Press, copyright 1962 by the Rand Corporation.

"Non-Western Intelligentsias as Political Elites" by Harry J. Benda is reprinted by permission from the *Australian Journal of Politics and History*, November 1960.

"Individualism and the Role of the State in Economic Growth" by Alexander Eckstein is reprinted from *Economic Development and Cultural Change*, January 1958, by permission of the University of Chicago Press.

# Preface

ECONOMIC DEVELOPMENT has become a world issue only since poor nations glimpsed the possibility that they might become rich. Before the English Industrial Revolution of the eighteenth century, nations quarreled over ideology, religion, territory, and commercial advantage, but they did not define their conflicts as disputes between the under-developed and the developed; poor nations did not expect rich ones to assist them; and rich nations recognized no moral obligation to share their abundance with their less fortunate neighbors.

In each of these respects the mid-twentieth century climate of opinion is significantly different. The nineteenth and twentieth century economic advances of England, the United States, Western Europe, Canada, Australia, New Zealand, and more recently Japan have demonstrated to the rest of the world that the fortunate and the energetic can enjoy a new abundance of consumer goods and services, widely distributed through entire societies. The much-described revolution of rising expectations in the underdeveloped world has fed upon the mass media, the boom in tourism, and the dispersion of American bases and American troops throughout much of the world. The least enlightened Latin American military juntas seize power in the name of economic development. The great Asiatic competition between India and China centers upon compara-tive rates of economic growth. Castro promises Cubans speedy industrializa-tion under socialism. If the spectacle of the affluence of others makes the underdeveloped nations yearn for rapid economic growth, their booming populations and limited natural resources render development absolutely essential to the preservation of social stability.

Few believe that under contemporary conditions the underdeveloped nations can achieve economic take-offs into "self-sustaining growth," to borrow W. W. Rostow's expressive language, without substantial financial, technical, and administrative assistance from the advanced nations and the international agencies. Indeed, not even the United States, blessed in the nineteenth century with a highly favorable ratio of land to population, geographical isolation from European quarrels, and comparatively stable political institutions, succeeded in industrializing itself without substantial injections of English and European capital—and a Civil War. In our time much of the assistance that the poorer nations have received from their richer brothers has been the consequence not of altruism but of cold-war rivalry between the West and the Soviet Bloc, a fact which explains disproportionate Russian disbursements to Cuba as well as lavish American allocations to Taiwan, South Korea, and South Vietnam.

Power politics are an old human story. What is new and encouraging is the timid beginnings of a general commitment by the advanced nations to the assistance of developing countries beyond the limitations of cold-war competition. Such concern is signalized by the General Assembly of the United Nations' adoption in December, 1961 of a resolution designating the 1960's the United Nations Development Decade. Among the multiplying signs of American engagement in the wider development problem are the Alliance for Progress, the Food for Peace Program, the economic portions of the foreign aid program, the great initial success of the Peace Corps, and the increasing American support for the international financial agencies. Although greater resources must be committed by the United States and the prosperous nations of Western Europe, some hope is justified that the 1970's will see a narrowing rather than a widening of the gap between the rich and the poor members of the international community. As Gunnar Myrdal has phrased it, we should be seeking a Welfare World, not simply a Welfare State.

Economic progress depends upon reliable technical knowledge. It demands administrative and organizational skills which are seldom plentiful even in the successful societies of the West. It requires attitudes towards risk and the postponement of immediate gratifications which appear novel to large numbers of the world's population. Economic development shuffles populations, transforms land tenures, and completely shatters traditional work habits. It asks often of new nations a political maturity which is rare anywhere.

Hence the understanding and the encouragement of economic development demand much more than the skills of the economist and the technologist. In economics writers like E. E. Hagen, who has drawn upon psychoanalysis and anthropology, W. W. Rostow, who has operated out of the economic historian's perspective, and Gunnar Myrdal, who has combined the insights of sociology and economics, have struggled with development as a social process. Other social scientists—sociologists, anthropologists, social psychologists, and political scientists—have written much that is valuable to the comprehension of economic change.

This anthology recognizes both the independent capacities of the economist and the role that other specialists must play. Part I, "The Economics of Development," concentrates upon economics in a fairly strict sense. It stresses basic economic concepts, theoretical models of analysis, and economic obstacles to growth. The readings in Part I identify the economist's part in the formulation of plans, the reconciliation of divergent objectives, and the organization of resources. Part II, "The Social Order," centers upon the sociological, psychological, anthropological, and cultural aspects of social change. The final portion of the volume, "The Politics of Development," examines the political conditions which facilitate or impede successful economic development.

Within inevitable limits of space we have tried to collect varied readings of use to teachers of economic development, political science, sociology, contemporary issues, and modern history. It is a pleasure to acknowledge the able research assistance of Miss Barbara A. Ruch and Miss Catharine Stimpson.

DAVID E. NOVACK

ROBERT LEKACHMAN

# Contents

xi

# Part One

---

# The Economics
# of Development

As THE EARLY twentieth century English economist P. H. Wicksteed put it, "A man can be neither a saint, nor a lover, nor a poet, unless he has comparatively recently had something to eat." Of nations it might be said that political enlightenment, social compassion, and cultural achievement are at the least made more possible by the attainment of minimal standards of diet, clothing, and shelter. Social progress is contingent upon economic development.

The economic aspects of development can be conveniently grouped around four questions: (1) What is "underdevelopment"; (2) What do we mean by economic growth; (3) What are the prerequisites of economic growth; and (4) What impedes growth in the underdeveloped areas of the world.

Underdevelopment as a term implies a comparison with more advanced nations. Countries whose real per capita income is markedly below that of the United States, Canada, Western Europe, and Australia qualify as underdeveloped. Japan, South Africa, Mexico and most of Southern and Eastern Europe, enjoying real per capita incomes somewhere between the advanced and the underdeveloped nations, are frequently placed in the category of "intermediate" development. It is still more illuminating, however, to distinguish the developed from the underdeveloped by the criterion of economic performance. The poor lands suffer not only from low real incomes but from low real incomes which fluctuate erratically around minimal average values. The developed countries, in contrast, enjoy both higher per capita real incomes and continuous growth in these incomes. It has been said that the poor are poor because they have been poor. Indeed the general ill-health, low levels of literacy, rapidly expanding populations, and brief life expectancies of the poorer nations are both consequences of poverty and barriers to overcoming poverty. Daily life for more than half the world's population is a desperate, bleak, nearly hopeless struggle.

Economic growth itself may be defined as continuous, substantial increases in per capita consumption of goods and services. This is a definition at least as old as Adam Smith's *Wealth of Nations*. Growth is the more general term applying to economies of many different varieties. Development, while partially synonymous with growth, emphasizes the impediments in the path of steady economic improvement in the poorer nations.

Growth generally depends upon the size and quality of the labor force, the natural resources available, the quality of technology, and the amount, character, and rate of accumulation of capital. It is the combination in any economy of these productive resources which decides the size and the nature of real output. And of the four, capital may be regarded as most important as a cause of change. For the underdeveloped countries the key issue often presents itself as the initiation of rapid capital accumulation. Economists generally agree that such accumulation in turn depends upon the appearance in sufficient quantity of innovation and work discipline, the development of social overhead capital, and agrarian reform.

From a slightly different angle of vision, these preconditions of sustained economic development often loom as major obstacles. When they are partially overcome, developing nations are likely to encounter next accelerated population growth, inflation, and foreign exchange shortages. In the appearance of these new barriers to smooth expansion is often found a cause of the chronic political instability of the developing nations.

# The Meaning
# of Development

THE THREE ARTICLES which follow are attempts to define precisely the concepts of economic development. After examining a number of alternative formulations, Viner concludes that the best definition of economic development incorporates the *possibility* of rising real per capita income as its central feature.

W. Arthur Lewis' closely reasoned essay analyzes the costs and the benefits of economic modernization. Lewis opts for growth primarily because growth promotes humanistic values. In any event, as he wryly observes, the pressure of population on resources is rapidly removing any bearable alternative to growth. The fate of underdeveloped lands that do not grow is increasing misery and perpetually declining living standards. William Letwin addresses himself to some of the defects of logic and language which have plagued development economics. Clearer terminology and abstaining from easy generalization would help economists to distinguish more reliably the relative merits of agriculture and manufacturing, capital saving and capital using techniques, investment in the private and investment in the public sectors, and rapid versus slow economic development.

# Jacob Viner

## The Economics of Development

THE OUTPUT OF LITERATURE on 'economic' development has in recent years reached massive proportions. The literature, however, is extraordinarily lacking in explicit definition of the basic terms it employs, and if one attempts to find from the context what definitions are implicit one discovers that a wide range of different and often conflicting concepts is being covered by a single verbal label. What, for instance, is an 'underdeveloped country'? Let me examine the most common criteria of 'underdevelopment' as they appear in the current literature.

1. A country is often labelled as underdeveloped merely or mainly because it has a low ratio of population to area. Since the term 'underdeveloped' always carries with it the implication that development is feasible and desirable, this usage overrates the importance of mere space, whether for economic or any other significant purpose. There are 'empty spaces' which it is not in anyone's interest to have filled. In the present state of knowledge, the Arctic and the Antarctic, the Sahara Desert, and even the great tropical jungles, are not properly to be regarded as underdeveloped areas unless 'underdeveloped' is to be used as synonymous with undeveloped.

It is a different matter if the sparsely settled area is 'rich' in natural resources in an economically significant sense. In the ordinary geography and travel books, and in the official handbooks of most countries, however, all areas tend to be labelled rich in resources, even when the 'resources' are unproven, or are of low quality, or are inaccessible, or are of a kind which has low economic value per unit of volume even at the point of consumption so that they are valuable assets only when located near important centres of population. The technique of discovery of hidden mineral resources is constantly improving, and new uses are constantly being found for organic and mineral materials which previously had no or limited serviceability. It is proper therefore to regard any extensive area as having potential value even if to date no one has found a way of making a decent living in it or from it. It nevertheless seems to be true that in the entire past century the only 'empty spaces' of any size which have been settled by a population which has succeeded in earning therein even a moderately high *per capita* income have been

4

areas with good soil and good climate, and no more of such large empty spaces seem to exist. There is no sense in wasting scarce resources in 'developing' areas which cannot provide a decent living for human beings, but a good deal of effort and wealth, and even a greater deal of talk, are being wasted on such areas.

2. Scarcity of capital as shown by the prevalence of high interest rates is often used as a sign that there is underdevelopment. This is not a decisive test, however. Until tight national controls on the export of capital became common, there was a high degree of international mobility of capital, with the consequence that borrowers of equal creditworthiness were able to borrow at not greatly dissimilar rates of interest regardless of their location. Before 1914, India, Canada, the United States, the Argentine, and Australia borrowed long-term capital in the London money-market at substantially similar rates of interest. Where debtors were charged high rates, it was not because they operated in underdeveloped countries but because their past records showed them to be uncreditworthy or because the prospects that they would be able to meet their debt obligations were unfavourable.

High interest rates, moreover, are an ambiguous test as to the kind of 'scarcity' of capital which is prevailing. Interest rates may be high because the risk premium is high, or because the marginal productivity function of capital is high and has high elasticity, or because capital has so far been available only for the most urgent purposes but would have low marginal productivity if more abundantly used. All three would ordinarily be regarded as instances of capital scarcity, but there would be important economic differences between them. It can be taken for granted that for substantial economic expansion increase of capital is always a necessary condition. But only in the second case would it be clear that substantially increased investment would be economically justifiable, that is, would add sufficiently to the national output to meet depreciation and reasonable interest costs.

Another type of criterion of scarcity of capital is often used, namely, the ratio of capital supply to the supplies of other categories of factors of production. As a practical test, this probably has a substantial measure of validity, although abstract theory gives only qualified support to the proposition that where the ratio of capital to other resources is low, the marginal productivity of capital will be high. Cases are conceivable, because of, let us say, an unfavourable climate, or of bad government, where the marginal productivity functions of all the factors taken seriatim, and therefore the overall productivity of the combined factors whatever the proportions in which they are combined, are low. The factors of production, moreover, are in some degree rival or competitive even if it is true that in general they are more complementary or cooperative than rival. It is for this and other reasons at least theoretically conceivable, therefore, that there may be national economies where the marginal productivity function of capital is low beyond a fairly early stage of investment even though natural resources are abundant and good in quality and even though the marginal productivity function of labour is high and has high elasticity, provided the marginal productivity function of labour is high even at low levels of investment. If such cases exist, increase in the amount of capital investment per unit of labour employed, or per acre, would not result in an appreciable increase in *per capita* output after allowance for the costs of the capital itself and its maintenance. These capital costs must not be neglected. Even if the capital came from abroad as a free grant, there would be the costs of maintenance, and of defraying time-depreciation, use-depreciation, product-obsolescence, and process-obsolescence. And when the capital is the result of domestic accumulation, or is borrowed from abroad, the interest charges have to be met, either as payments to the lenders, or as opportunity-costs reflecting the sacrifice of alternative uses of the capital.

3. The most commonly used criterion for classification of countries as developed or underdeveloped is the ratio of industrial output to total output or of industrial population to total population. In an earlier lecture, I pointed out that while it is true that the ratio of non-agricultural to total population tends to be highly correlated positively with *per capita* income, the degree of industrialization may be and often is a consequence rather than a cause of the level of prosperity, and that where agriculture is prosperous not only do tertiary or service industries tend spontaneously to grow, but there is widespread tendency to use disposable surplus income derived from agricultural prosperity to subsidize uneconomic urban industry, with the consequence that the overall level of *per capita* income, while still comparatively high, is lower than it would be if urban industry were not artificially stimulated.

I do not challenge the semantic sovereignty of economists or of anyone else, and if there is determination to continue to use 'underdevelopment' and 'non-industrialization' as synonymous terms, I must reconcile myself to the fact even if I do not approve of it. What I do have a right and a professional duty to insist upon, however, is that the practice is either arbitrary, or is more or less conscious question-begging, having as its consequence, and sometimes as its deliberate intention, the evasion of analysis which would lead to unwelcome conclusions.

4. I would question also the expediency of identifying 'underdeveloped' countries with 'young countries'. There are no satisfactory criteria for the 'age' of a country, and if, as is common, date of settlement by people of

European stock is taken as the test of age, Brazil is an older country than the United States, and China and India have not been born yet. Except for the United States, the countries outside Europe with the highest levels of *per capita* income are countries which were 'empty spaces' until fairly late in the nineteenth century, and some of the 'oldest' countries are the poorest. Time brings all things, but not to the same country. To some it brings prosperity; to others persistent poverty.

✓5. A more useful definition of an underdeveloped country is that it is a country which has good potential prospects for using more capital or more labour or more available natural resources, or all of these, to support its present population on a higher level of living, or, if its *per capita* income level is already fairly high, to support a larger population on a not lower level of living. This definition puts the primary emphasis where I would think it properly belongs, on *per capita* levels of living, on the issue of poverty and prosperity, although it leaves room for secondary emphasis on quantity of population. On the basis of this definition, a country may be underdeveloped whether it is densely or sparsely populated, whether it is a capital-rich or a capital-poor country, whether it is a high-income *per capita* or low-income *per capita* country, or whether it is an industrialized or an agricultural country. The basic criterion then becomes whether the country has good potential prospects of raising *per capita* incomes, or of maintaining an existing high level of *per capita* income for an increased population.

This definition, I am aware, would not be universally acceptable. It is not only that it would be objectionable to those who want 'economic development' even at the cost of a lowering of *per capita* income levels provided it brings the filling up of empty spaces, or urbanization, or industrialization. Patriotic citizens may want their national economies to grow in size of aggregate income or of aggregate output because of prestige considerations or strategic considerations even if this involves a lowering of average living standards. To others, living standards may be a weighty consideration, but in terms of the living standards—and conceivably also the size—of a particular class or a particular regional category of the population, rather than and perhaps to the total disregard of the average standard of living of the people as a whole. A colonial power may be interested in the economic development of a possession as an incident to its becoming an enlarged market for the mother country's export products or an enlarged source of supply of cheap foodstuffs, or raw materials, or military manpower, without regard to the economic welfare of the colonial population. All of these considerations have at one time or another been associated with the term 'economic development'. I do not question their claims to attention.

While the supplementing of data as to economic aggregates by *per capita* averages provides additional and often essential information, however, even this does not suffice for some purposes. Let us suppose, for instance, that a country which has embarked on a programme of economic development engages in periodic stock-taking of its progress, and finds not only that aggregate wealth, aggregate income, total population, total production, are all increasing, but that *per capita* wealth, income, production, are also all increasing. All of these are favourable indices, but even in combination do they suffice to show that there has been 'economic progress', an increase in economic 'welfare', rather than retrogression?

Suppose that someone should argue that the one great economic evil is the prevalence of a great mass of crushing poverty, and that it is a paradox to claim that a country is achieving economic progress as long as the absolute extent of such poverty prevailing in that country has not lessened or has even increased? Such a country, nevertheless, might be able to meet all the tests of economic development which I have just enumerated. If its population has undergone substantial increase, the numbers of those living at the margin of subsistence or below, illiterate, diseased, undernourished, may have grown steadily consistently with a rise in the average income of the population as a whole.

Not only this, but if immigration is a significant factor, these statistical tests are consistent with no native having undergone an improvement in his economic status beyond having more children survive to their teens instead of dying in infancy, and with no adult descendant of native parents having a higher level of income than did his parents or grandparents. It requires only one additional condition, that the immigrants shall not be as well off as they would have been if they had stayed in their native land, to make these statistical indexes of 'successful' economic development be consistent with no single individual being better off than or even as well off as his parents were.

Were I to insist, however, that the reduction of mass poverty be made a crucial test of the realization of economic development, I would be separating myself from the whole body of literature in this field. In all the literature on economic development I have seen, I have not found a single instance where statistical data in terms of aggregates and of averages have not been treated as providing adequate tests of the degree of achievement of economic development. I know, moreover, of no country which regards itself as underdeveloped which provides itself with the statistical data necessary for the discovery of whether or not growth in aggregate national wealth and in *per capita* income are associated with decrease in the absolute or even relative extent to which crushing poverty prevails.

There is a school of thought with respect to economic development which is aware of the point I have been discussing, but believes that to subject a national programme of economic development to the requirement that it shall prevent an increase in the absolute extent of severe poverty may doom the programme to failure without lasting benefit to any sector of the population. They hold that in many cases all that is practicable, at least for some time, is to increase the national area of economic health and strength, perhaps relatively but at least absolutely, without preventing or even retarding, and possibly even while stimulating, the growth of the area of desperate poverty. Eventually, they contend, the prosperity will trickle down to the lower levels of the population, and the national resources will become abundant enough to make possible large-scale programmes to rescue them from their poverty, whereas a direct and immediate attack on mass poverty would result only in the squandering of the limited national resources on temporary palliatives, with increases in the number of the desperately poor as the only important result.

This school is unaware, I suspect, that the views it holds are very close to one of Malthus's doctrines. Malthus was deeply concerned about the difficulty of raising the masses of the English poor from their level of desperate poverty, because of their tendency, as he believed, to absorb any increase in productivity in an increase in their numbers instead of using it to raise their standard of living. The remedy which he most emphasized was the limitation of births through postponement of marriage, with or without 'moral restraint', but without births, before marriage. He obviously did not have much confidence, however, in the practicality of this remedy, and he supported as an alternative or supplementary remedy the promotion within the English economy of what might be termed enclaves of economic privilege, whose members would be recruited from those sections of the population which could be relied upon not to absorb increases in income wholly in natural increase of population. It was largely on this ground that Malthus supported tariff protection for English agriculture as a means of increasing the prosperity of the landed classes and thus increasing the numbers of those who could be relied upon to use increased income either to raise their standard of living or for investment instead of to increase the size of their families. It is not an attractive doctrine. I am not aware, however, that where the population problem as Malthus envisaged it is a fact, and capital is scarce, patently superior alternatives are readily discoverable and applicable. . . .

# W. Arthur Lewis

## Is Economic Growth Desirable?

LIKE EVERYTHING ELSE, economic growth has its costs. If economic growth could be achieved without any disadvantages, everybody would be wholly in its favour. But since growth has real disadvantages, people differ in their attitude to growth according to the different assessment which they give to its advantages and disadvantages. They may dislike the kind of society which is associated with economic growth, preferring the attitudes and institutions which prevail in stable societies. Or, even if they are reconciled to the institutions of growing societies, they may dislike the transitional processes in the course of which stable societies are converted into growing societies; they may therefore conclude either that the benefits of growth are not worth the cost of the disturbance it involves, or also that growth should be introduced slowly, so that the society may have as long as possible to adjust itself to the changes which economic growth requires. We shall begin with the advantages of growth, and then consider the costs of growth in terms of the attitudes it requires, and in terms of the disturbances involved in the process of transition.

### THE BENEFITS OF ECONOMIC GROWTH

The advantage of economic growth is not that wealth increases happiness, but that it increases the range of human choice. It is very hard to correlate wealth and happiness. Happiness results from the way one looks at life, taking it as it comes, dwelling on the pleasant rather than the unpleasant, and living without fear of what the future may bring. Wealth would increase happiness if it increased resources more than it increased wants, but it does not necessarily do this, and there is no evidence that the rich are happier than the poor, or that individuals grow happier as their incomes increase. Wealth decreases happiness if in the acquisition of wealth one ceases to take life as it comes, and worries more about resources and the future. There is, indeed some evidence that this is the case; in so far as economic growth results from alertness in seeking out and seizing economic opportunities, it is only to be expected that it should be associated with less happiness than we find in societies where people are not so concerned with growth. There is evidence of much greater mental disturbance in the United States of America than there is in other countries, and, even when allowance is made for differences in statistical reporting, it is at least plausible that the higher suicide rate is causally connected with the drive for greater success in an already rich community. We certainly cannot say that an increase in wealth makes people happier. We cannot say, either, that an increase in wealth makes people less happy, and even if we could say this, it would not be a decisive argument against economic growth, since happiness is not the only good thing in life. We do not know what the purpose of life is, but if it were happiness, then evolution could just as well have stopped a long time ago, since there is no reason to believe that men are happier than pigs, or than fishes. What distinguishes men from pigs is that men have greater control over their environment; not that they are more happy. And on this test, economic growth is greatly to be desired.

The case for economic growth is that it gives man greater control over his environment, and thereby increases his freedom.

We can see this first in man's relations with nature. At primitive levels, man has to struggle for subsistence. With great drudgery he succeeds in wresting from the soil barely enough to keep himself alive. Every year he passes through a starvation period for several months, because the year's crop barely lasts out until the next harvest. Regularly he is visited by famine, plague or pestilence. Half his children die before reaching the age of ten, and at forty his wife is wrinkled and old. Economic growth enables him to escape from this servitude. Improved techniques yield more abundant and more varied food for less labour. Famine is banished, the infant mortality rate falls from 300 to 30 per thousand; the death rate from 40 to 10 per thousand. Cholera, smallpox, malaria, hookworm, yellow fever, plague, leprosy and tuberculosis disappear altogether. Thus life itself is freed from some of nature's menaces. Not everybody considers this a gain. If you think that it is better to die than to live, and best not to be born, you are not impressed by the fact that economic growth permits a reduction of death rates. But most of us are still primitive enough to take it as axiomatic that life is better than death.

Economic growth also gives us freedom to choose greater leisure. In the primitive state we have to work extremely hard merely to keep alive. With economic growth we can choose to have more leisure or more goods, and we do indeed choose to have more of both. The opposite impression is created if a comparison is made between impoverished agricultural countries and rich industrial countries, since in the former labour is idle through much of the year, when the weather is unfavourable to agriculture, whereas in the latter men work regularly throughout the year; but this is a false comparison. If we compare not industry with agriculture, but the industrial sector in rich with the industrial sector in poor countries, and similarly the agricultural sector in both countries, we shall find almost invariably shorter hours of work in each sector, as income grows; and also less drudgery, with increased use of mechanical power.

Also, it is economic growth which permits us to have more services, as well as more goods or leisure. In the poorest communities sixty or seventy per cent of the people are needed in agriculture to procure food; whereas in the richest countries twelve to fifteen per cent suffice to give a standard of nutrition twice as good. The richer countries can therefore spare more people for other activities—to be doctors, nurses and dentists; to be teachers; to be actors and entertainers; to be artists or musicians. Many of the 'higher' activities which philosophers value—art, music, the study of philosophy itself—are in a sense a luxury which society can afford to develop only as economic growth permits it to spare increasing numbers from the basic task of growing food. It is true that only a relatively small surplus is needed to support the arts, and that some of the highest artistic achievements date back to societies where the masses of the people were very poor. The raising of living standards over the past century has widened the opportunity to appreciate and practise the arts, without necessarily affecting the quality or quantity of the best art one way or the other. However, leaving aside the highest art, there has without doubt been an enormous increase in popular leisure and the popular opportunities for enjoying what were previously the luxuries open to very few. Relatively far more people hear the work of the best composers today than heard the work of Mozart or of Bach in their own times, or saw the work of Rembrandt or of El Greco.

Women benefit from these changes even more than men. In most under-developed countries woman is a drudge, doing in the household tasks which in more advanced societies are done by mechanical power—grinding grain for hours, walking miles to fetch pails of water, and so on. Economic growth transfers these and many other tasks—spinning and weaving, teaching children, minding the sick—to external establishments, where they are done with greater specialization and greater capital, and with all the advantages of large scale production. In the process woman gains freedom from drudgery, is emancipated from the seclusion of the household, and gains at last the chance to be a full human being, exercising her mind and her talents in the same way as men. It is open to men to debate whether economic progress is good for men or not, but for women to debate the desirability of economic growth is to debate whether women should have the chance to cease to be beasts of burden, and to join the human race.

\*     \*     \*     \*     \*

## THE ACQUISITIVE SOCIETY

If the benefits listed above were available without cost, nearly every-one would favour them. Many people, however, consider that the attitudes and institutions which are necessary for economic growth are undesirable in themselves; they prefer the attitudes and institutions which belong to stable societies.

In the first place, they dislike the economizing spirit, which is one of the conditions of economic growth. If other things are equal, growth is most rapid in those societies where people give their minds to seeking out and seizing opportunities of economic gain, whether by means of increasing earnings, or by means of reducing costs. And this propensity to economize, though it might equally well spring solely from a desire to reduce drudgery and increase the leisure available for enjoyment or for spiritual pursuits, seems in practice not to be well developed except when it is associated with a desire for wealth, either for its own sake, or for the social prestige or the power over people which it brings. It is arguable that economy is a virtue, in the sense that there is the same sacred duty imposed upon man to abhor waste and to make the best use of his resources as there is to abhor murder and to look after the widows and orphans—in fact the parable of the talents says that this is so. Not everyone agrees that we have a sacred duty to fuss and bother about resources, or about fleeting time; these would say that economy costs too much in nervous energy and human happiness, and is rather a vice than a virtue. They might admit a duty to economize or work enough to reach some minimum standard of living, necessary for health and comfort (a dubious concept) but would argue that economy beyond this level is not worth the effort. Moreover, even those who accept economy to be a virtue may nevertheless deplore the fact (if it is a fact) that this virtue is found only in association with the vice (if it is a vice) of materialism. It is possible to desire that children should be taught to make the best use of the resources and opportunities available to them (the virtue of economy), and at the same time not to want more than they already have (to avoid the vice of cupidity). If this were done, and if the teaching were effective, there would still be economic growth; only, instead of its showing itself in ever rising material standards of living, it would show itself in ever increasing leisure at constant material standards; and if this leisure were not to result also in the ever-increasing vice of idleness (if this is a vice), children would have also to be taught to use their leisure in ways which resulted neither in idleness, nor in the production of economic goods and services. We cannot, in practice, get very far by pursuing lines of enquiry which depend on assuming human nature to be other than it is. Man likes to have more wealth, likes to economize, and likes to be idle. None of these desires seems to be intrinsically either virtuous or vicious, but any one of them pursued to its extremes, in disregard of other duties, obligations or rights results in unbalanced personalities and also in harm to other persons. It is just as much possible for a society to be 'not materialistic enough', as it is for it to be 'too materialistic'. Or, to put the matter the other way round, economic growth is desirable, but we can certainly have too much of it (more than is good for spiritual or social health) just as well as we may have too little of it.

Exactly the same comment can be made in relation to individualism, which is the second score on which economic growth is attacked. It seems to be the case that economic growth is more likely if individuals attend primarily to their own interests and those of their more immediate relations than if they are bound by a much wider net of social obligations. This is why economic growth is associated, both as cause and as effect, with the disappearance of extended family and joint family systems; with the erosion of social systems based on status (slavery, serfdom, caste, age, family, race) and their substitution by systems based upon contract and upon equality of opportunity; with a high level of vertical social mobility; and with the decline of tribal bonds, and the reduced recognition generally of the claims of social groups. This is another problem which cannot be solved by making a virtue of one side of the argument and a vice of the other. There are some rights which all individuals ought to have, and which should be protected against all social claims; and at the same time every individual belongs to a group, or whole series of groups, whose existence is necessary to his own social health, and whose continuance depends upon his recognizing the claims of the group and loyally accepting its authority. The growth of individualism in the past five hundred years has had its evil side, but it has also been a valuable and liberating influence. Economic growth cannot therefore be attacked for being associated with individualism as if the only good things in human relations were tribalism, social status, extended family relations, and political authoritarianism.

A third line of attack upon economic growth derives from its association with reliance on reason. Economic growth depends upon improving technology, and this in turn is greatest where men have a reasoning attitude both towards nature and also towards social relations. Now the reasoning mind is suspect, either because it is believed to result in religious agnosticism or in atheism, or also because it is considered incompatible with the acceptance of authority. As for religious belief, it is an open question whether decline of belief in God or gods is to be blamed for the evils of our time, or even whether the evils of our time are greater than those of previous ages in which religious belief was commoner. But, in any case, it is not true that belief in the importance of reason is inconsistent with belief in God. The existence of God cannot be proved or disproved by rational means, so there is no reason whatsoever why the most rational of men should not also believe in the existence of God. Reason erodes not religion but authority, and it is only in so far as religion is based upon authority that the reasoning mind is hostile to religion. But in this sense the reasoning mind is just as hostile to science as it is to religion; for it is hostile to any attempt to claim that current doctrine is not open to re-examination from the roots upward, or that only the initiated have the right to question its validity. Here again, however, as with materialism and with individualism, so also with reason; truth is not to be found by identifying virtue with one only of two opposites. For, just as materialism and spirituality are both desirable, so also society needs to have both reason and authority. The good life is founded in weaving a pattern of opposite principles, not in rejecting some and using only the others.

A fourth line of attack is pursued by those who do not like the growth of scale which is associated with economic growth. The economies of scale show themselves, in the first instance, in the division of labour, and in the use of machinery. This is disliked by some who dislike machine made goods, and who prefer the products of the skilled handicraftsman. Economic growth destroys old handicraft skills, and though it creates even more new skills, machine skills and others (for specialization greatly increases the range of skills) there are many people who regret the passing of the old skills and the old craft products, and who find no consolation either in the growth of the new skills or in the multiplication and cheapening of output which mass-production makes possible. The principle of specialization is itself attacked, for specialization results in people having to do the same thing over and over again and this, whether it be turning nuts on bolts, or packing chocolates into boxes, or repeating the same university lecture, or practising musical scales, or taking out appendixes, is necessarily boring, until one gets so used to one's job that one can do it without giving the whole of one's mind to it.

The economies of scale show themselves also in the growth of the size of the administrative unit. Thus businesses, units of governments, and other organizations grow in scale. In the process, men are separated from the ownership of their tools, and are proletarianized. Large scale organization brings with it also peculiar social tensions; such organizations have to be run on hierarchical lines, which means that a few command while the majority obey, however much one may seek to democratize the process; these organizations have also to find some means of distributing work and reward which is at the same time efficient and accepted as just. We have not yet succeeded in learning how to run large scale organizations without creating unrest, and many people therefore think that we would be better off without them.

Large scale organizations are also disliked because of the discipline they impose; day after day men must rise at the same hour, arrive at their place of work at the same hour, do much the same things, and return home at the same time. Some think that this makes life drab and monotonous, and reduces human beings to the mechanical role of cogs in some vast wheel. They would prefer that men should not be tied to the clock, and should have greater freedom of choice from day to day, though it is by no means clear either that the man who works in the one-man business is less a slave of the clock, or that having regular habits is something to be deplored.

The economies of large scale organization also result in the growth of towns, especially when this is associated with growing real income per head, which increases the demand for manufactured products and for services relatively to the demand for agricultural products. In so far as the revolt against large towns is associated with a preference for agricultural occupations, it is really a revolt against technological progress. For it is technological progress which enables a country to produce with fifteen per cent of its population enough food to feed the whole, and if we are to return to the days when seventy per cent of the people were needed upon the land either we must abandon all that agricultural science has taught us, or else we must reduce hours of work to about ten a week. It is technological progress in agriculture which results in the growth of urban occupations, but it is the economies of large scale organization which result in these urban occupations being concentrated in ever larger towns. That this is undesirable is by no means clear. The majority of people, when given the chance of working in the town or in the village, choose the town—this is why towns grow at the expense of villages; only a minority prefer the village to the town, and many of those who denounce the town are in fact careful to avoid living in villages. If towns are thrown up in a great hurry, without proper planning or control, they can indeed be slummy, drab, ugly and unhealthy; but in these days there is no reason why new towns (or even old ones for that matter) should not be as beautiful, gracious, healthy and inspiring as any village, as well as providing far wider opportunities for exercising body, mind and soul than any village could ever hope to offer.

Finally, economic growth may be deplored in so far as it is dependent upon inequality of income. That this dependence exists cannot be denied since growth would be small or negative if differential awards were not available for hard work, for conscientious work, for skill, for responsibility and for initiative. It is arguable in any given situation whether the existing differentials are too great or too small, in the restricted sense of being greater or less than is required to achieve the desired rate of economic growth. But it is not arguable, as the rulers of the U.S.S.R. soon discovered, that significant economic growth could be achieved even if there were no differentials at all. Now, part of the revolt against economic growth on this score is no more than an argument that in some particular place or time the differentials existing are greater than are necessary for the achieved level of growth, and are due to faulty social organization. To this extent the argument simply becomes one of altering social institutions (inheritance of property, ownership of land, taxation, educational opportunities, etc.) in ways which alter the distribution of income or of property without reducing the rate of economic growth. But there are also situations where the degree of differentiation which economic growth demands is not acceptable even when it is fully admitted that smaller differentiation would reduce growth—for example, situations where foreign teachers or technicians cannot be had except at salaries which are high by local standards, or where pioneering foreign or domestic entrepreneurs are unwilling to initiate developments unless they are allowed the chance to make and keep profits at a rate far in excess of what is locally thought to be 'reasonable'. The economic test in such matters is that of supply and demand: 'reasonable' differentials are those salaries or profits which are objectively necessary in the situation to secure the required supply of skill or initiative. But what is 'reasonable' on this test may well be 'unreasonable' by some other standard of merit or social justice.

Three conclusions follow from this analysis. First, some of the alleged costs of economic growth are not necessary consequences of growth at all—the ugliness of towns or the impoverishment of the working classes, for instance. Secondly, some of the alleged evils are not in fact intrinsically evil—the growth of individualism, or of reasoning, or of towns, for example. As in all human life, such things can be taken to excess, but they are not intrinsically any less desirable than their opposites. From this it follows, however, thirdly, that the rate of economic growth can be too high for the health of society. Economic growth is only one good thing among many, and we can take it to excess. Excessive growth may result in, or be the result of, excessive materialism, excessive individualism, excessive mobility of population, excessive inequality of income, or the like. Societies are not necessarily wise to choose to speed up their rate of growth above its current level; if they do, they will enjoy substantial benefits, but they may also incur substantial costs, in social or in spiritual terms, and whether the potential gains exceed the potential losses must be assessed separately in each situation as best we may. It is because economic growth has both its gains and its losses that we are all almost without exception ambivalent in our attitudes towards economic growth. We demand the abolition of poverty, illiteracy and disease, but we cling desperately to the beliefs, habits and social arrangements which we like, even when these are the very cause of the poverty which we deplore.

### PROBLEMS OF TRANSITION

Special problems arise when it is a matter of introducing economic growth into societies which have existed for some centuries at low levels more or less of economic stagnation. For it is then necessary to transform beliefs, habits and institutions, and though in due course when the new beliefs, habits and institutions have been going for some time, and have become firmly rooted, a new dynamic equilibrium may be reached which is in every sense superior to the old static social equilibrium, nevertheless the transition may produce temporary but very painful situations.

One of the more obvious of these is changing peoples' habits of work. For example, suppose that copper is discovered in a very primitive country where all the people have land of their own which enables them to live to their own satisfaction, though at very low levels of health, of material standards, or of culture. These people do not want to work in copper mines, and it may be that they will not voluntarily accept employment at any wage which would make it remunerative to work the mines. On the other hand, it is also possible that if they were forced to work in the mines the wealth they could thereby produce would make it possible to give them very much higher standards of material well-being, of health, of education and of culture. Suppose also that if initially forced they would after a while acquire such a taste for the new kind of work, such an appreciation of their high standards, and such contempt for their previous ways of life that in due course they would be glad to work in the mines after the force was removed. Is the temporary use of force justified in these circumstances? This abstract example is by no means a mere academic exercise, since it is not at all dissimilar to what has happened in some parts of Africa, where the people have been forced to work in mines or on plantations, whether by orders issued through their chiefs, or because this was the only way of earning money to pay the taxes imposed on them for this purpose, or because they were driven off their lands. What actually happened in these cases is more complicated than the facts given in our abstract example, because of the additional fact that those who exercised force in these circumstances did it primarily to enrich themselves, and not because they wished to benefit the Africans. In some of these cases there is also the further fact that the Africans have not even benefited materially; on the contrary, their former villages are ruined economically, their way of life has been destroyed, while they themselves live in barracks, slums and shanty towns in material no less than in spiritual impoverishment. We have always emphasized in this enquiry that it is possible to have economic growth, in the sense of increasing output per head, without the majority of the people being any better off, because the increased output enriches only a powerful few. Most people in the world would agree that such developments are immoral, and would condemn economic policies which benefit the few at the cost of the many no matter how great the increased output that would result. This, however, is quite different from the abstract case we are examining, since it is one of the presuppositions of this case that the effect will be greatly to increase both the material and the cultural standards of the people involved, and that they themselves will in due course prefer the new way of life to the old. Faced with this example people react in different ways. Some rest their case on opposition to compulsion: however good the ultimate effects, they say, no man should be coerced for his own good, or for the good of his descendants. Others rest their case on happiness; even if the people come to prefer the new way of life to the old, they say, they are not really any better off because they are not any happier; hence they have had a painful transition to no purpose, since they have gained nothing that matters—a questionable argument, as we have already seen, since it is doubtful whether happiness is an appropriate test of change. Still others react differently, and would justify coercion if it greatly benefited the coerced. Thus, Negroes in the New World condemn the act of slavery which took them there, but in truth not all of them regret that their forefathers were not left in the jungle villages of West Africa. So also there will always be politicians and statesmen, while the world lasts, who will not hesitate to coerce their subjects for the ultimate good of the coerced.

*     *     *     *     *

Another painful transition is that which has to be made in social relations. The opposition of reason to authority, the movement from status to contract, and the change from social stability to vertical social mobility all upset existing relationships, whether in the matter of class, religion, political obedience, or family ties. This is clearly enough the case if the transition comes to a head in violent revolution, but even without this the transition is painful because it frustrates existing expectations and rights in every sphere. Many people are opposed to economic growth on this account. Some take the view that the old relationships are as good as the new or even better—they dislike the new freedom of family relations, the alleged 'rights' of the 'common man', and the destruction of the old social harmonies. Others, who do not believe that the old relationships were particularly harmonious, and who prefer the new, nevertheless question whether the difference is worth the cost. This, clearly, is an issue which can be decided only in terms of the valuation which one sets upon such matters as increased knowledge, equality of opportunity, better health standards, longer life, and the other fruits of economic growth.

Then there is the transition which has to be made in moral values. In the old society children are brought up into a code of behaviour, of duties, and of loyalties. The new society has a different code. Good behaviour in one society may be bad behaviour in the other. The duties and loyalties shift from one set of persons and institutions to another set—from the age-group to the trade union, or from the chief to an employer, or from the family to impersonal customers. In due course the new code may be established, and may work as smoothly as its predecessor, but meanwhile the community may pass through a trying time, during which the old morality has been cast off before the new has taken hold. Such transitions have been particularly painful in the past because we have not understood what was taking place. The transition is made much easier if the morality of the old society and the morality of the new society are both well known, and if those who are responsible for setting or guarding the moral standards of the community (especially the priests, the teachers and the legislators) deliberately set out to preach the new morality, right from the beginning of the change. But, in the first place, it is only recently that we have come to understand these matters, and to appreciate in particular the extent to which moral codes are bound up with and appropriate to particular social and economic patterns. In the second place, those who guard the moral standards of the community usually consider it to be their duty to guard the old code; they are hostile to the change, and regard the new code as immoral. And thirdly, even if they were won over to the new code, much of their authority disappears in the transitional phase, because of the growth of reliance on reason, and because of the public's loss of confidence in the institutions and practices with which these guardians have hitherto been identified. Thus the new code is not introduced systematically, or authoritatively. It is picked up only gradually, and in parts. New beliefs and old beliefs mix inconsistently. And there is much frustration and bewilderment when people do what they know to be the right thing to do, and find themselves ridiculed, scolded or punished for behaving in that way.

Painful transitions are inherent in the transformation of a society from one way of life to another; they cannot be altogether avoided except by avoiding change itself. This no one can do. The propensity to change is inherent in the nature of man. For man is essentially curious, and therefore forever accumulates knowledge, which alters his way of life. He is also prone to dissatisfaction, wanting more than he has, or moving about, or coveting his neighbour's status or possessions. He has also a sense of adventure, which makes him take chances, and a sense of rebellion, which is a constant challenge to hierarchical relations. It is therefore a waste of time to think in terms of stopping social change, and a waste of sentiment to regret that all established institutions must pass away. For social change arises just out of those parts of our nature which distinguish us from the rest of the animal kingdom.

All the same, though we cannot prevent change we can accelerate it or retard it. We have already emphasized that the rate of change can be too high, as well as too low. In the present context our problem is not the appropriate rate of growth of output, but rather the appropriate length of the period of transition from one pattern of social attitudes and institutions to another. Here there is no easy generalization; there is as good a case for getting transitions over quickly as there is for allowing plenty of time for adjustment.

In practice, we have no opportunity to choose retardation. The leaven of economic change is already working in every society—even in Tibet—thanks to the linkage of the world which has been achieved in the past eighty years by steamships, by imperialism, by aeroplanes, by wireless, by migration, by Hollywood and by the printed word. There have, in particular, been two developments which make it imperative not to retard but to accelerate further growth. One of these is the fact that aspirations have grown faster than production. And the other is the fact that death rates are falling faster than birth rates.

In all the under-developed world aspirations now greatly exceed production, and the gap is growing. The masses of the people are beginning to believe that their poverty is unnecessary, and that it could be ended by changing their allegiances. Some few believe that it could be changed by their own individual endeavour, but many more believe that the solution lies in repudiating their landlords, or their employers, their priests or their present political rulers. Some politicians also have great aspirations, whether it be to raise the material and cultural standards of their people, or also to raise the standing of their country in international affairs. Now a large gap between aspirations and production can be very dangerous, since it produces frustrations from which almost anything may emerge. Many people fear that the result will be 'communism' (a word which no longer has any precise meaning). Some fear the spread of native breeds of 'fascism' (a word which has to be interpreted to include the traditional warlordism of many eastern countries, as well as the Latin American 'caudillo'). Others again see a strong likelihood that power will pass to religious fanatics (to mullahs, Mahasabas, rabbis and the like). It is not therefore surprising that the leaders of many under-developed countries give a very high priority to measures for rapidly increasing production. Whether they will have the courage, and the necessary internal and external support, to raise the necessary resources may be doubted. And it is also doubtful whether in any case aspirations will not continue to outdistance production. But those who believe that it would be wrong to speed up production because of the effects on social relations, or on moral codes, usually forget both that these are already changing rapidly, and also that the results of frustrated aspirations may be even more dangerous to existing patterns than speeding up production would be.

The population dilemma is even less escapable. Under-developed countries untouched by external influences seem to have stable populations, with birth and death rates both very high by current standards. Once these countries are drawn into the modern world, with the consequent eradication of local famines and introduction of public health and medical care, the death rate begins to drop rapidly, and may fall from forty to ten per thousand in less than two generations. It then becomes necessary to begin to increase total production by rates of one or two or three per cent per annum, to keep up with rising population. Also, unless there is plenty of land available, it also becomes necessary to take steps to reduce birth rates to the same spectacular degree as death rates. This seems, however, almost certainly to require that production should grow even faster than population, since most of the explanations of the reasons why people adopt family limitation ultimately turn upon rising standards of living. In such a situation we cannot really choose to retard the growth of production; on the contrary in practically every one of the countries usually called under-developed the situation is that the current rate of growth of production is not adequate to permit the population problem to be tackled seriously. Again those who argue for retardation have usually overlooked what is happening to population, and have forgotten that the consequences of a population explosion may be much more damaging to existing social structures and moral codes than the consequences of any likely increase in production would be.

# William Letwin

## Four Fallacies about Economic Development

By FALLACY I mean a truism that has been misunderstood. It is a statement which, if hedged in by enough qualifications, would be correct, but which, as commonly understood, is false.

It cannot be demonstrated that the human mind is especially given to fallacies when exercising itself on problems of economic development. But the idea of economic development is so vague that it invites confusion. Development is generally understood as the going from an underdeveloped economy to a developed economy, and an underdeveloped economy is generally supposed to be less developed than a developed economy. This circularity in the definition leads to quite unnecessary paradoxes. For instance, the national income of Nepal (the most underdeveloped economy presently on record) has been growing recently; despite that, Nepal must now be considered more underdeveloped than ever before—because the highly developed economy of the United States has been growing faster. Nobody would be satisfied to have it said that a growing boy was becoming less developed because a bigger boy was growing faster. Such a paradox is not essential to the subject.

Economic development can be spoken of simply as the process by which a nation grows richer. An underdeveloped economy, then, is an economy that is poor in a special sense—by comparison with its own economic potential in the foreseeable future. A nation founded on a tiny island in the Antarctic wastes, its land consisting of naked volcanic rock, snow-bound, ice-locked, and wind-swept eleven months of the year; peopled by a race that is unskilled, untaught and unteachable, possessing no capital—that nation would be poor but not underdeveloped, for it might have reached the limits of its economic capacity. Most poor nations are not poor in quite so ultimate and hopeless a sense.

The practical problem of economic development is how to make poor countries richer absolutely. To make them as rich or nearly as rich as the United States or any other rich country is irrelevant and meaningless:

are they to be made as rich as the United States is now, was some time ago, or will be hence? We can hope to help the underdeveloped nations eradicate hunger; it is fatuous to hope that the citizens of all nations will some day eat the same amount of food; it is utopian to hope that all men will some day have the same incomes. In any event, to eliminate hunger and misery is a far more commendable and humane goal than to aim for mathematical equality.

The question then is how nations have become richer in the past and how others can become richer in the future. Much is known about this and much more surmised. The four fallacies cover only a small part of the ground, although all alike are fundamental and popular.

*The first fallacy:* Manufacturing is more productive than agriculture.

This fallacy underlies the widespread belief that the prime or exclusive cure for national poverty lies in industrialization.

Folklore has it that human beings, when they first appeared on the earth, earned their living by hunting. Later, understanding how efficient it would be to keep their prey in easy reach, men supposedly turned to grazing. As communities formed, peace and order were established, and with them the likelihood that a man could reap without hindrance where he sowed; thus cultivation began. And finally—so the legend goes—when farmers had become so proficient that they could raise more food than they needed themselves, the surplus was used to sustain urban workers who earned their claim to food by exchanging for it fabricated things, or manufactures, as they are still called.

Some such broad historical scheme—sketching a development from husbandry to industry—has been borrowed from folklore by social philosophers and social scientists, who by endorsing it and systematizing it have reinforced the public faith. This picture underlies the schematic views on economic history of men as diverse as Adam Smith, Thomas Jefferson and Thorstein Veblen, to mention only a few. It underlies also, for instance, the classification of goods that is part of an economist's everyday vocabulary: "primary" goods being those produced by agriculture and extractive industries; "secondary" goods, manufactures; and "tertiary" goods, those commodities and services generated by "service industries."

Although the notion of the historical priority of agriculture is embedded in folklore, it is not false. On the contrary, the fundamental assertion—leaving aside the details of the story—is more nearly correct than its opposite: it is certain that industry did not predate the extractive occupations, including agriculture. But the historical doctrine in its ordinary form is nevertheless fallacious, for the truth is that agriculture and industry have always coexisted; extraction and fabrication both have gone on together ever since the beginning.

Endless evidence exists for the early practice of manufacturing. Stone-Age arrowheads show that the act of capture was preceded by handicrafts; Stone-Age scrapers and knives show that the act of capture was immediately succeeded by acts of fabrication. Man is, among other things, a tool-making animal; and tools are essential because men are neither strong nor agile enough to capture many animals without tools, and also because Nature does not provide many raw materials that human beings can use, without first transforming them, for food, shelter, or especially clothing. Even the life of men as primitive as can be, is cluttered with spears, knives, pots, bags, huts, ropes and cloths—all fabricated things. Taking things from the earth and molding those things to human ends are equally essential parts of human activity.

History cannot clearly distinguish between agriculture and manufacture according to the order of their appearance; theory cannot more sharply distinguish between their natures. Both activities use land, labor, and capital in the production of commodities. The way each uses them and the character of the commodities that each produces do not fall into the neat and expected categories.

Does manufacture use more capital relative to labor than agriculture? Quite the contrary; it turns out that now, at least, and in many places, agriculture is more capital-intensive than manufacturing. Does manufacture use more power than agriculture? Some forms of it probably do; but on the other hand, the highly mechanized branches of agriculture use more power than an industry as advanced and complex as electronic-components manufacturing. Is the planning period for agricultural production longer than for manufactures? Possibly; but whereas it takes about four or five years from the time a particular automobile model begins to be planned until it comes off the assembly lines, agricultural processes such as mushroom culture take only a few weeks from seed to fruit. Does agriculture produce food, and manufacture other sorts of things? Obviously not, since manufacture produces bread, whereas agriculture produces jute, indigo, and beeswax. Does agriculture produce necessities, and manufacture luxuries? No; manufacture produces boots and brooms, but agriculture produces silk, strawberries, and orchids.

Everyone knows the difference between a farmer and a mill hand, but for the purposes of economic policy too much is usually made of that difference.

These caveats having been entered, it should be pointed out that all underdeveloped economies depend heavily on agriculture, whereas all highly developed economies generate very little of their income by agriculture. Only 5 per cent of the income of the United States arises in agriculture, forestry and fishery; and only 8 per cent of the American labor force is engaged in those activities. In Nepal, by contrast, 93 per cent of the labor force is engaged in agriculture. In India, about half of the national income derives from agriculture, forestry and fishery. But in New Zealand, whose citizens enjoy the third highest average income in the world, only one-sixth of the labor force is engaged in agriculture, and they produce only one-fifth of the national income. The other countries of the world arrange themselves more or less neatly on this scale, neatly enough so that one would be warranted in betting that a country which specializes in agriculture is a poor country and that a country which does not is relatively rich.

That this is not a mere happenstance, but an outcome of the general process of enrichment can be seen by examining the long history of the American economy. In 1840 probably more than half of American output was being produced in the agricultural sector; by the end of the Civil War the contribution of agriculture had shrunk to one-fifth; by the end of World War I to about one-tenth, and by now to less than one-twentieth. The same pattern could be exhibited in the history of the United Kingdom or of any other industrialized society. An inevitable concomitant of national enrichment is that agriculture ceases to be the single greatest contributor to national income and in time becomes, instead, one of the lesser contributors.

But the evidence should not be misread. Agriculture ultimately becomes less important when a nation has become fairly rich; although its agricultural output may continue to rise absolutely, the *fraction* of the national income produced by agriculture steadily declines because other forms of production take on greater significance. But this does not mean that agriculture is a crutch that can be abandoned. Although agriculture is superseded in rich nations, there is good reason to think that during the period of its primacy it was agriculture, above all, in nations such as the United States or New Zealand or Great Britain, which established the base for enrichment. At some points in the development of any economy, agriculture rather than manufacture *may* be the best means of enrichment.

Agriculture, then, though neither historically prior nor analytically distinguishable, tends to be superseded by manufacture in the course of enrichment. And it should be added, manufacture in turn tends to be displaced somewhat by service industries. For what reason?

The fundamental cause of this sequence is a fairly universal human taste for refinement. In the history of the Western world, for instance, white wheaten bread has always been preferred to wholegrain wheaten bread. But white bread is inevitably more expensive than dark—all else being equal—because the former uses up more wheat per ounce of bread; in consequence, the bread of the rich was always whiter than that of the poor. For similar reasons the linens of the rich have always been finer and whiter, their furnishings more delicate, their manners more elaborate. To refine nature's products to the standards which the human imagination invents requires much transformation, that is, much manufacture, which is costly. Hence, as men's incomes rise, they spend an increasing fraction of their incomes on the manufacturing processes that turn the immediate products of nature into the goods and services that fancy requires.

A poor savage, for want of better, sits in the sand eating meat of the bear that he has himself slain, quartered, and roasted over fire. The wealthy aesthete eats the meat of a duckling that has been reared in domestic tranquility, which has been pressed and cooked with the aid of ingenious machinery and talented labor and in the presence of artfully contrived wines, and which is served to him in a setting far from natural. The former, whose income is small, eats a meal the main ingredient of whose cost is an agricultural or extractive effort. The latter, in paying for his meal, pays mainly for the labor and capital that went into setting the dish before him, the refined dish in its refined setting; only a miniscule part of the cost is accounted for by the effort of producing the duckling, that is, by specifically agricultural costs.

The technical terms describing this behavior are that the income-elasticity of demand for agricultural products is low. It is not, of course, as low as all that. "Food" is not a homogeneous stuff. As their incomes rise, men choose to consume foods of the more tender and delectable sorts: spareribs and lamb forequarters are replaced by tenderloin, in the American version; in France, ordinary wine gives way to Burgundy; among Indian peasants, millet is abandoned in favor of rice. Nevertheless, in all places, the *fraction* of income devoted to the raw—that is, purely agricultural—ingredients of the diet falls as income rises. That is the chief reason why the fraction of income generated by agriculture—as "income" and "agriculture" are defined in national income statistics—is lower in rich countries than in poor countries.

This indisputable fact has been widely misinterpreted after the *post hoc ergo propter hoc* fashion. If rich countries do much manufacturing, does it not follow that a country wishing to be rich should expand its manufactures? Such reasoning is part of the doctrine, albeit only part, which suggests to impoverished nations throughout the world that to erect a steel mill is to make the first step toward national opulence.

It is easy enough to specify circumstances in which it would be anything but reasonable to set up a steel mill, or any other manufacturing enterprise. Imagine a very poor nation, very sparsely settled, absolutely closed off from the rest of the world; and suppose that each inhabitant had the same income, an income hardly sufficient to keep his family alive. In those circumstances agriculture and other extractive occupations would be the only ones; everyone would farm and fish and hunt, and in his spare hours everyone would be busy making clothing and housing, preparing meals, and fashioning implements. In such a setting, were incomes miraculously to rise a bit, nobody would think of spending the increase on anything but extra food. Nobody would think of buying any manufactured goods whatsoever, unless his income were to rise vastly beyond its existing range. Even if a foreign expert could demonstrate that the same effort required to increase the output of rice by one pound could produce instead one hundred pounds of steel, the demonstration would fall on deaf ears—for the inhabitants would want rice so badly that no amount of steel, or gold, would be an acceptable substitute. In a very poor and utterly closed economy, manufacture would be an inimical luxury.

Underdeveloped nations are neither so poor nor so closed as that hypothetical one. Since at least some of their inhabitants are not on the verge of starvation, the nation is already consuming a certain amount of manufactured goods, which may be made inside the country or imported from abroad. At that point it becomes plausible to ask whether the most efficient way to raise the average incomes of inhabitants is by investing capital—supposing there be some to invest—in agriculture or in manufacturing. The manufactured goods might, of course, find no buyers within the country; but that would be immaterial as long as the goods could be exchanged elsewhere in the world for additional food, if additional food were wanted. On the other hand, the manufactured goods might be of such a sort that they could find no buyers abroad; but that would be no fatal objection if they could be sold domestically to persons who until then had been buying similar goods imported from abroad. Whether the manufactured goods increased the nation's exports or decreased its imports, either way the foreign exchange acquired in the process could be used to buy extra food, if extra food were wanted.

In an open economy, in short, manufacturing may be a better way of getting food than the practice of agriculture. Similarly, agriculture may be a more efficient way of getting manufactured goods. The rational rule, then, is to pursue that activity which is most efficient. A nation that wants steel should not produce steel unless producing it is the cheapest way to get it; the possibility of international trade means that the cheapest way for some nations to get their steel is by producing butter or by catching fish.

Whether manufacturing is more productive than agriculture is therefore a question that cannot be answered in general, but only when one knows which branches of either group are being considered, and where, and when, and at what prices and costs. If an underdeveloped nation can produce radio circuits at a price far below world prices, but cannot produce its staple breadstuff as cheaply as others can, it will enrich itself more quickly by making the former and buying the latter. But which of these two, or of any other form of production it can carry on most efficiently, depends on the intricate relations, at each given moment, between such variables as the levels of income and rates of change of incomes throughout the world; of wage rates, interest rates, and rents at home and everywhere; of private tastes and diplomatic relations at home and abroad; and many more considerations of that sort.

All such qualifications being made, and in view of the fact that incomes have been rising throughout the world—despite the fears of neo-Malthusians who warn that the world's population will soon outrun the world's capacity to grow food—it is a safe general rule that *eventually* it will pay every nation to devote an increasing fraction of its productive efforts to manufacturing. But this is not all. The day may come when incomes have risen so high everywhere that manufactured goods too, like agricultural goods now, despite being more plentiful become insignificant in the budgets of consumers, who will begin to satisfy increasingly their desire for services.

*The second fallacy:* More capital is better than less capital.

This fallacy underlies the supposition that the problems of underdeveloped countries can be overcome merely by providing them with more capital.

A simple example will demonstrate the nature of the fallacy. Consider a small farm cultivated by farmer and ox. The man follows the plow from morning until night, under a hot sun: his life is hard. Imagine that the farmer acquires a tractor. The tractor chugs merrily through the day's work in an hour, the farmer driving it comfortably under an awning: his life has become easy and leisurely. The picture rightly comforts all humanitarian observers. The only difficulty is that the farmer is now starving. True, he has more leisure, but his crop is no larger than before, and the cost of keeping up the tractor (including as its main ingredient the interest charges on the loan with which he bought the tractor) is eating up a great deal of the food he previously had. The handy, efficient piece of machinery is impoverishing him.

The case of the farmer and his tractor, translated into technical terms, shows that the use of more rather than less capital is economically rational only if the labor saved by introducing an additional capital good is worth more than the costs added by using the capital good. As under-developed economies typically suffer from considerable unemployment, overt or disguised, the labor saved by introducing *certain* capital goods into *certain* occupations has a proper economic value of zero. That is to say that the real economic cost of using an hour's labor in any given enterprise is measured by its "opportunity cost," the additional output which that hour's labor would have produced in alternative employment. If Robinson Crusoe can gather a pound of brambleberries in an hour or catch half a pound of fish, then what the pound of fish really costs him is the two pounds of brambleberries he must forego for it. To return to the peasant and the tractor, the opportunity cost to the peasant of the hours of labor that the tractor saves him may be zero because he cannot use the saved time productively. In that case, the use of labor-saving capital goods is sheer waste.

The more general rule under which the peasant's case falls is that the most efficient combination of resources—efficiency being measured by costs—in the production of any goods is that which uses but little of the most costly resources and much of the cheaper resources. In an economy where wages are high and the use of machinery is cheap, goods that technically could be produced either by hand work or by machine work, will tend to be produced by machine. The converse would naturally hold in an economy where wages are low relative to the price of machinery.

The application of this rule explains, for instance, why Americans buy so many new cars. The American motorists' buying habits are generally thought to be a manifestation of lightheadedness, a proof that the consumer is enslaved by advertisers, and an illustration of conformism. By contrast, the tendency of motorists elsewhere to keep their cars for much longer stretches is supposed to result from a higher sobriety or more elevated taste. All that may be; yet the contrast can be explained simply in terms of economic rationality. In countries where labor is plentiful in comparison with producers' goods, the cheapest way to repair a car is by hand labor, that is, labor equipped with a minimal supply of simple tools. In a country like the United States, where labor is more expensive relative to capital goods, the cheapest way to keep a car up to a certain standard of performance is regularly to buy a new one from an automobile factory, where relatively little labor is combined with a vast supply of highly mechanized tools. The most efficient way to repair a car in the United States is to build a new car; the most efficient way to build a new car in most other places is to repair an old one.

In the same way it is equally sensible to build roads in the United States with bulldozers and diesel earthmovers and to build roads in China by using large gangs of laborers shifting gravel with no equipment other than picks, shovels and buckets. From the purely economic standpoint, to save much of that labor in China by using many bulldozers would be a sheer waste.

It is a fallacy, therefore, to believe that using more capital in any given enterprise is economically more efficient than using less. Capital goods, like other productive factors, are efficient only when they are properly allocated among all of the various uses to which they can be put.

The decision as to how much capital should be invested in any particular enterprise cannot be divorced from another decision, how much total capital a nation should accumulate, create or use.

At any given moment, to be sure, the amount of capital at a nation's disposal is not a matter of choice but of fact. Over any stretch of time, however, the amount can be expanded or contracted. Capital goods are produced, like all other goods, by the use of land, labor and capital. The only way a nation can by its own efforts expand its stock of capital goods, therefore, is by using resources that could otherwise have been devoted to making additional consumption goods. This interchangeability, in the production process, of capital goods and consumption goods is illustrated in a farmer's choice between eating his harvest and planting it as seed; the more he eats, the less he can plant; the more he uses for current consumption, the less he can use as capital. The monetary counterpart of this choice is that income can be spent on consumption goods, or set aside as savings; and in an economy that is working smoothly, the relative outputs of consumption goods and capital goods will match the ratio of consumption expenditures to savings. All that the people of an underdeveloped economy need do to expand the national stock of capital is to consume less than they produce. Leaving aside economic perturbations and peculiarities, the less they consume relative to current output, the faster their supply of capital will grow.

A slight defect in this prescription is that underdeveloped nations are so poor that they cannot generate much capital. The income of a very poor man hardly suffices for the ordinary needs of life; he cannot be expected to restrict his consumption in favor of future benefits; his needs press too urgently to allow much concern for the future. A man who is twenty and starving would be whimsical to invest in an annuity payable at sixty. A nation full of such men would not rationally do much saving, hence would not generate much capital. It would not, that is, if the voluntary individual choices of its citizens were allowed to prevail.

But the rate of capital formation in an underdeveloped economy can be speeded up by its government. Suppose the citizens are on the average currently saving 5 per cent of their incomes. If the government increases the tax rate and spends the added revenue on capital goods it can push the *national* savings rate, and the national rate of capital formation, up to any level it chooses short of the limit imposed by the size of national income. Programs of forced savings have been instituted by the governments of many underdeveloped nations. Insofar as the tax burden falls on the relatively wealthy citizens of those nations, the policy of forced savings is in effect a program of redistribution, open to approval or disapproval on the grounds generally applicable to schemes for equalizing income and wealth. Unfortunately, however, in very poor economies the national rate of capital formation cannot be raised much by any level of taxation applied to the wealthy few. Where that is the case, and it is probably a fairly typical case, the regime of forced savings may be extended to citizens who are poor absolutely, with the result that those who were already underfed are required to reduce their consumption further. The offer held out to them is that by making this coerced sacrifice now, by foregoing current consumption in order that extra capital may be created, they are guaranteeing themselves a higher income at some future time. But if it would be whimsical or mad for a very poor man voluntarily to save too much, it is surely whimsical or inhumane for a government to force him to save too much. One reads with shock of the aged bachelor brothers discovered lying dead of starvation on mattresses stuffed with money; the spectacle would be hardly more edifying had they died so because the state commandeered their income to build, for the national good, a splendid atomic power station.

There is still another way in which a nation can increase the supply of capital at its disposal, which is to borrow it from foreigners. This method, which has been used by underdeveloped nations for many centuries, is especially suitable since it can put at their disposal, quickly, capital far in excess of the amounts they could generate at home. Moreover, it is made feasible not only by the benevolence of foreign governments; the self-interest of foreign capitalists moves them, too, to invest in underdeveloped countries, for the rate of return in countries that as yet possess little capital is apt to be much higher than the rate capital can earn in richer economies. Unfortunately capital borrowed from private lenders is seldom or never received so warmly by the underdeveloped nation as when it is proffered to the government by other governments or international agencies. The reason is not only that public lenders are more likely to offer bargain rates. More often reluctance is dictated by the feeling that when foreigners invest in and own a country's facilities, especially its public services, they acquire too great a power in its political affairs. Whether this fear is realistic, and if realistic, so compelling that a nation should forego possibilities of more rapid enrichment in order to exclude the threat, is a question fruitless to consider in the abstract. It can be usefully answered, in concrete instances, only by the exercise of fine political prudence. As to the purely economic issue, there is no doubt that foreign financing is the quickest way for underdeveloped nations to expand their supply of capital. It is convenient, also, that transfers of capital, conceived as loans, sometimes end life as gifts.

To accumulate capital, no matter how a nation comes by it, means necessarily to defer current consumption. As men can be short-sighted, so too can they be excessively long-sighted; they can cheat the present as easily as they can cheat the future, and in that sense more capital is no better than less.

*The third fallacy*: More roads are better than fewer roads.

In this fallacy, "roads" stands as a symbol for all installations having to do with transportation and communications, or more broadly, all those commonly called public works. The fallacy urges that economic development is peculiarly dependent on a dense network of avenues and wires.

As all public works are capital goods, the general arguments given earlier as to getting and spending capital apply to them also. It is urged in extenuation, however, that public works have a special character, indicated by the technical titles commonly assigned them, Infrastructure or Social Overhead Capital.

Roads are called "Social" capital not only because they are generally owned by and used by the public, but mainly because a road bestows benefits on persons who have never seen it, much less travelled it. The parson in farthest Utah, as he drinks his morning's orange juice, drinks it cheaper because of a little road in Florida that enables the oranges to reach their market with less effort. It can be said, of course, that though he has not travelled that road in the flesh, he has travelled it vicariously by the motion of those oranges he consumes. Yet similar benefits will be realized also by persons who are utter strangers to the public improvement, such as the driver of a car who finds his journey to work eased because so many other commuters have taken to travel by subway, or the village gossip who sparing the expense of a telephone nevertheless feasts on the news it carries. Every public facility does social good far outside the circle of its users.

A road is "Overhead" capital because the cost of the road does not vary with the services it provides. Its cost is overhead in the same way that the cost of maintaining a factory building is no less or greater when the factory is working overtime than when it is standing idle. It is overhead cost by contrast with variable costs, such as the cost of the wood or labor that goes into table making, the total amount of it varying with the number of tables the factory constructs.

Because a road is overhead capital, and the amount of it required cannot be meted out in accordance with how intensely it is used, the investment required for it is said to be "lumpy." Some considerable investment is needed to build a length of road, whether one man or a hundred were expected to walk on it during any day. Moreover, the investment may take a long time to yield fruit. From the first moment capital begins to be sunk in the building of the road until the road is bearing enough traffic to justify its cost, years may elapse.

Now because of these three characteristics imputed to roads and other such facilities—the large investment, the long time elapsing before the investment yields commensurate benefits, and the enjoyment of benefits by people who do not in any direct or ordinary sense "use" the facility—some experts argue that social overhead capital must necessarily be provided or subsidized by the state. They argue that private investors cannot or will not make such big investments, that they cannot or will not wait so long to start earning a return on their investment, and that in any event they cannot get a sufficient return on their investment because so many of the beneficiaries are unknown, or even if known, could not be required to pay for their benefits.

Let us consider the arguments in order. A road needs a big investment, but private investors do not make big investments. But surely a big investment is only required for big roads. A short and narrow path does not need much capital. A long superhighway needs very much capital. But is it not surprising, then, that many of the biggest and longest superhighways in the United States, built by huge investments of capital, were financed by private capital, accumulated by the sale of turnpike-authority bonds in the open, competitive, private bond market? If it is said that in no underdeveloped economy could private citizens provide the capital to finance such a project, it might be answered that no underdeveloped country needs such roads at this point in its development—its scarce stocks of capital can be put to much more efficient uses.

The second argument is that private individuals will not wait as long as is required to realize returns on such investments. There is much evidence to the contrary. A young man freshly awarded his Ph.D. can be thought of as a capital good into which investment has been poured for a quarter of a century before it even begins to yield any monetary return. Shortly thereafter, the young man will begin investing about 5 per cent of his income in life-insurance, an investment guaranteed, on the average, to pay no return until half a century later. Orchards bear no fruit for five to fifteen years after planting; yet many private men invest in orchards. Private lumber companies plant seedlings that will not be harvested for thirty years. It is not clear that the state has a monopoly of patience.

The third argument is that the benefits of roads leak off, as it were, to many people who do not use them; hence the private investor could not capture an adequate return from investment in roads. The premise that leakage of benefits takes place is undeniable; but in the context it is fallacious because it implies that this is a special characteristic of roads as contrasted with other capital goods or other commodities. It is not special at all. A small boy who buys a chocolate for a penny may feel that he has been favored by a gift from the gods; he would gladly have given three cents or seven, had it been demanded. Every bargain in the eye of the buyer represents a leakage of benefits in the eye of the seller; the seller is prevented from charging a price exactly equal to the benefit only by force of the competition that presses prices down toward the cost of production. Moreover, in private production it also regularly happens that benefits leak off to persons that were not privy to the transaction. When the lady of fashion walks out in her latest creation, the boulevardier glories at the sight, but Mme. Chanel knows no way to levy a charge on him for the pleasure that her creation is occasioning. Neither can my neighbor who plants a beautiful garden.

If leakage of benefits were a fatal objection to private industry, there could not be any private industry at all. But private investors do not base their calculations on whether they can charge for *all* the utility their efforts give rise to, but only whether they can charge for enough to yield a suitable rate of return for the investment. It is true that were the leakage exceptionally severe, private investors would be dissuaded from investing, *even though* the total of all benefits realized by the whole community might amply justify the investment. In such cases, where the social benefit of an undertaking vastly exceeds the rate of return that the private investor could make it yield to him, there is occasion for the state to invest in the facility. A prime instance is a lighthouse.

Yet the abstract case that can be made for state investment in such projects encounters one great difficulty in practical application. The value of leaked benefits—or non-pecuniary social income—is difficult or impossible to assess: they are spread widely and nobody knows what precise value, in dollars, to attach to any one of them. To make investments in such cases is risky because the poverty of information subjects government officials to error, but safe because the critics of government investment cannot conclusively demonstrate that the investment was wasteful. For both reasons, the presumption ought to run against government investment in roads and other social facilities. The existence of privately financed railroads, turnpikes, airlines, canals, telegraph companies, newspapers, radio and the like demonstrates that private investors have not refused to construct social overhead capital.

Although, if the building of all public facilities were left to private enterprise, there would almost certainly be somewhat too few of them;

if government builds and operates them on a subsidy basis—that is, in such a way that the charges to direct users do not completely cover the costs—there will almost certainly be too many of them. This tendency will result inevitably from the fact that every individual has a private incentive to be subsidized by government, that is to have benefits conferred on him at the expense of other citizens. This incentive operates all the more forcibly to the extent that the citizens have been taught to make a sharp distinction between subsidies from government and subsidies from their fellow citizens; the former can be claimed proudly as of right; taking the latter could not fail to have an ethically dubious tone when the grantee knows that his fellow citizens are giving the gift under compulsion. It would be too much to say that every man looks forward with delight and an ardent sense of righteousness to receiving public subsidies; yet many do. Does the man living on top of a remote mountain doubt that his letters have an immutable right to be transported to the other end of the country for 5 cents, if that is the fee required of all other Americans, for instance of a New Yorker mailing an announcement to his next-door neighbor?

The private citizen demands that his government build better roads, better schools, better facilities of all sorts. There are many private citizens; taken together, they issue commands for facilities far beyond the resources available to satisfy them. Each, after all, is asking for something that would in fact benefit him considerably but that would cost him little or nothing. Would not the total demand for foodstuffs, housing, or automobiles be exorbitant if the price to the individual demanding it were a negligible part of its cost?

Faced with such demands, may not the government provide too much road? It is possible; to answer whether it is true would require a most exquisite calculation to determine whether the benefits to be realized by the community from an additional dollar invested in roads are at any moment greater or less than the benefits from that dollar's investment in any other capital good. The question cannot be answered.

But, since every one who talks about roads says that there are not enough roads, it is important to notice that there *can* be too many roads and that a democratic government may systematically err in favor of too many roads.

*The fourth fallacy:* Rapid economic development is better than slow economic development.

The need for rapidity is emphasized by those who point out that the impoverished masses in underdeveloped areas are impatient and that public impatience must lead to political disorder and perhaps to communism, unless it is soothed by quick and dramatic improvements in the standard of living.

Leaving aside important doubts as to whether the citizenry of the underdeveloped nations really are as impatient as all that, and whether the inevitable outcome of impatience is more likely to be political chaos than increased economic effort, one should nevertheless point out that the remedy proposed is impossible to achieve. It is impossible to accomplish simultaneously the *greatest* possible increase in the standard of living and the *speediest* increase.

The most feasible means—though neither a certain nor a unique means—to improve the standard of living is to build up one's stock of capital. But every addition to capital is necessarily made at the expense of current consumption; it is therefore impossible simultaneously to consume as much as possible in the present and to make the best possible arrangements for increasing future income. If a man wants to maximize consumption *this year,* he should consume all his current income and more: that behavior would reflect the extreme of impatience. If another one wants to maximize his consumption next year, ten years hence, or at any future date, he should consume nothing this year, next year, or any year up to the final one, but invest, invest, and invest; in the year when he finally turns to consumption, the income available to him will be the highest possible, a proper reward for uncommon patience. If one compares the standard of living of the two, it is clear that the first one is better off for each of the years while the other is biding his time and building his fortune, and after that the second is able to live much better. In short the *level* of consumption that can be achieved and the *speed* with which it is achieved stand in direct opposition to one another.

Economic policy, to be meaningful, must be based on a choice as to *when* the maximum level of consumption that the system is capable of producing should be achieved. To decide *when* is also to decide on *how high* the attainable level will be. These two variables are linked; they are the pans of a scale, and to raise one is necessarily to lower the other.

The choice of how much economic growth a nation should aim for and when it should start enjoying the fruits of that growth in increased consumption is not a single choice but a never-ending succession of choices. In order to make those choices rationally, a great array of tastes must be consulted. Each individual knows more or less well his own tastes about how much of his income he prefers to use now and how much he prefers to set aside for the future. It is not essential that this matter of individual choice be turned into a political question, to be decided by majority vote or the judgment of experts.

If rapidity of economic growth were not costly in terms of other human objectives, everyone should endorse it without qualification; as it is, no reasonable man can prefer it to the exclusion of all other goals. It is one of many objectives, and must be weighed against the rest.

However difficult and complex the whole problem of economic development is, one of its most confusing aspects is the difficulty of ascertaining exactly how poor the poor nations are.

There is no doubt that the standard methods of national-income accounting exaggerate their poverty. In rural and simple economies, people make for themselves many of the things that the inhabitants of complex industrialized economies do not make for themselves but buy from others. National income statistics usually and necessarily differentiate between goods exchanged in markets and identical goods that do not enter the market; the value of the former appearing in the total, the latter not. The textbook instance is that national income falls when a man marries his housekeeper, and rises when instead of shaving himself he goes to a barber. But in African villages, householders build their own huts; and throughout the underdeveloped world, neighbors sing and dance for each others' entertainment instead of going to concert halls to buy the services of paid performers. National income statistics cannot easily register the value of unbought services since those do not leave tangible traces in accounting records. The standard of living in non-industrial nations is much understated by ordinary statistics.

This is all the more true because national income statistics cannot and do not take into account the value of leisure. Imagine two identical farms, each producing one thousand bushels of wheat in a year, the only difference being that one farmer works fourteen hours each day and the other somehow manages to do the work in six; from the standpoint of national income statistics, the two farmers would be enjoying identical incomes even though it is obvious that the true income of the second is very much greater if he attaches any positive value to leisure. Time free from labor is not necessarily leisure, as it may yield nothing but boredom or frustration; but it should be remembered that men who live in industrialized societies have very assiduously trained themselves to attach a lower value to leisure than men have at other times and places. To the extent that people in underdeveloped nations do attach a high value to leisure, the statistics badly understate their total incomes by leaving out of account the psychic, non-pecuniary components of their incomes.

A further consideration suggesting that the poverty of underdeveloped nations is different in character than we suppose, arises from the reflection that the poorest nations are almost all tropical and tropical nations are poor. Not much is made of this beyond the platitude that men do not thrive in extreme heat, but insects and bacteria do. It seems a more plausible generalization, however, that a perpetually warm climate is highly favorable to human life; it reduces man's need for food, clothing and shelter; and at the same time it puts in his hands throughout the year—and not only in one short season—a plentiful supply of plants and animals.

From this standpoint the economic civilization that northern peoples have developed is a colossal exercise in irony. Having deliberately planted themselves in inhospitable regions, they have been forced to overcome the hazards of nature by donning heavy clothing, erecting bulky housing, and forcing crops from a reluctant earth. Then, having made all those things, the need for which was imposed only by the unsuitable setting in which they perversely decided to live, they have weighed all those goods, and finding them many, they call themselves rich.

But, if by contrast the inhabitants of perpetually warm places have Nature as an ally, why are they in fact so poor? The answer, perhaps, is that only in warm places can people as poor as they continue to live.

It cannot be denied that in the underdeveloped nations, however high a value the inhabitants may assign to leisure and the other pleasures of a simple life, many of them are too poor to enjoy anything at all. The entirely laudable desire to help relieve them will not have been very effective if, in the rush for a remedy, it urges cures that eradicate old miseries only to install new miseries in their place. A physician carried away by the pain of the victim and the impatience of the victim's friends does not work at his best.

# Theories of
# Economic Development

IN THE ECONOMICS of development, as in other areas of economic theory, generalization is inescapable. Economists prefer to generalize in the form of abstract models. At their best these models identify the important growth variables, invite empirical verification, and open the door to more powerful theories of economic change.

Perhaps the most widely known scheme of theoretical generalization is W. W. Rostow's. In this section's first article, Rostow explores the hypothesis that economic growth proceeds in several distinguishable temporal phases. The key stage is "take-off," the period during which an economy attains self-sustaining growth. Take-off generally follows the achievement of critical rates of growth in key sectors of the economy. A society that approaches take-off is in Rostow's framework a society that has already experienced basic structural changes in its social and political environment.

Rostow's approach is historical. H. J. Bruton prefers a deductive, non-institutional model. Moreover, his emphasis is upon the forces that support sustained economic growth *after* the economy has emerged from the pre-industrialization stage. Although his formal argument centers upon so-called mature economies, his analysis of the ways to avoid abortive development is highly relevant to the central concerns of this book. Bruton's model is post-Keynesian. It concentrates upon the interrelationship between increases in capital stock and increases in national income as these occur in economies undergoing basic structural shifts. Bruton concludes that sustained growth depends upon maintaining an appropriate ratio of capital stock to output. His mathematical mode of argument and the argument's abstraction from virtually all institutional data are characteristic of much contemporary development theory.

Gottfried Haberler, the author of the last essay in this section, dissents vigorously from some of the assumptions of contemporary development theory. Both empirically and logically, Haberler finds good reason to criticize such concepts as disguised unemployment, balanced growth, demonstration effects, and deteriorating terms of trade among the developing nations. Moreover, Haberler believes that attachment to such doctrines has encouraged over-sanguine expectations of state action and wasteful allocation of the slender resources of the poorer nations.

# W. W. Rostow

## The Stages of Economic Growth

THIS ARTICLE SUMMARIZES a way of generalizing the sweep of modern economic history. The form of this generalization is a set of stages of growth, which can be designated as follows: the traditional society; the preconditions for take-off; the take-off; the drive to maturity; the age of high mass consumption. Beyond the age of high mass consumption lie the problems which are beginning to arise in a few societies, and which may arise generally when diminishing relative marginal utility sets in for real income itself.

These descriptive categories are rooted in certain dynamic propositions about supply, demand, and the pattern of production; and before indicating the historical content of the categories I shall briefly state the underlying propositions.

### A DYNAMIC THEORY OF PRODUCTION

The classical theory of production is formulated under essentially static assumptions which freeze—or permit only onceover change—in the variables most relevant to the process of economic growth. As modern economists have sought to merge classical production theory with Keynesian income analysis, they have introduced the dynamic variables: population, technology, entrepreneurship, etc. But they have tended to do so in forms so rigid and general that their models cannot grip the essential phenomena of growth, as they appear to an economic historian. We require a dynamic theory of production which isolates not only the distribution of income between consumption, saving, and investment (and the balance of production between consumers and capital goods) but which focuses directly and in some detail on the composition of investment and on developments within particular sectors of the economy. The argument that follows is based on such a flexible, disaggregated theory of production.

When the conventional limits on the theory of production are widened, it is possible to define theoretical equilibrium positions not only for output, investment, and consumption as a whole, but for each sector of the economy.[1] Within the framework set by forces determining the total level

1. W. W. Rostow, *The Process of Economic Growth* (Oxford, 1953), especially Ch. IV. Also "Trends in the Allocation of Resources in Secular

of output, sectoral optimum positions are determined, on the side of demand, by the levels of income and of population, and by the character of tastes; on the side of supply, by the state of technology and the quality of entrepreneurship, as the latter determines the proportion of technically available and potentially profitable innovations actually incorporated in the capital stock.[2] In addition, one must introduce an extremely significant empirical hypothesis; namely, that deceleration is the normal optimum path of a sector, due to a variety of factors operating on it, from the side of both supply and demand.[3] The equilibria which emerge from the application of these criteria are a set of sectoral paths, from which flows, as first derivatives, a sequence of optimum patterns of investment.

Historical patterns of investment did not, of course, exactly follow these optimum patterns. They were distorted by imperfections in the private investment process; by the policies of governments; and by the impact of wars. Wars temporarily altered the profitable directions of investment by setting up arbitrary demands and by changing the conditions of supply; they destroyed capital; and, occasionally, they accelerated the development of new technology relevant to the peacetime economy and shifted the political and social framework in ways conducive to peacetime growth.[4] The historical sequence of business cycles and trend periods results from these deviations of actual from optimal patterns; and such fluctuations, along with the impact of wars, yield historical paths of growth which differ from those which the optima, calculated before the event, would have yielded. Nevertheless, the economic history of growing societies takes a part of its rude shape from the effort of societies to approximate the optimum sectoral paths.

At any period of time, the rate of growth in the sectors will vary greatly; and it is possible to isolate empirically certain leading sectors at early stages of their evolution, whose rapid rate of expansion plays an essential direct and indirect role in maintaining the over-all momentum of the economy.[5] For some purposes it is useful to characterize an economy

Growth," Ch. 15 in *Economic Progress*, ed. Leon H. Dupriez, with the assistance of Douglas C. Hague (Louvain, 1955); also, "The Take-off into Self-Sustained Growth," *Economic Journal* (March 1956).

2. In a closed model, a dynamic theory of production must account for changing stocks of basic and applied science, as sectoral aspects of investment, which is done in *The Process of Economic Growth, op. cit.,* especially pp. 22-25.

3. *Ibid.,* pp. 96-103.

4. *Ibid.,* Ch. VII, especially pp. 164-167.

5. For a discussion of the leading sectors, their direct and indirect consequences, and the diverse routes of their impact, see "Trends in the Allocation of Resources in Secular Growth," *op. cit.*

in terms of its leading sectors; and a part of the technical basis for the stages of growth lies in the changing sequence of leading sectors. In essence it is the fact that sectors tend to have a rapid growth phase early in their life, that makes it possible and useful to regard economic history as a sequence of stages rather than merely as a continuum, within which nature never makes a jump.

The stages of growth also require, however, that elasticities of demand be taken into account, and that this familiar concept be widened; for these rapid growth phases in the sectors derive not merely from the discontinuity of production functions but also from high price or income elasticities of demand. Leading sectors are determined not merely by the changing flow of technology and the changing willingness of entrepreneurs to accept available innovations: they are also partially determined by those types of demand which have exhibited high elasticity with respect to price, income, or both.

The demand for resources has resulted, however, not merely from demands set up by private taste and choice, but also from social decisions and from the policies of governments—whether democratically responsive or not. It is necessary, therefore, to look at the choices made by societies in the disposition of their resources in terms which transcend conventional market processes. It is necessary to look at their welfare functions, in the widest sense, including the noneconomic processes which determined them.

The course of birth rates, for example, represents one form of welfare choice made by societies, as income has changed; and population curves reflect (in addition to changing death rates) how the calculus about family size was made in the various stages; from the usual (but not universal) decline in birth rates, during or soon after the take-off, as urbanization took hold and progress became a palpable possibility, to the recent rise, as Americans (and others in societies marked by high mass consumption) have appeared to seek in larger families values beyond those afforded by economic security and by an ample supply of durable consumers goods and services.

And there are other decisions as well that societies have made as the choices open to them have been altered by the unfolding process of economic growth; and these broad collective decisions, determined by many factors—deep in history, culture, and the active political process—outside the market place, have interplayed with the dynamics of market demand, risk-taking, technology, and entrepreneurship to determine the specific content of the stages of growth for each society.

How, for example, should the traditional society react to the intrusion of a more advanced power: with cohesion, promptness, and vigor, like the Japanese; by making a virtue of fecklessness, like the oppressed Irish of the eighteenth century; by slowly and reluctantly altering the traditional society like the Chinese? When independent modern nationhood was achieved, how should the national energies be disposed: in external aggression, to right old wrongs or to exploit newly created or perceived possibilities for enlarged national power; in completing and refining the political victory of the new national government over old regional interests; or in modernizing the economy?

Once growth is under way, with the take-off, to what extent should the requirements of diffusing modern technology and maximizing the rate of growth be moderated by the desire to increase consumption per capita and to increase welfare?

When technological maturity is reached, and the nation has at its command a modernized and differentiated industrial machine, to what ends should it be put, and in what proportions: to increase social security, through the welfare state; to expand mass consumption into the range of durable consumers goods and services; to increase the nation's stature and power on the world scene; or to increase leisure? And then the further question, where history offers us only fragments: what to do when the increase in real income itself loses its charm? Babies; boredom; three-day week ends; the moon; or the creation of new inner, human frontiers in substitution for the imperatives of scarcity?

In surveying now the broad contours of each stage of growth, we are examining, then, not merely the sectoral structure of economies, as they transformed themselves for growth, and grew; we are also examining a succession of strategic choices made by various societies concerning the disposition of their resources, which include but transcend the income and price elasticities of demand.

## THE TRADITIONAL SOCIETY

The central economic fact about traditional societies is that they evolved within limited production functions. Both in the more distant past and in recent times the story of traditional societies is a story of endless change, reflected in the scale and patterns of trade, the level of agricultural output and productivity, the scale of manufactures, fluctuations in population and real income. But limitations of technology decreed a ceiling beyond which they could not penetrate. They did not lack inventiveness and innovations, some of high productivity. But they did lack a systematic understanding of their physical environment capable of making invention a more or less regular current flow, rather than a stock of *ad hoc* achievements inherited from the past. They lacked, in short, the tools and the outlook toward the physical world of the post-Newtonian era.

It followed from this productivity ceiling that food production absorbed

75 percent or more of the working force and that a high proportion of income above minimum consumption levels was spent in nonproductive or low productivity outlays: religious and other monuments; wars; high living for those who controlled land rents; and for poorer folk, there was a beggar-thy-neighbor struggle for land or the dissipation of the occasional surplus in an expensive wedding or funeral. Social values were geared to the limited horizons which men could perceive to be open to them; and social structures tended to hierarchy, although the traditional societies never wholly lacked paths for vertical mobility. The center of gravity of political power tended to reside in the regions, with the landowners, despite a fluctuating tension with those who—along with their soldiers and civil servants—exercised a degree of central authority.

## THE PRECONDITIONS FOR TAKE-OFF

The initial preconditions for take-off were created in Western Europe out of two characteristics of the post-medieval world which interacted and reinforced each other: the gradual evolution of modern science and the modern scientific attitude; and the lateral innovation that came with the discovery of new lands and the rediscovery of old, converging with the impulse to create new technology at certain strategic points. The widening of the market—both within Europe and overseas—brought not only trade, but increased specialization of production, increased interregional and international dependence, enlarged institutions of finance, and increased market incentives to create new production functions. The whole process was heightened by the extension to trade and colonies of the old dynastic competition for control over European territories, inherited from the world of traditional societies.[6]

Britain was the first of the European nations to move from the stage of preconditions into take-off, a fact capable of various explanations but certainly influenced by these circumstances: its achievement of a political and religious settlement by 1688; the area of social latitude and the limited but powerful incentives offered to nonconformists, who played a remarkable role in the process of industrial innovation; its naval and, thus,

---

6. This analysis shares with Schumpeter's the view that the ultimate causes of war were inherited from traditional societies, and were not a consequence of the more or less rational pursuit of direct economic interests. But, whereas Schumpeter tends to emphasize the persistence of irrational and romantic nationalist attitudes, this analysis would underline the structural fact that, once national sovereignty was accepted as a rule of the world arena, nations found themselves gripped in an almost inescapable oligopolistic struggle for power, which did have elements of noneconomic rationality.

trading advantages, partly determined by a greater freedom from commitments to land warfare than the French; an endowment in industrial raw materials superior to the Dutch.

The existence of the British take-off from, say, 1783, set in motion a series of positive and negative demonstration effects which progressively unhinged other traditional societies or accelerated the creation of the preconditions for take-off, where the preconditions process was already under way.[7] Before examining the manner in which these demonstration effects were communicated, however, the structural characteristics of the preconditions period should be defined.

Technically, the preconditions for sustained industrialization have generally required radical change in three nonindustrial sectors. First, a build-up of social overhead capital, notably in transport. This build-up was necessary not merely to permit an economical national market to be created and to allow natural resources to be productively exploited, but also to permit the national government effectively to rule. Second, a technological revolution in agriculture. The processes at work during the preconditions generally yielded both a general rise in population and a disproportionate rise in urban populations. Increased productivity in agriculture has been generally a necessary condition for preventing the process of modernization from being throttled. Third, an expansion in imports financed by the more efficient production and marketing of some natural resources plus, where possible, capital imports. Such increased access to foreign exchange was required to permit the less advanced region or nation to increase the supply of the equipment and industrial raw materials it could not then itself supply, as well as to preserve the level of real income while social overhead capital of long gestation period was being created. Framed by these three forms of sectoral development, yielding both new markets and new inputs for industry, the initially small enclaves of modern industrial activity could begin to expand, and then sustain expansion, mainly by the plow-back of profits.

These technical developments required, in turn, prior or concurrent changes in the noneconomic dimensions of the traditional society: a willingness of the agricultural community to accept new techniques and to respond to the possibilities of the widened commercial markets; the existence and freedom to operate of a new group of industrial entrepreneurs; and, above all, a national government capable not only of providing a

---

7. This article will not examine the preconditions process in the nations which, in Louis Hartz's phrase, were "born free" of traditional societies, mainly deriving from a British society already well advanced in the preconditions process or in regular growth. I refer to the United States, Canada, New Zealand, Australia, etc.

setting of peaceful order which encouraged the new modernizing activities but also capable and willing to take a degree of direct responsibility for the build-up of social overhead capital (including its finance); for an appropriate trade policy; and often, as well, for the diffusion of new agricultural and industrial techniques.

\* \* \* \* \*

## THE TAKE-OFF

As I have suggested in an earlier article,[8] the take-off consists, in essence, of the achievement of rapid growth in a limited group of sectors, where modern industrial techniques are applied. Historically, the leading sectors in take-off have ranged from cotton textiles (Britain and New England); to railroads (The United States, France, Germany, Canada, Russia); to modern timber cutting and railroads (Sweden). In addition, agricultural processing, oil, import substitution industries, shipbuilding, and rapid expansions in military output have helped to provide the initial industrial surge.

The take-off is distinguished from earlier industrial surges by the fact that prior and concurrent developments make the application of modern industrial techniques a self-sustained rather than an abortive process. Not only must the momentum in the three key sectors of the preconditions be maintained but the corps of entrepreneurs and technicians must be enlarged, and the sources of capital must be institutionalized in such a way as to permit the economy to suffer structural shocks; to redispose its investment resources; and to resume growth. It is the requirement that the economy exhibit this resilience that justifies defining the take-off as embracing an interval of about two decades.

A result—and one key manifestation—of take-off is the ability of the society to sustain an annual rate of net investment of the order of, at least, 10 percent. This familiar (but essentially tautological) way of defining the take-off should not conceal the full range of transformations required before growth becomes a built-in feature of a society's habits and institutions.

In noneconomic terms, the take-off usually witnesses a definitive social, political, and cultural victory of those who would modernize the economy over those who would either cling to the traditional society or seek other goals; but—because nationalism can be a social solvent as well as a diversionary force—the victory can assume forms of mutual accommodation, rather than the destruction of the traditional groups by the more modern; see, for example, the role of the Junkers in nascent industrial Germany, the persistence of much of traditional Japan beyond 1880. By

---

8. "The Take-off into Self-Sustained Growth," *op. cit.*

and large, the maintenance of momentum for a generation persuades the society to persist and to concentrate its efforts on extending the tricks of modern technology out beyond the sectors modernized during take-off.

## THE DRIVE TO MATURITY

After take-off there follows, then, what might be called the drive to maturity. There are a variety of ways a stage of economic maturity might be defined; but for these purposes it is defined as the period when a society has effectively applied the range of (then) modern technology to the bulk of its resources.

During the drive to maturity the industrial process is differentiated, with new leading sectors gathering momentum to supplant the older leading sectors of the take-off, where deceleration has increasingly slowed the pace of expansion. After the railway take-offs of the third quarter of the nineteenth century—with coal, iron, and heavy engineering at the center of the growth process—it is steel, the new ships, chemicals, electricity, and the products of the modern machine tool that come to dominate the economy and sustain the over-all rate of growth. This is also, essentially, the case with the later Russian drive to maturity, after 1929. But in Sweden after 1890 it was the evolution from timber to wood pulp and paper; from ore to high-grade steel and finely machined metal products. The leading sectors in the drive to maturity will be determined, then, not merely by the pool of technology but by the nature of resource endowments; and it may be shaped to a degree, as well, by the policies of governments. Although much further detailed analysis would be required to apply this definition rigorously, I would offer the following sample as rough symbolic dates for technological maturity.[9]

---

9. An oddity is to be noted. These dates, independently derived, come more or less sixty years after the dates established, on quite different criteria, for the beginning of take-off. There is no body of argument or evidence I can now offer to make rational such a uniformity. But it may be that when we explore the implications of some six decades of compound interest applied to the capital stock, in combination with three generations of men living under an environment of growth, elements of rationality will emerge.

| | |
|---|---|
| Great Britain | 1850 |
| United States | 1900 |
| Germany | 1910 |
| France | 1910 |
| Sweden | 1930 |
| Japan | 1940 |
| Russia | 1950 |
| Canada | 1950 |

The meaning of this technological definition of maturity—and its limits—may be better perceived by considering briefly a few specific problems posed by these particular dates.

Is France for example, on the eve of World War I, to be regarded as technologically mature, despite its large, comfortable, but technologically backward peasantry and its tendency to export large amounts of capital, despite certain technologically lagging industrial sectors? The case can, of course, be argued either way; but it does dramatize the need to allow, within the present definition, for regions of a nation or sectors of the economy to resist—for whatever reason—the full application of the range of modern technology. And this turns out to be generally true of nations which, by and large, one would judge mature. The United States of 1900 contained, after all, the South, whose takeoff can only be dated from the 1930s; and contemporary mature Canada contains the still lagging province of Quebec. The technological definition of maturity must, then, be an approximation, when applied to a whole national society. . . .

What about contemporary Russia, with more than 40 percent of the working force still in agriculture and much modern technology still unapplied in consumer-goods industries? Here again, the present definition of maturity would not predetermine how a society chooses to allocate its technological capabilities. By and large contemporary Russia is to be judged a mature economy despite the fact that its leaders have chosen for political reasons to bear the costs of a low productivity agriculture and have chosen to concentrate capital and technology in sectors other than manufactured consumption goods. Put another way, the obstacles to full modernization of the Russian economic structure do not lie in the supply of capital, entrepreneurial administrators, or technicians.

Finally, there is the case of Britain, mature on this definition as early, say, as the Crystal Palace Exhibition. How is one to deal with the long interval between the stage of its maturity, in terms of the effective application of mid-nineteenth-century technology, and the next stage of growth: the age of high mass consumption, when the radical improvements in housing and durable consumers goods and services become the economy's leading sectors? The reasons for the gap in the British sequence lie in the nature of this next stage. The age of high mass consumption represents a direction of development a society may choose when it has achieved both technological maturity and a certain level of real income per head. Although income per head—and usually consumption per head —will rise in the drive to maturity, it is evident that there is no fixed connexion between technological maturity and any particular level of real consumption per head. The course of these variables after take-off will depend primarily on the society's population-resource balance and on its income-distribution policy. The process of growth, by definition, raises income per head, but it does not necessarily lead to uniformity of per capita income among nations or, even, among regions within nations. There are—and there are likely to be—technologically mature societies that are, so to speak, both rich and poor. When historical data on national income are developed to permit systematic comparison, we are likely to find that incomes per head, at maturity, vary over a considerable range. Mid-century Britain would, presumably, stand low in that range. The improvements in real income and consumption per head that occurred in the second half of the nineteenth century took the form of improvements in diet, housing, and urban overhead capital which, while substantial, did not create within Britain new leading industrial sectors—at least down to the bicycle boom of the 1890s. . . .

As societies move to technological maturity, the structure and quality of the working force change. The proportion of the population in agriculture and rural life decreases; and within the urban population the proportion of semiskilled and white-collar workers increases.[10] This emergent working force is not only likely to organize itself with increasing effectiveness in the labor markets, but also to perceive that the industrial civilization of which it is a part can offer levels and types of consumption not previously regarded as a realistic possibility on a mass basis. And the rise in real income per head is likely to make these new tastes effective. Further, the new working force, increasingly born to the city rather than transferred from the lower margins of rural life, is likely to perceive that it can bring its weight to bear on the political process in such ways as to make the government increasingly provide measures of social and economic security. Moreover, the character of leadership in industry begins to change as well. The take-off is usually managed by relatively modest, creative men with an insight as to how output in their sector can be radically expanded: the Boultons' and Lowells'. In the drive to maturity men take over with more grandiose visions, with a more acute sense of scale and of power: although there are vast differences between post-Civil War United States and Stalin's Russia, there is, nevertheless, a distant family resemblance between some of the great entrepreneurs of the American drive to maturity and the men who administered the Five Year Plans between, say, 1929 and 1953. At maturity, however, the professional managers become more important: the nameless, comfortable, cautious committeemen who inherit and manage large sectors of the econ-

---

10. Although Colin Clark's categories—of primary, secondary, and tertiary activity—do not fit precisely this analysis, his pioneer compilations suggest that considerable uniformities in the structure of the working force of mature economies exist.

omy, while the society begins to seek objectives which include but transcend the application of modern technology to resources. . . .

## THE AGE OF HIGH MASS CONSUMPTION

There have been, essentially, three directions in which the mature economy could be turned once the society ceased to accept the extension of modern technology as a primary, if not overriding objective: to offer, by public measures, increased security, welfare, and, perhaps, leisure to the working force; to provide enlarged private consumption—including single family homes and durable consumers goods and services—on a mass basis; to seek enlarged power for the mature nation on the world scene. A good deal of the history of the first half of the twentieth century can be told in terms of the pattern and succession of choices made by various mature societies as among these three alternatives.

After a brief and superficial flirtation with the attractions of world power at the turn of the century and after imposing a set of mild measures of social reform, during the progressive period, the United States opted wholeheartedly in the 1920s for the second choice.[11] The boom of that decade was built squarely on the migration to suburbia, the mass extension of the automobile, and the household gadgetry which modern industry could provide. And these decisions to relocate the population and provide it with mobility, brought in their train not only new leading sectors—housing, automobiles, petroleum, rubber, electric-powered household devices, etc.—but also vast commitments to build new social overhead capital and commercial centers.

Down to 1914 Britain and Western Europe opted more substantially for public measures of social security, influenced perhaps by the higher proportions of urban population and by the greater power of socialist thought and political influence than in the United States. In addition, Germany was more seriously tempted than the United States to translate industrial maturity into enlarged world power; and in the inherently oligopolistic circumstances of the European arena of power, this decision led to a greater relative enlargement of military expenditures in Europe as a whole than in pre-1914 United States.

---

11. The time lag in the United States between the achievement of technological maturity in, say, 1900, and the high mass consumption boom of the 1920s is to be accounted for in part by the relative stagnation of industrial real wages in the pre-1914 trend period, due to rising living costs (*Process of Economic Growth*, Ch. VI). The more protracted lag of Western Europe is partly a consequence of the economic impact of World War I and of the public policies and dominant social attitudes of the interwar years.

During the 1920s Britain, in effect, took its favorable terms of trade in the form of chronic unemployment in the export industries. Only in the 1930s did a pervasive recovery occur. This phase did begin to exhibit a shift into the age of high mass consumption: suburban housing, automobiles, and durable consumers goods began to assert themselves more strongly as leading sectors. But rearmament and war postponed the immediate fruition of this trend.

Although the post-1920 terms of trade problem struck the Continent with less force than Britain, there too the return to relative prosperity, of 1925-1929, did not move the economies far beyond pre-1914 patterns. France, on the whole, continued to stagnate down to World War II, and German recovery, while reflecting certain symptoms of the new phase, was dominated by rearmament.

Svennilson presents calculations of motor-vehicle production (private and commercial) which suggest the relative movements of the United States and Western Europe between the wars. In 1929 the four major European nations (Great Britain, Germany, France, and Italy) produced 702,000 vehicles; the United States, 5.4 million. After a decade of protracted depression in the United States (marked by a compensatory turn to the welfare state), and a considerably greater degree of European recovery, the European figure was 1.1 million in 1938; the American, 2.5 million.[12]

In the decade 1946-1956 the United States resumed a pattern of recovery and growth markedly similar to that of the 1920s: the migration to suburbia, and the extension of the automobile and the standard mix of durable consumers household gadgets to 75 percent or more of American

12. Ingvar Svennilson, *Growth and Stagnation in the European Economy* (Geneva: United Nations, 1954), pp. 144-152. I am inclined to believe that the length of the American depression and its intractibility in the 1930s stems from the character of leading sectors in the age of high mass consumption. The diffusion of single-family housing, the automobile, etc. requires expanding levels of private income and, in effect, full employment. Moreover, until the diffusion process is actively under way certain major forms of investment are likely to be slack, because of idle capacity. Full employment is needed, in a sense, to maintain full employment when the leading sectors are consumption sectors. This was not true before 1914 when, even with unemployment high and incomes low, it might well pay to press on with railroadization, steel ships, etc. where the high expected rate of return over costs derived primarily from lowered costs. Put another way, in the age of high mass consumption a higher proportion of investment becomes endogenous, rather than exogenous, when the latter term is used to embrace investment stimulated by new technological possibilites.

families. And, after an interval of postwar reconstruction, Western Europe resumed with force the similar but more laggard development of the 1930s. By the late 1950s Western European growth was based on the fact that this region had at last fully entered the age of durable consumers goods and services, experiencing a version of the American 1920s. The patterns of consumption, as among the various European countries, emerge as largely explicable in terms of income and price elasticities of demand. And in Russia, as well, the inexorable attraction of the sewing machine, washing machine, refrigerator, and television was beginning to assert itself; and the first satellite town was under construction. It was evident, however, from the pattern of future plans that the Soviet government was not yet prepared to give the vast hostages to fortune that follow a society's commitment to the mass automobile.

## BEYOND CONSUMPTION

While Western Europe (and to a degree, also, Japan) were entering the era of high mass consumption and the Soviet Union was dallying on its fringes, an important new element entered the world economic system in the form of a quite unexpected tendency of birth rates to rise in rich societies. Although the tendency can be observed in a number of countries, it is most marked in the United States. During the years of World War II the American birth rate rose from 18 to about 22 per 1000. This was judged at the time, and to a large degree it certainly was, a phenomenon of resumed full employment and early wartime marriages. In the postwar years, however, it moved up and has stayed at about 25 per 1000. An official forecast in 1946 estimated that the American population would reach 165 million in 1990; an official forecast of 1958 estimated that the figure might be of the order of 240 million by 1980.

The human motivations and social processes which have yielded this extraordinary result are not yet well understood; but Americans have behaved as if diminishing relative marginal utility set in to the expansion of real income along the old paths. They have opted at the margin for larger families; and this trend may be related to the high rate of expansion in family trips to national parks, motorboats, do-it-yourself implements, and, even, to a widely noted tendency to turn away from the pursuit of income and authority within the large-scale bureaucratic establishments where a high proportion of the population do their work.

Whatever the motivation, however, an expansion of population on this scale will set up requirements for the lateral extension of the society's resources, including its requirements of social overhead capital. These requirements in any case had been enlarged by the consequences of the previous phase of extension in automobile ownership and suburban housing. There is a vast American backlog of investment to be carried out in roads and in the reconstruction of old depopulated urban centers. Finally, a quite significant change in the dependency ratio is under way. After falling for about a century, the number of persons under 20 and over 65 in the American population supported by each 100 members of the working force had reached 74 in 1935; by 1955 the figure was 81; and if present population patterns persist it is estimated that the figure will rise to 98 by 1975.

The pattern of American economic growth over the next several decades is likely to differ, then, from that of either the 1920s or the 1946-1956 decade; and it is likely to be based on somewhat different leading sectors. In any case, it is clear that American society, by its quiet collective decision about birth rates, has postponed the problems of a time of true affluence, when the full utilization of resources would not much matter.

The somewhat strenuous choice made by Americans as they pushed high mass consumption to a kind of logical conclusion, in the first decade after World War II, need not prove to be universal: the income elasticity of demand for children may vary. It is evident, however, that the march of compound interest is bringing some societies close to the point where the pursuit of food, shelter, clothing, as well as durable consumers goods and public and private services, may no longer dominate their lives. A new and revolutionary set of choices is being confronted, or is a mere generation or so over the horizon.

*Henry J. Bruton*

---

# *Contemporary Theorizing on Economic Growth*

. . . MODERN CONCERN with problems of growth cannot be attributed to a building up of a received body of thought which in recent years has required as its next layer of bricks a long-run theory. . . .

Rather there exists a wide variety of approaches to the problem of explanation. But rather than examine contemporary contributions to the growth literature in isolated groups, it would seem more useful—and more interesting—to attempt to examine them in the context of a single general framework. I propose therefore to examine modern growth theory in the following way: I shall begin with the simplest, and most formal, theory available—the capital stock adjustment theory, associated with the names of Harrod and Domar—and then, step by step, deepen, widen, and disaggregate, in an effort to include in the analysis the arguments and hypotheses of as many contemporary writers as seems warranted. Each section of this paper will therefore be an extension, in one way or another, of the theory described in the first section. I shall maintain the formal framework of the Harrod-Domar analysis throughout. This will not only provide a theme to hold the essay together, but has the additional merit of showing how various components, isolated and emphasized by the several authors, fit together (or do not fit together) and act on each other.

As the length of the paper must be finite, several difficult problems are solved by simple fiat. In the first place, I concentrate on the behavior of per capita real income. This means that I limit the problem of a theory of growth to explaining the time path of per capita income over a long period of time. Per capita income is chosen as the main measure of growth for two simple reasons: One, almost all writers direct attention to this variable; two, despite some obvious weaknesses in its use, there does not seem to be a practical alternative.[1]

Secondly, it is necessary to take an explicit position with respect to short-period fluctuations. In discussions of short-period phenomena, most authors assume that it is possible to ignore the slower changes going on in the economy. In an analysis of long-run growth, these slower changes must, of course, be examined and worked into the explanatory system. But then, can the short run fluctuations—frequently called cycles—be ignored? It is evident that the long-period behavior of an economy is not at all independent of what happens in the short run, but the nature of such interdependence is far from clear, and no simple assumption seems to be appropriate from all points of view. However, it is possible to recognize the interdependence of cyclical fluctuations and longer-run phenomena, while concentrating our attention on the latter, and to consider the former only in terms of how it affects the behavior of the system over a

---

1. It is to be emphasized that giving prime attention to per capita income is a limitation on the scope of the survey. Several writers are strong in their criticism of the use of per capita income as the strategic variable, but for the most part these writers offer no alternative. An exception is the work of Adolph Lowe, "Structural Analysis of Real Capital Formation," in *Capital Formation and Economic Growth*, Moses Abramovitz, ed., Princeton, 1956, pp. 581-635.

long period of time, without giving detailed examination to the *modus operandi* of the cycle itself. This is the procedure followed in this essay.[2] I have therefore ruled out discussion of the formal properties of the several types of cycle models currently extant, but I do recognize that the growth process is likely to generate fluctuations, and that these fluctuations act on the growth process in turn. I shall seek then to introduce into the analysis of the determinants of growth the effect of this interdependence on these determinants and hence, to some extent at least, on the long-run behavior of the economy itself.

Thirdly, attention is limited herein to the "real" aspects of growth, at the expense of the "financial" aspects.[3] And, except for minor deviations, the discussion is limited to a closed economy, and little attention is given to the growth process in a centrally planned economy. Omission of the international section seems reasonable, in light of the limited extent to which international relations have been introduced into the formal theories of economic growth.[4] I have excluded consideration of centrally planned systems simply because of space and time limitations.

Finally, it should be noted that although there has been a healthy emphasis on noneconomic aspects of growth in much of recent literature,

---

2. Some such procedure is implied in much of the literature. Perhaps the best discussion is contained in William Fellner, *Trends and Cycles in Economic Activity*, New York, 1956, chaps. 1 and 2. Evidently, those theories—chiefly Schumpeterian in orientation—which find the origin of growth in the cycle itself, would not fit into this approach.

3. Professor Fellner (*op. cit.*, chaps. 5 and 9) has a good discussion of the role of the price level in growth. Robert Solow ("A Note on the Price Level and Interest Rate in a Growth Model," *Review of Economic Studies*, XXI, pp. 74-79), and S. S. Alexander ("The Accelerator as a Generator of Steady Growth," *Quarterly Journal of Economics*, LXIII, 1949, pp. 174-98), also give some attention to the effects of price-level behavior. Economic historians have, of course, long been concerned with price-level behavior over substantial periods of time. For a recent examination of some of the hypotheses arising from these historical inquiries, see David Felix, "Profit Inflation and Industrial Growth: The Historic Record and Contemporary Analysis," *Quarterly Journal of Economics*, LXX, 1956, pp. 441-63. A specific discussion of some of the financial aspects of growth may be found in J. G. Gurley and E. S. Shaw, "Financial Aspects of Economic Development," *American Economic Review*, XLV, 1955, pp. 515-38.

4. Useful discussions of some aspects of the role of the international sector in growth may be found in Harry G. Johnson, "Equilibrium Growth in an Internationl Economy," *Canadian Journal of Economics and Political Science*, XIX, 1953, pp. 478-500, and Trygve Haavelmo, *A Study in the Theory of Economic Evolution*, Amsterdam, 1954, Part V.

discussion of this material is also omitted. This is to be regretted; in those countries where growth seems most essential for human welfare, problems outside the conventional limits of economics are surely paramount. Indeed, a strong argument can be made that the problem of underdevelopment will not be solved until economics has achieved a more compatible marriage than now prevails with other social sciences.

## THE CAPITAL STOCK ADJUSTMENT THEORY

By limiting his analysis to the short-run, Keynes was able to impound into *ceteris paribus* all those phenomena and characteristics of an economy that change more slowly than the immediate determinants of income. The short-run mechanism is assumed to work itself out in a setting in which capital stock, technology, market structure, saving habits, social and cultural environment, population, etc., remain unchanged. With all these given, the problem was to determine the equilibrium level of income.

It is possible by a comparative static technique to examine the effect on the equilibrium level of income of a once-and-for-all change in any of the occupants of the *ceteris paribus* pound. And, of course, this has been done. For example, much attention has been given to the effect of changes in income distribution on the consumption-income relationship, and to the effect of a change in the extent of monopoly on the rate of investment. But such changes in these "underlying" or "basic" characteristics are exogenous to the equilibrium conditions of the "static" Keynesian model. This statement is true, or approximately true, with respect to each member of the group in the preceding paragraph, except one—capital stock. Depending on the way the short-run system is established, if there is net positive saving, there is also net positive investment, and if there is net positive investment, the capital stock must be changing. Thus, the capital stock—surely a relevant determinant of the level of income—is not exogenous to the short-run mechanism, but changes in a way which is directly dependent upon how that mechanism works. Therefore, the first effort to extend Keynesian short-run theory into a growth problem was essentially to examine the effects of changes in the capital stock on the behavior of income.[5]

Since it is capital stock that is changed by investment, it appears reasonable to define equilibrium so that it involves the capital stock. Keynesian equilibrium requires equality between desired savings and

5. The pioneering papers are R. F. Harrod, "An Essay in Dynamic Theory," *Economic Journal*, XLIX, 1939, pp. 14-33; E. D. Domar, "Capital Expansion, Rate of Growth and Employment," *Econometrica*, XIV, 1946, pp. 137-47; and S. C. Tsiang, "Rehabilitation of Time Dimension of Investment in Macrodynamic Analysis," *Economica*, XVI, 1949, pp. 204-17.

desired investment, while the growth form of the model requires for equilibrium the continuing maintenance of the desired ratio between capital stock and the rate of output. In the early formulations, this ratio seems to be determined solely by technological considerations, i.e., it is a technological constant. It is convenient and helpful to label this kind of theory the capital stock adjustment theory.[6]

### The Aggregate Model

The capital stock adjustment theory may be stated in a variety of ways, but we may content ourselves with a single, simple form.[7] It was stated above that the central proposition of this theory is the explicit recognition that investment is capacity-creating as well as income-generating; it is therefore useful to develop the capacity effect and the demand effect separately, and then equate them to show the requirements for equilibrium.

The supply equations may be formulated in the following way: Let $O_t$ be the capacity rate of output during period $t$; let $K_t$ be the capital stock available to the system during period $t$; and let $k$ be the relationship between capital and output, a technological constant. Therefore:

$$O_t = \frac{1}{k} K_t$$

and:

$$O_t - O_{t-1} = \frac{1}{k}(K_t - K_{t-1}) = \frac{1}{k} I_{t-1}$$

---

6. R. C. O. Matthews, "Capital Stock Adjustment Theories of the Trade Cycle and the Problem of Policy," in *Post-Keynesian Economics*, Kenneth K. Kurihara, ed., London, 1955, chap. 7.

7. D. Hamberg (*Economic Growth and Instability*, New York, 1956), discusses the numerous forms the theory may take and the implications of these several forms. Professor Hamberg also makes extensive references to the literature on this general body of theory. The reader interested primarily in exploring the details of the Harrod-Domar model should consult the Hamberg volume; our problem is something else. In particular, it might be noted that much depends upon the pattern of lags that is assumed.

A word on references is appropriate here. It is impossible to refer to every item in the literature worthy of note, and I shall follow the practice of noting only what seems to me to be the earliest or clearest formulations and/or those sources that do present extended bibliographies on the subject under discussion. Professor Fellner's book, cited in footnote 3, above, contains the most useful general list of references that I have seen.

where $I_{t-1}$ is investment during the $t-1$ period which becomes producing capital in the $t_{th}$ period. Then:

$$(1) \qquad \frac{O_t - O_{t-1}}{O_{t-1}} = \frac{\frac{1}{k}I_{t-1}}{O_{t-1}} = \frac{v}{k}$$

where $v$ *is* the ratio of net investment to capacity output in the previous period. Equation (1) states that capacity will grow at a constant percentage rate, determined by the productivity of the additions to capital stock, $k$, and the proportion of the capacity devoted to the creation of new capital.

For the effect of investment on demand, we need an equation for consumption expenditures and one for investment expenditures. In an effort to maintain simplicity, we may write consumption as a function, $1-s$, where $s$ is average and marginal propensity to save of current income, and investment as a function, $b$, of the change in income over the immediately preceding periods, all in constant prices. Thus:

$$C_t = (1 - s) Y_t$$

and:

$$I_t = b(Y_t - Y_{t-1})$$

then:

$$(2) \qquad Y_t = (1 - s) Y_t + b(Y_t - Y_{t-1})$$

and by simple algebraic manipulation:

$$(3) \qquad \frac{Y_t - Y_{t-1}}{Y_{t-1}} = \frac{s}{b - s}$$

Equation (3) asserts that income will grow at a constant percentage rate, determined by the propensity to save and the extent to which changes in income induce investment.

Assuming that in period O equilibrium prevails, i.e., $O_0 = Y_0$, equilibrium growth requires that $\frac{v}{k} = \frac{s}{b-s}$. If $O_0 = Y_0$, then, since total savings equals total investment and the saving-income ratio is assumed to be constant, $v$ must equal $s$, and the achievement of equilibrium growth depends upon the equality $k = b - s$. Under these assumptions as to relationships and (especially) as to lags, $b$ must exceed $k$ by the amount of the saving ratio. For this reason and for others to be discussed later, it is of considerable importance to distinguish carefully between $k$, a supply parameter, and $b$, a demand parameter.[8]

Given these assumptions, the economy can achieve equilibrium growth; but if $k$, $b$, and $s$ are constants, the equilibrium path may be difficult to maintain. Suppose, for example, that the system is growing smoothly, but because of a shock of some sort, income suddenly fails to grow at the required rate, and excess capacity appears. Entrepreneurs may then seek to reduce their capital stock by reducing investment, but a reduction in investment leads to further reductions in the income, and the desired ratio between capital and output cannot be re-established. If income happens to grow faster than expected, entrepreneurs, finding themselves shy of capital, may seek to add to their capital stock, but this act leads to further increases in income, and the capital-output ratio remains less than that desired. This extreme instability obviously depends upon entrepreneurial expectations. For example, if decision-makers reacted to the sudden appearance of an undesirably large capital-output, not by reducing their rate of investment, but by increasing it, then the above result would not follow. And the way entrepreneurs react will depend upon what they think the future holds, i.e., upon their expectations. Thus, an expectation function could be introduced that would make the equilibrium growth path stable.[9] Unhappily, little is known about the expectation functions of entrepreneurs, and results that depend in a significant way upon a particular function must be interpreted with caution. It would seem that most discussions of capital stock adjustment theory assume it to be unstable, and since the theory, as described to this point, does not indicate what happens when equilibrium is disturbed, it cannot explain the time path of per capita income without further elaboration. Since it has been assumed that the purpose of a theory of economic growth is to explain the time path of per capita income, it is necessary to introduce some hypotheses that will either stabilize the equilibrium path, or that will indicate the route that instability imposes on the system. This is done at the end of this section, after some comments on the theory as it now stands.

It was stated earlier that the only modification made in Keynes' theory in its metamorphosis from a static, short-run theory into a dynamic, long-run theory was the recognition that net investment cannot occur without

8. Cf. A Kervyn, "A Note on the Accelerator and Constant Growth," *Review of Economic Studies*, XXII, 1954-55, pp. 61-66.

9. The role of expectations in this growth model are discussed in some detail by Diran Bodenhorn, "The Stability of Growth Models," *American Economic Review*, XLVI, 1956, pp. 607-31. See also W. J. Baumol, "Formalization of Mr. Harrod's Model," *Economic Journal*, LIX, 1949, pp. 625-29.

a change in the capital stock. This means that other strategic Keynesian concepts were retained, and are presumed to be appropriate in the long-run context. For example, the linear saving-income relationship that Keynes could draw fairly confidently as applicable for his static, timeless model was, without modification, plugged into a model designed to explain the long-run growth of an economic system.[10] It is useful, then, to begin the discussion of the capital stock adjustment theory of growth by an examination of the concepts of this theory with respect to their suitability as parameters of a growth model. Since we are interested in explaining—that is, in accounting for—the behavior of per capita income, the criterion of suitability is the effectiveness with which a given parameter contributes to this explanation.

The key new parameter in this formulation is the supply parameter, the capital-output ratio. In the simplest form of the theory it is assumed to be a technologically fixed constant. The conceptual problems involved in defining capital are made much more intricate than usual when the term is used to define the capital-output ratio. The most satisfactory approach to follow in computing the value of a stock is to discount the future stream attributable to that stock back to the present time. But to measure the capital stock in this way reduces the capital-ouput ratio to a tautological constant, devoid of explanatory significance. Moreover, of course, two accumulations of capital stock, although alike in every respect, may have different values simply because the discount factor is not the same in each case, and this leads to undesirable results when one attempts to determine capital needs. It is therefore necessary to rule out defining and measuring the numerator of the capital-output ratio in this way, despite the fact that this procedure has the most appeal in many other problems.

Thus, we must resort to the less satisfactory technique of defining investment as the difference between total output and consumption, and capital as the accumulated value of investment (with all variables measured in constant prices). Under ideal circumstances, this method is satisfactory. It implies that a quantity of resources are devoted to producing commodities that are not consumed, and that these commodities add to the capacity of the system to produce more commodities. Since all measurements are in "real" terms, investment may be assumed to measure resources allocated to the production of capital goods. Capital is thus thought of in terms of the resources (chiefly labor) required to reproduce the existing

---

10. The fact that the early forms of this model were all linear has led to the frightening result that income has to grow throughout eternity at a constant percentage rate or all is lost. Surely, in a long-run model the linearity assumptions are difficult to justify. See Solow, "A Note on the Price Level . . . ," *loc.cit.*, p. 75.

stock of machines, equipment, plants, buildings, etc. A capital-output ratio, technologically fixed, would then mean that production of a given increment in capacity will always require the application of an unchanging quantity of inputs to the production of the necessary capital equipment. In practice, this method results in valuing capital formation in each period at cost to the investor, and only in a perfectly competitive system with no uncertainty will such valuation equal that arrived at by use of the discounting procedure. Difficulties in deflating, in computing depreciation, and in evaluating the "initial" capital stock introduce additional problems of measurement and conceptual ambiguities which make the use of the capital stock notion troublesome.[11]

There is the further conceptual difficulty of the period of gestation with respect to capital goods whose productivity is indirect, at best. It is a simple matter to see that the production of one hundred new looms will have a specific and measurable effect on the capacity of the textile industry, which effect will be evident immediately upon the completion of the construction of the looms. But it is not as clear what the effect on the capacity of the economy will be if the new capital creation is in the form of schools, hospitals, highways (or government monuments). The capacity of the system to supply school, hospital, and highway services is of course increased immediately (assuming the availability of necessary labor), but, evidently, this is not the total effect of these activities. The total effect on capacity of such forms of capital will not be apparent until sufficient time has elapsed for the full effects of the new capital to be felt throughout the system. In a similar category with schools, highways, and so on, is investment in research facilities, an area which is currently attracting considerable quantities of funds in the United States.[12]

Not only does the choice of the time interval affect the capacity-creating effects of a given investment outlay, but so also does the composition of the new capital. Evidently, a capital stock is not a homogeneous

---

11. These problems are discussed in some detail by Joan Robinson, "The Production Function and the Theory of Capital," *Review of Economic Studies*, XXI, 1953-54, pp. 81-106, and in her recent book, *The Accumulation of Capital*, London, 1956, *passim*.

12. Another aspect of this same problem has to do with the life of the capital that is accumulated. This problem and the associated one of the effects of depreciation decision on growth are not considered in this essay. This, too, is a serious lacuna in the discussion. On the effects of depreciation decision on growth, see, for example, E. D. Domar, "Depreciation, Replacement and Growth," *Economic Journal*, LXIII, 1953, pp. 1-32, and Robert Eisner, "Depreciation Allowances, Replacement Requirements and Growth," *American Economic Review*, XLII, 1952, pp. 804-19.

whole; it has a structure, and the productivity of newly created capital depends in part upon how the new capital fits in with the existing structure. If capital is viewed as a heterogeneous composite of many types of capital services, an appraisal of the capital-output ratio requires consideration of potential complementarities which may have significant consequences for the capacity of the system. Especially relevant in this respect are external economies and "social overhead facilities." Both of these concepts are difficult to handle, but they are surely highly relevant in understanding the growth process, and the use of an aggregative capital-output ratio conceals, rather than reveals, the problem. More will be said on this point below, in the section on the disaggregated form of this model.

A final point on the capital-output ratio concerns noncapital inputs. The equilibrium rates of growth were determined above solely in terms of the behavior of capital stock. If input coefficients are assumed to be constant, there is not much more that can be said, since then the rate of growth of total output is limited by the rate of growth of the input, whose supply is growing at the slower pace. With constant input coefficients, the equilibrium rate of growth will be the full employment of labor rate of growth only if the rates of growth of capital and labor are equal. Thus, the assumption of the fixity of input coefficients is important in our attempts to explain what happens to the level of employment, as well as in our efforts to account for the instability of the equilibrium growth path.

The other supply parameter—the saving function—has, of course, been the subject of countless articles and books. Conceptually, it poses fewer problems than the capital-output ratio, but there is one point to which reference should be made in the present context. Interest in saving arises out of the fact that it is necessary in order to release resources from producing for current consumption, so that they may be used to create products which will increase the capacity of the system in the future. But, evidently, many forms of expenditure have an effect on the future capacity of the economy. This is especially true of expenditures for education and health services, but it is also true of other consumption. In effect, this means that saving and investment, as they are usually computed, do not measure the total amount of resources devoted to increasing the capacity of the economy. It appears that one of the major differences between consumption expenditures in high-income countries and in low-income countries is that only a very small proportion of total consumption outlays in the latter countries affects capacity, while in the high-income countries the percentage is of considerable magnitude. There are real difficulties here in separating net from gross expenditures, i.e., in separating out those expenditures which merely maintain capacity from those which augment it. Furthermore, expenditures on health and education may well reduce the incentive to save out of remaining income. Nevertheless, such considerations do introduce an ambiguity with respect to saving—for the growth problem—which may be expected to contribute to the unpredictability of the capital-output ratio, and consequently to the behavior of the capacity of the economy through time.

On the demand side of the problem, little need be said about the consumption function. Conceptually, it is unambiguous, although of course many writers question its use as a parameter in any kind of a model. With respect to the demand for capital accumulation, the chief conceptual problems are concerned with the appropriateness of the accelerator and the distinction between induced and autonomous investment.[13] A detailed account of the accelerator is unnecessary for our purposes here, and we need mention only one point.

The literature seems to concentrate on the technological relationship between output and capital. Thus, the equation is usually written as:

$$(4) \qquad\qquad I_t = b'(Y_t - Y_{t-1})$$

or:

$$(5) \qquad\qquad I_t = b''(Y_{t-1} - Y_{t-2})$$

where $b'$ and $b''$ refer solely to the technological requirement of capital in the productive process. These relationships express the concept that income has increased, and this increase then induces investment. In order for such equations to be meaningful, it is necessary to assume that it is possible to increase output briefly with no increase in capital stock. Firms maintain a higher rate of output than is desirable, given their capital stock, for a period or two, then increase capital accumulation to re-establish the desired relationship between stock and output. The argument is based on purely technological considerations: A given rate of output requires a given stock of capital; therefore, if output rises, new capital must be created. This kind of argument implies that investment demand is an automatic response to technological needs.

The other way of looking at the accelerator involves something more. One of two changes may be made. Rather than thinking of investment as

---

13. Autonomous investment was omitted from the equational system outlined above simply for ease of exposition, and because I later rule out the concept entirely. The literature on the accelerator is vast indeed, and specific references are hardly necessary: see Hamberg, *op.cit.* Many writers, of course, are reluctant to use autonomous investment as an acceptable theory of investment.

responding to a previous change in output, it may be argued that entrepreneurs estimate demand for output in the next period, and invest according to their expected needs. We would then write:

$$I_t = B''' \, (\hat{Y}_{t+1} - Y_t)$$

where $\hat{Y}_{t+1}$ is estimated income in the $(t+1)^{\text{th}}$ period.[14] Or we may argue that the change in income between periods results in entrepreneurial activity, but that behavior is induced by many factors in addition to technological considerations. Thus, we could write $I_t = b \, (Y_t - Y_{t-1})$, where the $b$ is the relation measuring investment response to changes in output, which response would depend chiefly upon expectations created by the difference between $Y_t$ and $Y_{t-1}$. These last two equations are, therefore, quite similar with respect to the kind of phenomenon they represent. They both make it clear that the investment decision is something more than an automatic technological response.

Earlier, we stated the capital stock adjustment theory in such a way that the capital-output ratio and investment demand parameter had to be different, if equilibrium growth were to be attained. Under this form of the model, it is possible to interpret the $b$ as a technological parameter, although there must be an assumption, explicitly stated, as to entrepreneurial expectations. However, it seems much more rewarding, in spite of the increased difficulty, to consider the $b$ as a behavioristic parameter, with certain technological limitations, and not merely as a technological coefficient handed to the economist by the engineer. If we do this, we are also required to say something more about the determinants of investment decisions. This we do later. The point here is that there must be a clear indication in the investment equation as to whether the accelerator is a purely technological parameter, or whether it is a behavioristic parameter as well; and, as just noted, it seems more acceptable to assume that it is a behavioristic parameter with certain technological limitations. . . .[15]

The final point in this section concerns the constancy of the relationships defined in the capital stock adjustment model. It was observed earlier that the chief innovation that turned Keynes' timeless theory into a

---

14. This is the way the accelerator is written by Paul G. Clark, "The Telephone Industry: A Study in Private Investment," in Wassily Leontief, *et al., Studies in the Structure of the American Economy*, New York, 1953, chap. 7.

15. This interpretation seems to be consistent with most of the literature. See, for example, Joan Robinson, *The Rate of Interest and Other Essays*, London, 1952, and Fellner, *op.cit.*

growth theory was the explicit recognition that investment results in increases in capacity. The maintenance through time of a Keynesian kind of equilibrium then required that demand grow so as to match the growing capacity. But now, with respect to each parameter, the further question must be asked as to whether the process of growth itself results in its changing in a systematic, predictable fashion. If it could be shown that a growing income did itself produce forces that resulted in systematic changes in the values of the parameters, then it would become necessary to explore further and to try to find the path of change that will be traced out. That is to say, if we are to understand the behavior of per capita income over time, it becomes necessary to deepen the explanatory system to the extent that these immediate determinants of growth are themselves explained, at least to the extent that these changes are functions of the growth process. . . . It may prove helpful to introduce some modifications into the above discussed model.

*Some Modifications*

The Keynesian setting of the capital stock adjustment theory has been emphasized, and it has been shown that several important results obtained are due to assumptions which are part of the Keynesian heritage. However, it is possible to change the setting from Keynesian to neo-classical, and when this is done it is not surprising that some of the more startling results obtained disappear. Such a resetting has been accomplished with great elegance by Professor Robert Solow.[16]

The strategic new assumptions are (a) at each instant of time all existing capital stock and all labor are thrown on the market; and (b) quasi-rents and wage rates adjust immediately to clear the market. With such a flexible productive system, the perfectly adjusting input prices would assure—under a wide range of conditions—that the capital output ratio, which did in fact obtain, was the desired one. The system could then always adjust to a given labor supply in such manner that the full employment of labor and the satisfying of entrepreneurs are achieved at the same time, not accidentally, but by a substitution of inputs responding to changed factor prices.

It is, of course, unlikely that factor prices and productive processes are such that the above assumptions can be considered realistic. However, it does seen reasonable to assume that, though not occurring instantaneously, such adjustments do tend to take place over a long period of

---

16. Robert Solow, "A Contribution to the Theory of Economic Growth," *Quarterly Journal of Economics,* LXX, 1956, pp. 65-94. See also H. Pilvin, "Full Capacity vs. Full Employment Growth," *Quarterly Journal of Economics,* LXVII, 1953, pp. 545-52.

time. In all countries which have experienced long periods of continued growth of per capita income, the evidence is strong that capital accumulation has proceeded at a faster pace than the labor supply has grown. Since the capital accumulated has been used—except for short interruptions, adjustments in the capital-labor ratio have evidently occurred. It is conceivable, of course, that such adjustments should be explained solely in terms of technological change, but this puts a burden on the rate and direction of technological change, a burden it seems incapable of supporting—for reasons to be discussed later. Further evidence that substitution takes place lies in the fact that it is possible to observe that different processes are being used by different firms to produce very similar products.

It therefore appears meaningful to accept the proposition that at all times there is an optimum input mix, which optimum is a function of technology and the relative prices of the inputs. When deviations from such an optimum combination develop, relative prices and productive processes begin to change in such fashion as to restore the optimum conditions. Since neither prices of inputs nor the productive process can adjust immediately, the system will not be constantly in equilibrium, but neither is it uselessly unstable. In particular, the knife-edge equilibrium path disappears, as do also the problems created by it. Especially important is the fact it now becomes meaningful to consider the equilibrium path as tracing out the actual time path of income for the economy.[17]

The introduction of flexibility into the system has another advantage as well. The above formulation of the capital stock adjustment theory stated the equilibrium conditions in terms of the continued maintenance of the desired relationship between the stock of capital and the flow of output. Under assumptions of fixed input coefficients, there is not much more to say on this subject (nor indeed is there much meaning to the notion of a "desired" capital output ratio). A more satisfactory approach appears to be to assume that the entrepreneur thinks in terms of achieving a satisfactory rate of return on his capital stock. What constitutes a satisfactory return depends upon many things, and the absolute magnitude of such a rate surely varies from time to time and from industry

---

17. There has been considerable discussion of the role of the fixity of input coefficients and the behavior of factor prices in accounting for the underemployment found in many underdeveloped countries. A recent useful discussion of this particular problem may be found in R. S. Eckaus, "Factor Proportions in Underdeveloped Areas," *American Economic Review*, XLV, 1955, pp. 539-65. For a detailed discussion of the process by which the technique of production becomes more capital intensive see Mrs. Robinson's *The Accumulation of Capital* (*op.cit.*).

to industry. To facilitate the analysis, it is convenient to introduce the simplifying assumption of a constant equilibrium rate of return, and to assume that, if this rate is maintained, entrepreneurs will feel that their investment is justified. This means that continuing equilibrium growth requires that the capital-accumulating process generate a total supply and a total income to enable the rate of return on capital to remain about constant through time.

The rate of return on capital is the ratio between the share of output going to capital (call this $q$) and the capital-output ratio ($k$), i.e., it is $q/k$.[18] Therefore, a constant $k$, along with an unchanging distribution of income, will produce a constant rate of return on capital. Thus, with fixed coefficients, the rate of return will tend to remain constant, and the growth path defined earlier meets this new equilibrium condition.

However, the situation is different when a more flexible system is assumed, and when it is also assumed—as is necessary—that capital accumulation is proceeding more rapidly than the labor supply is growing. These assumptions make impossible the conclusion that the rate of return remains constant through time, without specific reference to the comparative rates of growth of capital and labor and the behavior of technological change. This means then that the conditions for equilibrium growth require specification of those conditions to which reference has already been made, and to innovation behavior as well. In other words, the requirements of steady and continuous growth must include a specific innovational pattern.

\*    \*    \*    \*    \*

## Conclusion

How can this body of thought regarding economic growth be evaluated? At the aggregative level it was found that the concepts supporting the theory are defective in several respects; furthermore, the basic relationships of the theory—as with all economic theory—are also open to numerous doubts. When the theory is disaggregated, it becomes more realistic, at the expense, however, of introducing several new and intractable problems. It would seem that the usefulness of the theory depends not so much on any specific, rigorously demonstrated conclusion, but rather on the fact that the model does suggest some important requirements which an economy must meet if it is to enjoy smooth and continuing growth. In this respect, this set of ideas is of value.

Three characteristics of the theory are of particular importance. First,

---

18. If $Q$ is the total return to capital, and $K$ is the capital stock, then $Q/K$ is the rate of return on capital. If we then divide both numerator and denominator by output, we get $q/k$.

it is a short-run theory. It was emphasized earlier in this essay that the aggregative theory arose from a single alteration of the Keynesian model. And Keynes' model is of course short-run. This characteristic is especially apparent in the rigid form in which the model—aggregative and dis-aggregative forms—was first introduced. The assumption of fixed production coefficients, for example, can hardly be defended except in the very short run. When this and similar assumptions are relaxed—as they must be when the analysis includes a long interval of time—then it is evident that those items assumed constant in the theory (as presented up to this point of our discussion) are indeed strategic to the growth process, and must therefore be included in the explanatory framework. It then becomes profitable to explore somewhat the literature on these more slowly changing factors of growth in an effort to determine what light has been thrown on their behavior through time, and to inquire further as to how the short-run model responds to this behavior.

This approach is suggested by a second characteristic of the theory as outlined herein. The extension of the Keynesian model pointed up the fact that investment is capacity-creating as well as income-generating. It has also been shown that in those systems where growth is taking place, innovations are necessary to maintain the profit rate at the equilibrium level. Innovations have virtually unlimited ramifications in an economy; in particular, they may be expected to change the $a$'s, the $b$'s, and the $k$'s, i.e., change the structure of the economic system. Thus, economic growth results in rising income and rising capacity *and* in structural changes. These structural changes, in turn, change the environment within which the short-run mechanism functions. It then becomes necessary to examine the nature of these structural changes and the resulting effect upon the growth-generating powers of the economy. Thus both of the points mentioned here lead to the conclusion that the analysis, as presented up to this point, must be deepened, if it is to throw any light at all upon the truly long-run performance of an economy. . . .

The third characteristic of the set of ideas under discussion shall be cited here, but not discussed. In effect, the theory jumps into the middle of an economy that is already in motion. But in many economies in the world, growth is about to begin, and in such economies the problems focus on establishing the appropriate preconditions for growth, rather than maintaining an already established growth rate. Thus, one can conceive of the problems of an underdeveloped world in terms of creating an economy whose routine functioning produces growth. These problems bring us into contact with a whole host of difficulties distinct from those considered here; to attempt even a cursory review of current thinking on this subject would take us well beyond the time and space available.

## Gottfried Haberler

## Critical Observations on Some Current Notions in the Theory of Economic Development

I SHALL discuss critically four ideas that have played a great role in recent writings on economic development. 1) The notion of disguised unemployment in underdeveloped countries, 2) the notion of "balanced growth" or "big push," 3) the demonstration effect, 4) the theory of the secular deterioration of the terms of trade for underdeveloped countries.

I do not say that the whole literature on the subject is based on these notions. In fact it would be foolish to say that, if for no other reason than because I know only a small fraction of the immense literature on the subject. But it is safe to say, I believe, that these ideas have played a considerable role in a highly influential part of the literature and they permeate influential official thinking, e.g. many U.N. esp. E.C.E., ECLA and ECAFE publications.

### UNEMPLOYMENT IN UNDERDEVELOPED COUNTRIES

... To my mind, the claims of the proponents of the theory of widespread disguised unemployment are tremendously exaggerated. I can perhaps better explain what I think is wrong with the theory of disguised unemployment by stating positively what in my opinion is actually true in varying degrees in various countries, not only in underdeveloped but in developed countries as well: If it were possible to improve methods of production in agriculture; *if* the skill of farm laborers is increased; *if* social habits could be changed, a new spirit implanted and the resistance to moving to and living in cities and to working in factories could be overcome; *if* technology in industry could be changed so as to employ unskilled rural workers; *if* capital and other cooperating factors (entrepreneurs, managers, skilled foremen, etc.) could be provided in larger quantities and better quality; *if* and to the extent that all these things happen or are done, agriculture can release a lot of labor without loss of output and industrial output be stepped up at the same time.

Now there is no doubt that all these things gradually do happen and did happen all the time in developed as well as underdeveloped countries. In fact, economic development largely consists of these changes. Furthermore, few would deny that many of these changes and improvements can be speeded up by appropriate policies (although, if the measures taken are inappropriate or the dosage incorrect the result will be a slow-down rather than a speed-up) and that for some of these changes to happen Government action is indispensable. But it is very misleading to speak of disguised unemployment. In that sense there always was disguised unemployment in developed as well as underdeveloped countries and practically everybody is a disguised unemployed person, even in the most highly developed countries, because each of us will produce more ten years hence when technology has made further progress, skill and training have been further improved, the capital stock increased, etc.

The cases where after removal of a part of the labor force, output remains unchanged (or even rises) without capital having been increased, technology improved, social habits changed, etc., or where such changes can be expected to be the automatic and immediate consequence of a prior reduction in labor input, must be comparatively rare and inconsequential compared with the increase in output due to the gradual introduction of all those changes and improvements.

The theory of disguised unemployment is often associated with the proposition that the capital-labor proportion is fixed—forgetting conveniently other productive agents. In other words production functions (isoquants) are said to have rectangular (or at least angular) shape. In some modern highly mechanized industries one may sometimes find situations faintly approaching this case. But the assumption that this should be the case in more primitive economies (agriculture) and should be a chronic situation seems to me preposterous.

It is true one can sometimes observe in underdeveloped countries a tendency to introduce a few modern highly mechanized plants with imported machinery, foreign supervisors and mechanics and using very little native labor. But these instances of "show case industrialization"[1] can in no way change the general picture. It should also be observed that they are not instances of the operation of the "demonstration effect" but almost always the consequence of faulty policies which artificially foster (e.g. by

---

1. The phrase is W. H. Nicholls' in *Investment in Agriculture in Underdeveloped Countries*, "American Economic Review," May 1955.

means of exchange allocation at often fantastically unrealistic rates) the establishment of uneconomic plants and industries.

## THE THEORY OF "BALANCED GROWTH" OR "BIG PUSH"

This theory asserts that if the typical underdeveloped country wishes to develop, it must push ahead fast and far, all along the line or it will not get anywhere at all. There is no room for slow piecemeal improvements. Owing to the low income and lack of purchasing power, the market is too small to permit any one industry to expand unless all others expand at the same time—thus providing a market for each others' wares.

This theory, again, is based on preoccupation with, and exaggeration of the importance of, a few highly mechanized giant plants or industries. These show cases catch the fancy of the onlooker and make him overlook the great mass of small and medium size run-of-the-mill plants and industries which are the backbone even of most highly developed countries.

The theory is contradicted by the patent fact that industrial advance is usually limited by lack of capital, including "social framework investment," insufficient supply of entrepreneurship, of skilled, trained and disciplined labor and not by the insufficient size of the market.

The theory overlooks or discounts the possibility of increasing the size of the market by international trade.

On the basis of this theory, it is impossible to explain why any now developed country ever developed. How conservative and realistic, compared with modern theories, sounds the *Communist Manifesto* where the productive power of the unfettered capitalistic system and its capability of developing and industrializing backward countries are described in truly glowing terms.

## THE DEMONSTRATION EFFECT

Underdeveloped countries are supposed to be seriously handicapped by the operation of the "demonstration effect." The demonstration effect was introduced into economics by J. Duesenberry. He was, however, not speaking of underdeveloped countries and should not be held responsible for its use or abuse in that area.

The "demonstration effect" is supposed to work in the sphere of consumption as well as in that of production. . . .

The demonstration effect is best regarded as an explanation, motivation and excuse for inflationary policies. It is doubtful whether it would cause any troubles at all without lax monetary policies. It surely is not specifically related to underdeveloped countries. All of us, even in the most advanced countries, are under constant pressure by high power advertising to live beyond our means. Everywhere we see and read of things we should like to have and cannot afford. Instalment credit makes it easy to buy things that we should not buy. Some of us are tempted into making foolish purchases, which we later regret; but these slips are quickly corrected and no permanent harm results except if and to the extent that instalment credit intensifies inflationary expansion during the upgrade and deflationary contraction during the downgrade of the cycle; but this intensification of the cyclical swings is contingent upon the cyclical flexibility of credit in general and could be counteracted by monetary policy.

There is, however, an area in which the demonstration effect really operates and where it causes serious damage to the economies of under-developed countries. That is the area of public policy and collective spending.

Many backward countries have adopted and are still in the process of eagerly imitating the latest policies which it took the advanced industrial countries decades or centuries to develop. The latest most up-to-date legislation on social security, regulations of labor, minimum wages, working conditions, channeling of saving through governmental agencies and impounding them for public purpose—all these policies which the developed countries have adopted only in a late stage of their development are often introduced in underdeveloped countries as soon as they are freed from colonial status. Add equalization of income through progressive direct taxation, nationalization of existing enterprises and reservation for the Government of certain industries and you have an economic policy which greatly overtaxes the limited administrative capacities of underdeveloped countries.

## TERMS OF TRADE

The theory has become popular that the terms of trade have shown a secular tendency to deteriorate for the underdeveloped countries, the so-called "peripheral" world; more precisely for the raw material producing or rather exporting countries.[2] This alleged historical trend is supposed to be the consequence of deepseated factors and hence capable of confident extrapolation into the future.[3]

2. It should not be forgotten that there are some highly developed and industrialized countries, whose exports consist largely of raw materials and foodstuff. To this group belong, for example, Australia and Denmark.

3. See e.g. *The Economic Development of Latin America and its Principal Problems,* United Nations, 1950. For a more recent statement see Raul Prebisch in *National Policy for Economic Welfare,* Columbia University Bicentennial Conference. New York, 1955, pp. 277-280.

To my mind the alleged historical facts lack proof, their explanation is faulty, the extrapolation reckless and the policy conclusions irresponsible —to put it mildly.

The historical generalization suffers, first of all, from an excessive degree of aggregation. It is improbable in the extreme that it should be possible to make a valid generalization for the very heterogeneous countries which constitute the underdeveloped part of the world. To pick a few examples from the Western Hemisphere: Can anyone seriously maintain that the long run[4] change in the terms of trade is the same for (a) agricultural exporters (Argentina, Uruguay), (b) mining countries (Bolivia), (c) coffee exporters (Brazil), (d) petroleum exporters (Venezuela)? Many of these countries have undergone profound changes in their internal economy and trade structure which make long run comparisons extremely hazardous.

If we concentrate on a more homogenous group of countries whose export trade has not changed much, the fact still remains that the composition of their imports, that is of the exports of the industrial countries, has changed profoundly. Scores of new products are being produced and exported and the quality of those that existed 10 or 20 years ago has been improved to such an extent that they are virtually new commodities. No attempt has been made to allow for these quality changes. The above mentioned U.N. report confines itself to the remark: "It is regrettable that the price indexes do not reflect the difference in quality of finished products. For this reason, it was not possible to take them into account."[5] The report then proceeds as if this was a minor, quite unimportant qualification.

There has taken place another far-reaching structural change in world trade, the neglect of which completely vitiates long run comparisons in the terms of trade—namely, the revolution that has occurred in transport techniques and transport cost. When in the 1870's and 1880's the American Middle West was opened up and overseas wheat began to flow to Europe—the British terms of trade improved. But obviously that did not mean that the factoral terms of trade of the new exporting regions deteriorated. Agriculture in the old world was indeed hurt but surely not in the underdeveloped "regions of recent settlement" from where the new supplies originated.

In general, as has often been pointed out, if transport costs are reduced it is possible for the commodity terms of trade (exclusive of services) to improve for *both* importing and exporting countries or areas at the same time.

---

4. During the short run cycle a greater uniformity may be present.

5. *Loc. cit.* p. 6.

Waiving all these difficulties, or assuming that allowance has been made for them, there still remains the question of productivity changes. In other words, a given deterioration in the commodity terms of trade of a country need not reflect a deterioration of its single or double factoral terms of trade; it may reflect a differential increase in the productivity of the country's export industries.

No attempt has been made by the proponents of the criticized theory to grapple with any of the various defects which I have mentioned.

Suppose, however, we have satisfied ourselves that the terms of trade have in fact deteriorated in the last 100 years for a certain group of countries *posito non concesso*. No policy conclusions could be drawn unless it were possible to advance good reasons for assuming that this deterioration is likely to continue. In order to make such an extrapolation, it would be necessary to attempt an explanation of the alleged trend.

Two reasons are usually given why the terms of trade move against raw material exporters. The first is that prices of finished manufactured goods are bound to be kept high by monopolistic machinations of trade unions and cartels.

This argument, as it is usually presented, rests on a confusion of absolute and relative prices. It is true that industrial progress in the developed countries rarely takes the form of constant money wages and money incomes associated with falling prices, but rather the form of constant (or even rising) prices associated with rising money wages. This may be bad from the point of view of stability and is undoubtedly unjust for fixed income receivers. But there is no evidence that it has changed relative prices as between industry and agriculture or between finished goods and raw materials.

The second reason advanced for the alleged trend is the operation of Engel's law. When incomes rise the world over, demand for foodstuffs and raw materials rises slower than demand for finished industrial products. Hence the terms of exchange move in favor of the latter against the former.

Engel's law is certainly one of the best established empirical generalizations in economics. But it cannot bear the heavy burden which is placed on it by the theory under review. It applies to food but not to every kind of food. In the case of industrial raw materials, the situation is much more complicated.

The main objection, however, is that the operation of Engel's law is only one factor among many others. The exhaustion of certain raw materials in some of the developed countries (e.g. coal in the U.K.; iron ore in the U.S.) which necessitates the massive importation of raw materials is an example of a counteracting tendency.[6]

This development can be regarded as a concrete manifestation of a broad and supposedly all-pervading tendency which has played an important role in classical and neo-classical economics—viz. of the law of diminishing returns.

There is a pessimistic streak—pessimistic from the point of view of the industrial countries, as well as from the point of view of the internal income distribution within each country—going through classical economics from Ricardo and Torrens via J. S. Mill to Keynes (in his debate on the terms of trade with Beveridge) and recently Austin Robinson.[7] It is based on the doctrine that agriculture and extractive industries are subject to diminishing returns while this is not true of manufacturing. Hence the terms of trade must inexorably turn against the manufacturing industries and industrial countries.

This is evidently the exact opposite of the thesis that Engel's law will turn the terms of trade against the primary producers. We have thus Engel's law pitted against the law of diminishing returns.

Around the turn of the century an influential and vocal group of nationalistic and protectionist German economists (among them A. Wagner and Pohle) warned about the dangers of further industrialization and advocated higher protection for agriculture to arrest or slow down the rapid urbanization and industrialization of Germany which was then at full swing. Their case was partly based on the prediction that the industrial countries would find it harder and harder to obtain food and raw materials from abroad, because the food and raw material producing countries, too, would industrialize and use their food and raw materials themselves.[8] Austin Robinson's recent article is reminiscent of those German voices. He reaches the same conclusion for present-day Britain as Wagner and Pohle did for Germany of their time.

Until now these dire predictions have proved entirely wrong. Industrialization and urbanization have proceeded relentlessly everywhere but the supply of raw materials and foodstuffs have kept pace.

It will perhaps be objected that both parties, the champions of Engel's law and those of the law of diminishing returns, cannot both be wrong simultaneously. For the terms of trade must shift either in favor of one

---

6. There are, of course, examples on the other side, e.g. the substitution of "synthetic" for "natural" materials—which further illustrates the complexity and unpredictability of the broad development.

7. *The Changing Structure of the British Economy,* "Economic Journal." Sept. 1954.

8. See my *Theory of International Trade,* p. 285 *et seq.* for a brief summary and references to the literature.

or in favor of the other; it would be a strange coincidence if they did not change at all.

Now, the terms of trade may have shifted back and forth and this is probably what actually happened. But whatever the truth about the terms of trade, both parties can be wrong, and in fact are wrong, in my opinion, in the sense that a deterioration of its terms of trade does not prevent a country from being better off than before (although other things being equal a country would always be better off if foreign demand had been so elastic that a given improvement of technology in a country's export industry had left the commodity terms of trade unchanged instead of producing a deterioration).

Moreover, both parties cannot be right in their respective policy conclusions. For both groups recommend protection for contradictory reasons and purposes; the champions of Engel's law call for more severe import restrictions in underdeveloped countries in order to anticipate a deterioration of the terms of trade *against* the underdeveloped countries; the champions of the law of diminishing returns recommend more protection in the industrial countries in order to anticipate a deterioration of the terms of trade *against* the industrial countries.[9] The terms of trade cannot move in both directions at the same time. In fact, both parties are wrong in their policy recommendations, because it is irrational and irresponsible to base policy on highly uncertain guesses about future developments. Furthermore, even if we were sure that a certain change in the terms of trade was coming, there would be no sense in trying to anticipate it unless it was expected to come so suddenly that it would require a costly and rapid adjustment. In the German discussion 60 years ago much was made of the argument that industrialization and urbanization was an irreversible process. If by that is meant that once agriculture has been allowed to contract it is difficult to revive agricultural production, wartime experience seems to show that the argument is wrong. It is possible under modern conditions to expand agricultural production fairly quickly when the need arises.

Enough has been said, I believe, to demonstrate that the theory of the secular deterioration of the terms of trade for the underdeveloped countries is completely unfounded and the policy recommendations based on it are devoid of any solid basis.

## CONCLUDING REMARKS

What does it all add up to? We can perhaps say that the four criticized notions and the policy recommendations derived from them are based on three basic convictions.

---

9. It will be observed that the argument in question has nothing to do with the static, terms of trade or optimum tariff argument for protection.

1. A profound distrust of the judgment of individual producers and consumers. The individuals are said to be often irrational and ignorant. The consumer does not know what is good for him. He is typically a spendthrift and is subject to the demonstration effect. Producers are equally irrational and incompetent. They employ workers whose marginal product is zero or negative, they copy methods of production which are unsuited for the resource pattern of underdeveloped countries, they are ignorant of potential external economies and fail to foresee and to anticipate changes in the terms of trade.

2. The economists, both native and foreign consultants on their fleeting visits to some backward area, are alert and informed about all these things which individual consumers and producers are ignorant of. They foresee changes in the terms of trade, recognize disguised unemployment and external economies and are not subject to the demonstration effect.

3. Economists are not only omniscient, but also know what to do to correct the various defects. And there is no doubt about their capability of persuading governments and politicians and of carrying out policies according to the diagnoses and prognoses provided by the economists.

All this sounds fantastic and it is undoubtedly exaggerated, but not to such an extent as to rob the picture that emerges of its relevance for the understanding of actual economic policy in many underdeveloped countries. In almost all backward countries economic policy is highly interventionist and protectionist, verging in some on integrated central planning. The conclusion I wish to draw is not that an extreme *laissez-faire* policy is most conducive to stimulating economic development. The Government can certainly do much to speed up economic growth and there are many indispensable measures which only the Government take. My conclusion is rather that by doing too much, by trying to do things that individuals and the market can do better, Governments overtax their limited capacities and are forced to neglect their basic and indispensable functions.

In his keynote talk opening the Columbia University Bicentennial Conference on "National Policy for Economic Welfare at Home and Abroad," an address full of beauty and wisdom, Sir Dennis Robertson asked the question: "What does the economist economize?" His answer was that the economist economizes, or should economize, "that scarce resource, Love"— meaning that they should not act and predicate their recommendations on the assumption that love, goodwill, cooperative spirit are available in unlimited quantities.

Similarly, on a lower and more pedestrian level, we may say that Governmental know-how, administrative efficiency, political honesty are a scarce and precious resource, especially scarce in underdeveloped countries. The supply and quality of this resource has improved over the last

150 years in most countries. It can be further increased but only slowly and at a heavy cost in terms of manpower and brain power—another precious and very scarce resource. It cannot be as easily taught or copied and imported from foreign countries as many productive technologies can be. On the other hand, it can be depleted and its quality impaired by excessive use and above all it can be misallocated and be spread too thin.

This is what happens in many underdeveloped countries. Prevailing policies misuse and misallocate, spread too thin and deplete and impair the limited supply of Governmental know-how. If Governmental energies and the best brains serving the administrative apparatus are spent on thinking up and operating unworkable and infinitely complex systems of exchange control, rationing of imports, allocation of quotas, nationalizing, expropriating private enterprises, running grossly inefficient public enterprises—if Governments try to do things which private business, native or foreign, can do much more efficiently—it should be no wonder that those services, indispensable for economic growth, which only the Government can perform or which it can perform better, are sadly neglected. Such services and activities are elementary and higher education—if 40% and more of the population are illiterate as is the case, e.g. in most Latin American countries, economic growth must be retarded; public health; basic utilities such as water, communication, postal services, port installations as well as the elementary Governmental services of maintaining law and order. Many or all of these "social overhead investments" are sadly neglected in many or most underdeveloped countries; or they are not developed as fast as they should be in the interest of economic growth, because Governments pour a disproportionate part of their resources into activities which are either outrightly wasteful or could be performed more efficiently and cheaply by private business, and cause inefficient use of private capital; e.g. by stimulating by all sorts of protectionist devices (including exchange control) inefficient secondary industries.

Bad economic policies are, of course, not a monopoly of underdeveloped countries. But no doubt there they are especially bad and underdeveloped countries can least afford such waste. Economists in developed countries must take their full share of responsibility for this state of affairs.

# Obstacles
# to Development

How DOES A POOR NATION, apparently condemned by its poverty to remain poor, break out of the vicious circle of economic deprivation? How does it acquire the necessary margin of resources, beyond the needs of immediate subsistence, that is prerequisite to rapid capital formation and economic growth?

The first of the following six essays, written by Jacob Viner, classifies the bottlenecks and concludes that only foreign aid is capable of rescuing the poorer economies.

The late Ragnar Nurkse's essay concentrates on the danger that inadequate demand for capital goods will limit the pace of economic development. This seeming paradox is the consequence of the limited market in poor societies for final goods.

Supplementing Nurkse's analysis of the possible unattractiveness of investment in the underdeveloped economies is a discerning essay by Henry Aubrey. This essay investigates the nest of expectations and objectives which surround the entrepreneurial process in developing lands.

The authors of the UNESCO article emphasize land rather than capital as a development bottleneck. The result of their survey of existing agrarian arrangements is a plea for drastic land reform. They consider wasteful nearly all schemes of agricultural land tenure from small private holdings to large *latifundia*.

The next two articles discuss yet another obstacle to growth—the behavior of population. Ansley J. Coale's analysis of fertility, death rates, and determinants of real income leads to an urgent conclusion: birth control is absolutely indispensable if the emerging nations will ever be able permanently to improve their position. On population, Albert O. Hirschmann's judgment is somewhat less pessimistic. The experience of economic development may itself create the incentives needed to control the dangers of overpopulation.

# Jacob Viner

## Barriers to Economic Development

I PROCEED to an attempt at a schematic presentation of the obstacles to economic development, with the reminder that I use the term to signify not merely economic growth, but economic growth with which is associated either rising *per capita* levels of income or the maintenance of existing high levels of income. The classification of these obstacles about to be presented is admittedly a somewhat artificial one, since the categories of obstacles distinguished are not only not independent of each other but overlap and in some cases may represent the same factors looked at from different points of view rather than different factors.

First come low productivity functions. Foremost in responsibility for these are qualitative factors, physical or human. In the first lecture, I used, as an illustration of a type of assumption in the construction of economic models for theoretical analysis which was peculiarly destructive of the practical usefulness of economic theory, the assumption that each of the factors of production was universally homogeneous, so that the productivity functions were everywhere identical. Adherence to such a model would prevent consideration of the responsibility of international differences in the economic quality of factors, in their 'effectiveness', to use Taussig's term, for differences in the levels of *per capita* income as between countries.

Much obviously depends on the character of the physical environment, or the 'quality', in my terminology, of the natural resources considered as factors of production. Here are involved such things as the character of the soil, the forest resources, topography as favouring or hindering cheap transportation, mineral resources, the availability of water-power, and rainfall and temperatures. The geographical situation of a country is also significant with respect to its opportunities for profitable foreign trade, since proximity to foreign markets and sources of supply can be of great importance.

An unfavourable physical environment can be a major obstacle to economic development. That it need not be a fatal obstacle, however, that it can be overcome by high quality in its human resources, is demonstrated *inter alia* by the case of Switzerland. Except for the one advantage of its strategic location across some major trade routes, Switzerland has scarcely a single physical advantage for economic development; taking all physical factors into account, it is one of the most poorly endowed countries in the world. Nevertheless, in wealth *per capita* it ranks at or near the top, and it ranks high also in *per capita* income.

Of great importance also is the 'quality' of the working population, including the rank-and-file of industrial and agricultural labour, the entrepreneurial and managerial *élite,* and the skilled engineers and technicians. I have in mind here not biological or 'racial' differences, which authoritative scientific opinion overwhelmingly holds to be undetectable or of minor importance, but the differences which result from historical and cultural factors, from environment, quality of health, nutrition, and education, and from the quality of the leadership provided by government and the social *élite.*

The first requirements for high labour productivity under modern conditions are that the masses of the population shall be literate, healthy, and sufficiently well fed to be strong and energetic. In many countries, I feel sure, if this were achieved all else necessary for rapid economic development would come readily and easily of itself. I also feel sure that whenever this has not been accomplished and is not being strongly promoted to the utmost limits which the national resources permit, it is not necessary to look for the other factors, although they are certain to exist, to explain pervasive poverty and slow economic growth. . . .

The real bottleneck is likely to be not the lack of adequate responsiveness of the masses to the new teaching, but the scarcity of the teaching and of teachers able to impart it. The process can be greatly speeded, however, if there is initiative in importing teachers to train teachers, or in sending abroad selected nationals to learn how to train teachers. It is fortunate that modern industry is not as much dependent on the skills of the rank-and-file workers which can be learnt only slowly as was industry in the past or as agriculture in some of its phases continues to be. The difficult skills tend nowadays to be built into the machine, or to be concentrated in a relatively small number of supervisors and mechanics, and where these are not initially available locally, they can be readily imported through selective immigration. The higher levels of designing, engineering, and scientific 'know-how' are often needed only in small quantities. High-grade managerial and technological skill is always on sale at a competitive price, and provided it can adapt itself to local conditions, local materials, and the requirements of local markets, is cheap almost regardless of its price. Managerial and engineering 'know-how' are the most mobile internationally of economic goods, and where they are lacking it is because of the absence of genuine local demand, or unwillingness to import them, rather than because of unavailability. . . .

Scarcity of capital is the second type of obstacle to economic development which I will consider. Capital-scarcity may be absolute, or may be relative only to the opportunities for profitable investment. The United States was a relatively high interest-rate country and a borrower of capital until shortly before the First World War, but it probably even then had more capital per industrial worker than some of the countries from whom it borrowed. The amount of capital *per capita* in use within a country is probably more significant for present purposes than the amount of capital *per capita* owned within the country, since capital often, and probably usually, promotes the economic development of the country using it more than that of the country supplying it where these are not the same country. Canada provides an apt illustration. But the significance of international payments and receipts of interest and dividends on the economic growth of a country is not to be disregarded.

The domestic accumulation of capital in a poor country is bound to be slow. Income is the source of savings, and where income *per capita* is low, the annual rate of voluntary saving *per capita* will also tend to be low. It is generally agreed, however, that, in a given population at a given time, the percentage of income annually saved will be greater for higher-income than for lower-income groups, so that the greater the inequality in the distribution of income the greater will be the percentage of the aggregate income which will be saved. It may also be true that as average income through time increases, the percentage of the national income which will be annually saved will also increase. But empirical evidence in support of this is lacking, and there are some *a priori* reasons for being sceptical about it. What can be said with more confidence, however, is that as average income rises through time, the absolute amount of annual savings *per capita* will also rise. It is also to be considered that the greater the amount of *per capita* wealth and income, the better will be the credit status of a population, and the more therefore will it be able to borrow from abroad *per capita* if it wishes to. To him that hath more is available on loan.

I have been referring to general tendencies, and these may in particular countries or at particular times be offset or counteracted by special institutional or other factors. Before the Industrial Revolution in western Europe, and up to the present day in non-industrialized countries, the bulk of accumulated wealth has consisted of landed property.

\* \* \* \* \*

Wealthy landowners have greater opportunity to invest their savings in the improvement and embellishment of their own properties than does the ordinary urban saver. Peasant proprietors have notoriously been the greatest savers of all. For rural landowners spending and investing may be hard to distinguish, since improvement of an estate can be at the same time the most conspicuous way of displaying wealth and the most effective way of adding to it. As long as a country has a comparative advantage in the expansion of agriculture over the expansion of manufacturing, the investment in their own estates of their savings by rural landowners may be the most productive and the most efficient investment under way in the national economy.

The rate of savings depends, of course, on many factors in addition to the size of income, but we really have very little reliable knowledge about the psychological and other determinants of the volume of savings. It is generally held that inflation is an obstacle to private saving. This is probably true where the alternative to inflation is not mass unemployment. It is probably true also, under all conditions, for persons of middle incomes who are not able to find what they regard as effective hedges against the depreciation of the real value of their liquid assets and therefore flee from money and from assets having fixed money-values to consumable goods.

In past experience, however, the inflationary process has generally involved a shift of income and wealth from wage-earners, the salaried class, the holders of small pensions, savings accounts, government bonds, and life insurance policies, to the more wealthy classes, the landowners, entrepreneurs, middlemen, who automatically or by the exploitation of superior skill and opportunity were able to derive profit from the rise in prices which for the poorer classes brought only loss. Since those who profited from inflation were as a class those who saved larger fractions of their current incomes, it is conceivable, therefore, that in the net inflation as it has usually operated in the past has tended to increase rather than to decrease the proportion of national savings to national income.

Inflation, however, also operates arbitrarily to distort the direction of investment and also otherwise to generate economic waste. It brings profits to entrepreneurs even if they are inefficient, and thus dulls the incentives to efficiency. It artificially enlarges the field of operation of the middleman and the broker, and diverts talent and personnel from production to non-productive speculation. It puts a premium on investment in urban real estate and in idle inventories, and makes difficult the financing of enterprises whose prices because of regulation are not easily raised or which commonly obtain capital through the issue of bonds, largely regardless of the real productivity for the national economy of such enterprises.

If a government draws off from its citizens in taxes a part of what they otherwise would have spent for current consumption, and uses the proceeds in useful public works, the government is performing the saving function for the community. I do not think, however, that many well-authenticated instances of such procedures can be cited. In any case, it is much easier to cite instances where governments have either taxed away or borrowed private savings and used them to defray current expenditures of a non-investment, and often of a spendthrift, character. It is always incumbent on government in private-enterprise countries to create a favourable setting for saving and for private investment not only by providing a good example in its own financial housekeeping, but also by establishing an atmosphere of political and legal security for private investment, and by providing efficient and honest administration of the ordinary functions of government. The contributions which governments can make to sound economic development are often undoubtedly greater in these prosaic and old-fashioned fields than in the now fashionable 'plans' which have as their goals the diversion of private savings from the financing of routine private investment to the financing of spectacular and grandiose programmes of public investment not subject to the tests of profit-and-loss accounting.

In countries where the marginal productivity function of capital is high and elastic, capital scarcity can be a major brake on economic development, and its pace can be greatly speeded if capital can be borrowed abroad at moderate rates of interest. The obstacles to international investment, however, both on the creditor and the debtor side, have grown formidably in recent years, and while there has been no previous period in which as much reliance has been put on international investment as prevails today, it is long since the actual prospects for large-scale international investment have been as unfavourable as they now seem to be.

Main reliance is being placed today on governmental rather than on private international lending, both because debtor countries prefer to borrow from governments and because private capital shows great reluctance to go abroad except when it is fleeing from domestic perils. Through war losses, heavy taxation, and socialization, the fund of disposable private capital potentially available for foreign investment has been drastically reduced in some at least of the countries which formerly were important exporters of capital. The special hazards of foreign investment have increased and are increasing further by all appearances. Many capital-poor countries gave a grudging welcome to the private foreign investor, but if he nevertheless ventures his capital they give him cause to regret it. The popular prejudice which has always existed in all countries against the export of capital has become more effective in recent years with the decline in the political power of the propertied classes, the evaporation of *laissez-faire* objections to governmental regulation of capital flows, and the growth in the scale and the effectiveness of regulatory machinery.

There is no justification for more than very modest expectations as to the scale on which governmental foreign investment will take place, in the absence of pressure from political and strategic considerations which may tend to operate as much to make the potential borrowers unwilling to borrow as they do to convert otherwise reluctant lenders to willingness to lend. National economic planning has become general, and planning governments, as I have already found occasion to point out, tend always to get themselves into financial difficulties which foreign lending would alleviate in the short-run but augment in the long-run. The universal growth of national debts, moreover, makes all governments feel poor. Few governments have had substantial experience in foreign lending and most of such experience as they have had has been unhappy. The loans in the past have commonly brought neither lasting goodwill nor repayment. It is too early as yet for confident judgement that present-day governmental lending will have more gratifying results for the lenders. The number of potential lenders on a large scale is very small, scarcely larger than one, while the actual and potential seekers of credit number at least fifty. It would be easy to extend this list of reasons why it is not realistic for underdeveloped countries to place major reliance on foreign investment in their territories as an aid to their economic development.

*    *    *    *    *

The third category of obstacles to economic development which I will examine consists of conditions in foreign trade which have or are alleged to have peculiarly unfavourable impacts on relatively poor countries and on countries whose exports consist predominantly of primary products and whose imports consist largely of the products of industrially advanced countries. . . .

The terms on which a country trades depend on the scale on which it unloads its products on export markets as compared to the world demand for these products. The greater the increase in a country's population, other things equal, the greater will tend to be the volume of its staple export products which it will attempt to market abroad, provided these are not also its staple articles of domestic consumption, and therefore the worse will its terms of trade tend to be. But this will apply equally, as a tendency, to countries whether they are predominantly agricultural or predominantly industrial, and the appropriate remedy in either case would be to check the rate of growth of population. In a predominantly agricultural country rapid growth of population unaccompanied by proportionate growth in demand for its agricultural products will under free-market conditions bring spontaneously into action forces tending to industrialize the country, by making agricultural production relatively less remunerative. In industrialized countries it will have the reverse effect.

Primary commodities generally have a wider amplitude of fluctuation in their prices during the business cycle than do manufactured commodities. Countries exporting primary commodities are consequently squeezed during a depression by a greater drop in their export than in their import prices. This is true, and regrettable. But the obverse side of the shield should also be looked at. During booms, primary products rise more in price than do manufactures. The profits of the fat years should be balanced against the losses of the lean years. With good fiscal and monetary management, it would even be feasible—it has occurred without being planned in the past, notably in New Zealand—to conserve some of the boom-time profits in foreign trade to meet the deficits of the depression years. Still better, of course, would be, by international action, to iron out the cycles.

It is claimed that statistical data show a secular trend in the terms of trade between agricultural and manufactured products adverse to the former. As far as the data go, no such uniform trend can be shown. English economists have, indeed, often claimed to have found the reverse trend to have been operating in the past, and on the invalid assumption that the law of diminishing returns is peculiar to agriculture have often forecast the continuance of an adverse trend for the future for manufactures as against agricultural products. They are, in fact, making such forecasts now. For comparisons over long periods, moreover, the available data are largely irrelevant. The primary commodities whose average prices for broad categories are used in the computations of the terms of trade are for the most part, for averages so computed, not superior in quality, and in some cases are perhaps inferior, to the corresponding commodities of earlier years. The articles whose prices are used are always a much smaller sample of the total exports of manufactures than of agricultural products, and no weight is given to the gain in utility from the new commodities which have become available, such as the automobile, the tractor, and penicillin. Where the manufactures are nominally the same, moreover, they have over the years become incomparably superior in quality. It may perhaps take more pounds of coffee, or of cotton, to buy a lamp today than it did in 1900, but today's coffee and cotton are, I presume, not appreciably better in quality than those of 1900, whereas today's electric lamp is incomparably superior to the kerosene lamp of 1900. The decline in transportation costs, moreover, has made possible the seeming paradox of the commodity terms of trade improving simultaneously for both sets of countries.

It is claimed also that there is an historical 'law' of more rapid technological progress in manufacturing than in agriculture. If this were true, and manifested itself in a more rapid rate of improvement of the *quality* of manufactures than of agricultural commodities, it would operate to deprive an adverse trend of the terms of trade for agricultural products of its significance, for the adverse trend in prices would be offset by a reverse trend in quality. If this were true, and manifested itself in a relative decline in real cost of production of manufactures, it would tend to result in a favourable and not in an unfavourable movement in relative prices for agricultural products.

I know of no grounds, however, which justify acceptance of the proposition that there is any tendency for technological progress to be more rapid in manufacturing than in agriculture, except as such tendency is a consequence—not a cause—of countries which are more advanced technologically being often more industrial than agricultural. There is not, as far as I know, any marked backwardness in technology of the agriculture of Denmark, of England, of New Zealand, or of Iowa.

I will grant, however, that where agriculture is primitive in its methods it will tend to be resistant to more efficient procedures involving change in long-established practices and habits, and that this will not be equally true of manufactures, which are less susceptible to conservative adherence to obsolete methods. The more backward a country is in its procedures, however, the greater is the field for technological progress. A country with the most modern processes can advance farther only by new inventions and discoveries. A country which is backward technologically can make great advances merely by borrowing from the already existing stock of knowledge. For countries which have a comparative advantage in agriculture despite their failure to use advanced techniques, it is not a subsidized industrialization at the expense of agriculture which is the appropriate remedy, but education and training for a modernized agriculture. This will require capital, and capital is scarce, but industrialization will generally require even more capital per worker, or per unit of product. It is an important consideration, moreover, that whereas in international trade in manufactures the product of obsolete methods or styling is often absolutely unsaleable in a competitive market, so that for a country dependent to an important extent on exports of manufactures to finance its essential imports any lag in technological progress can be fatal, this is not true to anything like the same degree, if true at all, for a country which exports mainly primary products. . . .

The opportunities open to an underdeveloped country in the foreign trade field are certain to be a vital factor in determining the rate at which it can make economic progress. No country except the United States has attained a high level of *per capita* income which has not maintained a high ratio of imports to total national product, and no country, except possibly Russia, can in this respect make the United States its model without courting perpetual poverty. The high degree of self-sufficiency of the United States was due in part to a deliberate national policy of high tariff protection. But it was the continental character of the United States, its richness and variety of natural resources and the great obstacle which internal transportation costs presented to international trade, as well as the technical skills of its people, which enabled the American to dispense with foreign products without having to pay a heavy cost in terms of either deprivation of products of any important kind or of extreme expensiveness of domestic substitutes, and which thus enabled the United States to achieve economic prosperity despite its commercial policy and its low ratio of foreign to domestic trade.

The individual country has, as a rule, little control over the treatment its exports shall receive in foreign markets or over the terms on which it can obtain its imports. What it has full control of, however, is the extent to which imports shall be hindered from entering by its own artificial barriers. There is no underdeveloped country which has not a great stake in the removal or reduction of foreign trade barriers. . . .

The fourth and final category of obstacles to economic development, as I prefer to define the term, is associated with a rapid rate of increase of population. I have found it necessary already to refer to this factor as an obstacle to the attainment of economic prosperity in the sense of a high level of *per capita* income and the absence of mass poverty. Population increase hovers like a menacing dark cloud over all poor countries. It can offset, and more than offset, the contribution to economic prosperity which all other factors can make. Whatever the opportunities for economic betterment created by technological progress, by the discovery of new natural resources, by economic aid from abroad, and by the removal of foreign trade barriers, they can have as their chief consequence an increase in the number of children who survive to a short and wretched adulthood. Population increase may merely retard economic progress and under some circumstances may promote economic welfare, by increasing the number of those who share it, if it is a by-product of increasing *per capita* incomes operating, through better nutrition, better education, and better sanitary conditions, to enable more children to survive to a healthy and productive adult life. It will be most damaging if the increase in population is mainly the consequence of the application of modern public-health techniques which result in a decrease in infant mortality rates more rapid than the improvement in health conditions at later ages and more rapid than the rate of expansion of opportunities for productive employment.

What is most discouraging is that there are no easy and certain remedies for the overpopulation problem; that the remedy, birth control, which to most social scientists appears to be the only promising one requires a fairly high level of education and of income to be widely available and effective, and is moreover bitterly opposed by many on moral and religious grounds;

and that many persons, and many governments, refuse to recognize the existence of a problem here, or, if they do recognize it, to face it frankly and seek for a remedy.

It is a paradox of the population problem that on the grounds of historical experience and of theoretical analysis the attainment of high levels of *per capita* income and of education appear to be almost essential prerequisites of a cure of the problem and that the excessive rate of increase of population is itself the most important barrier to the establishment of these prerequisites. Here once more, the curse of the poor is their poverty, and no easy and certain way to break the vicious circle which is widely acceptable has as yet been discovered.

In this discussion of the obstacles to economic development, I have had occasion to deal with both external and internal obstacles. It is a natural and understandable tendency in underdeveloped countries to stress and to exaggerate the weight of the external obstacles, and to assign major responsibility for the removal of obstacles to economic betterment to governments and peoples other than their own. I do not wish to balance the exaggeration on one side by minimization on the other. The external factors are important, and I would wish to see the world at large, and the richer countries in particular, make their appropriate contribution to a solution of the world's greatest, most serious, economic problem: the problem of much over half the world's population living under conditions of acute poverty. The promotion of general reduction in trade barriers, the freer international movement of capital on reasonable terms, the facilitation of the general diffusion of the world's stock of technical knowledge and skills, these are the major contributions which the more favourably situated countries of the world can make to those less advanced and less prosperous. They are contributions of the greatest importance. But they will not suffice. Without genuine co-operation from the countries to be benefited they will not be effective, except perhaps in increasing still further the amount of hunger, sickness, premature mortality, and poverty in the world.

I do not contend that the underdeveloped countries have their economic futures in their own hands. On the contrary, in the absence of aid from external sources, I would have only pessimistic expectations with respect to the economic future of most of the underdeveloped countries. Given, however, the utmost help from these external factors which there is any reasonable ground to expect, the problem will not even begin to have a practicable solution unless the underdeveloped countries dedicate their own resources, human, physical, and financial, to a sound, large scale, and persistent attack on those basic internal causes of mass poverty which I have tried to identify and whose nature and method of operation I have tried to explain.

# Ragnar Nurkse

## The Size of the Market and the Inducement to Invest

OUR TOPIC has to do with the inducement to invest, such as it presents itself to the individual investor or entrepreneur. It is concerned, in other words, with the conditions that determine the demand for capital for use in the productive process. The dichotomy between demand and supply, so dear to economists, is fully applicable to the forces that govern the accumulation of capital. Capital formation is not entirely a matter of capital supply, although this no doubt the more important part of the problem. . . .

### THE VICIOUS CIRCLE OF POVERTY

In discussions of the problem of economic development, a phrase that crops up frequently is 'the vicious circle of poverty.' It is generally treated as something obvious, too obvious to be worth examining. I hope I may be forgiven if I begin by taking a look at this obvious concept.

It implies a circular constellation of forces tending to act and react upon one another in such a way as to keep a poor country in a state of poverty. Particular instances of such circular constellations are not difficult to imagine. For example, a poor man may not have enough to eat; being under-fed, his health may be weak; being physically weak, his working capacity is low, which means that he is poor, which in turn means that he will not have enough to eat; and so on. A situation of this sort, relating to a country as a whole, can be summed up in the trite proposition: 'a country is poor because it is poor.'

Perhaps the most important circular relationships of this kind are those that afflict the accumulation of capital in economically backward countries. The supply of capital is governed by the ability and willingness to save; the demand for capital is governed by the incentives to invest. A circular relationship exists on both sides of the problem of capital formation in the poverty-ridden areas of the world.

On the supply side, there is the small capacity to save, resulting from the low level of real income. The low real income is a reflection of low productivity, which in its turn is due largely to the lack of capital. The lack of capital is a result of the small capacity to save, and so the circle is complete.

On the demand side, the inducement to invest may be low because of the small buying power of the people, which is due to their small real income, which again is due to low productivity. The low level of productivity, however, is a result of the small amount of capital used in production, which in its turn may be caused at least partly by the small inducement to invest.

The low level of real income, reflecting low productivity, is a point that is common to both circles. Usually the trouble on the supply side receives all the emphasis. The trouble there is certainly obvious and serious, and some aspects of it will be thoroughly gone into later. But the possible block on the demand side, once one becomes aware of it, is also fairly obvious, though it may not be so serious, or so difficult to remove, as the supply deficiency.

Besides, let us remember that capital is not everything. In addition to the circular relationships that plague the capital problem, there are, of course, matters of unilateral causation that can keep a country poor; for instance, lack of mineral resources, insufficient water or barren soil. Some of the poorer countries in the world to-day are poor partly for such reasons. But in all of them their poverty is also attributable to some extent to the lack of adequate capital equipment, which can be due to the small inducement to invest as well as to the small capacity to save.

## WEAKNESS OF INVESTMENT INCENTIVES

It may at first be surprising to hear that there can be anything wrong on the demand side of the problem of capital formation in underdeveloped countries. Can there be any deficiency in the demand for capital? Are not the backward areas, almost by definition, greatly in need of capital for the efficient use of their labour and for the exploitation of their natural resources? Is not the demand for capital in these areas tremendous? It may well be; and yet in terms of private incentives to adopt capitalistic methods in the productive process there is the difficulty that stems from the limited size of the domestic market in the early stages of a country's economic development.

*The inducement to invest is limited by the size of the market.* This proposition is, in effect, a modern variant of Adam Smith's famous thesis that 'the division of labour is limited by the extent of the market.'[1] The

1. It was Allyn A. Young who suggested this re-interpretation in his well-known essay, 'Increasing Returns and Economic Progress,' *Economic*

point is simple and has long been familiar to the business world. It is a matter of common observation that in the poorer countries the use of capital equipment in the production of goods and services for the domestic market is inhibited by the small size of that market, by the lack of domestic purchasing power, not in monetary but in real terms, in a sense to be presently defined. If it were merely a deficiency of monetary demand, it could easily be remedied through monetary expansion; but the trouble lies deeper. Monetary expansion alone does not remove it, but produces merely an inflation of prices.

This simple point, that the incentive to apply capital is limited by the size of the market, has a certain validity not only in the exchange economy of the real world, but even in the economy of an isolated individual like Robinson Crusoe, well known to our forefathers from elementary textbooks. Suppose that Robinson Crusoe had two or three hundred nails (which he got, let us say, from a wooden box washed ashore on his island) and wanted to drive them into some trees in order to hang up his fishing nets or personal effects. It would pay him first to sit down and make a simple hammer with which to drive these nails into his trees. His total effort would be reduced; he would do the job more quickly. But if he had only two or three nails it would not be worth his while to make a hammer. He would pick up and use a stone of suitable size. It would be a slow and inconvenient method; but it would be uneconomic to produce capital equipment in the shape of a hammer just for driving in two or three nails.

In the exchange economy of the real world, it is not difficult to find illustrations of the way in which the small size of a country's market can discourage, or even prohibit, the profitable application of modern capital equipment by any individual entrepreneur in any particular industry. In a country, for instance, where the great majority of people are too poor to wear leather shoes, setting up a modern shoe factory may be a doubtful business proposition; the market for shoes is too small. Many articles that are in common use in the United States can be sold in a low-income country in quantities so limited that a machine working only a few days or weeks can produce enough for a whole year's consumption, and would have to stand idle the rest of the time. In Chile, for example, it has been found that a modern rolling mill, which is standard equipment in any industrial country, can produce in three hours a sufficient supply of a cer-

*Journal,* December 1928 (now reprinted in *Readings in Economic Analysis,* edited by R. V. Clemence, Cambridge, Mass., 1950, Vol. I). It is easy to see, and Adam Smith recognized it himself, that the division of labour is closely connected with the use of capital in production.

tain type of iron shapes to last the country for a year. In these circumstances the inducement to install such equipment is lacking. In some cases foreign branch plants which had been established in certain Latin American countries were subsequently withdrawn because it was found that the local market was too small to make their operation profitable.[2]

These examples may exaggerate the difficulty, but I do believe that, to some extent, the difficulty is real. To produce with more capital per unit of output means generally, though not invariably, producing on a larger scale, in the sense of a larger output per plant. This is what matters in the present context, though it may be noted that in a given line of production any increase in output, even when it maintains the old degree of capital-intensity, will be discouraged by the smallness of the market.

The economic incentive to install capital equipment for the production of a certain commodity or service always depends in some measure on the amount of work to be done with this equipment. Naturally the individual business man must take the amount of work to be done—the size of the market for his commodity or service—more or less as he finds it. He may hope to be able to deflect some of the present volume of consumers' demand in his own favour; but where real income is close to the subsistence level, there is little or no scope for such deflection. The limited size of the domestic market in a low-income country can thus constitute an obstacle to the application of capital by any individual firm or industry working for that market. In this sense the small domestic market is an obstacle to development generally.

How can this obstacle be removed? What is it that determines the size of the market? Some people may think, in this connection, of monetary expansion as a remedy, others of high-powered methods of salesmanship and advertising. Some may think of the size of a country's population as determining the size of the market; others, again, may have in mind the physical extent of the country's territory. All these factors are of secondary importance, if not irrelevant. A popular prescription is that small adjacent countries should abolish restrictions on trade with each other. But the smallness of a country is not the basic difficulty. The difficulty can exist even in very large countries such as China and India.

The crucial determinant of the size of the market is productivity. In an all-inclusive view, the size of the market is not only determined, but actually defined, by the volume of production. In the economy as a whole, the flow of goods and services produced and consumed is not a fixed magnitude. With a given population, it is a variable depending on people's

2. For these and other examples, see G. Wythe, *Industry in Latin America* (New York, 1951).

productive efficiency. It is sometimes said that, if only prices could be reduced (money incomes remaining the same), the market could be enlarged. That is true, but if this were to happen it would imply an increase in productivity and real income. The market would be similarly enlarged if people's money incomes could be increased while prices remained constant. Again, this would be possible only with an advance in productive efficiency, implying an increase in real income. We are here in the classical world of Say's Law. In underdeveloped areas there is generally no 'deflationary gap' through excessive savings. Production creates its own demand, and the size of the market depends on the volume of production. In the last analysis, the market can be enlarged only through an all-round increase in productivity. Capacity to buy means capacity to produce.

Now productivity—or output per man-hour—depends largely, though by no means entirely, on the degree to which capital is employed in production. It is largely a matter of using machinery and other equipment. It is a function, in technical terms, of the capital-intensity of production. But, for any individual entrepreneur, the use of capital is inhibited, to start with, by the small size of the market.

Where is the way out of this circle? How can the market be enlarged? Even though in economically backward areas Say's Law may be valid in the sense that there is no deflationary gap, it never is valid in the sense that the output of any single industry, newly set up with capital equipment, can create its own demand. Human wants being diverse, the people engaged in the new industry will not wish to spend all their income on their own products.[3] Suppose it is a shoe industry. The shoe producers cannot live on shoes alone and must depend on the exchange of shoes for the other things they need. If in the rest of the economy nothing happens to increase productivity and hence buying power, the market for the new shoe output is likely to prove deficient. People outside the new industry will not give up other things in order to buy, say, a pair of shoes every year if they do not have enough food, clothing and shelter. They cannot let go the little they have of these elementary necessities. If they *were* willing to renounce some of their present consumption in exchange for an annual pair of new shoes, these things would become available for the shoe workers to make up the balance in their consumption needs. As it is, the new industry is likely to be a failure.

The trouble is due by no means solely to discontinuities in the technical forms of capital equipment, though these will accentuate it. It is due above all to the inevitable inelasticity of demands at low real-income levels. It is

3. See Paul N. Rosenstein-Rodan, 'Problems of Industrialization of Eastern and South-Eastern Europe,' *Economic Journal*, June–September 1943, p. 205.

in this way that poverty cramps the inducement to invest and discourages the application of capital to any single line of production. The enlargement of the market through the rise in productivity that would result from increased capital-intensity of production is inhibited by the initial smallness of the market.

The problem of technical discontinuities, in turn, is due not merely to the fact that equipment produced in advanced countries is adapted to domestic mass markets there and is not, as a rule, best suited to conditions in the poorer countries. Even if equipment were devised particularly for the latter, discontinuities would still remain. Additions to capital equipment in any case are apt to come in relatively big units, and there is especially a characteristic lumpiness in the process of investment in overhead capital facilities such as railways, power plants and water works.

While thus the technical discontinuities may call for sizable forward 'junps' in the rate of output, the small and inelastic demand in a low-income country tends to make such jumps risky if not altogether unpromising in any given branch of business considered by itself. If, in the past, attempts at jumping forward in particular branches have for these reasons come to grief, individual enterprise is likely to take a dim view of future investment prospects; the demand for capital will be depressed.[4]

We recognize, in one of its aspects, the vicious circle of poverty. We perceive a constellation of circumstances tending to preserve any backward economy in a stationary condition, in a state of 'underdevelopment equilibrium' somewhat analogous, perhaps, to the 'underemployment equilibrium,' the possibility of which, in advanced industrial countries, was impressed on us by Keynes. Economic progress is not a spontaneous or automatic affair. On the contrary, it is evident that there are automatic forces within the system tending to keep it moored to a given level.

All this, however, is only part of the story. The circular constellation of the stationary system is real enough, but fortunately the circle is not unbreakable. And once it is broken at any point, the very fact that the relation is circular tends to make for cumulative advance. We should perhaps hesitate to call the circle vicious; it can become beneficent.

---

4. All this is superimposed on the fact that in communities afflicted with mass poverty the qualities of enterprise and initiative are usually in short supply to start with, and that the demand for capital tends to be sluggish for this reason alone. I am grateful to Mr. Robert G. Link for a detailed comment setting forth with more precision the possible ways in which the three factors—inelastic consumer demand, technical discontinuities and lack of enterprise—can keep down the demand for capital in low-income countries.

# Henry G. Aubrey

## Investment Decisions in Underdeveloped Countries

### CHARACTERISTICS OF ENTERPRISE

THE PROCESS of perceiving opportunities, evaluating them, and choosing between alternatives requires a number of qualities and attitudes which are subsumed in the concept of enterprise: intelligence and open-mindedness in discerning opportunities and appraising their various future possibilities; also perseverance in accepting sizable disutilities in the form of work and trouble in the execution of plans. In fact, the preliminary job of evaluation presupposes a series of steps rather than a single act of appraisal: forming judgments regarding the future course of yet-unexplored events, weighing the necessary adjustments to such a course, and devising and executing plans of adjustment.[1] While these steps require qualities which may be latent in a smaller or larger number of individuals, it may be well to recognize the importance of a suitable basis for the individual's confidence in his own judgment and his ability to carry out his plans. Past experience would seem to be the most favorable basis for such confidence. It may not be essential for this experience to be rooted in the individual's own past or to have been gained in precisely the same field of endeavor. If we talk of a "tradition" of entrepreneurship, its chief effective ingredient appears to be the degree of confidence provided by the subjective feeling of doing something that is new but not entirely so. It seems clear, without further elaboration at this point, that such a basis of subjective experience, or such easily accessible background for reference, is largely missing in early stages of development.[2] The gradual formation of such a framework of experience in the course of development may also help

---

1. Cf. Moses Abramowitz, "Economics of Growth," in *A Survey of Contemporary Economics*, B. F. Haley, ed., Irwin, 1952, Vol. II, p. 157, and Frank H. Knight, *Risk, Uncertainty and Profit*, Houghton Mifflin, 1921, pp. 241 ff.

2. Cf. H. W. Singer, "Obstacles to Economic Development," *Social Research*, Spring 1953, p. 23.

explain the emergence of native entrepreneurship within relatively short periods of time in countries where it had been conspicuously scarce for long periods of the past.[3]

This stress on limited and gradual innovation appears to conflict with the more heroic concept usually associated with the name of Schumpeter. His prototype of the entrepreneur is a man who perceives new methods of production which deviate deliberately from the pattern of past performance. History provides relatively few examples of such sharp breaks in contrast to the frequent, perhaps "normal," case of novel features superimposed on familiar technology.[4] The degree of technological discontinuity has, however, some bearing on the extent of entrepreneurship which backward areas require for their economic development; in this context the discussion concerned is of interest to the present paper.

## THE ROLE OF ENTERPRISE IN UNDERDEVELOPED COUNTRIES

At least two recent writers[5] have pointed out with great acumen that underdeveloped countries are not representative of a "Schumpeterian world." Their entrepreneurs are not original innovators because they obtain their technology ready-made from the industrial countries.[6] This process of adaptation would seem to rank lower in inventiveness than original innovation, but some comfort could be derived from the fact that the attribute of creativeness is occasionally applied to this process, too.[7] Our present interest in this discussion lies in two different directions. A lesser degree of initiative is needed to apply existing technical knowledge than to initiate complete innovation; moreover, the process of developing a new technology and nursing it from the drawing board to commercial success is not only frustrating and time-consuming, but extremely costly. It re-

3. E.g. in Mexico in the past twenty-five years.

4. Cf. Abramovitz, *op. cit.*, p. 142.

5. Henry C. Wallich, "Some Notes towards a Theory of Derived Development," paper presented at the third meeting of Central Bank Technicians, Havana, 1952, mimeographed; and Singer, *op. cit.*

6. Some implications of this fact will be discussed in section 3 of this paper. Cf. also Singer, *op. cit.*, pp. 24 ff.

7. Cf. Fritz Redlich, "The Business Leader in Theory and Reality," *American Journal of Economics and Sociology*, April 1949, p. 226. He also coins the terms "creative capitalist" and "creative manager" for people responsible for new ways in their respective fields. The difference between passive acceptance of and active response to external stimulation is stressed by J. A. Schumpeter in "Creative Response in Economic History," *Journal of Economic History*, Supplement, 1947.

quires capital and skills, both scarce in backward areas. Hence the "adaptive" type of enterprise ought to arise more easily in early stages of development than the more strictly Schumpeterian kind, however defined. In our context, then, the "adaptive" entrepreneur's task is finding and applying the most suitable known techniques; more will be said about this in the section devoted to the choice of technology.

The entrepreneurial activities required to start a new industrial enterprise in an underdeveloped country are not restricted to the choice of technology; different qualities are needed than those implied in the concept of an innovator who only once combines the factors of production in a new manner and at lesser cost. A "successful" entrepreneur under conditions of scarcity of entrepreneurship may turn out to be a man who does not permanently stay with the enterprise—a kind of professional promoter who withdraws when the new business is under way and starts another to which he applies his capital and both profits and experience acquired in his preceding promotional activities. This type of entrepreneur scouts for new opportunities, investigates them, and evaluates their potentialities. He has to define the nature of the product; assess the supply of materials, the scope of the market, and the proper organization to cover it; then decide on the size of the plant and the type of technology. Last mentioned, but often first in consideration, are schemes for financing, the distribution of risk, and remuneration for promotional services. . . . [8]

The purpose of drawing attention to the promoter type of enterprise in contrast to the owner-manager type with its permanent character was to emphasize a less publicized type of entrepreneurship. This may, incidentally, help to lay the ghost of the "Schumpeterian entrepreneur," which still haunts discussions of contemporary enterprise under conditions far removed from the original theoretical model. This statement, however, should not be interpreted to mean that the "Western" type of entrepreneurship has no place in underdeveloped countries. It exists in many forms, in persons ranging from owners of humble shops to industrial tycoons like Francesco Matarazzo in Brazil, who started out with a small store in the interior and built an industrial empire comprising 286 separate enterprises.[9] Like most socio-economic phenomena, entrepreneurship is too complex to be cast into a single type or pattern.

---

8. A. A. I. El-Gritly, "The Structure of Modern Industry in Egypt," *L'Egypte Contemporaine,* November-December 1947, p. 377.

9. George Wythe, *Industry in Latin America,* 2nd ed., Columbia University Press, 1949, p. 163, and George Wythe, Royce A. Wight, and Harold M. Midkiff, *Brazil, an Expanding Economy,* Twentieth Century Fund, 1949, p. 177.

## CRITERIA FOR INVESTMENT PREFERENCES

Up to this point this paper has adopted the customary implicit assumption that entrepreneurship can be treated like a scarce commodity indispensable for economic development. Perhaps it should be regarded as a human catalyst which transforms, by the process called investment, potentially available resources into additions to the stock of national capital. A mere change of ownership of a piece of real estate, to give an example, could not be considered investment in this aggregative sense. In the mind of the potential investor, however, such acquisition of existing assets presents a real alternative competing with the type of investment which will eventually increase the output of goods and services. A study of investment choice cannot ignore such a realistic alternative on the ground that it cannot be considered "investment" in the aggregative sense. True, much depends on the use the seller of the asset makes of the proceeds of this sale; it is, however, evident that a continuous chain of such "unproductive" investments is not a negligible phenomenon but frequently presents a very potent distraction from the kind of investment that may be favorable to economic growth.

A conceptual restriction is revealed by the frequently used term "unproductive investment." Never clearly defined, it seems to refer sometimes to the creation of assets which will not directly increase productive capacity or average national productivity. At other times, the term appears to involve some kind of judgment about balanced development. The building of luxury housing is a favorite target of criticism for this school of thinking while the construction of housing per se is accepted as essential; in other words, this type of "unproductive investment" would seem to provide an opportunity for luxury consumption in whose absence, presumably, both the investment in question and the future unconsumed surpluses would be used in a better manner—that is, one which furthers development. . . .

For the purpose of this paper, however, a different course is adopted. Since we are concerned with the determinants of the entrepreneur's investment decision, we must attempt to view them from his point of view, assessing the subjective and objective factors that motivate his action in underdeveloped areas. Then only—and this paper does not claim to move more than a step in this direction—can we hope to assess objectively the relative strengths of forces which oppose or favor "desirable" types of investment. In referring to subjective factors first, no a priori judgment regarding rank of importance is intended. No matter how tangible the objective criteria, such as factor supply or size of demand, appear, the investment decision will be based on the perception of opportunities which, while pointing to the future, exist only in the present in the investor's mind. The process of evaluation which precedes decision and action is, essentially, one of sifting impressions, of matching observable factors with anticipated alternatives—in short, of assimilating events into the structure of expectations. . . .[10]

## INVESTMENT DECISION AND UNCERTAINTY

Any investment decision involves a weighing of profits and risks attending, or believed to attend, various alternatives of investment in the future. Leaving risk estimates aside for the time being, the evaluation of profit can be made the point of departure for our deliberations.

Since profits are the difference between prices and costs, the level and future course of both of the latter will have to be estimated. The expected volume of sales will enter into an estimate of gross revenue, both volume and prices depending on the size of the market, type and intensity of competition, customs protection, etc. Prime unit costs of materials and wages will have to be assessed, appraisals of the latter depending on estimates of productivity; these presuppose alternative hypotheses regarding technology and size of plant which are also influenced by the size of the expected market and the availability and cost of finance. All of these factors tie in with assumptions about both the internal and the marketing organization of the firm, assumptions which in turn determine overhead costs and affect profits, considering once more the volume of sales. . . . This list—which is far from exhaustive—will serve to illustrate the variety of interlocking considerations which can be ignored only at the investor's peril. It is one of the main propositions of this paper that an awareness of this peril, however dim it may be in any individual investor's mind, is one of the greatest obstacles to positive investment decisions.

In industrially advanced countries the basis for estimating the factors enumerated above is infinitely wider and the requisite skill more generally available. A "Schumpeterian entrepreneur" need not worry about the market because he will, by definition, produce his goods at lower cost and find an outlet for them by underselling others. The "imitator" among entrepreneurs has, as a rule, some direct knowledge of the product and its markets; otherwise, expert information and advice can be obtained at reasonable hire from individuals familiar with the trade or from experts in market analysis. Such outside technical advice is available to the little fellow, while larger firms can also draw on their own technical or research staffs.

---

10. G. L. S. Shackle, *Expectations in Economics,* London, Cambridge University Press, 1949, pp. 70 and 75.

In underdeveloped countries the situation is very different. Experts for exploratory investigation are rarely available locally; foreign experts are costly and their advice is not always suited to different conditions. Often the lack of or deficiencies in statistics make estimates of consumption and markets, of costs and capital requirements, very difficult if not totally impossible. Worse yet, since many preliminary services which come ready-made in industrial countries are absent, the initial capital outlay is increased and a risk of running short or "making do" with regard to skills, parts, and sometimes even power and transportation is incurred. Planning deficiencies, caused by lack of means to carry out the required scrutiny of new ventures, appear as an almost inevitable danger. Some of the factual country reports picture this situation.[11] The lack of economic and technical research facilities is sorely felt in underdeveloped countries and keeps even basic knowledge of opportunities from maturing. Government research is frequently recommended as a remedy, but it cannot alone build the bridge between an idea and its execution since ideas rarely arise where there is a vacuum with respect to knowledge or experience. It does not come as a surprise to hear from Indian observers that industrialists rarely base their estimates on scientific calculation. As a substitute, they tend to take as a model another firm they consider profitable and approximate its organization with regard to size of plant, equipment, etc. If no such comparison is available, the characteristics tend to be set in an arbitrary manner without proper consideration of cost.[12]

It should be evident without further argument that the establishment of a new industrial enterprise in an underdeveloped country is fraught with great uncertainty, greater by far than that involved in the same kind of undertaking in a more advanced country. The greater the novelty of the enterprise in any one country, the slimmer the base of reference and experience in nearly all respects. The facts of such uncertainty will hardly be disputed; but is it possible to establish its degree and to discount it so as to leave sufficient incentive for a positive investment decision without depending entirely on a spirit of venture akin to that of the gambler? The theory of expectations seems to promise an answer to this question, and it appears desirable to investigate its relevance for our problem.

----

11. E.g. El-Gritly, *op. cit.*, p. 377; *The Economic Development of Guatemala*, Johns Hopkins Press for International Bank for Reconstruction and Development, 1951, p. 97; and *The Economic Development of Iraq*, Johns Hopkins Press for International Bank for Reconstruction and Development, 1952, p. 40.

12. D. R. Samant and M. A. Mulky, *Organization and Finance of Industries in India*, London, Longmans, 1937, p. 91.

## UNCERTAINTY AND PROBABILITY

Uncertainty is not identical with absence of knowledge. In practical contexts knowledge of some aspects may be combined with ignorance of others; it may be preferable to consider degrees of knowledge rather than its presence or absence.[13] Knowledge of future events is, of course, impossible and has to be replaced by a procedure of anticipation which consists of several elements: an expectation schedule of magnitudes assigned to each contingency or possibility for each future date, a probability weight for each such magnitude expressing the likelihood or range of probability that the anticipated contingency will actually occur, the degree of subjective confidence in the individual's ability to predict or to assign objective probability ranges to the several contingencies.[14]

Uncertainty is responsible for the lack of any unique future magnitude. Instead, there is a set of possible magnitudes of which one may be recognized as the most probable; the definiteness of this probable magnitude depends on the probability distribution and the width of the range which expresses this degree of uncertainty. After eliminating extreme values which lack high probability ranks, a practical range may be expected to emerge.[15]

Assuming for argument's sake that the above procedure of estimation can be carried out, how large can the expected practical range be in underdeveloped countries? Where the base of experience is narrow, can any extreme values be assigned such low probability ranks as to eliminate them from practical consideration? Perhaps no outcome within a range from extreme success to complete failure is so improbable that it can be dismissed altogether; it would certainly be dangerous to apply to *unexplored* situations a belief that extreme values carry less probability weight, a notion than can be derived only from *known* frequency distributions. It seems reasonable to assume that the practical range of probability distribution would be very large in underdeveloped countries, commensurate with the prevailing lack of knowledge and the resulting degree of uncertainty.

In any event, magnitudes in different future periods lack comparability unless they can be reduced to present values. According to theory, this

13. Knight, *op. cit.,* p. 199.

14. *Ibid.,* pp. 236 ff.; Albert G. Hart, "Anticipations, Uncertainty and Dynamic Planning," *Studies in Business Administration,* University of Chicago Press, 1940, Vol. xi, No. 1, p. 52; and Sidney Weintraub, *Price Theory,* Pitman, 1949, p. 345.

15. Oscar Lange, *Price Flexibility and Employment,* Cowles Commission, Monograph No. 8, 1945, pp. 29 ff.

may be achieved by discounting the future values by a factor equal to the difference between the most probable value actually expected and the equivalent value expected with certainty; this difference represents an uncertainty allowance or risk premium. Obviously, uncertainty is also related to time and will be the greater the more distant the future event; the risk premium increases accordingly and may become so large that it would discount present values to a point too low to be acceptable. Planning beyond this limit, which Tinbergen called the "economic horizon," is no longer possible.

Any critique of these theories need not rest on the manifest difficulty of carrying out such calculations in practice; this is a common shortcoming of economic theory. However, a difficulty of a different kind afflicts the concept of contingency or possibility which is implicitly based on the knowledge that similar occurrences have happened before under strictly comparable conditions. Applied to investment decisions, it is thus essential to ascertain the uniqueness or homogeneity of similar cases. This brings us back to the factual base of reference and of experience, which is, almost by definition, extremely slim in underdeveloped countries. A new industry in a partly explored environment comes as close to "uniqueness" as any innovation in a world where few things are entirely new.

A related argument carries rather more weight. Is it possible to square the concept of probability distribution with a businessman's thinking about his potential future profits?[16] Is the probability approach, based on a precise concept of frequency distribution, its shape and skewness, really applicable to decisions which lack the requisite wide actuarial base? The basic concept of probability involves the idea of a large number of repeatable tests by which ranks are assigned to various possibilities, thus substituting actuarial risk for knowledge. There may be some entrepreneurial decisions of a routine character which are repeated frequently enough to provide a basis of experience. Investment decisions are not of that nature. As a rule, there are only a few of them in a lifetime, often just one. Comparable experiences of others are still limited in underdeveloped countries. No such decision is repeatable in the strict sense of the probability concept. Probability reckoning, thus cannot be relied upon to facilitate investment decisions. Instead of "large numbers turning ignorance into knowledge," we are faced with a kind of uncertainty that is another form of ignorance.[17]

\*     \*     \*     \*     \*

16. Moses Abramovitz, *An Approach to a Price Theory for a Changing Economy*, Columbia University Press, 1939, p. 77.

17. Shackle, *op. cit.*, pp. 6 ff. and 115 ff.

## THE MOTIVATION OF "TRADITIONAL" INVESTMENT PREFERENCES

Turning to the practical aspects of the problems discussed, there are three basic sets of reasons why industrial investment may not be undertaken: (1) Lack of knowledge or experience is responsible for inability to recognize opportunities, for failure to plan with sufficient accuracy, or for fear of not being able to execute plans properly. (2) Inherent uncertainties, partly related to lack of experience, cause the investor to consider industrial investment as more risky than other alternatives. (3) The chances of profit are less, or are deemed to be less, than in alternative investments.

The lack of experience and knowledge has been discussed and need hardly be documented further. More should be said, however, about the effects of awareness of risk. Industrial enterprise is inherently of a long-term nature, while the preference for short-term ventures in underdeveloped countries is notorious. This preference can be linked with considerations of security and profit.

Dealing first with *security* as related to stability, the volatility of the political atmosphere in many countries makes it imperative that investors understand that a change in regime is often not restricted to the political scene; such a change may involve shifts in administrative personnel and policies, which may affect commercial operations through means ranging from placing of government orders to tax practice, economic controls, monetary policy, and development plans. A short-term rhythm of operations makes it easier to adapt to new situations and, especially, in the present context, to avoid unforeseeable dangers. An industrial enterprise cannot be adapted so easily or quickly. It lacks the security that lies in liquidity and flexibility.

While fear of political instability implies fear of risks which cannot be foreseen concretely, other pessimistic expectations are based on ample experience. The risk of devaluation may serve as an example of widespread factual significance. If the value of money declines year after year, distrust as to its future value favors investment which prevents loss. Hence, real estate becomes a favorite object of investment; this preference creates at the same time a highly active market, which confers greater liquidity on real estate than on other assets. This type of investment thus offers two elements of security: stability in real terms, and liquidity, a hedge against devaluation and also against unexpected contingencies. At the same time, it offers opportunities for quick and substantial profits. The conditions here described can be observed in a number of countries; they are mentioned most prominently in relation to Chile and Brazil.

Another cause of instability, less frequently mentioned, is related to the economic structure of many underdeveloped countries and therefore is very serious. Countries depending on the export of a few primary products for a large part of their national income have, in the past, experienced vehement swings of an exogenous nature whose effects they could not control. They cut so deeply into income and consumption that they are, in many countries, the major factor responsible for prosperity or depression. Clearly, long-term planning in the shadow of such contingencies is both difficult and risky. Capacity of the plant and size of the investment are placed at the mercy of unforeseeable events. Short-term investment offers a better chance to "get out from under," with liquidity and flexibility again being the controlling factors.

In addition to such cyclical fluctuations, the seasonal cycle of such products causes chronic economic insecurity in some countries. In Cuba nearly the entire economy is geared to the rhythm of sugar production. Shortly after the season, which lasts only two to four months, economic activity tapers off. Such seasonal instability makes industrial production very difficult and planning for it still harder. Superimposed on this instability is the anxiety about the price of sugar, in which most persons in the economy have a direct or indirect stake, creating a kind of "boom mentality" conditioned by short-term fluctuations. Such a climate is most unfavorable to long-term ventures and favors activities where the turnover is quick and the profit high.

Considerations of security affect not only the entrepreneur himself but the institutions or individuals to whom he may have to look for additional capital and credit. Banks will withhold credit if they consider the risks too high to be covered by normal interest charges; this, too, will be judged not by absolute standards but in relation to opportunities for lending funds for alternative investments. Lenders' risk is also determined by a desire to avoid such complications as litigation and foreclosure, which appear more likely in connection with untried ventures. In an unstable economy even "bankable" collateral is apt to become illiquid; banks prefer, therefore, to lend to trusted clients of old standing, and, unhappily, the innovators are less likely to be found among these members of the traditional commercial group.

Before the discussion of risk and security is concluded, reference should be made to the belief that risk is gradually becoming less problematic to business because business is steadily working at reducing risks by auxiliary services, market research, and other devices. Nothing could better illustrate the gulf between a developed country like the United States and in underdeveloped country, where, indeed, the absence of these facilities is one of the greatest obstacles to entrepreneurial initiative.

There are, of course, degrees of risk-taking in underdeveloped countries, too. Entrepreneurs entering existing trades find a stock of experience on which to draw, or they may be guided by reference to similar industries. It is being said that the cotton industry in India was not treading unknown paths because the raw materials and markets were at hand and the industry copied the jute industry. Almost everywhere, however, industrial enterprise encounters a powerful disincentive in the existence of other pursuits. Real estate investment, which is considered more secure and liquid than long-term industrial investment, requires less time and specialized knowledge for management of such investment and offers an opportunity for members of other professions to participate. Businessmen find inventory investment an attractive alternative to expansion of their own, or to investment in another, business. Inventories, too, are liquid and can be used as collateral for credit; their price is bound to rise in inflationary situations, when the supply of imports is likely to diminish as a result of balance of payment difficulties.

Real estate and inventory speculation and short-term commercial transactions, as well as the policy of commercial banks favoring such transactions, are the greatest traditional deterrents to industrial enterprise in underdeveloped countries. In descriptions of this situation, we note sometimes a trace of righteous indignation that "solid" investment is not preferred to "speculation," with its connotation of levity. A reason for this attitude is that instability itself induces a gambling spirit when the economy is controlled by short-term fluctuations. We have also seen that short-term transactions appear safer and more liquid than long-term ventures. Perhaps the best explanation of speculative preference for short-term transactions is found in the fact that "gambling" may actually appear safer than "solid" long-term investment, precisely because it is traditional and widespread. Moreover, a wide basis of reference and experience is the best antidote against fear or generally pessimistic expectations. The professional gambler could, if he cared, actually determine probability on the basis of actuarial risk. He has entered the market many times and has found that errors in judgment cancel out, to some extent, and leave a predictable return. The industrial investor lacks this kind of experience because he starts that particular industry only once. Moreover, in inflationary situations created by development spending under conditions of inelastic supply, any expectation of price rises appears actually built into the economy. No wonder, then, that nearly all arguments of security militate *quite "rationally"* against long-term industrial investment and in favor of those traditional pursuits which the puritan mind places lowest on the scale of desirability.

From the point of view of security, *profit* expectations tend in the same directions as investment choice. Short-term transactions of the types described appear not only safer but often more profitable. There is a factual basis for this belief. One of the oldest pursuits, moneylending, is widespread and lucrative. Statistics are usually lacking, but there is evidence that rates run from 18 to 60 per cent per annum and often much higher. Estimates of yield in inventory speculation run up to 70 per cent in not unusual or strongly inflationary situations. Clearly, industrial enterprises need to expect much higher returns than the rates considered satisfactory in industrial countries if they are to compete for capital with such profitable alternatives.[18]

## United Nations

# Land Reform: Defects in Agrarian Structure and Obstacles to Economic Development

## AGRARIAN STRUCTURE IN UNDER-DEVELOPED COUNTRIES

To A VERY LARGE EXTENT, the problem of the under-developed countries of the world is the problem of the poverty of their farm populations. Unduly low standards of living in rural areas are not confined to the under-developed countries; they can be found also in countries which have reached a high level of economic development. But in the under-developed countries the problem is of a different dimension, because the economy of these countries is mainly agricultural. Table 1 shows the proportion of

18. Cf., e.g., *The Economic Development of Nicaragua*, Johns Hopkins Press for International Bank for Reconstruction and Development, 1953, p. 10; *The Economic Development of Ceylon*, Johns Hopkins Press for International Bank for Reconstruction and Development, 1953, p. 515; and *The Economic Development of Iraq*, as cited, p. 278. Many other country sources report similar or higher figures.

agricultural population to total population in Asia, Africa, Central and South America as compared with the proportion in North America and Europe.

## TABLE 1.
*Proportion of World Population in Agriculture, 1949*\*

| AREA | TOTAL POPULATION (MILLIONS) | AGRICULTURAL POPULATION (MILLIONS) | AGRICULTURAL POPULATION AS PERCENTAGE OF TOTAL |
|---|---|---|---|
| North America[1] | 163 | 33 | 20 |
| Europe | 391 | 129 | 33 |
| Oceania | 12 | 4 | 33 |
| South America | 107 | 64 | 60 |
| Central America[2] | 50 | 33 | 67 |
| Asia | 1,255 | 878 | 70 |
| Africa | 198 | 146 | 74 |
| World total | 2,177 | 1,285 | 59 |

\*Source: Food and Agriculture Organization of the United Nations, *Yearbook of Food and Agriculture,* 1950, page 15.
1. Canada and the United States.
2. Including Mexico.

Of the total population of the world, some 60 per cent, or almost 1,300 million people, are dependent upon agriculture. Of these, over 1,000 million live in Asia, Africa, Central and South America, and only 162 million in Europe and North America. Whereas in Europe only one person out of three, and in North America only one person in five, is dependent on agriculture, in Asia and Africa three out of every four obtain their living from the land.

In the predominantly agricultural countries, the level of output per acre is generally lower than it is in the predominantly industrial countries; the level of output per person in agriculture is very much lower, because, generally speaking, the density of the farm population per acre is much greater, while the average yield per acre is less. As a long-term trend, these differences in productivity tend to become greater. The following table shows comparative levels of productivity in the agricultural and industrialized areas, by continents, before and after the Second World War.

The differences in productivity per person in agriculture give some indication of the range of difference in rural living standards. Where the output per person in agriculture averages approximately 2½ tons, as it does in North America, the standard of living of the farm population

## TABLE 2.

Productivity of the Agricultural Population by Continents and
for the World, Pre-war and 1947–48*

| CONTINENT | YIELD PER HECTARE PRE-WAR (METRIC TONS) | 1947–48 | 1947–48 AS PER CENT OF PRE-WAR | YIELD PER PERSON IN AGRICULTURE PRE-WAR (METRIC TONS) | 1947–48 | 1947–48 AS PER CENT OF PRE-WAR |
|---|---|---|---|---|---|---|
| World average | 1.24 | 1.30 | 105 | 0.42 | 0.42 | 100 |
| North and Central America | 1.07 | 1.50 | 140 | 1.80 | 2.57 | 143 |
| South America | 1.28 | 1.39 | 109 | 0.58 | 0.48 | 83 |
| Europe | 1.51 | 1.34 | 89 | 1.04 | 0.88 | 85 |
| Oceania | 1.06 | 1.20 | 113 | 1.94 | 2.38 | 123 |
| Asia[1] | 1.26 | 1.20 | 95 | 0.24 | 0.22 | 92 |
| Africa | 0.77 | 0.73 | 95 | 0.12 | 0.12 | 100 |

*Source: Food and Agriculture Organization of the United Nations, *Monthly Bulletin of Food and Agriculture Statistics*, vol. 2, No. 9, September 1949; arranged in order of yield per hectare in 1947–48.
1. Excluding the Union of Soviet Socialist Republics.

will clearly be higher than where it is less than one-quarter of a ton, as in Asia, or one-eighth of a ton, as in Africa.

The causes of low productivity in agriculture and of low standards of living of the farm population are many: poor soils and unfavourable climates; backward techniques and inadequate equipment; excessively high densities of rural population; low prices received by the farmer. All these are important in varying degrees.

Among the most important factors which affect rural living standards is the agrarian structure. This term is here used to mean the institutional framework of agricultural production. It includes, in the first place, land tenure, the legal or customary system under which land is owned; the distribution of ownership of farm property between large estates and peasant farms or among peasant farms of various size; land tenancy, the system under which land is operated and its product divided between operator and owner; the organization of credit, production and marketing; the mechanism through which agriculture is financed; the burden imposed on rural populations by governments in the form of taxation; and the services supplied by governments to rural populations, such as technical advice and educational facilities, health services, water supply and communications.

The different forms of agrarian structure and different systems of land tenure which exist in the under-developed countries of the world are the result in part of different forms of society and in part of the influence of foreign institutions. In many of the under-developed regions of the world, tribal or feudal institutions still form the social framework, even though under European influence the economic and political basis of tribal and feudal society has changed. . . .

*Farm Size and Layout*

The outstanding feature of the agrarian structure in many under-developed countries is the extremely small size of the average farm holding. The definition of what acreage constitutes a small farm varies greatly from country to country. In most parts of the United States and in England a farm of 30 hectares (75 acres) would be considered a small farm, while in eastern Europe, where the average size of farm holdings is 5 hectares (12½ acres), or in some Asian countries, where it is one hectare (2½ acres), such a farm would be considered very large indeed. Nor is it possible to establish a general criterion of what size of farm constitutes a minimum size for economic operation, since this standard must necessarily vary with the type of cultivation and land utilization in different countries. Clearly the minimum size for economic operation will be smaller if the plough is drawn by bullocks than if it is drawn by a tractor.

*Uneconomic holdings.* In many under-developed countries, however, the question of what acreage constitutes a minimum economic holding, in the sense of what acreage will permit full utilization of the farmer's equipment, is less important than the question of what acreage provides a subsistence minimum, either directly by growing food or indirectly by providing an income from commercial crops. The standard is measured not in terms of a necessary scale of operation, but of a minimum standard of food consumption. Even on this basis, acreage alone is not a sufficient criterion, since there are great differences in the intensity of cultivation, and differences in cropping rates: an acre of land in an irrigated double-cropped river valley in India may produce six times as much as an acre of nonirrigated single-cropped land.

None the less, even when allowance is made for differences in intensity of cultivation, it is possible to state that there are many countries in which large numbers of farms are too small to provide a subsistence minimum for the cultivator and his family, or to provide them with full employment; and too small also to permit of any improvement in methods of cultivation. This feature of the agrarian structure may be the result of the extreme subdivision of farms resulting from the pressure of population on the land, or of inequality in the distribution of land ownership, or it may result from the operation of both these factors together. Extreme subdivision of farm units tends to promote concentration of ownership and increase inequality in the distribution of property, because the small owners are generally unable to gain a subsistence from their farms, and in consequence become indebted to landowners and money-lenders who thereby acquire possession of the land.

Where the density of the agricultural population is extremely high, the average farm holding is as a rule extremely small. The relation of farm population to the cultivated area varies greatly between different countries, and between different continents. . . . It appears that the countries where density of total population in relation to the area of arable land is highest are, in order of highest density, Japan, Egypt, Haiti, Korea, Indonesia, Lebanon, Indochina, Ceylon, China and India.[1] In all these countries there is less than one-third of a hectare (less than one acre) per head of total population. The significance of these figures is clear if the relationship between rural population and land resources is considered on the basis of estimates of the rural population. Japan has a farm population of 34.5 million on 5.9 million hectares of arable land. Egypt has a rural population of between 14 and 15 million on 2.5 million hectares; in Indonesia, Java and Madura have a rural population of between 45 and 50 million on 10 million hactares of cultivated land; the average size of holdings in 1938 was 0.86 hectare. India has a rural population of 285 million living on 98 million hectares of arable land. Though the density of the rural population per hectare in India is lower than in the three countries mentioned above, the effects of a high density on the living standard are more acute, in that the level of productivity per hectare is far lower; crop yields are much smaller, and double cropping is only practised on a small proportion of the land, whereas in Egypt, Japan and Java, yields are very high and double cropping is general. In China, the density of the rural population is extremely high in many regions: surveys of 17,000 farms in twelve provinces reveal a farm population of some 1,500 persons per square mile, or half an acre of land for each person on farms. Thus the average density in these regions is twice as high as in India, but average crop yields are also twice as high. . . .

Table 3 shows the percentage of farm holdings which fall below the average in different Indian states. It should be noted that these figures refer to holdings and not to properties, and include tenants as well as owners. The figures indicate the scale of operations, not of ownership,

---

1. Three Latin American countries, Bolivia, Columbia and Peru, show a similar relationship. But here the area of arable land per person is not a sufficient indication of excessive density of farm population as it is in Asia, because pasture farming plays a much larger part in the economy, and also because much cultivable land is not classified as arable.

and show the effect of population pressure and inequality in the size of holdings, not the much greater inequality in ownership of land. . . .

TABLE 3.

*India: Percentage of Families with Different Sizes of Land Holdings*\*

| | NUMBER OF ACRES PER HOLDING | | | |
|---|---|---|---|---|
| PROVINCES | UNDER 2 | 2 TO 5 | 5 TO 10 | 10 AND OVER |
| Assam[1] | 38.9 | 27.4 | 21.1 | 12.6 |
| Bombay:[2] | | | | |
|   Gujarat | 27.5 | 25.7 | 22.3 | 24.5 |
|   Deccan | 19.8 | 16.7 | 18.8 | 44.7 |
|   Carnatic | 12.2 | 19.2 | 21.7 | 46.9 |
| West Bengal | 34.7 | 28.7 | 20.0 | 16.6 |
| Madhya Pradesh (Central Provinces)[3] | 49.0 | | 21.0 | 30.0 |
| Orissa | 50.0 | 27.0 | 13.0 | 10.0 |
| Madras | 51.0 | 31.0 | 7.0 | 11.0 |
| Uttar Pradesh (United Provinces)[4] | 55.8 | 25.4 | 12.8 | 6.0 |
| Punjab[5] | 37.9[6] | 17.9[7] | 20.5 | 23.7 |

\* Source: *Report of the Congress Agrarian Reform Committee.*
1. Based on a sample survey of 2,613 families in Darrang District, Assam. The size of the holdings in the original data were in *bighas;* the converted figures are only approximate.
2. Based on a sample survey by Shri Sankpal, Director, Bureau of Economics and Statistics, Bombay; indicates percentage of cultivators instead of families.
3. Figures based on information collected in 1938; indicates percentage of tenants.
4. Percentage of cultivators.
5. Figures refer to undivided Punjab; source, P. A. Wadia and K. T. Merchant, *Our Economic Problem* (Bombay, 1946).
6. Under two and one-half acres.
7. Two and one-half to five acres.

In greater or less degree, the problem of large numbers of extremely small farms affects India, parts of China, and all South East Asia except Burma. It is present also in the Caribbean countries, and in Egypt and Japan in an extreme degree. In so far as it results from an excessively high density of rural population, it is not a problem which can be dealt with by change in the agrarian structure alone.

Though it is in the rurally over-populated countries that this problem assumes its most serious dimensions, farms of non-economic size can also be found in countries which do not suffer from great congestion on the land. In the Philippines, for example, the average size of farm holdings is four hectares (10 acres) but more than half the farms are under two hectares, because of extremely unequal distribution of ownership and because of the concentration of population in Luzon and the Visayan islands.

Even in countries of very extensive cultivation with large reserves of land, over-cultivated small holdings exist. Their part in the economy is a different one, in that the small holding may not be the sole source of the cultivator's income as it is in some parts of Asia, but a subsistence holding to supplement wages. Where such holdings are the sole source of the cultivator's income, they are usually over-cultivated. . . .

In the sparsely populated countries of South America, there would appear good reason to believe that many holdings are uneconomically large. In Argentina, 85 per cent of the privately held agricultural land is in estates larger than 500 hectares (1,250 acres), while 80 per cent of the farm population own no land. . . .

*Fragmentation of holdings.* The splitting up of a farm holding into numerous different plots scattered over a wide area is a feature of the field layout in countries at all levels of economic development. It is not associated with any particular form of land tenure. It may be seen in countries as highly developed as Switzerland, France and southern Germany. In eastern Europe, notably in Poland and in the Balkan countries, the process has gone to extreme length; a farm of twelve acres, in Yugoslavia, for instance, may be divided into thirty separate plots. It is a widespread condition in Asia, particularly in India and China, and in the Middle Eastern countries.

Fragmentation has several causes. It originated in remote times from the traditional field layout in which holdings were divided into several strips located in different parts of a village. In the course of time these original strips have been divided and subdivided, as a result of the increase of the farm population, and of inheritance laws which encourage the subdivision of land among many heirs. In western Europe, where pressure of rural population is not acute, the principle of succession established in the Code Napoleon exercises a major influence, while in eastern Europe and in Asia, the pressure of population would appear to be the predominant cause, though laws of succession reinforce an inevitable trend.

The evils of fragmentation need no emphasis: waste of time and effort, the impossibility of rational cultivation are obvious effects. None the less, the consolidation of holdings is not an easy reform to carry through. The conservatism of the peasant is one obstacle, the high cost per acre of surveying and exchanging many small plots is another. Even in a country so advanced as Switzerland the process of consolidation has been slow.

\*     \*     \*     \*     \*

### Tenancy

Tenancy is a feature of the land tenure system in many under-developed countries. The proportion of tenants to the number of farmers varies widely from one country to another. In Asia, the proportion as a rule is very high. As a broad generalization, it would appear that in Burma, China, India and Japan, prior to the recent changes, about half of the land was worked by tenants cultivating small holdings leased to them by landowners and that the majority of the cultivators were either tenants or part owners and part tenants. In South East Asia, tenancy is an important feature of the land system in Burma, Cochin-China, the Philippines and central Thailand.

For the countries of the Middle East no estimate of the proportion of tenants to owners can be made owing to the lack of statistical data. There are some regions where peasant proprietorship is established. In Cyprus, Egypt, Lebanon and Turkey most of the farmers own land. Apart from these countries, tenancy is widely prevalent. In Syria, it is estimated that about half of the land is owned by large landowners, and cultivated by small share tenants; in southern Iraq, large landowners own most of the land, letting it to share tenants through a series of intermediary lessees. In Iran, also, tenancy is the prevalent form. It is estimated that only 15 per cent of the claimed land[2] belongs to small holders, as against about half to some 100,000 large landowners, the balance consisting of state domain or religious endowments. A sample survey conducted in 1949 showed that 60 per cent of rural families owned no land at all, 25 per cent owned less than one hectare and 10 per cent between one and three hectares. . . .

Although there is much variation in practice, some examples of the level of rents may be given. The most commonly practised division of the crop in India (before the recent changes) was half to the landlord and half to the peasant cultivator, who provided his own labour and that of his bullocks, while the landlord provided the land, and in some cases, half the seed. In Indonesia, the Philippines and Thailand, equal sharing of the crop between tenant and landlord seems to be a common practice. Rents in Ceylon vary from one-sixth to one-half of the crop, depending on the region and the type of crop.

---

2. Large areas are not claimed, and the ownership of many plots is in dispute.

In countries of the Middle East, 50 per cent is the usual division in Syria for dry crops; in southern Iraq, where landowner and sub-landlord provide water, their share in the crop may be higher. In Iran, there is great variation from district to district in the share taken by the landowner. For dry crops, which are grown only in certain parts of the country, the landowner's share, when land only is provided, varies widely. For irrigated crops, when the landowner provides water and the peasant labour, seed and oxen, there is also great variation: one-third, one-half, and two-thirds are customary divisions.

A description of the actual method by which rent is collected may serve to show the essential features of the share rent system as it is practised in these countries.

In those countries of Latin America where land is plentiful and labour scarce, share rents are considerably lower than they are in Asia and in the Middle East. Little statistical information on the subject is available, but from the 1948 legislation in Argentina for the compulsory reduction of rents to 20 per cent of the gross crop, it appears that before the introduction of the law the customary share of the gross crop payable as rent was 38 per cent for corn and 36 per cent for wheat. In the countries of Latin America where land is less plentiful, rents are higher, and in some countries reach levels comparable with those prevailing in Asia.

The payment of rent in the form of fixed amounts of produce, or payment in fixed sums of money, are less common forms of tenancy in underdeveloped countries. From the standpoint of the tenant, these forms are clearly preferable, since with a fixed rental he has an incentive to increase production and he gains the full benefit of any improvement on the land in so far as his tenancy is secure. Fixed produce rents were until recently the customary form of payment in Burma and in Japan; they are still prevalent in many parts of India. In Japan, rents were assessed each year in advance of the harvest, and varied from 50 per cent to 70 per cent of the gross product.

Where payment of rent is made on a fixed cash basis, the entire burden of risk is passed on to the cultivator. Cash rents are not, however, a general feature of tenancy systems in under-developed countries, and, as a rule, are found only in certain regions and for special crops. Such rents are extremely high. An investigation in Madras, for example, showed that in the districts of Guntur and West Godavari rents of 300 to 350 rupees per acre were charged on lands growing tobacco, and rents of 400 to 500 rupees per acre on lands growing sugar cane. In Egypt, a country of highly intensive farming and cash crop production, cash rent is the general form. Such rents are extremely high; in pre-war times they ranged from £E 4 per acre on newly reclaimed land to £E 10 per acre in the congested districts. During the war they rose in proportion to the price increase and in congested districts reached £E 25 per acre. These figures represent almost half the market value of the crops grown on an acre; most of the expenses of cultivation are borne by the tenant.

Labour rents are not a usual form of tenancy except in some countries of Latin America, in parts of India and in Iran. In Latin America, this form is common in Bolivia, Chile, Colombia, Ecuador, Peru and Venezuela, among estate labourers who receive a small piece of land from the estate owner in return for which they must work unpaid for a certain number of days per week. In remote regions of Iran, the feudal obligation of labour service on land cultivated by the landlord can still be exacted from villagers. In India, this form of payment is rare; it may be noted that the recent Bombay tenancy act prohibits it.

*Security of tenure.* Cultivators who hold land under these forms of tenancy as a rule hold it on a customary basis, with no legal agreement to define their obligations. In India, the rights and obligations of tenants with occupancy rights are defined by legislation, but the actual cultivators, in many cases share-croppers, enjoy no such legal protection. Where customary rights are not recognized, there is great insecurity and great poverty among the share-croppers. In Burma, where holdings are generally larger than in India, and tenants are better off, there is also great insecurity; investigations in different parts of the country in the nineteen thirties showed that the number of tenants who had cultivated the same plot of land for more than three years represented, in most cases, only a quarter to a third of the total, while the number of those whose tenancy did not go back more than one year ranged between a sixth and a half. In some countries of the Middle East, the peasant does not even cultivate the same plot of land from year to year; the landlord or his agent frequently gives the most fertile plots to favoured tenants who please him in one way or another. The peasant therefore has usually one aim, to get the best out of his land during his short tenancy, regardless of the effect on the fertility of the soil.

Great insecurity also characterizes the conditions of tenancy in Latin America. The term "tenant" in these regions covers many heterogeneous forms: the fixed money-rent tenant with some form of agreement; the tenant with a share-cropping arrangement of some type; paid migrant labourers who squat on small areas rent-free; permanent *colonos* or *inquilinos* settled on estates, paying for subsistence holdings by unpaid labour. Conditions of tenancy in all these forms are usually described as fluid or informal; there is possibly even less security than in Asia, because customary obligations are less powerful.

It is evident that the tenancy system in the conditions described above is a powerful obstacle to economic development, in three ways. In the first place, the tenant has little incentive to increase his output, since a large share in any such increase will accrue to the landowner, who has incurred no part of its cost. In the second place, the high share of the produce taken by the landowner may leave the peasant with a bare subsistence minimum, with no margin for investment; in a bad year, he gets more heavily in debt; in a good year, he can reduce his indebtedness. Thirdly, it means that wealth is held in the form of land, and that the accumulation of capital does not lead to productive investment. In Asia, the landowner is also a money-lender, and in this capacity depends more on interest on loans to small cultivators than on increased income from the improvement of land. . . .

### Estates and Plantations

In the Caribbean, throughout South America, in South East Asia, in Ceylon and in parts of East Africa, the agrarian structure is dominated by large estates. Unlike the large landholdings of Asia and the Middle East, referred to in the preceding section, these estates are large centrally managed and operated units of production, employing paid labour. This type of farm organization exists in widely differing conditions: in regions with much unused land and sparse population, and in regions where there is a great shortage of land and an excess of labour. In the former setting, the large estate may be a cattle ranch, covering great areas of grazing land. In the second setting, it is a plantation, with highly intensive cultivation, a large investment of capital and large labour requirements per acre. In their social effects both types of estate have a common feature: they offer the farm population unsatisfactory conditions of employment, and no degree of responsibility or initiative in management. In their economic effects they differ widely and must be considered separately.

*Large estates with extensive agriculture.* This type of farm organization, the *latifundia*, is a special feature of the agrarian structure of Latin America. With the exception of parts of Costa Rica, El Salvador, Haiti and Mexico, large estates take up the greater part of the cultivable land area throughout the continent. In Latin America as a whole, about one and one-half per cent of the individual landholdings exceed 15,000 acres. The total of these holdings constitutes about 50 per cent of all agricultural land. While much of the land is not suitable for crop production, a substantial proportion consists of idle lands that have been held for generations. Large plantations are also included in these great land-holdings, but do not account for the greater part of the land so held. At the other extreme are the small landowners who practise subsistence farming on a few overcultivated or unproductive acres. While there are also farmers with medium-sized holdings, the bulk of the remaining rural population consists of small tenants and landless labourers.

A peculiarity of the agrarian structure in Latin America is the absence of a clear line of division between the last two categories. In the more advanced countries, a proportion of the land is leased to tenant farmers on fixed rentals. But elsewhere tenancy arrangements are less systematized. When labour is scarce, squatters settle temporarily on the borders of an estate, cultivating a small area for their own requirements, and working on the estate without paying rent. A characteristic feature in many countries, notably in Bolivia, Chile, Guatemala and Peru, is the patron-tenant relationship, under which the tenants (*colonos*) receive a piece of land for cultivation in return for a specified number of days' work per week on the estate. This relationship is associated with a low social status and an extremely low living standard for the farm workers.

Clearly, high levels of productive efficiency and rising standards of living are not likely to be achieved in an agrarian structure of this kind. Some of the effects of the tenancy system on farm productivity have already been considered in the preceding section. Here attention may be drawn to the broad effects of this form of agrarian structure on the utilization of land.

One obvious effect of this type of structure is that agricultural production is not adjusted to the demand for food, particularly foods of high nutritional value. The prevalence of large estates devoted to extensive grazing prevents an expansion of food production to meet the needs of the urban population, as well as the needs of the rural population itself. Throughout Latin America there is a shortage of dairy produce, which could be overcome by the introduction of better breeding stock, more attention to soil conditions and better pasture management. Several South American countries, with a predominantly agricultural population and large land resources, import food for their urban population, part of which could be supplied by more intensive cultivation of the land, or by bringing idle land into cultivation. In Venezuela, for example, within easy reach of the capital now there are fertile regions utilized for extensive grazing which, with a different system of land tenure, could become a market garden area for Caracas. In other regions, all the produce from the areas of intensive cultivation on less fertile and steeply sloping hillsides has to be transported by human beings or pack animals across less intensively cultivated fertile areas to the town.

The pattern of land utilization is thus the reverse of that which market conditions and natural resources require. The hillside land, which is best suited for pasture and woodland, is intensively cultivated for subsistence crops by hoe culture which destroys the top soil, while the valley floors, more suited for arable cultivation, are used for grazing. . . .

If the medium-sized farms played a larger part in the economy, there is reason to believe that the volume of agricultural production would rise, and that standards of living, both urban and rural, could be raised also. Provided that such farms could be established in the grazing lands, methods of land utilization could also be improved. In Brazil, the pattern of agricultural production would appear to be changing in favour of the small and medium-sized farms, of which the numbers are increasing, chiefly as a result of the tendency to sell off land from the older coffee plantations. Market conditions also favour this change. The only limiting factor to a further expansion of small and medium-sized holdings is everywhere the shortage of capital, which prevents the small tenants or subsistence cultivator from increasing the size of his holding. At present, however, the provision of capital to the small farmer is not adequately organized. Co-operative credit societies play very little part in the credit system. If this obstacle were removed, the conditions for the development of family farms in many regions would be highly favourable. Shortage of land is not a limiting factor in most Latin American countries, and, given adequate credit facilities, farms in the more advanced countries should be able to attain an economic size. In the less advanced countries, and in non-cultivated areas, the provision of educational and technical assistance by the government and the extension of health services would be a necessary accompaniment of any change in the agrarian structure.

*Plantations.* Large estates which practise intensive farming cannot generally be said to impede economic development; on the contrary, large increases in land productivity and high yields per acre are usually a feature of the plantation system. The demand for a reform of the estate system in plantation economies is motivated by social considerations: the need for more equal distribution of income and greater possibilities of social advance. . . .

The sugar plantation economy of the West Indies is one example among many which might be given of the conflicts which now centre on this type of agrarian structure. In this region the disproportion between population and natural resources is very great. The density of the farm population in the islands is among the highest in the world, ranging from thirty to fifty persons in agriculture for every hundred acres of cultivated land. The cultivated land is owned predominantly by large estates, either centrally operated or leased to tenants on small holdings. Such holdings are fragmented and occupy only a minor part of the total area. The sugar industry has been subject to long periods of depression, in which estates have gone out of cultivation and unemployment has increased.

In this situation the demand for land reform has taken the form of a demand for land settlement, as a means of relieving unemployment, and as a means of improving the conditions of employment. That there is possible scope for increasing employment by the division of the sugar-cane plantations seems unlikely since the cultivation of sugar-cane requires an intensive use of labour to the acre. With the existing density of farm population it would appear that no reorganization of the agrarian structure is likely to increase the employment possibilities. None the less, from the social point of view, the plantation system is everywhere unpopular.

The sugar industry in the West Indies has reached a political impasse. It cannot continue on its present basis because that basis gives too much political offence. This offence shows itself not only in a general atmosphere of hostility, but also in strikes, riots, the burning of canes, and in some colonies even in uncertainty from year to year whether the state of labour relations will permit the whole crop to be taken off. This state of tension is a luxury which the West Indies cannot afford. New forms of organization must be tried, and must be tried urgently.[3]

Since the need for maintaining employment must be a paramount consideration in these overcrowded islands, whatever new forms of organization are created must aim at promoting intensive use of the land. It is generally believed that the division of the plantations into small farms would be likely to reduce the area planted to sugar-cane, which would reduce the demand for labour and also the volume of agricultural production. So far as plantation crops other than sugar are concerned, the difference in yields between large and small farms is not great enough to outweigh the social advantages which would be gained by resettlement on smaller farms. So far as sugar-cane is concerned, the division of plantations under present conditions would probably result in a decline in yields. The yield of sugar per acre is from 50 to 100 per cent greater on the plantations than it is on small farms. Whether it is possible to conclude from these figures that small-scale production is not an economic alternative as a long-run development is uncertain. The small farm at present produces on inferior land and with insufficient capital. The experience of the United States Farmers Home Administration has shown that it is possible for small farmers, given adequate technical assistance and credit, to produce crops, as for instance cotton, in which the large estate was considered to have an uncontested superiority. None the less,

---

3. W. Arthur Lewis, *Issues in Land Settlement Policy*, a report to the Caribbean Commission West Indian Conference, 1950.

unless such assistance were forthcoming, it seems certain that a division of the estates would be followed by a decline in yields.

\* \* \* \* \*

In the Caribbean region, the main objections to the plantation system are social. In other regions of the world, however, the plantation system, in addition to similar social consequences, has had serious economic disadvantages. The sugar plantations of Java, for example, though successful in that they produced a high return on private capital, dominated the whole economy of the districts in which they were situated, and had adverse effects on crop rotation by facilitating the cultivation of sugar at the expense of rice. They also had unfavourable effects on food production for local needs and on the volume and conditions of employment. As a result, the area of sugar production in Java has long been a "classical stage for social unrest" as it has been in the Caribbean.

In certain areas of Africa—particularly in eastern, central and southern Africa—there has been a development of plantation agriculture mainly under the auspices of non-indigenous enterprise. These plantations are devoted almost exclusively to the production of cash crops, most of which are for export. In the main, the labour force on which these plantations depend is drawn from indigenous tribal and village groups. Formerly, these workers depended entirely on subsistence agricultural and pastoral activities for their livelihood; most of them are still rooted in their subsistence tribal and village groups, from which they come as migrant workers, often on temporary contracts. In some parts of eastern and southern Africa, plantation crops have been developed on the basis of immigrant labour from Asia, particularly the Indian sub-continent, as, for example, in the case of the Natal sugar industry in the Union of South Africa. In Kenya and Tanganyika, where the labour corps is largely African, plantations are mainly owned by European and Asian immigrant settlers.

The most important plantation crops in Africa are sisal, sugar, tea, coffee, tobacco, wattle, rubber, pyrethrum and essential oils. Sisal, sugar, tea and pyrethrum are at present almost exclusively produced on non-indigenous plantations as export crops. Coffee, wattle and tobacco are grown for sale both on plantations and by peasant cultivators. Certain other crops, such as sisal, are likely to continue as plantation crops on account of the relatively large capital outlays required in their production and the economic advantages which they offer through mechanized methods of cultivation. Apart from these special considerations, however, the general trend of African commercial agriculture appears to be toward peasant rather than plantation forms of cultivation.

There is no clear indication from the available evidence on Africa whether plantation production is likely to prove more advantageous to the territories concerned than peasant production. The kind of crop cultivated undoubtedly has a bearing on the question. Equally, if not more, important is government policy in respect of assistance to indigenous agriculture through such agencies as, for example, credit institutions, co-operatives and marketing facilities. Other relevant considerations are wage rates and conditions of labour on plantations as compared with the lot of individual, and in some cases co-operatively organized, peasant producers. The effect of either type of agrarian structure on production of food for local consumption is also a crucial question.

*     *     *     *     *

### Communal Tenure

A type of agrarian structure entirely different from those which have hitherto been described is the system of communal tenure in which control over land is exercised through a social group. Systems of this kind are to be found surviving in parts of South East Asia, India and the Middle East, in some of the Caribbean countries and in the northern and western republics of South America. The question of settlement of title which arises when such a system has already disintegrated has been mentioned in the previous section, with reference to the Middle East. In the following paragraphs the relation of economic development to this form of tenure is considered as it is seen in Africa south of the Sahara, where communal tenure is the most widespread form of agrarian structure.

In this region communal tenure exists in a variety of forms, with certain fundamental features in common. Land is held on a tribal, village, kindred or family basis, and individuals have definite rights in this land by virtue of their membership in the relevant social unit. Hence, title to land has a communal character and it is usufructuary, rather than absolute. A chief, for example, may be the custodian of the land but he is not its owner. The normal unit of land ownership is generally the extended family or kindred group, and once the land is granted to such a group it remains its property. In theory land may be pledged and redeemed, but only in such manner that it shall not be permanently lost.

Though different physical conditions result in a variety of forms of cultivation in various parts of Africa, communal tenures have been most frequently associated with shifting subsistence agriculture. Shifting cultivation in any of its forms implies a relatively plentiful supply of land in relation to population. As the area of land in relation to the population declines, more intensive methods of cultivation become necessary. This has already happened in many parts of Africa as a result of a number of closely related factors, including population increase, the introduction of commercial crops and the alienation of land either on a concession basis or to immigrant settlers. Soil deterioration and soil erosion, already serious problems in these areas, further reduce the available land. New techniques of agriculture are thus imperative, not only for the purposes of commercial cropping and subsistence production, but also for maintaining the fertility of the soil and for reconditioning land already eroded.

Under the pressure of these influences, traditional systems of land tenure are necessarily being adjusted. Frequently, however, conflicts of interest arise between the development of commercial cropping, and the requirements of farming methods designed to prevent loss of soil fertility, since overcropping for commercial reasons is a common danger and may contribute seriously to soil deterioration. Moreover, commercial crops may be developed at the expense of local food crops. New methods also frequently involve some capital expenditure—for example, for the fencing of pasture lands, for fertilizer and for new agricultural implements. In many instances, the lack of proved experience tending to show that the additional returns justify new forms of effort and expenditure may be more important obstacles to change than the existing form of land tenure.

Indeed, available data suggest that the communal systems of land tenure in Africa have not proved in themselves so inflexible as to prevent adaptation to new conditions. In certain parts of Africa, for example in the Gold Coast and Uganda, the traditional communal land system has been changing rapidly to one of individual private holdings in land, mainly in response to the desire to exploit land for commercial purposes. In other areas of Africa, the communal system has been less completely modified. In the Belgian Congo commercial and subsistence crops have been developed under government direction, without fundamentally affecting the customary system of land tenure in force. In the Gezira Scheme in the Sudan, where private rights to land in this area had long been recognized, the right-holders largely retained ownership of their land, although they leased it to the Government for a forty-year period, and acquired rights of tenancy when the Government obtained control over the land for purposes of development. The question of the influence of land tenure in Africa is therefore not whether traditional systems present *per se* a powerful obstacle to economic development, but rather whether the new forms arising from the increasing invasion of subsistence economy by an economy based on exchange will lead to economic development, without in the long run destroying much of the land for agricultural production, or resulting in abuses detrimental to the social and economic welfare of the community.

## Ansley J. Coale

# Population and Economic Development

MOST UNDERDEVELOPED AREAS of the world have birth rates of forty per 1000 or higher and an average number of children born at the end of the fertile period—at age of forty-five or fifty—of at least 5. This fertility contrasts with experience in Europe, where birth rates are, with only two or three exceptions, below twenty per 1,000, and total fertility is two to three children. The fertility of Japan is at the low end of the European scale. Other highly industrialized areas outside of Europe—the United States, the Soviet Union, Australia, New Zealand and Canada—have birth rates between twenty and twenty-eight per 1,000 and a total fertility of three to four children.

As a consequence of the invention and application of low-cost techniques of public health, underdeveloped areas have recently experienced a fall in mortality more rapid than ever seen before. They have not had to wait while the gradual process of developing medical science took place; nor have they had to depend on the possibly more rapid but still difficult process of constructing major sanitary engineering works and building up of a large inventory of expensive hospitals, public health services and highly trained doctors. Instead, the underdeveloped areas have been able to import low-cost measures of controlling disease, measures developed for the most part in the highly industrialized countries. The use of residual insecticides to provide effective protection against malaria at no more than twenty-five cents per capita per year is an outstanding example. Other innovations include antibiotics and chemotherapy, and extend to the discovery of relatively low-cost ways of providing a safe water supply and adequate environmental sanitation in villages that in other ways remain little touched by modernization.

The result of a precipitous decline in mortality while the birth rate remains essentially unchanged is, of course, a rapid acceleration in population growth, reaching in some instances rates of three to three and one-half per cent per year. The underdeveloped areas with more moderate growth rates of one and one-half to two and one-half per cent per year are typically in the midst of a rapid decline in death rates, and are experiencing steep increases in the rate of growth of their populations.

The high fertility of low-income countries produces a large proportion of children and a small proportion, in consequence, of adults in the economically most productive ages. The underdeveloped countries have forty to forty-five per cent of their population under age fifteen, in contrast with a maximum of twenty-five to thirty per cent in the highly industrialized countries. Differences in mortality among countries, whether industrialized or not, have only slight effect on the distribution of the population by age, and specifically on the proportion of the population that children constitute. Indeed, the effect of a lower death rate on the proportion of children is in a surprising direction. Mortality is typically reduced the most in infancy and early childhood; and if fertility remains unchanged, a reduction in mortality of the sort usually occurring increases the proportion of children and reduces rather than increases the average age.

There are great variations in population density from one low-income area to another, with fewer than ten persons per square mile in Bolivia, and more than 600 in Korea.

In this chapter we shall consider how these characteristics of the population affect the process of industrialization or modernization to which the low-income areas aspire. Their populations at present suffer from inadequate diets, enjoy at best primitive and overcrowded housing, have a modest education or no formal education at all (if adult) and rarely attend school (if children), and are often productively employed for only a fraction of the year. These populations suffer all of the misery and degradation associated with poverty. They naturally wish to enjoy the universal education, adequate diet, housing equipped with modern amenities, the long and generally healthy life, the opportunity for productive work and extensive voluntary leisure that the highly industrialized countries have shown to be possible. To do so the underdeveloped countries must modernize their economies.

The changes in social and economic structure that make up the process of modernization or industrialization are many and profound. More productive techniques must displace traditional methods of manufacturing, agriculture, trade, transport and communications. Economic activity must become more diversified and more specialized. The emphasis in production must shift from extractive industries, especially agriculture, to manufacturing, trade and communications. The interchange of goods through a monetary medium on widespread markets must replace local consumption of goods produced on the farm or exchanged only in small village markets. The labor force must be transformed from illiteracy to literacy. A sufficient supply must be found and trained of what has become to be known as "high talent manpower"—doctors, lawyers, engineers, entrepreneurs and managers. Production must shift from small, family-oriented enterprises into large, impersonal, professionally supervised organizations. However, many of these essential changes are related only indirectly to demographic characteristics such as growth and age distribution.

Here two important aspects of industrialization or modernization will be considered. One aspect is increasing income per person as a consequence (and an index) of industrialization, and the other is the attainment or maintenance of productive employment for the labor force.

## POPULATION AND INCOME PER HEAD

Examining the implications of population change for the growth of real income we shall consider nations rather than areas within nations. The selection of the nation as the unit for analysis implies that gains or losses of population through migration can generally be considered of negligible importance. There are a few exceptions (perhaps four or five small countries that can expect gains or losses from migration of important magnitude compared to natural increase), but for the majority of underdeveloped countries and certainly for the larger ones there is no such realistic likelihood.

For somewhat different reasons, the possibility of alternative courses of mortality can also be ignored, at least for a generation or two. The basis for paying little attention to different possible courses of mortality is that the technical feasibility of reducing mortality to lower levels—of increasing expectation of life at birth at least to some fifty or sixty years— has been widely demonstrated in the underdeveloped areas themselves. Unless the effort to start and continue the process of modernization fails completely, or unless there is a breakdown in world order, the attainment and maintenance, at least for a short time, of low mortality rates seems potentially within the reach of most low-income countries. It does not appear that widespread famine or even severe increases in malnutrition are a necessary consequence in the next few decades, even if the low-income countries experience population growth rates of two to three and one-half per cent.

The agricultural and industrial technology that can be introduced into low-income countries is, in a sense, parallel to the medical technology that can be imported to achieve a rapid reduction in mortality rates. Rates of increase in agricultural output of at least three or four per cent a year appear technically feasible, even in such a densely settled, highly agricultural country as India. If the birth rate in India is not reduced, the population will probably double in the next generation from about 450 million to about 900 million persons. Agricultural experts consider it feasible within achievable limits of capital investment to double Indian agricultural output within the next twenty or twenty-five years. In the short run, then, it can be assumed, provisionally at least, that mortality reduction can be achieved and maintained.

Finally, if sickness can be reduced and death postponed within the resources available to the health authorities in the underdeveloped countries, assisted by the World Health Organization, UNICEF, and directly by the industrialized countries, it is scarcely imaginable that by deliberate policy these opportunities would be foregone. In other words, the only factor that can be realistically considered as variable in causing population change by deliberate policy is fertility. We shall be concerned here with the implications, for the growth in per capita income and for the provision of productive employment, of alternative possible future courses of fertility. The specific alternatives to be considered are the maintenance of fertility at its current level (which would involve in almost all underdeveloped countries the continuation of an essentially horizontal trend that has already continued for generations) and, as the contrasting alternative, a rapid reduction in fertility, amounting to fifty per cent of the initial level and occupying a transitional period of about twenty-five years.

\* \* \* \* \*

## Economic Development and Demographic Variables

We shall consider primarily the implications of our demographic variables for the capacity of the economy to divert effort and resources from producing for current consumption to producing for the enhancement of future productivity. In other words, it will be assumed that to accelerate the process of modernization an economy must increase its level of net investment. Net investment here means additions to factories, roads, irrigation networks, fertilizer plants and other productive facilities. It also can include in a broad definition resources and effort devoted to education and training. It is not an intended implication that merely stepping up the rate of new investment automatically insures a major speed-up in industrialization, or assures the attainment of the fastest possible pace of modernization. Resources mobilized for productive purposes must be wisely allocated. Adequate leadership must be found for the new forms of productive organization that an industrialized society requires. Long-standing customs and traditions must be altered if new and more effective techniques of production are to be employed. In other words, a high level of net investment is a *necessary* but not a *sufficient* condition for a rapid pace of industrialization. In the ensuing analysis it will be assumed that the other crucial elements in modernization are present.

## Age Distribution and Investment

At the end of twenty-five years there is only a four per cent difference in the size of the labor force or, more precisely, a four per cent difference in the number of persons fifteen to sixty-four. Let us suppose that productive employment can be found for all males of labor force age seeking employment and for all females who are not bound to housekeeping duties by lack of education, tradition, and the necessity to care for small children and who also are in search of productive employment. Let us assume further that twenty-five years from now the progress toward modernization has included the establishment of virtually universal primary education, so that the effective age of entry in the labor force is not before age fifteen. Let us also make the provisional assumption, which we shall re-examine shortly, that national income is, in the twenty-fifth year, the same for the two projected populations. If the reader objects that this provisional assumption seems unrealistic because the high fertility population would have some four per cent more persons of labor force age, let him consider the offsetting fact that the low fertility population would contain only about half as many young infants and half as many pregnant women. If allowance is made for the greater number of women free to work outside the home, the number of persons actually available for productive employment would not really be four per cent less in the low fertility population but might actually be slightly greater. It is certainly reasonable to disregard the small difference in size of population over age fifteen.

If there were the same total national income to be utilized by the two projected populations, the pressure toward utilizing nearly all of it for consumption would be substantially greater in the high fertility population, as a direct result of the greater burden of dependency that must be borne by the labor force. In the high fertility population after twenty-five years, there would be ninety-six persons in the dependent ages for every one hundred persons in the productive ages, while in the low fertility population there would be only sixty-five dependents for every one hundred persons fifteen to sixty-four.

The pressure to spend a higher fraction of national income on consumption can take many forms in different kinds of economies. In a capitalist economy, where investment is financed out of private savings, the fact that families with a large number of children find it more difficult to save reduces the volume of savings and hence the level of investment.

When low-income families are not an important source of savings, higher fertility creates social pressure to increase the share of national income received by the poorest earners (the non-savers) in order to maintain minimum standards of consumption.

High fertility can depress private savings in two ways: (1) by reducing the volume of savings by individual families when such savings are an important component of the national total; (2) by increasing the proportion of national income that must accrue to non-savers if standards of consumption play any part in determining the earnings of low-income families.

When it is the government rather than individual entrepreneurs that provides a large proportion of national investment, fertility affects the level of investment through its effect on the capacity of the government to raise money through taxation. Suppose the government attempts to maximize the fund it mobilizes for net investment. For any given level of deprivation that it is prepared to impose, it can raise more taxes from a low fertility population than from a high fertility population with the same national income and the same number of adults in each. Even if the government does not calculate the maximum revenue it can assess, the existence of such factors as exemptions for children would automatically reduce income tax revenues.

After this lengthy review we reach a simple conclusion. Given the same labor force and the same total national income, a low fertility population will achieve a higher level of net investment than a high fertility population. It will therefore be able to make larger additions to the productive capacity of the country and achieve a higher national product in the next year. In addition, the population with a higher burden of child dependency feels a constant pressure to divert investment funds to less productive or at least to less immediately productive uses. To meet given target dates for achieving universal literacy or universal primary education, more funds must be spent on education. In a population of large families rather than small, more construction must be diverted to housing rather than to factories or hydroelectric plants.

During a short-run period of twenty-five to thirty years, the age distribution effect of declining fertility enhances the capacity of the economy to increase its net investment, and to utilize investment in more immediately productive ways. The labor force available for productive employment during the short-run period is the same, or perhaps a little larger during the first fifteen years because persons over fifteen would be the same in number and more women could participate in productive employment. Actual numbers available for employment probably become equal in the two projections some time between twenty-five and thirty years after the decline of fertility starts. The resources available would presumably be identical. In consequence, there emerges a conclusion that may seem paradoxical. During a period of twenty-five or thirty years, at least, after fertility reduction begins, the population reducing its fertility would produce a more rapidly growing national product than a population which kept its fertility unchanged. This more rapid growth would cumulate into a consequentially higher total product at the end of the thirty-year period. In other words, in the short run not only does a population with reduced fertility enjoy the benefit of dividing the national product among a smaller number of consumers, it enjoys the additional benefit of having a larger national product to divide.

## Effects of Labor Force Growth

After twenty-five or thirty years declining fertility begins to cause major differences in the growth rate, and later on major differences in the size of the adult population. The difference in dependency burden reaches a maximum by about forty years, thereafter remaining unchanged. The high fertility labor force must continue, as in the short run, to share what it produces with a distinctly greater number of dependents, and this necessity continues to impair the capacity of the economy to attain a high level of investment. But after the short run a new element, the different rate of growth of the labor force itself, assumes important dimensions.

The significance of the growth of the labor force for income per head is that higher rates of growth imply a higher level of needed investment to achieve a given per capita output, although there is nothing about faster growth that generates a greater supply in investible resources. A larger labor force requires a larger stock of productive facilities in order to have the same productivity per head. The per cent of national income that must be invested merely to keep productivity from declining is some three times the annual per cent rate of increase of the labor force. In other words, if the labor force were growing by three per cent a year, a level of net investment of nine per cent of national income would be required to prevent declining productivity, while if the rate of growth of the labor force were one per cent a year, the needed level of investment for this purpose would be only three per cent of national income.

This rule of thumb assumes that the stock of capital must increase as much as the labor force to prevent a decline of productivity, and assumes further that the stock of capital is roughly three times as large as the current level of national income. Yet the faster growing labor force has no intrinsic advantages in achieving a high level of savings to finance the needed higher level of investment. It needs more investment but has no inherent advantages in achieving more.

Another way of presenting the difference between a rapidly growing and a slowly growing labor force is to consider the effect of net investment at the respectable rate of fifteen per cent of national income. A population with a rate of growth of three per cent in its labor force can with such a level of net investment add about two per cent per year to the endowment of capital per worker. If the labor force were growing at one per cent, the annual increase in the stock of capital per worker would be four per cent.

An economy where additional members of the labor force settle on empty land, a "frontier society," is a partial exception to the above line of reasoning. If frontier settlement provides an outlet for the growth in the labor force, it is possible that new members provide most of their own capital—by clearing land, constructing roads, building log houses, etc. Under these hypothetical circumstances the rate of capital formation might be automatically higher with a more rapidly growing labor force. However, it is uncertain whether there are genuine instances of this kind of frontier settlement in the world today. Indonesia has attempted to re-settle families from densely populated and rapidly growing Java to the relatively empty land in Borneo. However, the Indonesian government has felt impelled to make a generous capital investment in the form of tools and equipment for each family, the numbers involved have been at most a trivial fraction of the annual increase in Java's population, and many of the pioneers have returned to Java after a short period.

Most underdeveloped countries find it difficult to invest as much as fifteen per cent of their national incomes, and hence will find it necessary for the next generation to utilize more than half of their investment merely to provide capital for the growing labor force. In the short run a reduction of fertility would not affect this necessity. However, even in the short run the age distribution advantages of reduced fertility would in-crease the level of net investment that would be attained. During the intermediate period, when reduced fertility results in a substantially slower growth of the labor force, the age distribution advantage would continue. A greater capacity to allocate output to investment would be combined with a less imperative necessity to invest merely to keep up with the growth of the labor force.

### Effect of Density

The question of population density tends to be the dominant concept in most casual thought about the population problems of underdeveloped areas. The notion of excessive density is certainly implicit in the term "overpopulation." The underlying idea is that when there are too many workers relative to the available resources, per capita output is smaller than it would be with a smaller number of workers. Given gross enough differences in the numbers of workers being compared, it is certainly possible in principle to establish that overpopulation in this sense exists. For example, in 150 years the high fertility population that we projected would be eighteen times as large as the population that would result from fifty per cent reduction in fertility. Even the labor force with reduced fertility would imply a density more than twelve times greater than at present, while the population with sustained fertility would involve a density more than 200 times greater than at present. There is little doubt that in most countries a density 200 times greater would have a depressing effect upon per capita output compared to a density twelve times greater.

There are, however, two reasons for doubting the immediate usefulness of the concept of density in considering population problems of underdeveloped areas. The first is that in this period of human history few countries have any genuine freedom of choice of policy that would have an important effect on population density (or, more specifically, on the density of the labor force) in the short run. There are few areas where realistic alternatives of promoting or retarding international migration would have an important effect upon density. It is unlikely, and I would argue strongly undesirable, that an underdeveloped country should contemplate a deliberate restraint on its public health programs in order to retard the decline of mortality and thus prevent an increase of population density. . . . a reduction in fertility does not have an important effect on density for a long time in the future. The difference in the size of the labor force is less then ten per cent thirty years after a rapid and extensive decline in fertility begins. After thirty years, however, the difference in density between sustained and reduced fertility rapidly mounts, reaching a factor of two in about sixty years, a factor of three in seventy-five years, and a factor of eighteen after 150 years. In other words, so far as acceptable and attainable policies are concerned, only in the relatively distant future can the density of the labor force relative to resources be affected. In the meantime the policy that would have a long-run effect on density, namely one that reduces fertility, would through changes in dependency and differences in the annual rate of growth of the labor force have produced major economic effects.

A second reservation about the relevance of density is that it is of clearcut importance only in a closed economy—i.e., one that does not trade extensively—or in an economy where the principal industry is extractive. Only in extractive industries—mining, agriculture, and forestry—are resources as related to numbers of workers a dominant element in productivity. For example, if India were compelled to continue to employ seventy per cent of its labor force in agriculture, increasing density would inevitably mean smaller average holdings. The average holding today is only about two acres per person aged fifteen to sixty-four dependent on agriculture, and the possibility of bringing new areas under cultivation is limited.

In non-extractive industries international trade can greatly reduce the effect of limited resources. In all industries, extractive or otherwise, productivity is determined to a large degree by the stock of capital per worker. The underdeveloped areas have in common a small endowment of productive equipment per worker relative to the industrialized countries; in other words, the underdeveloped countries all have a "high density" of workers relative to capital, whether the country appears to be sparsely or densely settled relative to land and other resources.

*       *       *       *       *

In the normal course of industrialization the proportion of the population engaged in agriculture and other extractive industries steadily declines. In the history of every highly industrialized area a period was reached during which the number of persons dependent on agriculture was stabilized so that all increases in population of labor force age caused increases only in non-agricultural employment. The period of unchanging numbers engaged in agriculture has typically been followed by a shrinkage in the absolute number. This sequence has been typical both in countries where the initial density of agricultural settlement was very high, such as Japan, or where it was relatively low, as in the United States or New Zealand. The implications of this sequence for employment in industrializing countries will be considered later. Here its relevance is that for countries in the earlier stages of economic development some of the increases in the labor force must seek employment in extractive industries. If the agricultural population is already densely settled (as in India), this necessity undoubtedly constitutes a greater hardship or barrier to rapidly increasing incomes than in a less densely settled country.

As was noted earlier, the underdeveloped countries all suffer from what might be called a high density of population relative to *capital*. Therefore the effects not only of the age distribution but also of the rate of growth of the labor force (with their respective implications for the ease with which capital formation can proceed and for the rate at which it must proceed to attain given objectives in per capita output) operate in sparsely settled as well as in densely settled countries. In very sparsely settled countries the adverse effect upon the possible reduction of density relative to capital of rapid growth of the labor force may be partially offset by an increasingly advantageous relationship between numbers and land area and other resources. A larger population may, when original density is unusually low, permit the use of more efficient large-scale operations. This possibility does not imply, however, that the more rapid the rate of growth the better. Additional capital for the additional labor force is still essential, and rapid growth prevents an increase in the capital/worker rates. Moreover, from a strictly economic point of view the most advantageous way to attain a larger labor force is through immigration, because it is possible by this means to obtain additional labor without incurring the expense of childhood dependency.

*Declining Fertility and Per Capita Income*

A reduction in fertility has the immediate effect (during the first generation after the decline begins) of reducing the burden of child dependency without any major effect on the size of the labor force. After twenty or twenty-five years the decline in fertility begins to effect a major reduction in the rate of growth of the labor force. In the more remote future, beginning after forty or fifty years and with increasing importance with the further passage of time, reduced fertility produces a population of lower density—with a smaller labor force relative to the available resources. The age distribution effect of reduced fertility operates to produce during the first generation a larger total national product than would result if fertility had not been reduced. The greater rise in total output results from the fact that the same number of producers— the same number of persons eligible for participation in the labor force —is accompanied by a smaller number of consumers. The smaller number of consumers decreases the fraction of national output that must be allocated to current consumption, and thus promotes the mobilization of resources for economic growth. Both private savings and the ability of the government to raise funds for development are increased.

In addition, a smaller number of consumers (especially children) permits the expenditure of savings and tax receipts in ways that raise national output more (or more immediately) than other uses. Less must be spent for primary education, housing and "social overhead" purposes generally.

Another indirect effect of reduced fertility is that, as a result of larger per capita consumption, the labor force is perhaps more productive because of better nutrition, and because of the effects of rising consumption in combatting apathy, and in providing better work incentives. These effects of a reduced number of consumers relative to the producers in the population caused in the short run by a decline in fertility continue into the future so long as fertility remains below its former level. Starting after twenty-five or thirty years is the additional effect of reduced fertility in slowing down the growth of the labor force. A reduced rate of growth of the labor force means that a given level of net investment can be used to add more to the per capita endowment of the labor force in productive equipment than if the labor force were growing more rapidly.

In the long run the slower rate of growth that reduced fertility brings would result in much lower density of population than with the continuation of high fertility. Even with a fifty per cent reduction in fertility, the population in most underdeveloped areas would grow very substantially during the next two or three generations. For example, in the projection presented earlier showing typical prospects for Latin American countries, with fertility falling by one half, density would be multiplied by 2.46 in thirty years and by 1.71 in the ensuing thirty years, a total increase of 4.2 times in sixty years. In spite of greatly reduced fertility, the density of workers relative to resources would increase by a factor of something like four in the next two generations.

Brazil is often cited as a country that might derive economic benefits from more dense settlement. Even with a fifty per cent reduction in fertility, the population of Brazil aged fifteen to sixty-four will have increased from 38 million to 161 million in the next sixty years. This would give Brazil a population at these ages sixty years from now forty-two per cent larger than that of the United States today. It is hard to argue that this density would be too small to achieve an efficient exploitation of Brazil's resources, especially since much of Brazil's vast area is of uncertain economic value. Not all underdeveloped areas have as high a current growth potential as Latin America. Current fertility is in many instances below that found in Mexico or Brazil, and in other instances success in reducing mortality is somewhat behind the achievements of the more advanced Latin American countries. . . .

The population density that would result from a fifty per cent reduction in fertility in the next twenty-five years would in almost every underdeveloped area be at least adequate for the efficient exploitation of the resources available. The much *higher* density that would result from sustained fertility, a margin of higher density that would increase with ever greater rapidity the further into the future one looks, might in the most favorable circumstances cause no insuperable difficulties for a few decades. It might be possible, for example, to offset a high density of population in some areas, as Hong Kong has done, by engaging in trade, provided there remain areas of the world prepared to supply agricultural products and raw materials in exchange for finished goods and services. But in all areas, a prolonged continuation of rapid growth would lead to intolerable overcrowding.

\*　　\*　　\*　　\*　　\*

## Delaying Reduction in Fertility

There is a persuasive *laissez-faire* position on population policy in the pre-industrial countries, based on the following argument. Every country that has become highly industrialized has experienced a decline in fertility amounting to at least fifty per cent of the pre-industrial level. Therefore, the argument runs, public policy should be concentrated on achieving the maximum pace of industrialization. The decline in fertility will take care of itself.

The generalization upon which this argument rests is well founded. All countries that have become predominantly urban, that have shifted away from agriculture as the source of employment for as much as half of the labor force, and that now have adult populations that are at least eighty-five per cent literate have experienced at least a fifty per cent decline in fertility. Included among these countries are: all of Europe (except for Albania); the overseas industrialized countries with predominantly European populations—Australia, New Zealand, Canada and the United States; Japan and the Soviet Union. However, it is far from clear precisely what aspects of industrialization have been instrumental in causing the decline in fertility in these countries. In some instances industrialization had preceded for a long time and had effected major changes in the economy and society before any tangible reduction in fertility occurred. For example, a marked decline did not begin in England and Wales until the 1880's, nor in Japan until about 1925. For countries that are as yet in the early stages of modernization, having very low current per capita incomes, it might take at least thirty to sixty years to attain a state of industrialization that would in itself cause a rapid decline in fertility. In fact the adverse effects of continued high fertility in the interim might in itself postpone the attainment of the needed state of advanced industrialization.

\* \* \* \* \*

## POPULATION AND THE LABOR FORCE

It is of course a drastic oversimplification to treat industrialization and modernization wholly in terms of increases in income per head. Such increases are surely a valid and necessary objective of economic development, but there are other goals widely shared in the underdeveloped areas, including better health and improved and more widespread education, rightly viewed as values in themselves, as well as means of achieving larger incomes. A nearly universal goal is that of providing productive employment for male adults and for a proportion of adult women that steadily increases as modernization proceeds. This goal, like those of better health and education, is considered as valuable in its own right, because of the degrading effect of unemployment or of unproductive employment.

The problems of "unemployment" and "underemployment," which are the subject of so much comment in the underdeveloped areas, are essentially reflections of the poverty and low productivity to which these areas are subject. Underemployment is sometimes defined as a situation in which a reduction in the number of persons engaged in a given activity would not cause an important reduction in total output from the activity in question. Examples are the presence of more porters in a railway station than are needed to carry the normal load of luggage, farming operations where a traditional set of tasks are divided among whatever family members have the responsibility for operating the farm, or a cluster of small retail shops carrying essentially identical merchandise in which the clerks or proprietors are idle most of the day because of the scarcity of customers. In most underdeveloped areas such examples are common. The existence of essentially redundant manpower that these examples indicate is called "underemployment" rather than "unemployment" because the redundancy does not show itself in the form of large numbers actively looking for work. The measurement of unemployment (and the technical definition of unemployment) has become increasingly a matter of determining the number of persons actively seeking jobs.

In most underdeveloped areas a major increase in the number of productive jobs would be needed to make serious inroads into current underemployment and unemployment. The prospective rapid growth in the labor force that such countries face adds greatly to the difficulties of achieving satisfactory employment goals. During the first generation the number of additional productive jobs that must be provided is scarcely affected by the course of fertility. The labor force thirty years following the start of a fifty per cent reduction in fertility spread evenly over a twenty-five year period is less than ten per cent smaller than the labor force resulting from a continuation of unchanged fertility. In a typical Latin American population the labor force would increase in thirty years by a factor of 2.44 should fertility be reduced, and 2.67 should fertility remain unchanged. In either case the provision of adequate employment opportunities is a job of frightening proportions. An annual increase of about three per cent or more in the number of jobs is required if unemployment and underemployment are not to increase.

In underdeveloped areas the barrier to more adequate employment opportunity is not primarily that lack of sufficient effective demand which many economists see as the source of the apparently chronic problem of attaining full employment in the United States. The simultaneous existence of unemployed persons and idle capital equipment in the United States (a conspicuous example is the steel industry) is not the situation typical of the underdeveloped countries. The absence of opportunities for productive employment is primarily the result of insufficient productive equipment and resources for labor to work with, compounded by the lack of education and training on the part of the labor force itself.

In the earlier discussion it was seen that a population with reduced fertility has important advantages in its capacity to accumulate capital. It also can more readily provide a rapid attainment of specified educational standards. Consequently, even during the first twenty-five or thirty years following the start of fertility decline, when the number of new jobs needed each year is not much affected by reduced fertility, the advantages in reduced dependency that lower fertility brings would, by enabling higher levels of investment, permit the more rapid expansion of employment opportunity. In the longer run the reduced rate of growth of the labor force resulting from lower fertility would make the achievement of adequate employment opportunities much easier. After sixty years, for example, the rate of increase in the labor force in our model projection for a Latin American country would be 3.7 per cent if fertility were sustained, and only 1.3 per cent if fertility were reduced. By that time the number of persons sixteen to sixty-four in the lower fertility projection would be nearly 4.2 times as great as today, and with sustained fertility it would be eight times as great.

The magnitude of the problem of providing future jobs in the underdeveloped countries can be better appreciated when one considers the typical change in the composition of employment that accompanies the process of industrialization. In general terms the change in patterns of employment is one of increasing diversity, with reduced proportions in the traditional occupations, especially in agriculture. If the employment history in the industrialized countries is examined, the universal trend during the process of industrialization is found to be a steadily decreasing proportion in agriculture. In fact all of the more highly industrialized countries have reached or passed through a phase in which the *number* in agriculture remains constant, so that all of the increases in the population of labor force age are absorbed in the non-agricultural sectors of the economy. This phase has then typically been followed by a decline in the absolute number of persons dependent on agriculture. It is not surprising that such a decline has been experienced in countries such as England and Wales, known for their emphasis on manufacturing and for their exports of manufactured products and imports of agricultural products. It is somewhat unexpected that a decline should have occurred in Denmark, a major exporter of agricultural produce. Decreases in the absolute number in agriculture have also been recorded in countries of very different densities, ranging from England and Japan on the one hand to the United States, the Soviet Union, and New Zealand on the other.

At some stage, then, an industrializing country must, if it follows the sequence common to the history of the now industrialized countries, look to the non-agricultural sector of the economy for the provision of employment opportunities sufficient for the whole increase in the labor force. . . . In most underdeveloped countries it will be impossible to achieve these rates of increase in non-agricultural employment. They will be forced to continue to increase the number of persons engaged in agriculture. Such continued increases are at best a necessary evil. In fact these unavoidable increases in agricultural employment show the cost of an initial high level of density in a country that has a high proportion of its labor force engaged in agriculture. Such countries cannot provide non-agricultural employment opportunities for the whole of the increase in their labor forces, and because of the small land holdings that high density implies, additions to the labor force in agriculture add mostly to underemployment in this sector.

It is a reasonable, almost an essential objective that within a generation most countries should plan to provide non-agricultural employment for the whole of their additions to the labor force. . . .

This sketchy analysis is sufficient to show that the reduction of fertility would play an even more crucial role in attaining the goal of adequate employment opportunities than in the closely related but not identical goal of insuring a more rapid increase in income per consumer.

## Albert O. Hirschman

# Population Pressures as a Force for Development

FEW TOPICS in the theory of economic development have evoked such unanimity as population growth. With increases in per capita income widely accepted as the objective of development or as the best available approximation to it, population is firmly relegated to the denominator of the expression which we want to maximize and any increase in numbers can only be considered a setback on the road to development. Such expressions as the population growth that "swallows up" increases in output in whole or in part, such images as walking up a downward moving escalator, and the virtually obligatory quotation from Lewis Carroll: "Here it takes all the running you can do, to keep in the same place,"—all testify to the universal assumption that the exclusive effect of population growth is to frustrate economic development. Some writers are of course aware of the fact that demographic stagnation or declining population growth were high on the list among the explanations for the falling behind of France as a major political and economic power, and were one of the three pillars of the stagnation thesis in the United States. But any disturbing ideas on that account could be quickly discarded by the reassuring, if somewhat shapeless, thought that the problems of developed and underdeveloped countries are entirely distinct.

In the face of such unanimity, we shall present with considerable reluctance some reasons which make us think that population pressures are to be considered forces that may stimulate development. We are fully aware that this is a dangerous thought—dangerous not so much for the world at large as for the reputation of the author; and in order not to expose ourselves too long to the heavy fire which will certainly be opened on us, we shall dispose of what we have to say with the utmost brevity.

Let us start out by again invoking Dusenberry's "fundamental psychological postulate," which says that people will resist a lowering in their standard of living. If they do this as a result of a cyclical depression why should they not also react in some way against their incomes being squeezed by an increase in population? Our first proposition is therefore that *population pressure on living standards will lead to counterpressure, i.e., to activity designed to maintain or restore the traditional standard of living of the community.* Leaving the validity of this proposition for later consideration, we shall assume for the moment that this counterpressure is partially or wholly successful in restoring per capita incomes. Thus far, then, the psychological postulate yields at best a mechanism of equilibrium, i.e., of stagnation rather than development.

But the situation is not really the same after this process, for in its course the community has *learned,* through wrestling successfully with new tasks. Our second proposition is therefore that *the activity undertaken by the community in resisting a decline in its standard of living causes an increase in its ability to control its environment and to organize itself for development.* As a result, the community will now be able to exploit the opportunities for economic growth that existed previously but were left unutilized.

In short, the learning a community does when it reacts to population pressures increases the total stock of its resources much as investment adds to total productive capacity. To revert to the images mentioned earlier: walking up downward escalators or running in the same place is excellent exercise and practice for people who need to improve their walking or running performance. Anyone who has watched attempts by public and private bodies to cope with the traffic, water supply, electric power, housing, school, and crime problems of a growing city can have little doubt that the qualities of imagination and organization developed in these tasks of *maintaining* standards of living in the face of population pressures are very similar to those that are needed to *increase* per capita incomes. The basic determinant of development which we have called the "ability to invest" is decisively enhanced in the course of the struggle to accommodate more people.

Returning to our first proposition, we cannot claim that it is more than a variant of an old idea. Many writers, Malthus among them, have remarked on the incentive effects of the need to provide for one's wife and children. Others have examined the stimulating effect of population increases, not on the individual's "natural indolence," but on society's. In this respect, much that is incisive has been said, in particular by the Belgian sociologist and philosopher Dupréel[1] who has traced the many ways in which an increasing population leads to improved performance of the administrative, political, and cultural processes. But while these direct positive influences and actions of population growth on individual motivations and economic and political developments are of interest, we think it more useful to stress the *reaction* mechanism that is set up when population growth depresses, or is about to depress, living standards, for the recognition of this reaction mechanism permits us to go beyond the following somewhat unsatisfactory summary of the problem by Schumpeter: "Sometimes an increase in population actually has no other effects than that predicted by classical theory—a fall in per capita real income; but at other times it may have an energizing effect that induces new developments with the result that per capita income rises."[2] By viewing the "energizing" effect as potentially induced by the "classical" effect, we can at least attempt to reduce the complete indeterminateness of this statement.

Our affirmation that a society will attempt to react to the "dilution" of total income that comes with larger numbers is of interest only if

1. E. Dupréel, "Population et progrès" in *Deux essais sur le progrès*, Brussels, 1928.

2. J. Schumpeter, "The Creative Response in Economic History," *Journal of Economic History*, 7 (Nov. 1947), 149.

the reaction can be successful, i.e., if there is some "slack" in the economy that can be taken up. This assumption is of course contrary to the basic hypothesis of the neo-Malthusian models, *viz.* "all productive forces are fully utilized, i.e., there are no unemployed resources—the supply of land and capital is fixed."[3] This formulation is not even sufficiently strong if we wish to stipulate that it is impossible to squeeze more output from the available resources without a prior increase in per capita incomes out of which new savings can be extracted. We must then also suppose that production is *optimally* organized, that all existing technological and organizational knowledge that does not require capital outlays is fully applied. Obviously, even in densely populated underdeveloped areas, such a situation will be exceedingly rare.[4]

The panorama changes abruptly if it is granted that a margin of possible improvements exists, and if, more generally, we revert to our diagnosis of underdevelopment as a state where labor, capital, entrepreneurship, etc. are potentially available and can be combined, provided a sufficiently strong "binding agent" is encountered. . . . Then an increase in incomes is by no means the only way of starting the economy on an upward course. Nevertheless, there is some question whether population pressure can be considered an "inducement mechanism" in the sense in which we have used this term. How will it cause the possible improvements to be made? How will it call forth the latent resources of the economy?

Among the inducement mechanisms we have studied, from the various complementarity effects on down, population pressure must rank as the least attractive one. In the first place, it works through an initial decline in per capita income rather than through, e.g., an uneven expansion in output. Secondly, it is less reliable than the other mechanisms we have considered. In our previous, vaguely similar mechanism, i.e., losses in foreign exchange income leading to indus-

---

3. Alan T. Peacock, "Theory of Population and Modern Economic Analysis," *Population Studies,* 6 (1952-53), 115.

4. Malthus can be quoted in support of this view: "There are few large countries, however advanced in improvement, the population of which might not have been doubled or tripled, and there are many which might be ten or even a hundred times as populous, and yet all the inhabitants be as well provided for as they are now, if the institutions of society and the moral habits of the people, had been for some hundred years the most favourable to the increase of capital, and the demand for produce and labour." *A Summary View of the Principle of Population,* reprinted in *Introduction to Malthus,* ed. D. V. Glass, London, Watts, 1953, pp. 151–2.

trialization, we could point to several solid links in the reaction chain: specific, now unsatisfied, needs; "forced savings" of a kind; the interest of the heretofore importers or foreign suppliers, etc.

In the case of population pressures, on the other hand, we are provided only with an aspiration to return to the status quo ante, but generally not with specific means or intermediate reaction links for doing so. Nevertheless, in some of the following situations, the passage from aspiration to reality becomes plausible or is more readily visualized than in others.

1. The probability of a strong reaction is greater if the population increase comes as a sudden shock. A community may not feel impelled to "make a stand" when population increases and declines in living standards are slow, just as workers will sometimes experience greater difficulty in maintaining their real wages in the face of creeping inflation than when prices rise a good 20% a year. For this reason, the dramatic decline in mortality rates and the consequent massive increase in numbers that is taking place today in underdeveloped areas holds greater promise of a vigorous reaction than the far slower increases of previous epochs.

2. A population increase is likely to be more action-stimulating if it is combined with increased urbanization and therefore leads to obvious needs and pressures for more overhead facilities, such as housing, schools, and public utilities.

3. Again, the reaction may be facilitated if population growth takes place in underdeveloped countries which as a result of the increase in numbers pass minimum production thresholds in a number of important industries, as compared to more populous countries where these thresholds have long been passed or to much smaller countries where they remain far away.

4. The reaction may be easier to accomplish if the increase affects primarily the upper classes of society, or at least the upper classes along with the lower classes, for the need to provide for one's children is in this case more likely to take the form of increased entrepreneurial activity.

5. Finally, the closer a country actually is to the rigid assumptions of the neo-Malthusian models which we mentioned above, i.e., the more fully and perfectly its resources are already utilized, the less room there is for any reactions outside of the most direct ones—namely, birth control and postponement of marriage. Precisely because of the assumption of fixed resources, this reaction to population pressures has virtually monopolized the attention of demographers. From our point of view, the "preventive checks" are only one of the many forms which the reaction mechanism can take. Under present conditions, in fact, it

is in many countries more difficult to visualize population pressures resulting in effective birth control measures than in improvements of agricultural techniques and in stepped-up capital formation in industry and public utilities. In any event, our second proposition applies here also, even though perhaps somewhat indirectly: for a people that is induced to exercise foresight to the point of adopting effective birth control techniques is again learning that one's environment can be controlled and changed and will therefore be better equipped for coping with the tasks of development.

All in all, population pressure still qualifies as an inducement mechanism in the sense that it presents the developmental forces within a society with an opportunity to assert themselves. It supplies "the motive and the cue for passion" (though admittedly it fails to provide many cues for action). Thus it seems wrong to say that population pressures act as an obstacle to development. There are circumstances under which these pressures are unsuccessful in performing their stimulating role just as relative price increases are at times ineffective in calling forth increases in the supply of the "signaled" commodities.

The view that has been presented is consistent with the fact that population pressures have demonstrably been an integral part of the development process in all countries that are economically advanced today. It would surely be most unrealistic to look at the population increases in Europe in the nineteenth century and at those in, say, Brazil and Mexico today as a depressing influence on economic development. But if this is granted, then we must ask the partisans of the classical view to explain why population growth, like some of the lesser Homeric gods who throw their support to the winning side at the height of battle, suddenly becomes a stimulant to economic development after having long played the role of obstacle. In our view, no such switch ever occurs; rather we are able to account by a single hypothesis for a stream of events within which we might distinguish three periods: during the first, per capita incomes do not increase, but countries, in reacting to population pressures, acquire the abilities to launch undertakings that will lead to genuine economic growth; during a second period, per capita incomes begin to rise, with economic growth continuing to draw strength from population growth; and only at a later stage does economic growth wean itself from population growth and becomes self-sustained.[5]

---

5. With population still growing in all economically progressive countries, we actually have no conclusive empirical evidence about the existence of this stage.

What conclusion can be drawn from the preceding remarks for population policy in underdeveloped countries? Certainly not that they should institute a system of generous family allowances. In the first place, we have already stated our view that population pressures are a clumsy and cruel stimulant to development. Actually, underdeveloped countries are today abundantly supplied with this stimulant, whether they want it or not, as a result of the universal and rapid decline in mortality rates. Secondly, we consider the spread of birth control as one important form which the reaction to population pressure can take, and one that, if it occurs, brings with it basic attitude changes that are favorable to development.

Our policy conclusions, then, are somewhat anticlimactic. Any practical usefulness of our reasoning lies in the fact that it leads to a less alarmist attitude toward the population problem than is displayed by the current literature with its "traps" and the need for a huge jump to break out of them. This kind of reasoning derives of course from the comparisons of population growth with output growth rates. A highly sophisticated version of this approach is given by Leibenstein; he demonstrates that if a country has a population growth rate of, say, one per cent per year, it is not sufficient for it to achieve an output growth rate in excess of one per cent; for when output and therefore income rise, population may rise even more; so that to overtake population growth for good, the country may have to achieve a rate of output growth that is a multiple of the initial rate of population growth; and it must achieve this rate not gradually but in one jump, for at any intermediate point the country's rate of income growth will be dragged down again to its low-level starting point.

Our approach leads us to take a far calmer view of the situation. We have shown that if a country is at all able to offset, be it even partially at first, the effect of the population increase, then we may have confidence that, through the learning acquired in this process, it will be able to do progressively better in marshaling its productive forces for development so that eventually output growth will overtake population growth. If a community makes a genuine effort to defend its standard of living in the face of population pressures, it need not be afraid of imaginary traps, for cumulative growth is then already in the making: just as income can rise in advance of consumption, so can economic progress get under way before being registered in per capita income increases.

# Part Two

---

# The Social Order

Economists have traditionally regarded development mostly as a set of relations among productive resources and distributive institutions. Here the primary variables are the nature and behavior of tangible inputs and outputs (especially capital), technological change, and the size of markets. It is natural enough for economists to concentrate upon the *operating* mechanism of economic development. Professional training and specialization persuade most economists that the useful contribution their profession can make is of this nature. Moreover, the tremendous difficulty of understanding posed by traditional societies is itself a temptation to division of labor among the academic disciplines.

Within this framework of preferences economists have accomplished a good deal. The major drawback is the difficulty of disentangling in practice economic from noneconomic elements of development. Economic modernization of traditional societies requires the reconstruction of entire life-styles. The civilization based upon technology is radically different from the civilization dependent upon handicraft skills and attitudes. From the standpoint of *total* transformation, such questions as *who* promotes economic growth and *why* economic growth succeeds or fails appropriately supplement the more limited inquiries of economists.

Understandably, economists have hesitated to venture too far into investigations that involve the identification of social values, the class structure of developing nations, political attitudes, legal structures, and religious attachments. The world is full of analogues to the observant Hindu's reverence for the cow as a sacred animal. And in each case the belief has its influence on economic life. But if anything is plain it is that economists and other social scientists must comprehend development as a total process or in the end fail in their twin missions of assistance and comprehension.

# Society, Personality, and Entrepreneurship: Three General Approaches

THIS SECTION consists of three attempts to construct more general systems of social and economic change. All three emphasize the social, cultural, and psychological forces which facilitate the emergence of entrepreneurs.

Hoselitz's approach owes a considerable debt to the sociologist Talcott Parson's investigations of the theory of social action. Hoselitz stresses the precarious and exceptional role that entrepreneurial personalities play in traditional societies. Thus, development depends upon the appearance of socially deviant personalities who, given appropriate institutional opportunities, can initiate the productive and distributive shifts which are one of the meanings of development.

As Everett Hagen's essay demonstrates, the linkages among society, personality, and economic change can be regarded as still more complex phenomena. Hagen constructs a classification of personality types and relates it to a corresponding array of social situations. At the center of his analysis are those social and psychological drives which operate to produce the "innovative" personality.

David McClelland's analysis is somewhat less comprehensive than Hagen's. Although he also seeks to identify the variables that produce entrepreneurial personalities, he concentrates upon psychological elements. Using both history and contemporary observation, he locates the origin of innovation in the psychological drives that underlie the individual's "need for achievement." The parallel to Weber's famous association of Calvinism and capitalism is close and fully acknowledged by McClelland.

Bert F. Hoselitz

# A Sociological Approach to Economic Development

ALTHOUGH IN RECENT YEARS the study of economic development has made great advances, the mutual dependence between changes in economic activity and organization and in social structure is as yet relatively little explored. This is not due to the lack of recognition of the dependence of successful economic growth on social change. Ever since economists concerned themselves with problems of economic progress, but certainly since Marx stated in clear and unmistakable language that the origin and development of the capitalist mode of production was the outcome of the transformation of society resulting in the elevation of the bourgeoisie to the position of leading social class, the mutual interaction between social-structural change and economic development has been recognized. For, in spite of the many criticisms which have been levied against the Marxian theories, Marx's interpretation of capitalism as a social-economic system and of its changes as alterations in the relations between social classes and in the forms and organization of production has been quite generally accepted, even by his most ardent critics. The acceptance of these interrelations was doubtless aided by the spectacular economic progress made in capitalist countries. It may be said not unfairly that capitalism was the first socio-economic system under which the mass of the population was enabled to enjoy a level of consumption effectively elevated above that of sheer subsistence. Whereas the mass of people in all previous civilizations were periodically threatened with severe famines, epidemics, and other life-destroying scourges, the societies of Western Europe were able to raise productivity, and to advance scientific and technological knowledge sufficiently to escape living in the permanent shadow of fear of want.

This unique achievement of capitalist society in the field of technology, production, and economic organization has been so impressive that scholars were drawn to investigate its causes. They were motivated not merely by an interest in the social history of their own civilization, but also, especially in the last few decades, by the desire to derive general or generalizable sociological and economic propositions which would be applicable to societies in which economic growth was as yet stagnant and the level of economic advancement unsatisfactorily low. It is not surprising, therefore, that in the study of the interrelations between sociological and economic factors which are associated with economic development much attention was paid to the experience of the capitalist countries of the western world, and that scholars were inclined to draw heavily from that experience especially in their discussion of changes in social structure accompanying or conditioning economic growth.

*   *   *   *   *

. . . Generally and almost unconsciously the assumption is made that modernization and the adoption of western technology and forms of economic activity require the simultaneous transformation of a society to exhibit western social structure and even to assume most of the social values of the West. Yet there exist, so far as I am aware, two theories which attempt to provide a general theoretical explanation of this process of change. One is the Marxian theory of economic and social development, particularly under capitalism, and the other is the theory of social deviance which is built upon some propositions of modern social theory and, to the extent to which it relates to economic development, also on the work of Joseph Schumpeter.

The Marxian theory is too well known to require extensive restatement here. Its application to the economically underdeveloped countries is the work not so much of Marx himself, but of some of his followers. In brief outline this theory may be stated as follows: The underdeveloped countries contain societies which are either entirely pre-capitalist or, under the influence of capitalist imperialism, have adopted features of incipient capitalism. The extension of capitalist-imperialist dominance in the under developed countries is inevitably supported by the native bourgeoisie and its political parties, by reformist middle class elements, and by intellectuals who see in this policy a means of bringing their societies under the complete dominance of the bourgeoisie. But the extension of capitalist and imperialist control in the colonial and dependent countries results in the expropriation of the masses of the people and the imposition of manifold barriers to the rising middle classes. This sows the seed of revolt which is expressed in its initial stages by the rise of national liberation movements led by the emerging bourgeoisie and middle class elements in these countries. The colonial bourgeoisie thus finds itself in an ambivalent situation. With respect to its own proletariat it is an exploiting class and hence allied with the foreign imperialists; with respect to these imperialists themselves it is the chief carrier of nationalistic movements antagonistic to the imperialist interests of the great powers. This makes the social situation in colonial and imperialistically exploited countries more unstable, and improves the changes of success of a revolutionary movement which will lead to the political and social emancipation of the masses, the overthrow of imperialist power, and the chance for an unfettered development of the productive forces of the underdeveloped country. To be sure, there is some debate as to whether all countries have to pass through a stage of native capitalism in order to reach a socialist form of social organization, or whether they can jump over this stage. There is also some debate of whether the social revolutions in underdeveloped countries are purely or even predominantly proletarian revolutions, or whether they may be based upon other classes also, especially the poorer and middle peasants. But these questions are problems of strategy and not of the general theory applicable to the transition of a society from a situation of economic backwardness to one of economic advancement.

Although this theory is expressed usually in terms of political struggles and hence abounds in a terminology of revolutionary strategy, the underlying conception is clear. Stripped of the purely political and strategic appendages, it sees the economic development of underdeveloped countries to be associated with a series of social transformations which are identical with those postulated by Marx for the countries of the West. This theory postulates, therefore, a single-line process of social and economic development and states that, with minor deviations, all societies must go through analogous transformations of social structure in order to reach higher levels of productivity and economic organization.

Let us now turn to a brief examination of the theory of social deviance. Although deviance may occur in many fields of social action, we are concerned here primarily with deviant behavior in areas which are relevant to the production and distribution of goods and services. As I have shown elsewhere, we may characterize societies at different levels of economic development by describing them in terms of contrasting pairs of pattern variables as these were defined by Talcott Parsons.[1] Economic development may then be considered as being associated with a transformation of social behavior from a form which in its economically relevant aspects it is oriented towards ascription, particularism and functional diffuseness to a form of social behavior oriented towards achievement, universalism, and functional specificity. In somewhat different terms this may be stated by saying that a society on a low level of economic development is characterized in the main by the following features: Economic roles are distributed on the basis of what status a person has rather than whether he has shown the necessary competence to fill the role; and economic relations in general, for example, exchanges of goods and services, are based

---

1. On the pattern variables themselves and their definition, see Talcott Parsons, *The Social System* (Glencoe, Illinois, 1951), pp. 58 ff.

often on traditionally prescribed and sanctioned acts and performances rather than on attempts to arrive at a balancing of values through bargaining or the use of a price mechanism. (An example of the principle of ascription in the realm of a system of exchanges is the medieval doctrine of just price.) But in the little advanced country the attainment of and selection for certain economic roles is based merely on ascription rather than achievement; the overall pattern of distribution of roles between classes of the society is particularistic rather than universalistic. Mobility is difficult or, in extreme cases, absent, both between social groups, different professions, and often also between different localities. A society with a strong and vigorous caste system exhibits particularistic patterns in a clear form. Finally, the types of economic roles performed in a society on a low level of economic advancement are typically diffuse, whereas in a developed economy they are, typically, highly specific. This is an outcome of the increasing division of labor, which implies greater and greater specialization of tasks as the economy develops. The primitive farmer does everything from producing his crops, to building his house, fixing his implements and constructing roads and other means of transport and communications whereas the modern worker in a factory or office is occupied with one specific, often clearly circumscribed task to which he devotes his full attention.

A society on a low level of economic development is, therefore, one in which productivity is low because division of labor is little developed, in which the objectives of economic activity are more commonly the maintenance or strengthening of status relations, in which social and geographical mobility is low, and in which the hard cake of custom determines the manner, and often the effects, of economic performance. An economically highly developed society, in contrast, is characterized by a complex division of social labor, a relatively open social structure in which caste barriers are absent and class barriers not unsurmountable, in which social roles and gains from economic activity are distributed essentially on the basis of achievement, and in which, therefore, innovation, the search for and exploitation of profitable market situations, and the ruthless pursuit of self-interest without regard to the welfare of others is fully sanctioned.

If we consider that societies with the characteristics described in the preceding paragraphs stand at the beginning and at the end of the process of economic development several additional questions are raised. What are the mechanisms which lead from one stage to the other? Is there only one path by which the transition may occur or are there several? Is the transition process continuous or discontinuous? What relationship, if any, exists between the form and nature of the transition process and the relative emphasis on different factors in the social structure that results? For even if we may assert that a developed economy exhibits in its economic roles orientations towards achievement, universalism, and functional specificity, we are making a very general statement and the concrete social relations which may be subsumed under this very general description may vary considerably. Nobody would deny that there exist significant differences in the social structures of Germany, Britain, Japan, and the United States, and yet all these countries are economically fairly highly developed and present economic role structures which are oriented toward achievement, universalism, and functional specificity.

The questions which we have posed would require, for a full answer, a discussion of such length as cannot be presented within the confines of this essay. Rather than attempting a full and detailed treatment, I shall present some thoughts which may be regarded as a general outline along which some answers may be obtained. Let us turn first to the question of the mechanism of transition from a stage of economic underdevelopment to one of advancement. Here the theory of social deviance has found its main application. Rather than stating it in a general form, I will concentrate on its applicability to the problem of economic development. Here also the influence of Schumpeter's analysis of the role of the innovating entrepreneur in economic growth has found wide and fruitful application.[2]

The entrepreneur, especially the capitalistic entrepreneur as he was known in the economic history of late medieval and modern Europe, is regarded as the prototype of the social deviant. By definition he is an innovator, a finder and applier of new combinations and hence, in a society where innovation is at best tolerated but hardly carries high approval, anyone engaging in innovating behavior is, by this very fact, a deviant.

Now if the concept of deviance is to have any meaning, it cannot be

---

2. The "classical" statement of Schumpeter's theory of entrepreneurship is a passage in *Die Theorie der wirtschaftlichen Entwicklung*, 2nd ed. (Muenchen, 1926), pp. 110 ff. It is interesting to compare this with an exposition of this same theme made not long before his death. See Joseph A. Schumpeter: "Economic Theory and Entrepreneurial History" in Research Center in Entrepreneurial History, *Change and the Entrepreneur* (Cambridge, Mass., 1949), pp. 63-82. See also the essay by Arthur H. Cole: "An Approach to the Study of Entrepreneurship" in F. C. Lane and J. C. Riemersma: *Enterprise and Secular Change* (Homewood, Ill., 1953), pp. 181-195; especially the statement on p. 187, that "to study the 'entrepreneur' is to study the central figure in modern economic history, and to my way of thinking, the central figure in economics."

interpreted as signifying simply behavior which is new, but it must imply that this set of innovating acts is opposed in some way to existing social norms or to approved forms of behavior. In other words, a deviant always engages in behavior which constitutes in a certain sense a breach of the existing order and is either contrary to, or at least not positively weighted in, the hierarchy of existing social values. If we apply this concept to the behavior displayed by businessmen and merchants in the course of the economic history of Western Europe, we find that we can speak of true or genuine deviance only in those periods in which entrepreneurial behavior did not belong in the category of social actions which were considered as constituting the "good life." Thus during the later Middle Ages, when the official Christian doctrine still regarded the practice of usury as objectionable, any person who engaged in financial entrepreneurship must be regarded as a deviant.[3] Further evidence that in the Middle Ages financial activity may be considered to constitute deviant social behavior can be gained from the manner by which it spread among the peoples of Europe in the period from the ninth to the twelfth centuries. In Italy, in the period of Gothic and Langobard rule, moneylenders were almost all foreigners: Syrians, Byzantines, Jews. The same was true in the realm of Charlemagne. Later when Italians turned to financial entrepreneurship on a large scale, the Genoese and Pisans, Sienese and Florentines, who were all lumped together under the name of "Lombards," became the financial entrepreneurs in the countries north of the Alps.[4]

Gradually in France, and later in Germany, England, and the Low Countries, native financiers arose and forms of economic activity which before had been almost exclusively carried on by foreigners became domesticated in one country after another. The earliest native financiers were surely still deviants. But at some point financial entrepreneurship must have lost its deviant character. Would we be justified to call moneylending in the Siena of the Buonsignori a form of deviant behavior? Can

---

3. On the canonist doctrine concerning usury see W. J. Ashley: *An Introduction to English Economic History and Theory* (New York, 1901), I, 126 ff., and in particular the stimulating essay by Benjamin N. Nelson, *The Idea of Usury*, (Princeton, 1949).

4. As concerns the later history of moneylending, especially in England, Ashley shows (*op. cit.*, I, 195 ff.) that in the 12th century the Jews, in the 13th the Caursines, and in the 14th the Lombards controlled this type of business. Similarly in Germany, moneylending was, before the 13th century, almost entirely in the hands of Jews, Italians, and other foreigners. (Cf. R. Koetzchke: *Grundzüge der deutschen Wirtschaftsgeschichte bis zum 17. Jahrhundert* (Leipzig, 1921), pp. 103 ff.

we say that the granting of vast public loans in Augsburg at the time of the Fugger was deviant behavior? Unambiguous answers to these questions are difficult because the practice of "usury" was as yet concentrated in only relatively few centers and the hierarchy of values was oriented still toward a largely self-sufficient economy dominated by agriculture. Moneylending loses its deviant characteristics clearly and unmistakably with the breakdown of the old medieval values in the period after the Renaissance. The famous letter of Calvin to Claude de Sachins of 1545 on the subject of usury constitutes a true landmark. Here a man whose words were acknowledged as an authoritative interpretation of the structure of values justified a form of action which hitherto had been considered sinful.

It has sometimes been held that Calvin's discussion of the legitimacy of interest was not revolutionary, but merely an explicit statement of a situation which had been tacitly recognized and condoned by many canonist casuists long before his time. It is, of course, agreed that loans for interest were given among Christians before the Reformation, and precisely because such financial operations were practiced we can speak of deviant social behavior. But there is a vast difference between even the most latitudinarian interpretations of the casuists who yet viewed usury as, in principle, wicked, and the explicit acknowledgement of this as permissible in practice under the laws of Christian morality. This view has been stated excellently by Benjamin Nelson when he says that "not even the most accommodating of the casuists presumed at any time in the medieval period to call in question the historic assumption that the taking of usury was antithetical to the spirit of brotherhood," whereas in Calvin's teaching, "the specific gravity of the claim of brotherhood is radically altered by his support of the taking of interest and . . . impels our use of the phrase " 'Universal Otherhood.' "[5]

The case of usury exhibits the development of deviant social behavior and its eventual transformation into approved behavior. The role expectations of a lender since the 16th century presumes not only his desire for interest, but also attaches a positive valuation to this practice. A similar transition of valuation took place in the case of commerce, especially large-scale foreign commerce. Here the record is not as clear as in the case of usury because the prohibition of, and sanction against, usury was more explicit than against trade. Yet, if we compare the statements of some interpreters of medieval Christian morality, we find here also first a general antipathy to trade with a more permissive attitude later and finally full acceptance not only of the desirability of commerce but even of its character as a virtuous and God-pleasing occupation.

---

5. Nelson: *op. cit.*, pp. 27-28 and 81.

If we can explain the emergence of important new forms of economic activity through the presence of socially deviant behavior, we are immediately drawn to enquire how this pattern of change operated in other cases and whether or not we may stipulate the hypothesis that innovations in the economy leading to improved output and living standards are in all cases the consequence of social deviance. It appears that some of the fundamental attitudes and practices of capitalism originated in such a way. But once "capitalist modes of behavior" were generally accepted, how can the further development of capitalism be described as an outflow of deviance? Can we, for example, find a process of social change underlying the evolution of industrial capitalism similar to that which seems to have been present in the development of commercial and financial capitalism? This question is of paramount importance, because many underdeveloped countries today seem to have developed fairly well functioning commercial and financial enterprises, but appear to encounter their most serious difficulties in the development of industry and an industrial society.

*   *   *   *   *

I have indicated before that one of the processes by which social deviance was introduced was the presence and growing participation of, what has been called, culturally marginal individuals. The Jews and the Greeks were characteristically such culturally marginal persons in the Middle Ages, and the Jews, at any rate, seem to have retained characteristics of marginality all through their history.[6] As Park, the inventor of the concept and of the significance of social marginality has stressed, marginal men are—precisely because of their ambiguous position from a cultural, ethnic, or social standpoint—peculiarly suited to make new creative adjustments in situations of change and, in the course of this adjustment process, to develop genuine innovations in social behavior. Although some of Park's very general propositions about marginality have been somewhat refined in the work of his students and followers, the theory of social marginality has not advanced enough to supply sufficient evidence for the role it may play in the explanation of instances of social deviance wherever they occur. Even if it is admitted that marginal individuals tend to make creative adjustments more often than to relapse into new or old orthodoxies, the record is not at all clear, and there are some students who warn us that marginal individuals are more prone than others to experience *anomie,* and thus to become carriers of trends

---

6. On the concept of "marginal man" and a more explicit discussion of cultural, ethnic, and social marginality see the work of Robert E. Park: *Race and Culture* (Glencoe, Ill., 1950), pp. 345-92, esp. pp. 345-56, and E. V. Stonequist: *The Marginal Man: A Study in Personality and Culture Conflict,* (New York, 1937).

leading towards social disorganization rather than to innovations of a creative type.

* * * * *

In order to supplement the explanation of social change associated with economic growth which is provided by the theory of social deviance we must add other variables which are either aspects of, or impinge upon, the social structure. When I discussed the emergence of industrial capitalism in eighteenth century Britain I listed several such variables, and it appears to me that two are of especial relevance for our problem. One is the ratio between population and non-human natural resources of an area and the other is the degree of constraint exerted by a central political authority. The former has sometimes, somewhat loosely, been called also the man-land ratio, and the latter is an index of the presence of authorization tendencies in the political structure of a community.

It would appear at first sight that these variables are related only very tenuously to the social structure. But if we look at these variables not as general data describing a society but rather as factors impinging upon the manner and facility of economic development, we will soon find that they are closely related to social structures.

Consider first the man-land ratio. This is an expression of the density of population per resource unit at the beginning of the growth process. Stated in somewhat different terms, this variable indicates whether the growth process is primarily intrinsic, i.e., whether it consists primarily in an intensification of economic activity within a given geographical space, or whether it is primarily expansionist, i.e., whether it consists primarily in an extension of the economic "frontier" and a gradual spatial expansion of the area in which more advanced technology and economic organization are applied.

The process of capitalist development in the western world, as a whole, exhibits both the intrinsic and the expansionist growth patterns, and I consider it to be the chief merit of W. W. Rostow's recent book, *The Process of Economic Growth*,[7] to have shown not only the existence of these two patterns of economic development, but also to have related them to fluctuations in other variables of profound economic significance, such as prices, etc. But if the growth process of western capitalism as a whole may be said to exhibit both intrinsic and expansionist features, different countries in the Western world show wide variations. In some of them, for example, Germany, or Switzerland, intrinsic patterns are considerably more important than in other countries, such as, for example,

---

7. Walter W. Rostow: *The Process of Economic Growth* (New York, 1952).

the United States or Australia, where an extension of the frontier is a clear characteristic of the development process.

It would, of course, be a mistake to assume that any country or region whose economic history has been surveyed exhibits either an intrinsic or expansionist growth pattern in pure form. The case of Britain is an example where a neat balance between intrinsic and expansionist development prevailed. Although in the older industrial centers—London, Bristol, Sheffield, Birmingham, for example,—intrinsic patterns of development preponderated, several expansionist episodes are clearly discernible. The draining of the Fens must be regarded as a process of internal colonization; and the growth of coal and iron production in South Wales, Northeast of England, and Scotland, as well as the development of cotton textile and other industries in the new industrial centers of Lancashire and elsewhere, which set in motion a vast movement of internal migration, must also be considered as an extension of the internal geographical frontier. Finally, in the nineteenth century, the growth of foreign investment and the impact of the returns from this investment had profound influences upon further British economic growth. . . .

. . . The growth pattern of the United States, Canada, and Australia is profoundly different. It is not necessary to recount here in any detail the history of the settlement of North America or Australia, but the greatness of the population shifts and associated expansion of settlement may be gauged, if we recall that in 1860, on the eve of the vast industrial upsurge in the United States, Chicago had barely more than 100,000 inhabitants, Minneapolis, Cleveland, and Detroit were little more than villages, and Los Angeles, Denver and Seattle, only dots on a map. The importance of this development pattern for our purposes is not so much to point to the addition of vast areas to the economically effective area of a country, nor to derive inspiration from the heroism and romance of the westward movement. It is important rather because it depended on the appearance of a singular mass phenomenon: the willingness and, indeed, the eagerness of entire communities of persons to relinquish the security of familiar surroundings and to settle in the wilderness or almost-wilderness.

The significance of these differences in expansionist versus intrinsic patterns of development for the social structure of the countries which followed either of the two paths is twofold. In the first place, the settlement of a large area, unless achieved by forced migration or planned relocation of large populations, must depend upon an ideology holding out important rewards for the migrant. To leave one's home and to face the hardships and uncertainties of settling in a wilderness will only be undertaken by persons—whatever their own personal motives may be which impel them to follow such a course of action—who live in an intellectual climate where this type of venturesomeness and initiative is highly positively valued. But an ideology of this type is in itself the result of a social structure which is relatively open and in which vertical mobility is not made excessively difficult. It also is a social structure in which emphasis is placed on the attainment and possession of material goods and in which a man's worth is judged, at least in large part, by the command which he exercises over such goods. A second important feature is the impact exerted by an expanding pattern of economic development on the social structure. The migrants will almost invariably tend to set up social institutions in the newly settled areas identical with those they left behind. Although there may be some subordination of the newer parts of a country under the older ones, there will exist strong tendencies towards the establishment of relations of co-ordination. That is, the new portions of a country will develop a social hierarchy similar to that of the older portions and there will be strong forces at work to intermesh these social structures. Expansionism thus has the tendency of even further increasing the potentiality of vertical mobility in the social structure and to lead to a relatively high degree of equality in social relations.[8]

Contrast this with the social relations which are associated with intrinsic development. Here the intensification of economic activity in a number of limited centers leads to a concentration of population. The newly arriving persons come into a place in which internal class relations are already well developed. The new immigrants often only find a place at the periphery of the society; they form the membership of the lowest layers of the proletariat and the lumpenproletariat. There are, of course, a few newcomers who rise in the social scale, but the great mass of the new immigrants is forced to content itself with positions on the lower margin of the social structure. Moreover, there seems to develop often a tendency, in situations where in-migration of new proletarian or quasi-proletarian populations takes place, for the existing social structure to take on greater rigidity. This occurred to some extent in medieval European cities, where the growth of the city through the influx of former serfs and other migrants from the countryside was accompanied by a strengthening of the status and power of the urban patricians, and in several countries of continental Europe with a predominantly intrinsic

8. For the United States, a thesis similar to that stated here has been developed by F. J. Turner and his school, although they applied it primarily to political institutions rather than to social structure. The two are obviously interrelated. Cf.: F. J. Turner: *The Frontier in American History*, (New York, 1920).

pattern of economic development (e.g., Germany) where in the course of the later nineteenth century class conflict tended to become more bitter than it had been before.

There is some connection between the impact of an intrinsic or expansionist pattern of economic development on social structure and the degree of central guidance of, and responsibility for, the development process. For it is clear, that the more open a social structure and the less the inequality between the various classes, the more widely diffused will be the locus of economically relevant decisions. On the other hand, the more strictly hierarchical the class structure and the narrower the socially dominant groups, the greater will normally be their responsibility for such decisions. Thus when we speak of autonomous development—as against planned or induced development—we have in mind a process in which economic growth is affected by a multitude of individual decisions, each made with primary reference to the objectives of the person making it. Autonomous development is thus found most frequently in societies which experienced some form of expansionist economic development, whereas planned development is found more often in societies which followed a pattern of intrinsic development. But there are, of course, some exceptions. Although the Swiss class structure is fairly rigid, economic development in Switzerland has been fairly autonomous and political processes have been democratic throughout. On the other hand, Russian economic development was certainly expansionist, but at the same time, highly planned and occurred in a country in which the political process was under a harsh centralized authoritarian regime. This is not the place to enter deeply in the explanation of these apparent exceptions, but it should be pointed out that both in Switzerland and in Russia very clear forms of political organization had been established before economic development (especially industrialization) on any significant scale occurred. Variations such as these constitute a confirmation of the proposition implied earlier that the ratio between population and natural resources at the beginning of the development process and the degree of centralization in decisions affecting it are independent variables.

Our analysis of interrelations between the process of economic growth and concomitant changes in social structure is furthered if we introduce these two additional variables and establish clearly their impact upon the class relations of a society. These variables perform a different role in our system than the pairs of pattern variables which were derived from Parsons. The pattern variables, as applied to social action in the fields of production and distribution, determine the distinctions between social roles and role expectations in societies on different levels of economic advancement. The former determine the more specific differences in the-social structures of societies experiencing economic growth which are associated with different paths of economic development.

The introduction of these two additional variables permits, moreover, a more precise evaluation of the function performed by social deviance or the presence of marginal individuals as factors explaining social change. For the chances for certain forms of deviance to develop will depend, *ceteris paribus,* upon the flexibility and openness of the social structure and the degree of centralization and authoritarian control in the field of decision-making, especially of decisions relevant to economic growth. In fact, it is conceivable that, in the limiting cases, the degree of centralization and control of decision-making is so great that deviance is made impossible and that any change which does occur is the result of a change of objectives or aims of an elite controlling the allocation of resources and economic activities of the society. This process is not likely to occur very frequently, especially not in any very pure form, but there are instances on record where rapid economic development took place with an apparently astounding degree of "orderliness" and a minimum of social disorganization. The chief example which comes to mind is the experience of Japan. Another example, which, however, is much less well explored, is the rapid transformation of the New Zealand Maori economy in the period between 1840 and 1860. . . .

These instances thus present us with examples of a mechanism of social change which differs from both the Marxian approach and that which I have called the "theory of social deviance." It is granted that the social structures of the Maori and the Japanese, before these people embarked on the road to economic change, embodied features which may be regarded as propitious for the alternatives taken.[9] It is also granted that in both cases there existed important external stimuli to make the type of development which was followed, attractive, and there existed technological devices which could be adapted with relatively little difficulty to the needs of the developing economies. But in applying any theories derived from the analysis of historical experience to the problems of presently underdeveloped countries, the experience of the Maori and Japan is perhaps more pertinent than that of the European countries in which the modern economy was first evolved. It may, of course, be that social structures in some underdeveloped countries are such as to favour the development of social deviants or to allow wide scope for "creative adjustment" of marginal individuals. On the other hand, there

9. On Japanese social structure before the fall of the *Shogunate* and the features it exhibits which facilitated the kind of change which occurred, see Marion J. Levy, Jr.: "Contrasting Factors in the Modernization of China and Japan." *Economic Development and Cultural Change,* Vol. 2, No. 3, (Oct. 1953), pp. 161 ff.

may be situations, in which a reinterpretation of social objectives by already existing elites may be the dominant mechanism for setting the process of economic change in motion. Which particular form of social change is applicable to any one society can only be determined by a careful analysis of its social organization and the forces in it which tend to promote economic growth. If we do not prejudge the issues by applying ready-made theoretical formulations, and if we admit that various paths of growth and various patterns of social reorganization are possible we will be able to provide more appropriate theoretical guides for the sociological dimension in economic development.

# Everett E. Hagen

## Personality and Economic Growth

### INNOVATIONAL PERSONALITY

#### The Quality of Creativity

When it is stated that innovation requires creativity, the reader should not assume that the term "creativity" refers to genius. Creativity exists in varying degrees; the man who conceives of an improvement in a can opener as well as the man who conceives of the theory of relativity is creative. Technological progress results from the actions of men characterized by varying degrees of creativity. The discussion of creativity refers, therefore, not merely to the limiting case of genius but to the quality of creativity in general, in whatever degree it may be found in a given individual.

The major qualities that constitute creativity are easy to list imprecisely: openness to experience, and, underlying this, a tendency to perceive phenomena, especially in an area of life that is of interest to the individual, as forming systems of interacting forces whose action is explainable; creative imagination, of which the central component is the ability to let one's unconscious processes work on one's behalf; confidence and content in one's own evaluations; satisfaction in facing and attacking problems and in resolving confusion or inconsistency; a sense that one has a duty or responsibility to achieve; intelligence; energy;

and, often, related to several of these, a perception that the world is somewhat threatening and that one must strive perpetually if one is to be able to cope with it. The type of creative personality that is driven by a sense that the world is threatening sometimes seems to belong to a different category from the person characterized by some of the other qualities listed. I shall discuss first the ideal or pure type of unanxious creative person, and then indicate how the sense of living in a threatening world qualifies the characteristics described.

Poincaré has suggested the "capacity to be surprised" and Carl R. Rogers "openness to experience" as essential to creativity.[1] I would judge that the meaning of the two is almost identical. What is referred to is an unconscious alertness that leads the individual to note that some aspect of an everyday phenomenon differs from the expected and to appreciate the significance of the difference. This is the capacity that leads an individual to note that, contrary to the body of scientific authority in his time and the conclusions of common sense, bodies fall at the same rate regardless of their weight if air resistance is the same; to have his curiosity aroused by the fact that iron filings adhere to a coil of wire as an electrical current passes through it; to observe that some men with paralyzed limbs handle them in ways that suggest that the paralysis of function begins at a point at which there is no physiological reason for it to begin—to note such a thing and say to himself, "What an interesting force must have caused that! I wonder what its implications are."

Basic to this quality of observation is assurance in one's own evaluation of experience, freedom from a tendency to take a generally accepted evaluation for granted and overlook facts inconsistent with it. Basic to it also is a tendency to assume that one can understand experience. The creative individual has a sense, deeper than any rational acceptance of cause and effect, that the world is orderly; that every phenomenon of life or of some large area of experience is part of a system whose operation can be understood and explained; that if he approaches the sphere of life in which he is interested it will respond dependably, even though perhaps in a complex fashion, so that if he has enough information he will be able to understand the response. If the world were not orderly, or if the individual were not confident and content in his ability to

---

1. Poincaré's phrase is quoted by Erich Fromm in Harold H. Anderson (ed.), *Creativity and Its Cultivation* (New York: Harper & Bros., 1959), p. 48. "Scientific genius," said Poincaré, "is the capacity to be surprised." Rogers' phrase is in *ibid.*, p. 75. Several essays in this interesting volume are pertinent to the present discussion.

understand its order, he would not be unconsciously alert to unexpected aspects of phenomena, for they would contain no lessons for him.

Openness to experience, then, refers to a capacity to note phenomena that are starting points for new analyses. Creative imagination refers to a tendency to leap far afield from a starting point, to note relationships where others had not thought to find them. In part it is the product simply of superior innate intelligence, of a mind which can hold many factors in simultaneous consideration and analysis. But it is more than this. It embraces two kinds of mental activity. One is the capacity to use an interesting or unsatisfactory situation as a springboard from which one's imagination roams, apparently uncontrolled and seemingly un-directed, in varying associational bypaths, regressions, and far reaches, then returns to the matter at hand either with a workable conception for the reconstruction or transformation of the unsatisfactory situation or with a novel analytical model of the significance of the observed fact. Conscious movement from one step of analysis to the next is at a min-imum; the individual does not ask consciously whether the wandering is pertinent to the problem.

The other is the capacity to let one's purely unconscious processes work for one without any conscious awareness or acknowledgment of the activity and to admit the results to consciousness. Unaware that his mind has been working on the problem, the individual finds that a solution, an appropriate ordering, an explanation has come to him. Visualization occurs as he wakes from sleep, when he has been daydreaming, on rare occasions in a dream while sleeping, or perhaps while he walks his dog. "It came to me," the scientist sometimes says, or, "As the problem returned to my mind, I saw how it could be done." Subsequently he demonstrates to himself the logic of the solution. The solution was pre-sumably reached by a sequence of logical steps or chain or association of thoughts (how else could it have been reached?), but these were unconscious, or, sometimes, in more precise psychological terminology, preconscious.

Such creative imagination is often stressed as a part of literary or, more generally, aesthetic creativity. But there is ample evidence from biographies of scientists that it is important in their creative achievement also.[2] There is less evidence concerning strictly technological creativity,

2. An interesting brief discussion of its presence in scientists is pre-sented by Professor Donald W. MacKinnon of the Institute of Person-ality Assessment and Research of the University of California, in a paper delivered at a convention of the Western Branch, American Public Health Association, at San Francisco, June 2–5, 1959, which I have from him in mimeographed form.

but it is reasonable to suppose that this is because of absence of documentation rather than because of a difference in the creative process.

These two aspects of creative imagination have two important elements in common: the unconscious processes of the individual are productive rather than distractive in nature, and the individual is unafraid or little afraid of them. The aspect of a problem that some individuals react unconsciously to is a sense of frustration at not having an answer at hand. As a defense against that sense of frustration, the individual, if he lets himself go, experiences fantasies of magic achievement, crushing victories over persons who have slighted him, sexual conquest, the attainment of position so high that all of his wishes are gratified, and the like. Even if he does not let himself go, such fantasies occur in his unconscious processes. The unconscious processes of some individuals, on the other hand, react to the substance of a problem or surprising phenomena at hand, and aid in logical and imaginative analysis of it. When the individual "floats," his mind rearranges elements of thought in bold ways but ways which, when he returns to the details of reality, are fruitful. Every individual responds in some degree in both ways. Creative individuals are those who primarily respond productively.

The individual who responds with unacceptable fantasies may shut them out from his conscious mind, but he senses dimly the emotional surges within him and fears what is going on in his unconscious. Finding impulses in himself which he regards as evil or foul or dangerous, he is afraid of letting his unconscious processes come to the surface for fear that dangerous or evil or vile urges will appear. Hence his unconscious processes are not only primarily unproductive; even insofar as they are productive, they are unavailable to him. The results do not appear in his conscious mind. The creative individual, on the other hand, is not afraid of his unconscious processes, and their results appear in his conscious mind. In the technical terms of psychoanalysis, he can "regress in the service of the ego."[3]

More than other individuals, he understands his unconscious motivations.[4] It is commonly recognized that ability to understand one's unconscious motivations is an important element in artistic and especially literary creativity; one understands others and can portray them only to the

---

3. Ernst Kris, *Psychoanalytic Explorations in Art* (New York: International Universities Press, 1952).

4. Which include passive, so-called "feminine" needs, needs to be dependent and to be nurtured, needs for aesthetic gratification. These needs are greater in him, as measured by psychological tests, than in the average person. Professor Donald W. MacKinnon, *op. cit.*, discussed relevant research at the Institute of Personality Assessment and Research.

degree that one understands oneself. It is less well recognized that the same understanding of self may be conducive to understanding of the physical world as well. The man who understands something of his unconscious motivations understands his interaction with phenomena outside him as a system in which there is causality. He is self-conscious; he watches his own behavior as an observer. This understanding seems to be the model for the individual's perception of the external world as a system and subject to analysis, the perception which gives him openness to experience, which makes him wonder creatively why some everyday phenomenon is as it is.

Such an individual is somewhat detached from himself and from his society. To some degree all that goes on is something he watches from the outside. This detachment seems to be an integral part of creativity. It does not imply lack of interest in the world or of concern about it. In fact, it is often peculiarly associated with a sense of moral obligation, of responsibility for society and the world, to be discussed later.

This sense of detachment has often been observed in creative workers in science as well as in literature and art. It must also be associated with technological innovation. It is difficult to see how any person can manipulate the world about him, put its elements together in new ways to obtain new order, except as he sees it as a system outside himself, detached from himself. Even the tinkerer who merely improves a machine must see the machine as a system to be analyzed rather than simply taking it for granted as an instrument if he is to be free to conceive of changes in it. The business administrator, whose function is to manipulate other men, often gives little overt evidence of this detachment; yet his understanding of how other men function is evidence of such understanding of himself, which again is a symptom of this detachment.

Because the creative individual assumes that the world will respond dependably to his judicious initiative, he does not feel threatened by unresolved situations. He has no need to turn to the judgment of others for reassurance or relief from anxiety, for the facing of unresolved situations arouses little anxiety within him. He trusts his own evaluations of them. His "locus of evaluative judgment" is within himself.[5] This does not mean that he is always sure that he is right, but only that he does not have anxiety about his own observations and evaluations. Knowing that the comments of others may suggest new avenues of approach or added relationships in a complex problem which has no one solution, he may turn to them, but as instruments to help him, not for reassurance.

He feels satisfaction at the prospect of testing his capacities against a

---

5. Carl R. Rogers, in *Creativity and Its Cultivation*, p. 76.

problem and is drawn toward the attempt. If the solution does not readily appear, and the problem is of relevance to his interests, it remains a matter on a shelf in his mind, and he will anticipate the possibility of realizing a solution later.

Because he is not afraid of problems or of the world, he has a tolerance for recognizing apparently contradictory or discrepant facts. He will not unconsciously and conveniently ignore one of them because the discrepancy alarms him. But, because he perceives the world as orderly, he assumes that two discrepant facts, both having been verified as true, are not really contradictory but are part of a higher order whose nature he does not yet realize. Their apparent inconsistency, like any problem, is therefore a challenge to him, and he feels satisfaction in seeking a higher order within which they will both rest comfortably. He feels a need to place them in a logical or pleasing relationship. Too simple order is uninteresting and somewhat unpleasant to him.[6] He may have some fondness for disorder and conflicting logic since they suggest to him that a higher order is available.

As his experience and confidence in his ability grow, he will lose interest in simpler problems and will seek to attack more and more difficult ones, or sometimes merely different ones. The former trend is manifested by a painter who as his career proceeds passes from simple symmetry to balance of colors and forms so complex that the picture is confusing to the novice but brings the greatest aesthetic pleasure to the individual whose comprehension has grown until he can appreciate it, and the latter in a painter who moves from simple realism to impressionism to expressionism toward abstraction, as Rembrandt did. It is also readily noticeable in the other arts and in literature. In business the process is one of moving up the ladder to positions which are more difficult as well as more responsible.

In mathematics the peak of creativity usually comes early; almost all of the great mathematicians made their most original contributions before the age of thirty, whereas in some other fields creative activity reaches its peak later in life. The difference seems to be associated with some degree of difference in the locus of the creative process. In mathematics the immediate creative act is more largely unconscious; the new concept presents itself to the conscious mind in largely finished form; whereas in many other fields a greater element of conscious judgment en-

---

6. This is indicated by studies at the Institute for Personality Assessment and Research of the University of California of individuals from the arts and sciences whose careers demonstrate a high degree of creativity. See Frank Barron, "The Psychology of Imagination," *Scientific American*, Vol. CXCIX (September, 1958), pp. 150-66.

ters. Perhaps almost no one has within him more than one great new view of the world. In a field unrelated to the complex facts of life, one in which abstract logical relationships alone constitute the materials, one may encompass the known logic and realize his new view in his twenties. Then, his mind being drawn thereafter to the area which proved so satisfying, he spends the rest of his life tidying up and making minor advances here and there. However, in fields in which the complex details and relationships of real life are pertinent to the creative act, accumulation of knowledge by strengthening the basis for judgment provides increasing grist for one's unconscious (as well as conscious) processes to work on as the years pass, and creativity matures later in life.

The innovator not only feels pleasure in solving problems; he also feels a duty to achieve. The avowed goal of economic innovators, the purpose which they have felt it their duty to serve, has varied greatly among societies, but the sense of duty is a constant. Often this sense is religious in nature. The doctrine that the specific religious dogma of the Protestant Dissenters is peculiarly associated with innovational activity is obsolete,[7] but a number of scholars observing economic growth in various societies have noted that innovators in the early stages of growth seem to be characterized by a common ethic which is appropriately termed religious in nature, whatever their religious dogma. They feel a personal responsibility to transform the world that far transcends a profit motive.

To these qualities should be added intelligence and energy.[8] Intellectual capacity is in part inherited, and no doubt innate capacity is higher among innovators than among the population in general. In part, however, the intellectual capacity of innovators is due to the qualities described above. An individual with a given intellectual endowment will use it the more effectively the greater the degree to which he perceives the world as an orderly system, the greater his contentedness in his own judgment and reactions, the greater his satisfaction in attacking problems or in resolving inconsistencies, and the less the degree to which his energy has to be used to suppress unacceptable impulses within himself. The person with lack of these attitudes toward the world will be inhibited from attempting to use his capacities. But these attitudes are not simply the products of high innate intelligence; they derive primarily from conditions

7. Perhaps it never was held by scholars. Max Weber in *The Protestant Ethic and the Spirit of Capitalism,* trans. Talcott Parsons (New York: Charles Scribner's Sons, 1956), at times seems to argue this thesis but then backs away from it.

8. For an analysis of leading American business executives which stresses their energy, see Osborn Elliott, *Men at the Top* (New York: Harper & Bros., 1959).

of the individual's environment as he grows up, and especially in childhood, that are quite independent of his innate capacities.

Much the same factors determine the individual's level of energy. No doubt there are innate or, more broadly, constitutional determinants of energy just as there are of intelligence. The individual who is constitutionally endowed with an ampler than average reserve of energy stands a better than average chance of accomplishing creative deeds. But to a large degree the ability to draw on a great store of energy seems to depend on an individual's freedom from doubt and mistrust of himself, on his sense that the world is orderly and will respond dependably and pleasingly to his initiative. It is as though, not having to use his energy in conflicts within himself, he has it available to direct toward the world outside him.

The creative individual is not necessarily a happy man who faces problems with pure pleasure. Rather, most creative individuals are driven to creative activity by an incessant anxiety; their perception of the world as a threatening place leaves them only while they are active, then returns to drive them on again. Yet in other individuals anxiety is associated with rage that provokes urges and fantasies which persist in the unconscious and cause an individual to seal over his unconscious processes for fear of what he will find in them. (The anxiety is also largely unconscious; if questioned, the individual would probably deny its existence.) The two types of personality must be distinguished.

An individual acquires persisting anxiety if in his early life he faces a sequence of situations important to him that he cannot resolve satisfactorily or can resolve satisfactorily only by repeated attempts and with great difficulty—hunger, pressure on him to walk, and so on. The anxiety-creating situations may, however, be of two types which convey to the child differing perceptions of the world. He may become anxious because persons important to him, for example, his mother, seem willing to hurt him. If so, combined with his anxiety will be rage directed at her and fantasies of revenge. However, he must suppress these from consciousness since his mother is so important to him that he dares not admit that he hates her. He then seals over his unconscious processes, and their inaccessibility to him prevents him from being creative, or greatly cripples his creativity.

Suppose, however, that his experiences of infancy and early childhood give a firm and satisfying impression of the loving nurturance of his mother, but that repeatedly he is unable to achieve as she seems to wish him to. He may then feel that the fault must lie in him, and there may become built into him anxiety that he may not accomplish enough, anxiety that drives him all his life to achieve in order to regain fleetingly that temporary feeling of security conveyed by his mother's praise and caresses. In this case, little rage and hatred may be provoked in him, and his unconscious processes will remain accessible to him. Given the other necessary qualities, he becomes the anxious creative individual.

Of course the perceptions sketched here as arising from his relationship to his mother may arise also in relationships to other persons important to him in early life.

He may not be quite as open to experience as the unanxious creative individual because he is more fearful of experience. The accessibility of his unconscious processes to him may be somewhat less than to the unanxious individual, since the tensions of his childhood may have caused some reactions in him which were fearful or unacceptable and had to be repressed permanently. But these handicaps to creativity are compensated for by his incessant scanning of the horizon and by the great energy which he is incessantly driven to exert in defense against his anxieties.

Indeed, innovational activity is always a reaction to some degree of anxiety. The individual who is not in the least pushed toward creative activity as a relief from anxiety but is only drawn toward it by the great pleasure it gives him is an ideal case; he does not exist in life. Creativity does not require complete access to one's unconscious processes, complete confidence in one's own judgment, and so on. It requires only somewhat more of these qualities than characterizes the average person. Moreover, some types of innovation may require only a moderate degree of creativity combined with dogged determination or a high degree of motivation to dominate other men. Thus the characteristics of creativity described may not be high in some economic innovators. Often, however, they are greater than appears on the surface, especially since in business it is often desirable to keep one's inner life to oneself and to cast an image of oneself as a highly conventional extrovert.

## The Determinants of the Innovational Field

The discussion to this point has referred only to creativity in general. However, an individual is never creative in general; he is creative in some specific activity or activities. His being attuned to one or another sort of activity is therefore an element in his creativity.

Perhaps we may think of the characteristics which channel and release creativity into one field or another as being of three types: one's values concerning activities, one's anxieties or satisfactions in relationships with other men, and the scale of activity or influence in which one feels content or secure.

Perhaps there is, first of all, a rather direct attachment to one activity or another. In some sense an individual may enjoy for its own sake tilling the soil or tinkering with machinery or contemplating mathematical relationships. Second, one may have one or another attitude toward relationships with other men. One may find satisfaction in competition with them; the act of inner or outer aggression may give one pleasure or temporarily relieve one's anxiety. Or one may find a sense of security in being able to influence other men by one's logic or persuasiveness or in gaining a position of control over them. Or on the contrary, one may feel uneasy in any close competition or co-operation with other men and may turn toward working in isolation. In combination these characteristics plus the alternatives objectively open to him will determine the occupation in which a man chooses to work. Third, if one is characterized by a drive to influence or direct other men, he may be content to do so on a small scale or, on the other hand, he may feel that he has not sufficiently proved himself or made himself secure so long as there are wider groups against which he has not tested himself. One may therefore be content to work in his own pond—perhaps intellectually or technically or socially a very important pond—or one may be driven to seek national influence in his profession or in society as a whole and reform all society.

The choice of technology as a field in which to innovate of course requires one or another of certain combinations of these attitudes. It was noted [earlier] that the sense of identity of a member of the elite classes in traditional society makes him unable to function effectively in work which he associates with the menial classes. In general, the authoritarian personality of traditional society is uncreative. If, however, a deviant individual of the elite classes became creative, he would nevertheless be unable to innovate in technology so long as he retained the elite antipathy to manual labor, work with tools and machinery, and interest in the physical world.[9]

In recapitulation, then, the creative individual is unconsciously alert to new aspects of phenomena; he assumes that the phenomena of the area of experience of interest to him form a system that he can understand and manage, and that therefore encountering unexpected aspects will lead him to new understanding, not to frustration. He responds imaginatively to the stimuli that new observations provide; his unconscious mental processes deal with the substance of the problem rather than reacting to a sense of frustration with angry or aggressive fantasies or fantasies of magic solutions. And since he does not fear the content of his unconscious processes, their results are available to his conscious mind. He observes with detachment his own interactions with the world

---

9. Of course the same forces in his immediate environment which caused him to become deviant in ways that made him creative would probably also impinge on some of these attitudes.

outside him; his recognition that both the reactions of the world to him and his reactions to the world have understandable causes, that he himself is a system, is probably the basis of his assumption that the larger world is orderly and understandable. He trusts his evaluations of the world. The prospect of resolving a problem therefore attracts him; he approaches rather than evades it. Many effective innovators are oppressed by a pervasive anxiety concerning life. Their anxiety, however, is not the result of conflicting urges whose balance creates paralysis; rather, it is a gnawing feeling that they are not doing enough, or not well enough. Repeatedly, they escape from their anxiety temporarily by creative achievement. Effective innovators also typically feel a sense of duty to achieve.

## AUTHORITARIAN PERSONALITY

*     *     *     *     *

One gains an understanding of most of the facets of authoritarian personality if one assumes that as a child the authoritarian individual acquired no perception of the phenomena around him as elements in systems whose operation is amenable to analysis and responsive to his judicious initiative. Instead he must have gained two other impressions of the world that were overwhelmingly important in disciplining his later behavior. One of these is a perception of the world as arbitrary, capricious, not amenable to analysis, as consisting of an agglomeration of phenomena not related by a cause-and-effect network. The other is that the caprice of the world is not accidental but the play of willful powers far greater than his which serve their own purposes and disregard his unless he submits his will to theirs. These perceptions, we must assume, because the experiences which gave rise to them were very painful, have been pressed down out of his conscious mind; but he retains them in his unconscious, and they guide his adult behavior.

These perceptions breed in him a fear of using his initiative, an uncertainty concerning the quality of his own judgment, a tendency to let someone else evaluate a situation in order to avoid frustration and anxiety. Out of these perceptions also grows uneasiness at facing unresolved situations. Rather than rely on his own analysis to solve problems of the physical world or his relations to other individuals, he avoids pain by falling back on traditional ways of behavior that his parents and other earlier authorities taught him, and by relying on the judgment or will of individuals superior to him in authority or power.

To an individual guided by such perceptions it would seem to serve no satisfying purpose to be open to experience. Since phenomena and the forces that control them seem arbitrary to him, there are no useful deductions to be drawn from them. Moreover, a novel phenomenon would be disturbing since if it posed a problem it would arouse the anxiety associated with prospective initiative on his part. Hence for both positive and negative reasons he wears blinders to the interesting details of the world. He finds it safer to rely on traditional rules or on the judgment of older, wiser, and superior persons.

The painful experiences which gave rise to these perceptions must have created hatreds in him which shocked those around him. We shall see . . . that they also tend to arouse in him both doubt of his manliness and homosexual inclinations and desires. He presses these fears and unacceptable urges out of his conscious mind and seals over his unconscious processes as best he can because he is uneasy about what thoughts and fears they include. Hence his unconscious processes are inaccessible to him. In addition, they would not be useful if they were accessible, for instead of reactions to the phenomena he has currently observed they consist of the inadmissible impulses and desires which he has repressed and which are activated anew by the anxiety created by facing a problem.

But rage and pain, though repressed, are still within him. He dared not express his rage against the superior authorities who early in life directed him arbitrarily, but once he is an elder in the community, or a father, or even an older brother, he can somewhat satisfy his aggressiveness by his dominance over his inferiors. Moreover, as he moves to successive positions of authority at successive stages in his life the anxiety he feels in ambiguous situations causes him to insist that his own authority not be questioned, just as it earlier required that he submit his judgment to superior judgment and will. Thus each traditional adult individual in traditional society presents strong resistance to the questioning of authoritative decisions or traditional ways. That resistance is an important obstacle to change.

\* \* \* \* \*

## THE EMERGENCE OF VALUES CONDUCIVE TO ECONOMIC GROWTH

If the social change that occurs is to be a transition to economic growth, it is necessary that values conducive to technological innovation and other activities pertinent to economic growth should appear in personalities. They are less apt to appear in reformers than in other innovators, for reformers are concerned with moral questions and power rather than with efficiency. Institutional changes favorable to economic growth are apt to be made by innovators who are not reformers, though these men may influence reformers and work through them.

I have suggested how the personality of a member of a group from which respect for its status has been withdrawn may become creative. How does he simultaneously come to hold new and radical values?

## Identification and the Search for a New Identity

In the normal course of events, we say, a son identifies with his father. This statement, however, is elliptical. The son internalizes an image of a satisfactory role in life if he can find one. In normal circumstances his father's role as the son understands it serves this purpose. In the circumstances of withdrawal of expected status, however, his father casts an image of satisfaction in his role in life as conflicting with satisfaction in the regard other members of the society have for him. This conflict is the source of his father's anxiety. The son has the problem of deciding what is good in life in the face of this conflict.

As has been suggested, individuals of the first generation—perhaps the first several generations—that face this problem can find no better solution to it than to repress the conflicting values. From one generation to the next they become increasingly retreatist. But when an individual with a higher degree of creativity, and specifically higher need achievement and need autonomy, emerges, his creativity is conducive to a more effective solution to the problem.

Even the most self-reliant son will internalize his father's values in some degree. His father is so important in his life that this is inevitable.

But if the son is creative, he may hold in abeyance a commitment concerning some of his father's values, questioning them because they lead to an unsatisfying identity in his father, but not yet knowing quite what to do about them. Later he will be able to observe models of behavior beyond his father, and, observing that they are more satisfying, he may be able to interpret them as extensions of certain of his father's values. If so, he may find in them promising paths to an appropriate role in life, and not an abandonment but rather a fulfillment of his early purposes.

Early in life, if he has high need autonomy, he holds commitment in abeyance, not merely because of a general sense that he must look for more satisfying models but for a specific reason: the rage and disappointment which he feels at his father's behavior.

His mother's nurturance and the image of his father's motivations which he receives directly and which his mother also presents to him create guilt in him at his rage. He can relieve his guilt by directing his rage not at his father but only at some quality of his father which does not seem an essential part of his father. By presenting the perception that he himself is not at ease about some of his values, the father invites the son to find this solution. Similarly, a little later in life the son feels rage at the aggressor group, yet he cannot reject their values outright and completely since that would leave him with an incomplete frame of reference for an identity in his society. He can solve his problem if he can denounce and abandon certain elite values yet take hold of some aspect of life which will satisfy other of their values and offer greater promise than does his father's life of giving him satisfactory status.

Looking around his universe, he may be able to find some group or individuals who do not threaten him, who have power or status recognized and respected by the group which does disparage and threaten him, and whose role in life is not closed to him. If he sees the possibility of proving his worth (to himself and to his society) by adopting the values and some aspects of the way of life of that group, then he has a promising solution. If the new values can be interpreted as extensions of values which are a part of his father's personality and thus of his child-hood model, so that by superimposition he partly replaces the old values without really losing them, then he has the best of the worlds which are possible in his circumstances: He can reject the low valuation of him by his father and the aggressor group, divert his rage toward imperfections in them which are a permissible target, gain a new promise of security, and yet in intent act in accordance with the more general values of his society after all.

Indeed, if he is clever enough he can serve yet another purpose. With part of himself he identifies both with his father and with the aggressor group and knows that they identify with him. They presumably scorn some of the values of the group he has now adopted as his model, for if some of its values were not contrary to theirs, selection of the group as a model would not have satisfied his rage. If now he can safely reject values which his father and the society accuse him of not measuring up to, and adopt others which they scorn, he will have his revenge on them; for he will thus destroy his identity and, in his view of the world, by his identification with them destroy their identity also. This is the phenomenon, writ large, of the child who, angry at his mother for scolding him, injures himself to make her feel sorry. But he can safely do all this only if in the same operation he can also find some new values, extensions of old ones, which will promise him recognition and preserve his identity. Otherwise, in his view, he will truly destroy himself.

I trust it is clear that new values are not adopted by a process of rational choice either by children or adults. Rather, the process is a largely unconscious one of responding to needs and finding the mental model which will justify holding the values that promise to satisfy the needs. The environmental pressures which initiate the process of the adoption of new values are not those of the larger society but the complex of pressures which impinge immediately on the individual in childhood. I suggest, for example, that no individual in any underdeveloped country decides on a business career merely because of a mental judgment, after he has learned of Western technology, that such a career would be profitable and would yield economic power. (He may think that he decided on such a basis, but I would not take the individual's testimony as good evidence in the matter.) Rather, he turned in this direction only if the activity itself (not its results) gives him a sense of power and of a satisfying identity. This it will do only because of images he has in mind of the worthiness of the type of people who pursue such activity.

### The Selection of Technology: Religious Ethic

There is nothing in the process of search for new values to suggest that groups who are under pressure of withdrawal of status respect will everywhere turn to prowess in technology to prove their worth. They will do so only if, among the models of activity they see in the world around them, this type of activity provides a more satisfying sense of identity, a better prospect of attaining regard and respect by the reference groups whose opinion one values, than any other. Throughout history groups whose status is no longer respected have chosen various new roles, usually roles which they thought would lead to social power. Once a model of technological progress and of the power it yields existed, it was inevitable that this course to proving one's worth would be sought by many groups denied status respect.

In Japan, to various unhappy groups in the population the occupations in which the warriors of the Western world found the sources of their military strength met the requirements perfectly. They promised status greater than that of the Tokugawa; they were an extension of the traditional military values of the samurai; and they defied the Tokugawa aggressors. In Colombia the technological prowess of groups in foreign countries served the purpose well. It was an extension of the manual-technical occupations of the Antioqueños; engaging in it flaunted the values of the other Colombians; and it promised economic status greater than that of the other Colombians. Indeed, it is obvious that groups in traditional societies who are at the present time rebelling against the lack of respect of elites for their purposes are apt to turn to the way of life in which foreigners (of West or East) have found prestige.

It is less obvious where the Protestant Dissenters and lowland Scots found a model which led them to technological prowess; the model was not so obviously at hand. . . . Let it merely be noted here that these groups had earlier reinterpreted their religious beliefs so those beliefs first provided an acceptable channel for need dependence, and that when the devotion of energies to technological progress proved attractive it was possible to extend the religious reinterpretation to sanction the activity.

This dual result of a reinterpretation of religion occurred also in Russia. Although the Old Believers were formally the upholders of the old faith rather than sponsors of a new one, the schism undoubtedly led them to a closer personal responsibility to God than they had previously felt. The religious decree which brought the breach with the higher church authorities in the seventeenth century may reasonably be regarded as initiating the entire subsequent sequence of personality change.

Even if prior religious change has not occurred, the individual who has found a new identity will probably project it onto his religion and interpret his religion so as to provide sanction for his new purpose in life.

In Japan the change in interpretation of the role of the emperor, though not religious in form in the usual sense of the term, may reasonably be regarded as a reinterpretation of a religious ethic. In Colombia there has been neither any break with the established religious tradition nor any manifest reinterpretation of the meaning of religion, but inner reinterpretation may have occurred. Observers have noted that many Antioqueños seem to feel a special sense of their obligation in life.

### Eating One's Cake and Having It

Following their success in economic prowess, unless the old social order has been largely disrupted, the innovators are apt to turn to acquiring traditional symbols of status which their economic affluence makes possible. For they have not rejected the general status values of their society. They have only temporarily abandoned the old values as not open to them. The economic innovators of Colombia make no attempt to conceal their nostalgia for the land and their desire to "keep one foot on it" when economic success in industry has made this possible. Satisfaction at landed status and titles of honor and nobility in England was felt by business leaders of the Industrial Revolution and their descendants as well as by the old aristocracy and gentry. In Japan the old feudal economic system broke down with revolutionary speed. By the time the economic innovators had succeeded, no place in that system could be sought because the system no longer existed. But their satisfaction at a place in a social hierarchy modeled after the old one in most essentials, though without the economic-military trappings, is obvious.

In these ways, then, creative and reformist personalities may emerge out of retreatism. In cultural circumstances in which creative individuals see technological prowess as a promising path to satisfaction of their needs, the values of the new generation will tend to turn in this direction. Innovations in production will then appear, innovational individuals will guide institutional reforms in favorable directions, and economic growth will gain momentum.

# David C. McClelland

## The Achievement Motive in Economic Growth

FROM THE BEGINNING of recorded history, men have been fascinated by the fact that civilizations rise and fall. Culture growth, as Kroeber has demonstrated, is episodic, and sometimes occurs in quite different fields.[1] For example, the people living in the Italian peninsula at the time of ancient Rome produced a great civilization of law, politics, and military conquest; and at another time, during the Renaissance, the inhabitants of Italy produced a great civilization of art, music, letters, and science. What can account for such cultural flowerings? In our time we have theorists like Huntington, who stresses the importance of climate, or Toynbee, who also feels the right amount of challenge from the environment is crucial though he conceives of the environment as including its psychic effects. Others, like Kroeber, have difficulty imagining any general explanation; they perforce must accept the notion that a particular culture happens to hit on a particularly happy mode of self-expression, which it then pursues until it becomes overspecialized and sterile.

My concern is not with all culture growth, but with economic growth. Some wealth or leisure may be essential to development in other fields—the arts, politics, science, or war—but we need not insist on it. However, the question of why some countries develop rapidly in the economic sphere at certain times and not at others is in itself of great interest, whatever its relation to other types of culture growth. Usually, rapid economic growth has been explained in terms of "external" factors—favorable op-

---

1. A. L. Kroeber, *Configurations of Culture Growth* (Berkeley, California, 1944).

portunities for trade, unusual natural resources, or conquests that have opened up new markets or produced internal political stability. But I am interested in the *internal* factors—in the values and motives men have that lead them to exploit opportunities, to take advantage of favorable trade conditions; in short, to shape their own destiny.

This interest is not surprising; I am a psychologist—and, furthermore, a psychologist whose primary research interest is in human motivation, in the *reasons* that people behave as they do. Of course, all people have always, to a certain extent, been interested in human motivation. The difference between their interest and the twentieth-century psychologist's interest is that the latter tries to define his subject matter very precisely and, like all scientists, to measure it. How can human motives be identified, or even measured? Psychologists' favorite techniques for conducting research in this area have always been the interview and the questionnaire. If you want to know what a man's motives are, ask him. Of course, you need not ask him directly; but perhaps, if you talk to him long enough in an interview, or ask him enough in a questionnaire, you can infer what his motives are—more or less the same way that, from a number of clues, a detective would infer who had committed a crime.

. . . About ten or twelve years ago, the research group in America with which I was connected decided to see what we could learn about human motivation by coding objectively what people spontaneously thought about in their waking fantasies.[2] Our method was to collect such free fantasy, in the form of brief stories written about pictures, and to count the frequency with which certain themes appeared—rather as a medical technician counts the frequency with which red or white corpuscles appear in a blood sample. We were able to demonstrate that the frequency with which certain "inner concerns" appeared in these fantasies varied systematically as a function of specific experimental conditions by which we aroused or induced motivational states in the subjects. Eventually, we were able to isolate several of these inner concerns, or motives, which, if present in great frequency in the fantasies of a particular person, enabled us to know something about how he would behave in many other areas of life.

Chief among these motives was what we termed "the need for Achievement" (*n* Achievement)—a desire to do well, not so much for the sake of social recognition or prestige, but to attain an inner feeling of personal accomplishment. This motive is my particular concern in this paper. Our early laboratory studies showed that people "high" in *n* Achievement tend

---

2. J. W. Atkinson (Ed.), *Motives in Fantasy, Action, and Society* (Princeton, N.J., 1958).

to work harder at certain tasks; to learn faster; to do their best work when it counts for the record, and not when special incentives, like money prizes, are introduced; to choose experts over friends as working partners; etc. Obviously, we cannot here review the many, many studies in this area. About five years ago, we became especially interested in the problem of what would happen in a society if a large number of people with a high need for achievement should happen to be present in it at a particular time. In other words, we became interested in a social-psychological question: What effect would a concentration of people with high *n* Achievement have on a society? . . .

Let us discuss the precise ways that higher *n* Achievement leads to more rapid economic development, and why it should lead to economic development rather than, for example, to military or artistic development. We must consider in more detail the mechanism by which the concentration of a particular type of human motive in a population leads to a complex social phenomenon like economic growth. The link between the two social phenomena is, obviously, the business entrepreneur. I am not using the term "entrepreneur" in the sense of "capitalist": in fact, I should like to divorce "entrepreneur" entirely from any connotations of ownership. An entrepreneur is someone who exercises control over production that is not just for his personal consumption. According to my definition, for example, an executive in a steel production unit in Russia is an entrepreneur.

It was Joseph Schumpeter who drew the attention of economists to the importance that the activity of these entrepreneurs had in creating industrialization in the West. Their vigorous endeavors put together firms and created productive units where there had been none before. In the beginning, at least, the entrepreneurs often collected material resources, organized a production unit to combine the resources into a new product, and sold the product. Until recently, nearly all economists—including not only Marx, but also Western classical economists—assumed that these men were moved primarily by the "profit motive." We are all familiar with the Marxian argument that they were so driven by their desire for profits that they exploited the workingman and ultimately forced him to revolt. Recently, economic historians have been studying the actual lives of such entrepreneurs and finding—certainly to the surprise of some of the investigators—that many of them seemingly were not interested in making money as such. In psychological terms, at least, Marx's picture is slightly out of focus. Had these entrepreneurs been above all interested in money, many more of them would have quit working as soon as they had made all the money that they could possibly use. They would not have continued to risk their money in further entrepreneurial ventures. Many of them, in fact, came from pietistic sects, like the Quakers in England, that prohibited the enjoyment of wealth in any of the ways cultivated so successfully by some members of the European nobility. However, the entrepreneurs often seemed consciously to be greatly concerned with expanding their businesses, with getting a greater share of the market, with "conquering brute nature," or even with altruistic schemes for bettering the lot of mankind or bringing about the kingdom of God on earth more rapidly. Such desires have frequently enough been labeled as hypocritical. However, if we assume that these men were really motivated by a desire for achievement rather than by a desire for money as such, the label no longer fits. This assumption also simplifies further matters considerably. It provides an explanation for the fact that these entrepreneurs were interested in money without wanting it for its own sake, namely, that money served as a ready quantitative index of how well they were doing—e.g., of how much they had achieved by their efforts over the past year. The need to achieve can never be satisfied by money; but estimates of profitability in money terms can supply direct knowledge of how well one is doing one's job.

The brief consideration of the lives of business entrepreneurs of the past suggested that their chief motive may well have been a high *n* Achievement. What evidence have we found in support of this? We made two approaches to the problem. First, we attempted to determine whether individuals with high *n* Achievement behave like entrepreneurs; and second, we investigated to learn whether actual entrepreneurs, particularly the more successful ones, in a number of countries, have higher *n* Achievement than do other people of roughly the same status. Of course, we had to establish what we meant by "behave like entrepreneurs"—what precisely distinguishes the way an entrepreneur behaves from the way other people behave?

The adequate answers to these questions would entail a long discussion of the sociology of occupations, involving the distinction originally made by Max Weber between capitalists and bureaucrats. Since this cannot be done here, a very brief report on our extensive investigations in this area will have to suffice. First, one of the defining characteristics of an entrepreneur is *taking risks* and/or innovating. A person who adds up a column of figures is not an entrepreneur—however carefully, efficiently, or correctly he adds them. He is simply following established rules. However, a man who decides to add a new line to his business *is* an entrepreneur, in that he cannot know in advance whether his decision will be correct. Nevertheless, he does not feel that he is in the position of a gambler who places some money on the turn of a card. Knowledge, judgment, and skill enter into his decision-making; and, if his choice is justified by future developments, he can certainly feel a sense of personal achievement from having made a successful move.

Therefore, if people with high *n* Achievement are to behave in an entrepreneurial way, they must seek out and perform in situations in which there is some moderate risk of failure—a risk which can, presumably, be reduced by increased effort or skill. They should not work harder than other people at routine tasks, or perform functions which they are certain to do well simply by doing what everyone accepts as the correct traditional thing to do. On the other hand, they should avoid gambling situations, because, even if they win, they can receive no sense of personal achievement, since it was not skill but luck that produced the results. (And, of course, most of the time they would lose, which would be highly unpleasant to them.) The data on this point are very clear-cut. We have repeatedly found, for example, that boys with high *n* Achievement choose to play games of skill that incorporate a moderate risk of failure. The game was adapted from one used by the psychologist Kurt Lewin. Each child was given a rope ring and told that he could stand at any distance that he preferred from the peg, to try to throw the ring over the peg. The children with high *n* Achievement usually stood at middle distances from the peg, where the chances of success or failure were moderate. However, the children with low *n* Achievement evinced no particular preference for any position. They more frequently stood at extremes of distance—either very close to the peg, where they were sure to throw the ring over it, or very far away, where they were almost certain not to. They thus manifested behavior like that of many people in underdeveloped countries who, while they act very traditionally economically, at the same time love to indulge in lotteries—risking a little to make a great deal on a very long shot. In neither of the two last examples do the actors concentrate on the realistic *calculated* risk, as do the subjects with high *n* Achievement.

We have recently concluded a somewhat analogous study, which indicated that boys with high *n* Achievement tend to perform better and to work harder under conditions of moderate risk—boys not only in the United States, but also in Japan, Brazil, and India. In each of these countries, the boys with high *n* Achievement did not invariably perform a laboratory task better than the boys with low *n* Achievement. They did better only under conditions involving some degree of competition, some risk of doing worse than others or of not getting a sense of personal achievement. There was still another group of boys in the sample from each country. These boys were identified by their optimistic attitude toward life in general, as manifested in their answers to a questionnaire. The members of these groups always had more success than the others, no matter what the competitive or risk situation was. I like to think of these boys as the conscientious ones, who will do their work cheerfully and efficiently under any kind of incentive conditions. They may form the backbone of the civil service, because they can tolerate routine; but they will not be the business entrepreneurs, because the latter constantly seek situations in which they can obtain a sense of personal achievement from having overcome risks or difficulties.

Another quality that the entrepreneur seeks in his work is that his job be a kind that ordinarily provides him with accurate knowledge of the results of his decisions. As a rule, growth in sales, in output, or in profit margins tells him very precisely whether he has made the correct choice under uncertainty or not. Thus, the concern for profit enters in—profit is a measure of success. We have repeatedly found that boys with a high *n* Achievement work more efficiently when they know how well they are doing. Also, they will not work harder for money rewards; but if they are asked, they state that greater money rewards should be awarded for accomplishing more difficult things in games of skill. In the ring-toss game, subjects were asked how much money they thought should be awarded for successful throws from different distances. Subjects with high *n* Achievement and those with low *n* Achievement agreed substantially about the amounts for throws made close to the peg. However, as the distance from the peg increased, the amounts awarded for successful throws by the subjects with high *n* Achievement rose more rapidly than did the rewards by those with low *n* Achievement. Here, as elsewhere, individuals with high *n* Achievement behaved as they must if they are to be the successful entrepreneurs in society. They believed that greater achievement should be recognized by quantitatively larger reward. . . .

There are two successful, and one unsuccessful, methods by which the business community recruits people with the "entrepreneurial spirit"— with high *n* Achievement. The unsuccessful way is easiest to describe and is still characteristic of many underdeveloped countries. In a study of the occupational likes and dislikes of boys in Japan, Brazil, Germany, India, and the United States, we found that (as Atkinson had predicted on theoretical grounds) the boys with high *n* Achievement usually aspire toward the occupation of highest prestige *which they have a reasonable chance to enter and to succeed.*[3] For example, their ambitions will be centered on the professions, which are the highest prestige occupations in most countries—*if* the boys themselves are from the upper class and thus have the opportunity and backing to enter the professions. In other words, when the business leadership of a country is largely recruited from the

---

3. J. W. Atkinson, "Motivational Determinants of Risk-Taking Behavior," *Psychological Review*, LXIV (1957), 359-372.

élite (as it is in many countries, because only the élite has access to capital and to government), it will *not* tend to attract those with high *n* Achievement who are not from the upper class.

Developments in many of the Western democracies were quite different. In the most rapidly advancing countries, business leadership was drawn, at least in the early stages, largely from the middle classes. A business career was the highest prestige occupation to which a middle-class boy with high *n* Achievement could aspire—especially if he were a member of a disliked minority group, like the Protestants in France or the Jews in many countries, to whom other channels of upward mobility were closed. Thus a constant "natural" flow of entrepreneurial talent from the middle classes provided economic leadership of a high quality.

The other successful method of recruiting entrepreneurial talent is the one that has been adopted, for example, in the U.S.S.R. There, the central government took a severe, achievement-oriented, "pass-or-fail" attitude toward its plant managers, so that only the "fittest" survived. We believe that those "fittest" were the ones with the highest *n* Achievement, although we have no supporting evidence as yet. In the free enterprise system, the recruiting method may be compared to a garden in which all plants are allowed to grow until some crowd the others out. In the Soviet system, it is comparable to a garden in which plants that have not reached a specified height by a certain time are weeded out. In many underdeveloped countries, it is comparable to a garden where only certain plants are permitted to live in the first place, so that the gardener has to take them whatever size they attain. Of course, no country represents a pure type; but perhaps the analogy, oversimplified though it is, helps to illustrate my point.

What produces high *n* Achievement? Why do some societies produce a large number of people with this motive, while other societies produce so many fewer? We conducted long series of researches into this question. I can present only a few here.

One very important finding is essentially a negative one: *n* Achievement cannot be hereditary. Popular psychology has long maintained that some races are more energetic than others. Our data clearly contradict this in connection with *n* Achievement. . . .

However, there is substantiating evidence that *n* Achievement is a motive which a child can acquire quite early in life, say, by the age of eight or ten, as a result of the way his parents have brought him up. Winterbottom's study of the importance of early self-reliance and achievement training has been supplemented by a much more detailed inquiry by Rosen and D'Andrade. . . .[4]

---

4. B. C. Rosen and R. G. D'Andrade, "The Psychosocial Origins of Achievement Motivation," *Sociometry*, XXII (1959), 185-218.

. . . There does seem to be one crucial variable discernible: the extent to which the religion of the family emphasizes individual, as contrasted with ritual, contact with God. The preliterate tribes that we studied in which the religion was the kind that stressed the individual contact had higher $n$ Achievement; and in general, mystical sects in which this kind of religious self-reliance dominates have had higher $n$ Achievement.

The extent to which the authoritarian father is away from the home while the boy is growing up may prove to be another crucial variable. If so, then one incidental consequence of prolonged wars may be an increase in $n$ Achievement, because the fathers are away too much to interfere with their sons' development of it. And in Turkey, Bradburn found that those boys tended to have higher $n$ Achievement who had left home early or whose fathers had died before they were eighteen.[5] Slavery was another factor which played an important role in the past. It probably lowered $n$ Achievement—in the slaves, for whom obedience and responsibility, but not achievement, were obvious virtues; and in the slave-owners, because household slaves were often disposed to spoil the owner's children as a means for improving their own positions. This is both a plausible and a probable reason for the drop in $n$ Achievement level in ancient Greece that occurred at about the time the middle-class entrepreneur was first able to afford, and obtain by conquest, as many as two slaves for each child. The idea also clarifies the slow economic development of the South in the United States by attributing its dilatoriness to a lack of $n$ Achievement in its élite; and it also indicates why lower-class American Negroes, who are closest to the slave tradition, possess very low $n$ Achievement.[6]

I have outlined our research findings. Do they indicate ways of accelerating economic development? Increasing the level of $n$ Achievement in a country suggests itself as an obvious first possibility. If $n$ Achievement is so important, so specifically adapted to the business role, then it certainly should be raised in level, so that more young men have an "entrepreneurial drive." The difficulty in this excellent plan is that our studies of how $n$ Achievement originates indicate that the family is the key formative influence; and it is very hard to change on a really large scale. To be sure, major historical events like wars have taken authoritarian fathers out of the home; and religious reform movements have sometimes converted the parents to a new achievement-oriented ideology.

---

5. N. M. Bradburn, "The Managerial Role in Turkey" (unpublished Ph. D. dissertation, Harvard University, 1960).

6. B. C. Rosen, "Race, Ethnicity, and Achievement Syndrome," *American Sociological Review*, XXIV (1959), 47-60.

However, such matters are not ordinarily within the policy-making province of the agencies charged with speeding economic development.

Such agencies can, perhaps, effect the general acceptance of an achievement-oriented ideology as an absolute *sine qua non* of economic development. Furthermore, this ideology should be diffused not only in business and governmental circles, but throughout the nation, and in ways that will influence the thinking of all parents as they bring up their children. As Rosen and D'Andrade found, parents must, above all, set high standards for their children. The campaign to spread achievement-oriented ideology, if possible, could also incorporate an attack on the extreme authoritarianism in fathers that impedes or prevents the development of self-reliance in their sons. This is, however, a more delicate point, and attacking this, in many countries, would be to threaten values at the very center of social life. I believe that a more indirect approach would be more successful. One approach would be to take the boys out of the home and to camps. A more significant method would be to promote the rights of women, both legally and socially—one of the ways to undermine the absolute dominance of the male is to strengthen the rights of the female! Another reason for concentrating particularly on women is that they play the leading role in rearing the next generation. Yet, while men in underdeveloped countries come in contact with new achievement-oriented values and standards through their work, women may be left almost untouched by such influences. But if the sons are to have high *n* Achievement, the mothers must first be reached.

It may seem strange that a paper on economic development should discuss the importance of feminism and the way children are reared; but this is precisely where a psychological analysis leads. If the motives of men are the agents that influence the speed with which the economic machine operates, then the speed can be increased only through affecting the factors that create the motives. Furthermore—to state this point less theoretically —I cannot think of evinced substantial, rapid long-term economic development where women have not been somewhat freed from their traditional setting of "Kinder, Küche und Kirche" and allowed to play a more powerful role in society, specifically as part of the working force. This generalization applies not only to the Western democracies like the United States, Sweden, or England, but also to the U.S.S.R., Japan, and now China.

In the present state of our knowledge, we can conceive of trying to raise *n* Achievement levels only in the next generation—although new research findings may soon indicate *n* Achievement in adults can be increased. Most economic planners, while accepting the long-range desirability of raising *n* Achievement in future generations, want to know what can be done during the next five or ten years. This immediacy inevitably focuses attention on the process or processes by which executives or entrepreneurs are selected. Foreigners with proved entrepreneurial drive can be hired, but at best this is a temporary and unsatisfactory solution. In most underdeveloped countries where government is playing a leading role in promoting economic development, it is clearly necessary for the government to adopt rigid achievement-oriented standards of performance like those in the U.S.S.R.[7] A government manager or, for that matter, a private entrepreneur, should have to produce "or else." Production targets must be set, as they are in most economic plans; and individuals must be held responsible for achieving them, even at the plant level. The philosophy should be one of "no excuses accepted." It is common for government officials or economic theorists in underdeveloped countries to be weighed down by all the difficulties which face the economy and render its rapid development difficult or impossible. They note that there is too rapid population growth, too little capital, too few technically competent people, etc. Such obstacles to growth are prevalent, and in many cases they are immensely hard to overcome; but talking about them can provide merely a comfortable rationalization for mediocre performance. It is difficult to fire an administrator, no matter how poor his performance, if so many objective reasons exist for his doing badly. Even worse, such rationalization permits, in the private sector, the continued employment of incompetent family members as executives. If these private firms were afraid of being penalized for poor performance, they might be impelled to find more able professional managers a little more quickly. I am not an expert in this field, and the mechanisms I am suggesting may be far from appropriate. Still, they may serve to illustrate my main point: if a country short in entrepreneurial talent wants to advance rapidly, it must find ways and means of insuring that only the most competent retain positions of responsibility. One of the obvious methods of doing so is to judge people in terms of their *performance*—and not according to their family or political connections, their skill in explaining why their unit failed to produce as expected, or their conscientiousness in following the rules. I would suggest the use of psychological tests as a means of selecting people with high *n* Achievement; but, to be perfectly frank, I think this approach is at present somewhat impractical on a large enough scale in most underdeveloped countries.

Finally, there is another approach which I think is promising for recruiting and developing more competent business leadership. It is the one called, in some circles, the "professionalization of management."

---

7. David Granick, *The Red Executive* (New York, 1960).

Harbison and Myers have recently completed a world-wide survey of the efforts made to develop professional schools of high-level management. They have concluded that, in most countries, progress in this direction is slow.[8] Professional management is important for three reasons. (1) It may endow a business career with higher prestige (as a kind of profession), so that business will attract more of the young men with high *n* Achievement from the élite groups in backward countries. (2) It stresses *performance* criteria of excellence in the management area—i.e., what a man can do and not what he is. (3) Advanced management schools can themselves be so achievement-oriented in their instruction that they are able to raise the *n* Achievement of those who attend them.

Applied toward explaining historical events, the results of our researches clearly shift attention away from external factors and to man—in particular, to his motives and values. That about which he thinks and dreams determines what will happen. The emphasis is quite different from the Darwinian or Marxist view of man as a creature who *adapts* to his environment. It is even different from the Freudian view of civilization as the sublimation of man's primitive urges. Civilization, at least in its economic aspects, is neither adaptation nor sublimation; it is a positive creation by a people made dynamic by a high level of *n* Achievement. Nor can we agree with Toynbee, who recognizes the importance of psychological factors as "the very forces which actually decide the issue when an encounter takes place," when he states that these factors "inherently are impossible to weigh and measure, and therefore to estimate scientifically in advance."[9] It is a measure of the pace at which the behavorial sciences are developing that even within Toynbee's lifetime we can demonstrate that he was mistaken. The psychological factor responsible for a civilization's rising to a challenge is so far from being "inherently impossible to weigh and measure" that it has been weighed and measured and scientifically estimated in advance; and, so far as we can now tell, this factor is the achievement motive.

---

8. Frederick Harbison and Charles A. Myers, *Management in the Industrial World* (New York, 1959).

9. Arnold J. Toynbee, *A Study of History* (abridgment by D. C. Somervell; Vol. I; New York, 1947).

# The Clash
# of Cultures

THE ESSAYS in this section share a common theme: the clash between traditional and emerging cultural values. On this topic anthropologists like Linton and Mead have written much that is illuminating to economists. Linton's essay discusses the conditions under which cultural factors may enhance or inhibit economic transformation. He stresses the "digestability" of foreign values, meaning by the word a measure of the capacity of older cultures to absorb new values. Margaret Mead's description of the Manus Islanders features a somewhat unusual view of change. She argues persuasively that the sweeping character of transformation demands *total* rather than selected change. It is Miss Mead's conviction that the center of resistance to change is in the technical culture. For her, development is beneficial only if the new pattern of life promotes integral, autonomous personality.

Sadie's case study marks an instance of much less successful cultural adaptation. His description of the discouraging pace of modernization among South Africa's Bantu tribesmen partially corroborates Mead's insistence upon the necessity of comprehensive change. Bantu tribal society has been only peripherally affected by change. Deeply imbedded values and the institutional forms that embody them have produced a milieu highly intractable to economic change. Hence, Sadie concludes, only a "social revolution" can overcome the passivity and inertia which up to this point have rendered capital investment unproductive.

# Ralph Linton

## Cultural and Personality Factors Affecting Economic Growth

. . . There is good evidence that any personality configuration which can be found in one society can be matched in any other. In the small "primitive" groups which anthropologists prefer to study, all personality types may not be present at all times, but any type can be relied upon to show up eventually. However, the frequencies of various personality types vary enormously from one society to another. Thus, a type which is the most frequent in one society may be so rare in another that individuals who show it are regarded as pathological. An anthropologist friend told me that, when he settled in a village in the Admiralties, the local natives pointed out one of their number as insane. As he came to know the man, he found him not only sane but much more likeable than any of the others. He discovered that he was regarded as insane because in an emergency, say, a drowning child, he would help a neighbor without waiting to drive a bargain as to how much he should get for the assistance.

In small, culturally homogeneous societies a large majority of members usually belong to one personality type, while other types are represented by scattered individuals. The basic personality type shows a close relation to the society's techniques of child care and to the demands which the society makes upon its adult members. From numerous clinical studies in our own society we know the effects of certain sorts of early experience on the developing personality. In each of the "primitive" societies studied to date, the methods of child-rearing have been such as might be expected to produce the basic personality type. Moreover, individuals with this sort of personality find themselves at home in the society's culture. They are able to accept its values and fulfil the obligations which it imposes with a minimum of psychological difficulty.

We do not know whether the same conclusions apply to large, heterogeneous societies such as modern nations. A modern nation always includes numerous communities and classes which may differ markedly in their customs. Although a number of interesting and suggestive books have been published on the subject of national character, none of them rests upon study of an adequate sample of individuals from the various subsocieties within the nation in question.

Fortunately, the question of national character is not of paramount importance for our present discussion. Individuals normally behave in accordance with the culture of their societies, and, given a knowledge of this culture, one can predict their reactions to most situations without knowledge of their personality configurations. Let us suppose, for example, that I am in Norway and have no change with which to tip a porter. I give him a hundred-kroner note, asking him to get it changed for me. On the basis of a knowledge of Norwegian culture, I can predict with a high degree of probability that he will be back with the change. If I did the same thing in Italy, I could predict with an even higher degree of probability that I would never see the porter again.

Most of the factors which affect the adoption and integration of new ideas by a society can be phrased more effectively in cultural than in psychological terms. If we know what a society's culture is, including its particular system of values and attitudes, we can predict with a fairly high degree of probability whether the bulk of its members will welcome or resist a particular innovation. We can also predict what parts of the society's economic or social system will be affected first and where the resulting disorganization will be most extensive. In any such predictions the circumstances surrounding the innovation, such as its source, external pressure toward its acceptance, and immediate utility, must, of course, be taken into account. The one variable which cannot be reduced to exact terms and which always interferes with exact prediction is the presence of particular individuals.

Our studies of the processes of culture change have revealed the extreme importance of innovators, persons who for some reason espouse a new idea and devote themselves energetically to "selling" it to their society. Both the motives and the personalities of such individuals appear to be varied, but it is safe to say that their personalities are rarely of the basic type. Opposed to them are, in most cases, a group of equally vigorous conservatives, persons who are contented with the status quo because, often unconsciously, they derive advantage from it. The social position, force of character, and intelligence of particular individuals belonging to one or the other of these groups may have a very real effect on patterns of economic growth. They not only may hasten or retard the growth itself but also may determine which of several possible lines it will follow.

In addition to the active innovators, the social disruption which inevitably accompanies extensive culture changes always brings to the fore numerous individuals who find the innovations congenial and are ready to exploit them. This is even more true in cases where the innovations are not congruous with the pre-existing culture than in those where they are. In fact, such persons are very frequently misfits in their societies, handicapped by atypical personalities. If the innovations are accepted, these former misfits become a new elite, and there is a strong tendency for them to transmit their advantage to their descendants, thus becoming the founders of a new hereditary ruling group. The current situation in Russia provides a good illustration for this.

Turning from questions of personality and its influence, there are two factors effecting economic growth which are universal. First, all societies and most individuals welcome improvement in their economic condition as long as such improvements do not involve more trouble than they are worth, that is, necessitate too many changes in established behavior patterns and controvert too many accepted values. In a research undertaken by sociologists some years ago, it was discovered that nearly everyone in our own society believes that he could live comfortably on an income one-third larger than that which he actually has. This attitude seemed to be present irrespective of the actual level of income. In the same way, all societies would like to improve their economic condition, although the ceilings which they would initially set for the improvement might vary greatly. Where a society no longer tries to improve economic conditions, this attitude can be traced to a series of past failures and frustrations. . . .

Unless a society has had adverse experiences of this sort, its members will be interested in improving their economic condition; but we must remember that many of the people whom we hope to help have had such experiences. Many colonial peoples and the sharecroppers and tenants who form a large part of the population in even independent "backward" nations know from sad experience that, every time their income increases, so do their rents and taxes. After each advertised economic advance they find themselves with very much the same standard of living they had before they underwent the trouble and uncertainty involved in practicing new techniques.

One also finds that the members of the average peasant community view any attempts to improve their economic condition which originate with their rulers with considerable and not unjustified suspicion. This holds whether the rulers are foreign imperialists or a native upper class. The peasant feels that anything which his rulers offer as a chance to improve his condition is probably much more to their advantage than to his own. Since his rulers have always mulcted him in the past, he assumes that they will continue to mulct him in the future. So much for the desire for economic betterment which is obviously basic to any attempt to improve economic conditions.

The second factor which is universally significant in connection with any attempt to improve economic conditions is the ability of any society's members to handle machines. In spite of a few humorous examples, as in the often-cited case of the African natives who, when given wheelbarrows to move earth, carried the loaded barrows on their heads, there is abundant evidence that the members of any society can be taught to use mechanical and even scientific techniques. Many of these techniques can be learned without any understanding of the principles involved. They do not even entail surrender of established beliefs in magic. I was in Cairo at the time when model-T Fords were in process of replacing donkeys as the preferred means of transportation. Around the radiator caps of most of the Fords were draped strings of large blue beads. These had previously been worn by donkeys to avert the evil eye, and the native drivers felt that they were equally necessary with the new carrier.

One of the greatest contributors to the diffusion of mechanical skills and technological ability has been the automobile. This contrivance seems to have a fascination for people everywhere. It has penetrated into many out-of-the-way parts of the world, bringing new crafts in its train. Since these frontier regions are where bad cars go when they die, it requires no mean degree of skill to keep them running, and I would back certain Polynesian and Swahili mechanics of my experience against nine-tenths of American garagemen for ingenuity and mechanical know-how.

It is obvious that any individual can learn mechanical skills more readily if his training is begun while he is young. People brought up with machines learn to use them almost unconsciously, while those who do not encounter them until they are adult have more trouble. People reared in societies which have a manipulative tradition also learn mechanical skills more readily than those from societies which are indifferent to good craftsmanship. Most of the unmechanized civilizations do have such a tradition, while it is by no means lacking among "primitive" groups. A friend of mine who had spent many years in the Arctic told me that, if an outboard motor got out of order, he simply found an Eskimo and turned it over to him. The Eskimo might never have seen an outboard motor before, but he would be delighted at the chance to take one to pieces and put it together again. It might take him several days, but, if there was anything broken or out of place, he would be sure to locate it. Similarly, Polynesians have a manipulative culture. In ancient times skilled craftsmen enjoyed great social prestige, and today much of this carries over to the mechanic.

Needless to say, in societies where the technology is crude, or where the social position of the skilled craftsman is low, it takes much longer to diffuse mechanical skills. Nevertheless, it can be done. We have abundant evidence that, as far as intelligence and learning ability are concerned, there is no group in the world which cannot be mechanized.

Unfortunately, industrialization presents another problem even more complicated than that of technical training. If modern machinery is to produce an improvement in economic conditions, it has to be operated by labor which will be on the job even though it is a wonderful day and the fish are biting. It is much easier to train an intelligent man to diagnose and repair an injury to a machine than to get him to spend day after day tightening Nut 36 on an assembly line.

*      *      *      *      *

In summary, every society would like to improve its economic position, and every society is capable of learning to operate the machines and follow the scientific procedures which might lead to such improvement. Let us turn now to the cultural and social factors which may operate to inhibit or retard economic growth.

The first and perhaps most important of these is unrestricted breeding. This is no more and no less natural than other features of human behavior. It is intimately wrapped up with the society's culture, and birth control is infinitely older and more widely distributed than the use of rubber. Where such relatively humane methods of keeping down population are not in use, the balance between societies and their food supply has, until recently, been maintained by periodic famines and plagues. What happens when modern science and charity step in to prevent these can be seen in the case of the Navaho.

When I first visited the Navaho in 1912, there were supposed to be about twenty thousand of them. Exact figures were lacking, since many of those living in the back districts could not be caught to be counted. Today there are over sixty thousand, with no signs of a letdown in the rate of increase. Since there are already enough Navajo to weave all the blankets and herd all the sheep for which white Americans can provide a market, no solution to the problem is in sight. . . .

The problem of how to deal with human fertility is by no means limited to "backward" societies, so let us turn to cultural factors more immediately related to economic growth. Since culture change of any sort is heavily dependent upon individual initiative, the values which are attached in any society to individual industry and to individual accumulation of wealth will become important factors in determining the extent and direction of economic changes. If one goes over the whole range of the world's societies, one can find weird and wonderful patterns of ownership, wealth distribution, goods exchange, and other economic activities. Most have probably heard of the Northwest Coast potlatches, in which a man humbles rivals by destroying his own property or of the amazingly intricate rules governing division of an Australian hunter's kill among his relatives. However, such cultural aberrations have little to do with the great oriental populations which are of paramount importance in the world of today and tomorrow. These groups have civilizations which are actually older than our own in most cases. They are habituated to city life and a mercantile economy even though this economy rests upon an economically depressed peasantry and hand industries. What these people need is mechanical skills and scientific techniques. On other aspects of economic life they are well able to take care of themselves. I have not heard of any suggestion in Washington that, as part of the Point IV program, we should send a delegation to Armenia to teach the natives how to trade.

Fortunately for any plans which we may have for encouraging economic growth, China, Southeast Asia, the Islamic cultures of the Near East, India, and, although these are often ignored, the high native civilizations of West Africa are all thoroughly familiar with trade, credit, banking, and private property. In the Islamic countries in particular, one is struck by the resemblance of these patterns to those of medieval Europe. China also seems familiar to an American in these respects. India avowedly has a different value system from the rest, but anyone who has done business there will recognize that indifference to economic gains is largely limited to ascetics.

In spite of these resemblances there are certain significant differences which can hardly fail to influence both the speed and the direction of economic growth. One of the most important of these is the varying patterns of individual as against communal ownership of land and other natural resources. Ownership always involves a conflict of values—the claims of the individual against those of the group. In the Near East in particular there are areas where the desire to give all families in a village equal economic opportunity results in the redistribution of village land every few years. At this time each family will get an allotment based on its size. A family which has grown from eight to ten will get more land this time than it did at the last division; one which has shrunk from eight to five, less. Whatever the social justice of such a practice, it robs the family of any incentive to improve the land it is working. It is, in effect, a renter from the community with no assurance of tenure.

Closely related to this is the practice, widespread even in some parts of Europe, of subdivision of land through inheritance. At the death of a landowner, his fields are divided as equitably as possible among his sons. Since all his land is not of equal value or usable for the same purposes, the desire to give every heir a fair share results in repeated fragmentation until a man may find himself owner of fifty or sixty tiny plots spread over an area of several square miles. Under such conditions individual ownership and use of modern machinery becomes uneconomic and, in practice, impossible.

To continue with cultural factors effecting possible improvements in agricultural techniques, one of the main initial blocks to improvement is the widespread institution of absentee landlords. The tenants of such landlords are nearly always sharecroppers rather than renters, and the oriental landlord really shares. The tenant usually pays anywhere from a quarter to a half or more of his crop each year for the privilege of remaining on the land. Under such circumstances it is hard to persuade him to expend the extra labor required to install modern methods while he lacks the capital needed for fertilizer and modern tools. Only fundamental changes in the system of land tenure will make modern agricultural methods possible in most of the unmechanized civilizations.

Ownership of natural resources other than land, especially minerals, may also stand in the way of economic development. Government ownership is a long-established pattern in most of the civilizations under discussion. Mining claims are leased but never owned outright by the operators. In many cases the countries in question have not enough capital to modernize mining operations or the trained personnel required for this. At the same time, if they bring in foreign capital and experts, demagogues will immediately raise the cry that that party in power is selling the nation's birthright. The current difficulties over Iranian oil would be a case in point.

Another series of factors influencing economic growth are directly connected with social structure. One of the most important of these is the extent and nature of kin claims and the extent of the kin group. In all the unmechanized civilizations such groups are much more extensive and functionally much more important than they are among ourselves. In China and India, in particular, the ideal family is the "joint family." This is a technical term used to refer to a family which functions as a corporation and survives generation after generation without division of the family property. Members of such a family who do not live in the common establishment are expected to contribute part of their income to the family funds. In return, all members of the family are entitled to support and care in case of old age or disability.

Where the family structure is of this sort, economic improvement presents certain specific problems, while changes in the established economic system are unusually disruptive socially. Joint families function under the direction of the oldest living male, unless he is obviously senile, in which case the next oldest takes over. Their reactions thus tend to be highly conservative. Moreover, kin claims within the joint family are so strong that in the establishment of a new commercial or manufacturing enterprise they have to be given precedence over actual ability. All relatives have to be taken care of before outsiders can be employed in other than menial positions. This situation plagued the Imperial Chinese government, which recognized the inevitability of nepotism in administrative offices and did what it could to counter it by appointing administrators to provinces as far as possible from those in which their joint families lived. In recent times the Japanese have been able to work out a fairly effective adjustment between joint family claims and business efficiency. The families controlling large enterprises marry daughters to their most promising employees, who then take the family name. However, this method will not work everywhere. Even in Japan able young men are reluctant to become adoptive husbands, since it means separation from one's own family group and little control over one's wife.

On the other side of the picture, economic change is always destructive to a joint family system. This can be seen even in Europe, where the early Roman and Germanic families were not unlike the oriental joint families. Such families broke down under the impact of developing mercantilism with its increase in individual opportunity, while their complete destruction came with the rise of modern mechanized civilization. Here in the United States we have reached the low point in a process of breakdown of kin structure which has reduced our functional kin group to the primary, biologically determined one of parents and children. However, now that most skilled trades are becoming hereditary through union policy, and influence is becoming increasingly important for getting a start in a profession, we may expect a recognition of more extended kin ties and an increased persistence of family groups. It may be doubted whether the joint family pattern will re-establish itself as long as its usual function of providing social security is taken care of by government agencies and its other once important function of keeping working capital intact is invalidated by taxes and inflation.

It can be stated as a theorem, valid in a very high percentage of cases, that the greater the opportunities for individual economic profit provided by any social-cultural situation, the weaker the ties of extended kinship will become. Modernization of the unmechanized cultures, with their unexampled opportunities for individuals with intelligence and initiative, cannot fail to weaken or even destroy joint family patterns. This in turn will entail a whole series of problems for the societies in question. They must develop new mechanisms to provide for the economic and psychological needs now taken care of by family organization.

Social values connected with class structure may also have a profound effect on economic change. While the members of any group can learn to use machines, there are great differences in their eagerness to learn. Societies and even the members of different classes within a society may differ profoundly in their attitudes toward trade and work. In most of the unmechanized civilizations, including those of our own not very remote ancestors, the upper classes derived their wealth from either (1) owner-ship of land and exploitation of the peasants on it or (2) pre-emption of governmental posts and the consequent profits from salary and "squeeze." Most civilizations employ both sources of wealth, but owner-ship of land is, generally speaking, more important in Europe and gov-ernment office more important in Asia, especially China. It is a curious and rarely recognized survival of this old culture pattern which makes western Europe and the United States the only places in the world where an honest and able man has to accept serious financial loss if he works for the government. Outside these regions the men who hold government office are the ones who get the largest incomes. Their salaries are huge in comparison with the earnings of craftsmen or even merchants and are supplemented by recognized and regulated graft.

Whatever the basis of wealth and power, one finds that in all the un-mechanized civilizations the trader and the mechanic rank far down in the social scale. The farmer, while actually the worst exploited of all, is usually accorded a somewhat higher position socially, especially if he is a landowner. As a result, attempts at economic improvement are caught on the horns of a dilemma. Foreign experts sent in to implement such programs immediately arouse hostility and suspicion, but there are not enough native experts and little chance to train them. The upper classes, who are the only ones who can afford to give their sons a foreign educa-tion, prefer to have them trained in white-collar occupations, preferably law. Even when they do go into such fields as engineering, they prefer theory to practice and feel that any sort of manual work, even as a part of training, is socially degrading.

It may be added that members of the upper classes who are uncon-ventional enough to take technical subjects in Western universities very often show a strong disinclination to return to their own countries when their training is complete. The type of mind which makes such aristocrats critical of the social values of their own civilizations seems to predispose them to appreciate the creature comforts of the West. Very much the same reluctance to return will be found among the students who have gone abroad for study under government scholarships or missionary auspices. Although this situation will no doubt be overcome eventually, lack of trained native personnel will continue to be one of the serious problems for some time to come.

# Margaret Mead

---

## From the Stone Age to the Twentieth Century

. . . WHAT CAN WE LEARN from this single historical experiment, this one detailed account of how a handful of people on an isolated South Sea island entered our modern world, and about their efforts to stay here, and our efforts to keep them here? Before attempting to draw conclusions, it is perhaps necessary again to consider to what extent their experience can be generalized—for the people of undeveloped countries, for the mid-twentieth century, for mankind. Because one people have shown, under very special and quite unrepeatable conditions, a capacity to learn very rapidly, does this change our ideas about how rapidly other peoples can learn? To what extent can this unique little experiment be shrugged off with the statement that one swallow doesn't make a summer, that all over the world we have examples of people who are less developed technically, politically, socially, religiously, than others, and who, far from coming enthusiastically into the modern world, resist and withdraw, sabotage machinery, boycott schools, or put coal in bathtubs, retreat into ideas of witchcraft or sorcery or cheaply attained apocalyptic solutions, or deteriorate into forms of criminal sub-humanity? Isn't "civilization" something that it takes a very, very long time to learn, perhaps many, many generations?

This question is the more important because of the special contribution that anthropological studies have made to our conceptions of change, of how fast and in what ways people could change, and what the ethic of changing people should be. For the first four decades of the twentieth century, anthropologists were concerned with demonstrating a series of propositions which had not, for some time, been regarded as to any degree self-evident: that the human race was one, and that the various "races" of mankind were specializations without any measurable differences in their capacity as groups of individuals to take on any civilization; that each people has a shared, learned way of life—a "culture"—of its own, within which dignity is accorded the individual, and continuity provided for the group, and that this "culture" should be respected in the same way that individual human beings should each be respected; and, finally, that, although the behaviour which differentiated an Eskimo from a Frenchman, a Hottentot from an Englishman, a Burmese from an American, was learned, the circumstance that it was learned and not inborn did not mean that, once learned, there were not very great differences between the members of these different societies.

\*　　\*　　\*　　\*　　\*

Even after World War II, when the non-industrialized peoples of the world began clamouring for the blessings of the modern world, machine technology, universal literacy, medicine, the clamour was all too often seen as inevitable but regrettable, an unfortunate by-product of European contact which had made people discontented with their own way of life, or as the necessary answer to Communist propaganda. It was recognized that with the Communists promising the delights of progress to the villagers of the world, it would be necessary for us to accede to their requests for this same progress, to go in and help induce technological change.

And now our old sense that all change was one-sided and came from a misuse of power suffered a new transformation. All change was now seen as terribly difficult and against the real will of the people, who only thought they wanted tractors because these were symbols of Western superiority but who really hated regular hours, clocks, machines, hospitals, the dictates of nutritionists, sitting still in school, and learning to think in realistic Western terms. So the anthropologist on the technical assistance team tended to remain, in most cases, an expert on difficulties, who, while he insisted on taking the culture into account, also insisted that change must be slow, cautious, tentative, if resistances were not to be aroused, if social and personal disorganization was not to result. However much it had become clear that change was now inevitable, that it would be rapid, that we must have as our goal the making of some members of every culture world-mobile in one generation, we were still trapped in a one-sided picture that something was being done to people, and that by insisting on working as slowly as possible, and through their own cultural values, we were protecting and cherishing them. So one important contribution of this record of change among the Manus is that it points up the completeness with which a people may want to change rather than merely submit to being changed; it shows culture contact as an active choice of the emigrants from the Stone Age as it is for the representatives of highly industrialized countries, and it points up the "resistance" to giving in the members of the more developed "culture" as well as the resistance to receiving in the members of the "under-developed culture."

How often has our Western attempt to preserve native dress, old customs, different styles of architecture, to respect native laws and customs, been only a thin disguise over an unwillingness to admit a people, newly entering into our way of life, to a full participation in the culture which we claim to value so highly? Yes, we want them to go to school; "education" is a beautiful thing, but we don't want too many of them to become aspiring white-collar workers; we want them—peoples of other countries, or of racial, ethnic, and economic enclaves in our own countries—to improve their standards of living, have better nutrition and running water, to be clean—but not to dance at our dances, join our clubs, or hold the offices of greatest sacredness and prestige in our societies.

Whether it is the white official saying of the New Guinea native, "It's such a mistake for them to wear trousers in this climate, you know; *laplaps* are much cooler, cheaper, and more practical, and so much healthier," or the commentator who regrets the disappearance of the lovely blue of traditional Chinese dress, or the old abbot, who after seventy-five years of presenting a picture of life of high religious abstinence into which no Australian native was considered fit to be inducted, remarks, "They just don't want to take our more complex ethical standards; their minds aren't able to deal with them. Generation after generation we educate the children here, the sisters teach them good habits, and then—they go back to the bush to live as their parents lived," each in his way is refusing to share the whole pattern, however willing he is to give bits of it. Resistance in the grudging and selective giver turns out to be as important as resistance in the grudging and selective receiver.

Once this is recognized, it is possible for us to scrutinize with newly opened eyes each situation in the world where people of a different sex or race, class or culture, seem to fail to accept or to use the opportunities which are offered them, to become "like" the members of another class or race or culture. Many different kinds of failure and refusal become intelligible—of girls to learn physics, of bright-eyed little African children who learn so quickly as small children and turn apathetic and disinterested at puberty, of new immigrants in model housing developments who don't "appreciate" their excellent plumbing, of the contrast between the adjustment of Negro boys and their sisters when both are asked to meet the middle-class standards of a high school in a small Pennsylvania town, of the restlessness and refusal of regular employment by modern Maoris in New Zealand or by American Indian immigrants to the big cities. The situation in which children are taught by individuals whose full status—as men, or members of an excluding race, or nuns, or persons free to travel—they cannot hope to attain makes the goals held up to the pupils seem not to be the wonderful opportunities which they are so often represented to be. So bright girls strangely have no "ambition," and children of discriminated-against minorities turn "dull" at adolescence, not because of intrinsic incapacity, but because the desire to learn is blocked by the knowledge that part of the pattern to which they aspire will be denied them.

Furthermore, as part of the pattern is denied—as for instance specially selected individuals from Africa or Asia are sent to school in the West and offered full "academic" but no "social" participation—the terms in which the participation is denied—physical self-identification as a "mere woman" or a Negro, or a national identification as an Indonesian or a Thai, religious identification as a member of a different creed, class identification as a member of "the masses" or "the proletariat"—are strengthened and intensified and become heavily loaded with both positive and negative feeling. The sex or race, nation, religious or class membership, overstressed and omnipresent, determines the lines of identification, so that individual children will quickly learn that they can only do what a woman, a Negro, the foreign born, a Jew, or an unskilled dock worker can do. Each such limitation of natural gift and aspiration carries with it a kind of constriction, a denial of the self, which, if once relaxed, provides channels through which great energy can be mobilized and released. So we find that the first groups of women who are admitted to some male occupation perform astonishingly well, learn faster than the norm for men, while women who enter the same occupation after it has been defined as something done by men and women will show no such conspicuous superiority. Throwing off colonial yokes which have included definition as second-class human beings has the same releasing effect on members of former colonial states.

The movements which spread from people to people—the good news that is shouted from housetop to housetop until whole sections of the people of the earth become one in religion or political philosophy—characteristically rest on a reaffirmation that all men are brothers. Those peoples who deny such brotherhood to men are characteristically members of shrinking, partial, or limited societies, without the expansionist zeal of those who greet all men everywhere as potential converts or comrades or partners, because all are members of the human race.

"All men are brothers," say the Manus, "black, white, green, red men, all are brothers." The addition of the words *red* and *green* adds an extra blaze of glory to the statement which ennobles each of them in his own eyes as he makes it. All men are brothers, not only the black and white men who are known to exist, but the green and red men who somewhere, somehow, might exist—all are brothers.

A second contribution of the Manus experience is the suggestion that rapid change is not only possible, but may actually be very desirable, that instead of advocating slow partial changes, we should advocate that a people who choose to practise a new technology or enter into drastically new kinds of economic relationships will do this more easily if they live in different houses, wear different clothes, and eat different, or differently cooked, food. Looked at from this point of view, the speed with which European immigrants adapted to American life will be seen not only as due to some problematical factor of selection through which all those who were willing to emigrate had more energy and flexibility and capacity to change than those who remained at home, but also to the transforming experience of entering a world where everything was different, to which one brought only the clothes in which one stood and which were easy to discard.

There was no old house style to remind one that the old social relationships no longer held. Instead, a different kind of house, lived in by those who practised the different kind of relationship, was ready to support the change. Children who came home from school to insist that a good American breakfast contained orange juice and cereal stormed up American steps and banged American doors; children, become far more active and free in the American environment, jumped on American sofas —if the springs were damaged there was at least no physical reminder of three generations of ancestors who had never jumped on any sofa as children. Unfamiliar foods were cooked on a new kind of stove, and served in a new kind of dish, whose pattern and design evoked no nostalgia for the old. Each detail of the new life supported each other detail. Peasants, unused to depending on an urban money economy, did not have to learn new attitudes toward the old money, which had been buried in the garden or hidden in old socks, but instead were confronted with a quite different-looking money, with different values, different shapes and sizes and names.

Partial change—installing new kinds of office furniture in out-of-date reconverted dwelling houses, turning carriage houses into garages, putting the engine of a car where the horse once stood—can be seen not as a bridge between old and new, something that permits men, slow to learn and fumbling at the unfamiliar, some respite from the unbearableness of change, but rather as the condition within which discordant and discrepant institutions and practices develop and proliferate—with corresponding discrepancies and discordancies in the lives of those who live within them. The alternative to the culture which has existed so long and changed so slowly that every item of behaviour is part of a pattern so perfect that it seems as if it must have sprung complete from the head of Jove, is seen to be not the culture in which necessary and wanted change is artificially slowed down and retarded but rather the culture in which—if there is to be purposeful change, by an Ataturk, an enterprising Maharajah, or the agricultural extension department—the whole pattern is transformed at once, with as little reminder of the past as possible to slow down the new learning, or make that learning incomplete and maladaptive.

As an analogy we may consider the new trends in the treatment of certain kinds of sprains, in which the injured foot is injected with a local anesthetic so that the foot may be walked on at once, because walking is actually beneficial, and the adjustments to the pain were the elements which did the harm and the reason why rest had to be pre-scribed, or the new post-operative treatment which gets the patient out of bed at once before crippling maladaptation can develop in response to the operation. In the same way, attempts to deal with some drastic altera-tion in a culture—to substitute wage labour for subsistence farming, assembly-line manufacture for handicrafts, democratic voting procedures for feudal rule, land ownership for sharecropping, non-segregation among castes for a former rigid segregation—may well work best if they are accompanied by as many other congruent changes as possible.

Just as the survival of some parts of an old pattern tends to reinstate the rest, and so continually acts as a drag on the establishment of new habits, so also the establishment of part of a new pattern calls for other congruent elements, facilitates their establishment, and each element sup-ports the other. Let us consider the simple matter of the introduction of cloth or clothing among a people who have only worn G-strings or grass skirts. If cloth is introduced without soap, habits of handling cloth may grow up in which the infection rate rises; but if cloth and soap are intro-duced together, a pattern of sanitation can be established immediately. If fashioned clothes are introduced without sewing skills, a style of rags and tatters may be set up, simply because the art of mending, a by-product of sewing, is missing. But if the sewing machine is introduced with the ready made clothes, this can be avoided.

Similarly, the acquisition of tailored cotton clothes without starch or irons means the possible establishment of a style of dress which will be greeted with ridicule by the very people—the Western model-setters—from whom it was meant to elicit a recognition of the human worth of the new wearers. The possession of clothing means that the clothing has to be stored. If new styles of housing with closet space are designed, it is possible to prevent the stage in which pieces of string are stretched across a house, once kept neat as a pin when only grass skirts had to be hung, tightly rolled, from the rafters. And with the introduction of clothing comes the need for some kind of handkerchief, for the old methods of nose-wiping accord poorly with the use of cotton cloth. If cloth is worn, and washed and starched, then sitting on a floor on which people walk either barefoot or in shoes becomes unfeasible, and it is necessary either to have furniture on which people can sit or new habits of taking off or changing footwear at the door.

The regularity with which most peoples who change from a life of highly traditional handicraft to one of dependence on the purchase of European-manufactured objects become slum dwellers, can be explained by the number and type of discrepant changes—in which wash basins become food bowls, objects are introduced without appropriate ways of keeping them clean or storing them. Each misuse breeds a new form of abuse, the whole in turn evoking contempt and ridicule as the aspirants toward a new way of life sink instead into one far lower than that from which they came.

As in such a concrete matter as clothing, so at every level the same rule may be seen to apply. Practically, this means that whenever a people wish to take over some invention or discovery or practice of another people, the real alternatives should be seen as between taking over the new idea in the most abstract form possible, so that it may be incorporated within the old pattern with a minimum of change, or else taking over as much of the culture in which the new idea is imbedded as possible.

The spread of the science of nutrition provides a good example here. If another people whose food and ways of cooking and eating are completely different from our own, who through all the centuries of their ancestral life have only considered food within a set of ideas quite different from those of the modern nutritionists, wish to learn to feed themselves and their children better, how can they most painlessly learn what we know? There seem to be two answers. Some of them can become highly trained nutritionists, able to analyze foods into their constituents and able to study the human beings who eat those foods and show where their diet is deficient. Then, armed with the knowledge of how to measure calories, assay proteins, spot vitamin deficiencies, they can readjust the food patterns of their traditional culture so that the missing ingredients are preserved or provided. This may have to be done by making a brew of pine needles or a jam of rose haws to provide the vitamin C which we get from oranges, or by feeding infants the water in which vegetables are cooked in place of cow's milk. If the adjustment is to be done this way, it is very important that none of our special ideas about kinds of food, number of meals, ways of cooking, should be included in the training which the young nutritionist from Japan or Burma receives. Otherwise, the mixture of a few of our ideas—like the sacredness of three meals a day, or the insistence that cow's milk is the only proper substitute for mother's milk—may confuse the picture disastrously. They should have only the purest and most abstract principles, and then be left alone to work within their own way of life with their own kinds of food, their charcoal fires or clay pots, to develop their own way of meeting the aspiration which they now share with us—a self-conscious application of the principles of nutrition to the problem of keeping their people alive and well.

The other alternative is to share as much of our pattern as possible. While the old civilizations of the world with ancient institutions of markets, banking, credit, and government may have a pattern within which they can take the new principles of medicine and nutrition and industrialism and develop their own style within the coherencies of their old way of life—as, for example, Japan did to a great extent—the more primitive peoples do not have such a pattern on which to build. Once the buffalo is destroyed, the once open plains enclosed, the spear and bow and arrow rendered useless, or, on the other hand, any need for real relationship with high civilizations develops, the very primitive and some of the simplest peasant peoples of the world have to change. Neither their clothes nor their manners, their economic ideas nor their political habits, fit them to live in the modern world as they are. It is then up to those societies which already have invented ways of living with these modern inventions to share their patterns in entirety with the peoples who wish to have them.

So this study of the Manus suggests the great importance of whole patterns, that it is easier to shift from being a South Sea Islander to being a New Yorker—as I have seen Samoans do—than to shift from being a perfectly adjusted traditional South Sea Islander to a partly civilized, partly acculturated South Sea Islander, who has been given antiquated versions of our philosophy and politics, a few odds and ends of clothing and furniture, and bits and pieces of our economics. I used to marvel at an individual Samoan, accustomed at home to go about barefoot, clad (except on Sundays) in a loincloth, and to sit cross-legged on the ground, who would turn up in my office perfectly and comfortably dressed in Western clothes, speaking English with grace and style. Without fully realizing the importance of changing from one whole pattern to another whole pattern, I used to attribute the Samoans' successful adjustment to their sense of style and to some particular security in their character. These are indeed there, but making a total shift seems now to be even more important. The same sense of style, which made Samoans refuse to speak *broken* English and insist on their few words of English being perfect, guided them in handling this total shift.

If we realize that each human culture, like each language, is a whole, capable of accommodating within it the wide varieties of human temperament, and that learning another culture is like learning a second language, or a third or fourth, then we can see that if individuals or groups of people have to change—leave their island homes, their mountain valleys, their remote fishermen's coves, give up their shell money, their old joint families, their hand nets, change because they wish to share, and to have their children share, in the benefits the great civilizations have made possible for mankind—then it is most important that they should change from one whole pattern to another, not merely patch and botch the old way of life with corrugated iron or discarded tin cans, in political peonage in the great cities of the world. While it is dreadfully difficult to graft one foreign habit on a set of old habits, it is much easier and highly exhilarating to learn a whole new set of habits, each reinforcing the other as one moves—like a practised dancer learning a completely new dance—more human even than one was before, because one has been able to do one more complicated human thing, learn something completely new.

But is this not a lonely path, to leave behind all the familiar sounds and sights, tastes and smells of childhood, and proceed alone, however perfectly, into another world? Here another suggestion from the Manus experiment comes in. For the people of Peri are not lonely or disoriented. They remember their past; their only poor memory is for the period of the nineteen-thirties when they were sharing little bits and pieces of Christian civilization, a little literacy with nothing to read, reading without arithmetic, Christian valuation of human life but no modern preventive medicine to keep it going, money but no economic system which made money function efficiently, aspirations to be civilized which were blocked by the fact that the white men they met both refused to treat them as equals, as human beings, and to believe that they were capable of sharing in the white men's superior civilization. But once they had taken their own modernization in their own hands, redesigned their culture from top to bottom, asserted their full dignity as modern Manus, the continuity with their personalities as they had been developed in the past was not broken, nor were their relationships with each other destroyed.

For here we have another part of the secret of felicitous change. The people of Peri all changed together as a unit—parents, grandparents, and children—so that the old mesh of human relations could be rewoven into a new pattern from which no thread was missing. As living individuals remembering their old ways and their old relationships, they could move into a new kind of village, live in new kinds of houses, participate in a new form of democracy, with no man's hand against another, no child alienated from the self or from the others.

It cannot be claimed, of course, that because a whole village or many villages act together as a group they will necessarily act progressively. We have ample evidence from groups like the Amish and the Hutterites that a radically new system, once established as a whole pattern among a group of related families who then live as closed communities, may be able to resist any further changes, may become indeed a fortress against the introduction of any new ideas, far more strongly walled than communities which have undergone no such radical initial alteration. The effort that goes into consolidating a change, combined with the reinforcement which is given each member of the family, each family in the group, because all move in step, may prove to be such a powerful condition of conservatism that it may well be too expensive for the world to encourage. While the mental health of each member of an isolated Hutterite community or a kibbutz may be protected by this strong group spirit, the protection given may be of a sort that disqualifies the individual member of the community from participating in other societies, and that keeps the group in an archaic or static state of adjustment, dependent after a time on a defensive attitude toward the rest of the world.

\*     \*     \*     \*     \*

This Manus record is presented as the material which the research scientist owes to the society of which he is a member, carefully collected materials on which considered decisions may be based. It is the story of a handful of men who twenty-five years ago seemed destined to live a life of anonymity and lack of wide significance. A series of historical accidents has transformed them—as any small group of individuals may be transformed within our reverberating world—into a group with world significance.

The Manus experiment itself is unique. The Manus were a people most favourably inclined toward change, conscious that cultural forms differed and could be changed, infused by their upbringing with an aspiration congruent with the more universal and humane forms of Western democracy, with the rare accident of a very gifted leader, and the unique experience of having a million men, members of a modern society intent on their own affairs, enact a large part of the pattern of Western democracy before their eyes. Whether they themselves survive, whether this unique attempt to move thousands of years in twenty-five is doomed, depends on that fantastic interlocking of world events which makes the existence of any individual who ties his identity to anything less than the human race hazardous in the extreme. The Manus have entered the modern world. As Manus, their humanity is dependent upon the preservation, in some sort of identified wholeness, of the small communities which they have built. In this respect they do not yet belong, nor do most members of the human race, to the age of the air, when the world becomes one great highway, and in any inn along the way there must be room and welcome for each and every guest.

## J. L. Sadie

# The Social Anthropology of Economic Underdevelopment

IN THIS PAPER evidence is submitted to support the thesis—which has evidently been gathering force during the past few years—that the economic condition of the underdeveloped community is fundamentally a function of its social-cultural customs and institutions, in consequence of which the generation of economic development of a people by themselves[1] is neither more nor less than a socio-psychological process. This represents a "venture into the preserves of other social scientists" as Belshaw puts it,[2] but it is a venture which economists can ill afford not to undertake.

Although our conclusions are based on a study of a specific African people in the southern part of the continent, it is believed that their validity is not thus restricted.

## THE PEOPLE AND THEIR ECONOMY

The underdeveloped people in question are South African Bantu, approximately 4,500,000 in number, scattered over 58,000 square miles of territory, called Bantu Areas, which adjoin the areas constituting the developed sector of the South African economy. Nowhere in the Bantu territories do the concentrations of population assume the proportions or the character of a town in the customary sense of the word. The natural rate of population growth, at 1.6 per cent per annum, is the result of a

---

1. The qualification "by themselves" is necessary, since it is conceivable that an underdeveloped people could be developed by means of factors of production from developed economies.

2. Belshaw, *Population Growth and Levels of Consumption* (Allen and Unwin), 1956, p. viii.

high fertility rate, limited to some extent by the observance of the traditional custom of spacing, and a fairly high rate of mortality. The growth of their numbers is not prescribed by the ability of their economy to accommodate an increased population, since the adjacent developed sector takes care of the overflow.

For all practical purposes they can be described as an exclusively agrarian people. Ninety-two per cent have a stake in the land, which, compared to that of the developed sector, is mostly of a good quality and has for the greatest part the benefit of very favourable climatological conditions. By the standards of the surrounding developed areas this land could yield at a minimum £90 million worth of agricultural production per annum. In actual fact the value of the annual production varies around £13 million,[3] and has shown, until quite recently, no increase since the time the first statistics have become available. As the subsistence farming does not provide adequate sustenance for the population, their income is supplemented by wages earned during intermittent spells of work in the developed sector. These and other contacts with a developed economy have had some effects on the life of the African communities which will be described at a later stage. Thus far they have, however, made little impression on the traditional social and cultural habit patterns which inhibit economic progress.

## THE TRADITIONAL SETTING

The tribe, which is based on a nucleus of families descended from a common ancestor(s) (as the result, among some tribes, of fairly rigid marriage rules calculated to strengthen mutual ties) and which has a chief as its binding force, is the social unit. Since chieftainship is an inherited status, the chief is often not endowed with the attributes of a leader. The mental horizon of the people is limited by their allegiance and loyalties, which extend no further than the tribe, and is directed towards the smaller family group in the first instance. The latter forms the economic unit, which is self-contained. Intra-tribal trade is negligible; inter-tribal trade is non-existent. No indigenous medium of exchange had been developed, since there was no need for it. Theirs is the well-known subsistence economy.

Their agriculture has evolved in circumstances in which no store was

---

3. This is in terms of conventional calculation. When the calculation is in terms of the amount of products consumed, which include certain plants, roots, small animals, etc., found in the fields, and the meat of cattle and other animals which died, the figure can be put at approximately £30 million.

set by the long-run fertility of the soil because movement to new territory was always possible, and in which the male adult occupied himself with hunting and warfare. Thus the cultivation of the soil became primarily the responsibility of the mother of the family, assisted to some extent by her children. Assistance by the husband is an exception. He and his sons tend the cattle, sheep and goats. It is not good form for the man to "burrow" in the soil. The effect of this custom on agricultural productivity must be obvious.

The success of a crop is promoted by means of ceremonial rituals in which the aid of magic is invoked. The seed may be specially treated by the chief, who may also determine the time of planting and sowing in accordance with the witch doctor's reading of the constellations. Rituals are performed to ensure adequate rain, and certain taboos are to be observed to prevent failures or catastrophes. Thus the manipulation of supernatural forces in the interest of the cultivator takes the place of methods which harness the forces of nature to increase productivity. Instead of using manure as a fertiliser, it is dried and used as fuel. Once again the consequences are obvious.

Stock-breeding, in which cattle predominate, is a way of life: its economic functions are completely overshadowed by its social significance. To each person, while still young, is assigned a specific steer, whose praises will be sung in songs dedicated to it and which may be sacrificed when the person to whom it has been assigned falls seriously ill, or as a means of keeping on good terms with the ancestral spirits. "The God with the wet nose" it is called in one eulogy. Cattle are very seldom slaughtered for consumption in the ordinary course of events. That is mostly reserved for ceremonial and ritual purposes. In so far as the population does consume a fair amount of meat, it is because the carcasses of domestic animals which have died are not wasted, unless such animals constitute the totem of the tribe. The number of cattle determines the status and dignity of the owner, since it allows him to dispense hospitality and generosity, to repair strained relations and to generate good relations among the living and between the living and the dead, and to procure wives. Cattle are the traditional media for the payment of "lobolo," *i.e.,* the goods to be handed over by the family of the bridegroom to the family of the bride when a marriage is contracted. The more cattle in a person's possession, the more wives he can afford.

In these circumstances it is the quantity of animals that is important, not the quality. For all the functions decimated animals will be as appropriate as any other. Scrub cattle, overstocking, denudation of the veld and soil erosion are the inevitable outcome. Capital formation through a process of increments in the value of the stock is obviated.

As an integral part of their culture, many habits and customs are calculated to promote the propagation of children. Although most marriages are monogamous, it is partly so because the majority do not have the necessary "lobolo" at their disposal to enter into polygamous unions which are the accepted system. The consummation of the marriage is in the procreation of children; girls are the means whereby the family increases its stock of cattle when they are old enough to marry. Procreation is the fundamental condition attached to marriage. Large families are regarded as good performance. Its realisation is promoted by the system of "lobolo." If the bride is barren, or dies young without issue, a sister or younger relative may in some tribes be supplied to make good the deficiency. A widow may be assigned to a younger brother of her deceased husband so that she can propagate children for the deceased. Apart from the economic effects arising from the size, growth and composition of the population, these customs make for limited interests, diverting the attention and endeavour from the pursuit of other, including economic, ends.

In their religion these Bantu communities are ancestor-worshippers. The ancestors act as the mediators between human beings and the Supreme Being (God), who has the power of life and death and brings prosperity to, or visits catastrophes upon, human beings, and must be accorded the necessary offerings to prevent their anger. This religion is anti-rationalistic; it is antipathetic towards a spirit of inquiry and demands only conformism. It is not a stimulus to a higher level of material well-being. The *summum bonum* is the honouring of the traditional usages and beliefs. Their own system of education, which amounts to the instruction in age-old customs, mores and institutions, ensures the transmission of traditions from one generation to the next and the perpetuation of the inherently conservative culture.

In sharp contrast with the individualism which characterises all or most Western peoples, and which has been an outstanding factor in their economic development, the tribal people form organic and integrated societies with a strong community-consciousness, and in which the rights and obligations of the individual are well defined and adhered to. Mutual ties, interdependence and responsibility are established by the system of consanguinity, worshipping of the same ancestors, the possession of the same totems, the system of land tenure and other institutions. Social care is the responsibility of each and all, extending from the family through the household and the family group to the whole tribe. There are no special institutions to cater for the poor, the hungry, the sick, the disabled and the aged. They are cared for by the more privileged. Thus the community guarantees the security of the individual. Mutual aid is extended on numerous occasions, such as the harvesting of crops, the building of huts, weeding, etc. A person may lend-lease part of his wealth to a less-privileged neighbour to enable him to make a better living. Food, housing accommodation and other living arrangements will always be shared with the most distant of relations, even if the latter are strong and healthy and able to fend for themselves but do not feel inclined to do so.

Community-centredness and the absence of individualism are nowhere more strongly reflected than in their economic system. Land is communal property, administered by the chief or headman. For each wife the husband is granted a piece of land for the growing of crops, and each has the right to graze his cattle, sheep, goats or other animals on the commonage. They prosper together and they go hungry together.

However commendable the social security which arises from this type of socio-economic organisation, it is inimical to economic development. It obviates, or greatly diminishes, the necessity for continued personal exertion. Social care and mutual aid coupled with a low standard of living mean that the disappearance of a source of income, or of personal earnings, does not have the significance for the individual it would have in an individualistic culture. Friends and relations can be relied on to come to the rescue or shoulder the extra burden. The progressive individual can never be sure that he will be able to enjoy in full the fruits of his own exertions. If some were to cultivate their piece of land better than the others the increase in the crops would be shared by others; if they improve their land the improvements do not become a negotiable commercial asset. Communal grazing severely limits the possibilities of scientific husbandry by individuals.

A philosophy of life which sets little store by an abundance of material things fits into this social setting. Their needs are relatively few. There is no strong urge to attain ever-increasing standards of material welfare. They do not have the acquisitive instinct. An increased standard of living is preferably realised in the form of greater leisure. Although the backward-sloping supply curve of effort is not unique to the tribal Bantu, the backward movement starts at a fairly early stage because of the limited and inelastic demand for income. The equivalence of marginal utility of income and the marginal disutility of effort is reached very soon. Nourishment that can be obtained from wild fruit and roots in the fields need not be earned in other ways. There seems to be at the back of his mind some doubt about the necessity and sense of all the urgency, striving, efficiency and high-speed activity of modern industrial life. Work for its own sake is not part of this scheme of things. We have here all types of under-employment imaginable: visible, disguised and potential, and most of it voluntary.

There are in this society no distinctive social classes stratified according to income. In the result a factor is missing which could have acted as an incentive to economic advancement as a means toward social advancement.

A characteristic which more than anything else distinguishes the tribal people from technologically developed communities is the absence of a regard for, and concern about, the future. "The lobotomised personality" —in the phraseology of the psychologists—would not be an inappropriate term in this connection. The future as a concept which elicits action is not part of their culture. The "sufficient unto the day" approach does not make for an inclination to accumulate for the sake of sustaining life at some future time. It is not an unknown phenomenon that good crops in one season may lead to the abstention from ploughing and sowing during the next. This has serious implications for capital formation: there is no, or little, purposeful accumulation of capital. More than that, it means that capital goods put at their disposal are not maintained but allowed to fall into disrepair, without being used as the basis for further capital formation. Maintenance of the fertility of the soil for future production is not a consideration.

In the search for a meaningful definition of the term "underdeveloped community," the above characteristic could be used as a strategic explanatory factor.

In the light of the above and with peace and quiet—except when interrupted by faction fights—representing the dominant note of tribal life, it is not surprising that psychologists find them lacking in self-assertiveness, self-confidence and initiative, and in ability to organise, to plan a course of action and to put plans into action. Understandable too is the deficiency in their psychomotor attributes, which may be in the receptor mechanism—the organising process dealing with the incoming data—and/or in the motor or effector mechanism—which translates perception or assimilation into muscular movements. In the absence of daily contact and acquaintance with the devices of technological civilisation, the actions and experience which can attune the psychomotor mechanism to the requirements of industrial development are lacking. The realisation of their innate intellectual capacities, which are no doubt on a par with those of other peoples, is inhibited by the totality of environmental influences.

## THE TRANSITION

Change-inducing factors have been introduced into tribal life as a result of contact with the developed sector and its technological culture. The contact is established, directly, through the periodic temporary emigration of men to industrial towns and cities in the surrounding area, and, indirectly, through the missionaries, traders, civil servants, teachers and development personnel who endeavour to transmit the ideas, knowledge and procedures of the technological civilisation to the people. Of the two channels of contact the former appears to have been, outwardly at least, the more potent. Periodically subjected to the individualistic, rationalistic urban culture, they return to their homelands to find the traditional ties and mores irksome. Their protest is in the first instance directed against parental and tribal authority, either because they have come to dislike authority *per se* or because they consider the persons concerned as too orthodox. Some leave the tribal areas permanently; others retain their domicile, and for them the migratory labour system becomes part of a way of life until the "retiring" age—just after forty—has been reached. In the long run this contact, reinforced by the presence and endeavours of representatives of the developed sector, has an influence which extends over a broader front. But the effects have not been so radical or fundamental as to reach down to the roots of economic under-development.

The development personnel who have been trying to change the economic habits of the people have had a hard and uphill struggle, and their success has been slow in coming. The all-pervading social climate remains a powerful counter-force. Grafting new economic habits on to traditional tribal culture does not lead to abundant growth, where the indigenous underdeveloped agricultural entrepreneur is to be harnessed as the leader in economic change.

The most marked changes induced by the contact with the developed sector have been in outward appearances of an imitative character. Clothing habits, consumption patterns and housing styles have changed to a considerable extent; technologically more advanced implements are being used in the home and on the lands. These are the most conspicuous elements in the technological culture; they can be visually appreciated and are therefore most easily adopted. The new needs which have evolved in this way spelled the end of the self-sufficiency of their economy. The amount of trading has increased. Much of it is still barter trade, but money as a medium of exchange and as a store of value is growing in importance, and the money sector of the economy is gradually expanding. A class of tradesmen emerged which grew in size as the policy of protection of the "infant entrepreneur" took effect and the entry of general dealers from the developed sector was limited or prohibited. By ordinary standards this new class is not very successful as yet, hampered as they are by the lack of experience and know-how. But as a means of initiating change it is a most useful agency, inasmuch as some members of the underdeveloped people assume the strategic role, however inadequately, of entrepreneur outside the traditional agriculture industry, and help to increase the size of the market sector and to transform the subsistence economy into a money economy.

The acquired needs also act as an incentive to earn more cash. Encouraged by stock fairs which are specially organised for them, they participate in the selling of cattle on a small scale, while some have proceeded to the slaughtering of animals for commercial purposes. Even so, for the greatest part the necessary cash is still obtained through the performance of wage labour in the developed sector.

The impact of the new habits has, by and large, not extended to the pattern and mode of production. While the men tend to give some aid in the cultivation of the soil, women and children still constitute the predominant labour force. Cattle retain their attribute as a most precious possession. Culling is not yet generally and spontaneously accepted and practised, and soil conservation remains the obligation and function of the developing authority. While some inhabitants are prepared to pay high prices for certain vegetables and other foodstuffs, the prices do not stimulate production of these goods by themselves, even though there is no climatological or physical reason why they should not do so. They prefer to adhere to their traditional crops. Where the agricultural yields are above the average it is invariably a function of the degree of supervision by the extension officer and the aid given by the development personnel in the actual ploughing, sowing and fertilising.

It is not an unusual experience for the agricultural officers to have to persuade the peasants who have been allocated land in new irrigation schemes to start planting every time a new season has arrived.

Neither is it unusual for the Bantu who is employed as demonstrator to instruct his people in all the principles of scientific farming, but to ignore completely all these principles, and to revert to the traditional methods when cultivating his own plot of land.

The institution of private individual tenure of land, where it was experimented with, did not meet with the success hoped for. Very often the land thus allocated became overcrowded with "relations," some of them very distant ones, who attached themselves to the household of the owner or occupier. Evidently the superimposition of private tenure on a communal-tenure habit pattern cannot make for a great measure of success. Farming does not gain either by the facilities for formal education and training. The vast majority who go through school, even those specially trained for agricultural pursuits, shun this industry. The prevailing view among those who have had four or five years of schooling seems to be that they have been adequately prepared for "white-collar" jobs and that manual labour does not have the necessary status to match their education.

As the activities of the development personnel increased, so did the dependence of the inhabitants on a distant body, "the government," as represented by the personnel. Rather than assume the responsibility for soil conservation, the maintenance of wire fences, of boreholes, etc., it was much more comfortable to leave it to the authorities. The phrase "that the government be respectfully requested" invariably prefixed the motions introduced in their Councils. In fact, the untiring efforts of the developing authority rather than those of the inhabitants themselves have been responsible for the measure of development that has taken place.

There has been no fundamental change in the social structure, habits and institutions of the people. Although nearly half of the population has been converted to the Christian faith, superstition has not lost its grip. The youth is still educated in the customs, mores and folk-lore of the tribe, and is required to conform. Polygamy, though diminished as a result of the missionaries' influence and of economic pressure, is still practised. The system of lobolo, though disliked by the younger generation and often paid in the form of cash instead of cattle, has been retained. Stock-breeding has largely remained a way of life rather than become a commercial activity, even while the quality of the animals has been improved.

In so far as there has been some change in their philosophy and way of life, it has been confined to the fringes of society. These fringes have not yet produced a body of economic leaders sufficiently strong and experienced and willing to act as initiators within tribal society, to set a cumulative process of change in motion. In other words, the exogenous factor, in the form of the outside body of developers, has not yet engendered a virile endogenous factor, the repercussions of whose activities could permeate the whole of society, which is caught up, economically speaking, in the fetters of its own traditional culture. The social and cultural milieu has proved to be very intractable and has retained its predominance.

## CONCLUSIONS

There is much to be gained, and many misconceptions can be avoided, if the economic problem of an underdeveloped community of the type described above is framed, not in terms of the vicious circle of poverty, Malthusian pressure or inadequate capital formation, etc., but in terms of the strategic factors of an ultimate character, namely its social and psychological inertia. Here economic elements as such are not limiting factors of the first order; by assigning them to the category of mediate factors, the accent is put where it should be, and the difference between the underdeveloped and the developed community is clearly pointed up. In the latter the human material can be taken for granted in the sense that it can be assumed that various economic stimuli will evoke fairly definite reactions; and on the basis of this assumption economic progress can be considered a function of economic factors in an ultimate sense. Even if changing psychological attitudes cannot be ruled out as causal factors in the developed economy, they are of a nature completely different from those obtaining among some underdeveloped peoples.

Economic development of an underdeveloped people by themselves is not compatible with the maintenance of their traditional customs and mores. A break with the latter is a pre-requisite to economic progress. What is needed is a revolution in the totality of social, cultural and religious institutions and habits, and thus in their psychological attitude, their philosophy and way of life. What is, therefore, required amounts in reality to social disorganisation. Unhappiness and discontentment in the sense of wanting more than is obtainable at any moment is to be generated. The suffering and dislocation that may be caused in the process may be objectionable, but it appears to be the price that has to be paid for economic development; the condition of economic progress.

If economic progress is deemed desirable and necessary and policy is to be formulated to achieve this end, the cart could in a certain sense be put before the horse in that economic changes can be utilised to generate the social revolution. Such a policy requires an outside agency or agencies from the developed countries which are prepared to supply the entrepreneurs, the capital and the highly skilled technical labour, who will take the initiative in establishing enterprises in the secondary and tertiary sectors. Providing the capital without the entrepreneurial initiative and manageral abilities to direct its economic exploitation will only lead to the waste of such capital. These agencies are to introduce the elements of technological culture into the pre-industrial societies. The industrial and business enterprises, which draw the underdeveloped people into their labour force and provide opportunities for them to rise in the hierarchy of the organisations, bring them into contact with new ways of doing things and new ways of life and standards of living. They should form the nucleus of urban development. The milieu of the town and city is *par excellence* conducive to a break with tradition, and as the ideas and values evolved in the industrial city permeate through the surrounding rural areas, the attitude of their inhabitants towards farming tends to change, so that it is no longer regarded only as a way of life and a means of supplying a minimum of subsistence. In particular, the proximity of a regular market in the form of the town or city will foster the growing of cash crops.

This approach, which could be termed "development from above," implies that the development of the underdeveloped people is not generated by themselves, and does not emanate from within except in so far as the outside agencies have been brought in at the request of the leaders of the underdeveloped community; which request can be taken as a reflection of the desire for economic development. However, this exogenous factor is used as a means to spark off an endogenous process of growth. To attain this effect and to ensure the self-perpetuation of the progressive disequilibrium, the policy of "development from above" must be accompanied by a policy of "development from below," which involves the measures usually applied in the community project approach.

What needs to be stressed in the implementation of the latter policy is the indispensability of the services of the social anthropologist who has made a thorough study of the community concerned in each case. Not only should he be able to give advice on the basic growth-inhibiting factors and thus to indicate the strategic elements that have to be influenced, but also to make recommendations regarding the *modus operandi* which will yield optimum results. Thus the waste of much effort can be prevented.

# Status and Mobility

SOCIAL DIFFERENTIATION, that is, the characteristic distribution of roles to different members of a society, is almost a definition of that society. Economic modernization inevitably entails profound changes in the stratification system. Where class depends upon occupation, then development has an especially disruptive impact upon old class relationships.

The initial selection, by Melvin Tumin, discusses the consequences to economic development of superimposing upon a traditional society the status pyramid of an industrialized community. Tumin suggests that when social positions are analyzed according to the hierarchy of rewards it is easier to identify areas of harmony and areas of strain in changing societies. Men and women accept new roles in an industrial society according to the gains or losses of power, prestige, or property which these new roles enforce. No development scheme has much chance of success if it ignores the importance of changes in the self-images of members of the industrializing society.

Thomas W. Shea's case study of the obstacles to economic development in the Malabar region of India describes the inhibiting nature of the area's caste system. This system throttles human mobility and inhibits the dissemination of new ideas. Land tenure arrangements and inheritance laws are closely linked to the caste system and reinforce that system's constricting effects.

# Melvin M. Tumin

## Competing Status Systems

TWO MAJOR THEMES are found in several of the papers presented in this symposium. The first theme forcefully asserts that the processes by which modernization takes place are numerous and diverse and that our knowledge of these is still so limited that the time is not yet ripe to attempt any all-embracing generalizations. The second theme acknowledges the diversity of the experiences of various societies, but strains toward provisional generalizations about the evolutionary processes of change and about the proper model of a modernized society.

The tension between these themes reminds us that we must view with suspicion any attempts to seal off questions by laying down propositions on what *must* take place in history, or what is sociologically unavoidable in the efficient arrangement of institutions. At the same time, the prolixity and incomparability of the data in the several papers remind us just as strongly that some genuine effort must be made to develop a more adequate comparative framework of concepts, and to attempt at least some provisional models of the relations among relevant variables.

A second noteworthy feature of these papers is the apparent ease and responsibility with which persons trained in one social science have managed meaningfully to utilize and incorporate data gathered by students trained in other disciplines. It is, for instance, impressive to discover how effectively a cultural anthropologist can take account of numerous political and economic factors while keeping kinship a central variable in his model of transformation. Political scientists similarly manage to keep various aspects of the political system in focus while considering the bearing of economic and cultural factors on political organization and process. And economists have not been insensitive to the numerous cultural and political factors that affect economic organization and reorganization. That these different scholars have taken the data and concepts of other disciplines out of the matrix of their original formulation does not mean they have done injustice to or distorted the facts.

### RELEVANCE OF STRATIFICATION THEORY

Considerations such as those sketched above make it easier to deal with a rather large body of political, economic, cultural, and social psychological data within a framework of theory about social stratification and to try to apply these to the process of modernization. Two things must be said of any such theory: (1) Stratification is only one feature of any social system, and no approach through stratification theory can include or exhaust the phenomena relevant to the full analysis of a social system. (2) The study of stratification is primarily concerned with inequalities in the distribution and utilization of the good things in life. These are ordinarily subsumed under the rubrics of power, property, and prestige.[1] Study of such inequalities is therefore concerned with political structure and process, economic forms and functions, the cultural arrangements by which persons are differently evaluated in regard to their worth and desirability, and the social psychological dynamics underlying these arrangements.

The successful use of such diverse bodies of data requires the construction of some analytic apparatus that, while unavoidably compressing much detail, makes it easier to discern the interrelations of these materials. At this point in the development of our theory, no complicated or complex model of stratification that is relevant to modernization can be formulated. However, it is possible to list the aspects of social structure and action that are most pertinently involved in the recruitment of talent in any social system. With a schematic presentation of these aspects, it is possible to indicate the places at which political, economic, cultural, and sociological data may best be included, so that their more general relations can be analyzed.[2]

Although stratification is concerned with inequalities in power, prop-

---

1. Certain problems are created by the use of only these three categories. For instance, only by stretching the common connotations of the term "property" can we include such a valued item as "job satisfaction." Yet, in at least one theoretically possible major variant of stratification systems, job satisfaction must be considered a major "reward" in the system, and hence has to be allocated to one category of rewards. Other more complex matters, such as "style of life," similarly resist being subsumed by these rubrics. But for present purposes we assume that anything that does not refer primarily to the ability to get others to adopt one's own means and ends (power), or to a favorable position in some rank order of evaluation (prestige), is to be included under property. Thus property is used to mean "rights over goods and services, both tangible and intangible," and the term "goods" obviously refers to much more than is ordinarily connoted by it.

2. The traditional view of the function of stratification in the efficient recruitment of talent is best stated in Kingsley Davis and Wilbert E. Moore, "Some Principles of Stratification," *American Sociological Review*, 10:242–249 (April 1945). The sharpest difference of opinion is expressed in Melvin Tumin, "Some Principles of Stratification: A Critical Analysis,"

erty, and prestige, the focus of interest here is on the recruitment of labor and the development of its commitment to a new form of work and a new set of social relations. Our special interest, then, is with the recruitment of talent for the occupational sector of the society and the hierarchical distributions of occupations and incomes. We are concerned with the general questions that must be asked about any such system of recruitment and any such hierarchy of positions and rewards. These questions and the distinctions involved do not exhaust the relevant materials but are central to any case study and to any theory of stratification.

In the following outline of variables relevant to the location of individuals on occupational and income ladders, nine features of stratification systems are listed. The major possible variations appear under each of these:[3]

    I. Degree of proliferation and specialization of statuses
       1. Much specialization among many statuses
       2. Division into only two or three major statuses
   II. Manner of entrance into statuses
       1. Through competition (equal or unequal)
       2. Through maturation or assumption
       3. Through inheritance

---

*American Sociological Review*, 18:387–394 (August 1953). Bernard Barber's version of Parsons' theory of stratification, as found in *Social Stratification* (New York: Harcourt, Brace and Company, 1957), adds nothing to previous theoretical statements. Indeed, as Barber presents the case for the "inevitability" of stratification, it becomes clearer than in either Parsons' formulation or that of Davis and Moore that there is nothing inevitable at all about the need for unequal rewards for unequal work. Between the universal facts of differentiation of function and differential evaluation for moral conformity, on the one hand, and the "unavoidability" of unequal rewards for and invidious distinctions among such functions, on the other, there are no necessary and sufficient connections that have been described in any theoretical work.

    3. Surely this list by no means exhausts the relevant variables. The limits of the paper do not permit me to give a variety of illustrations, even hypothetical ones, which would clarify the ways in which these variables are strategically relevant to analysis of the process of recruitment of labor. Numerous other questions that are ordinarily asked about any stratification system, viz., concerning the degree and types of mobility and the barriers to mobility, do not appear in this list. But most, if not all, of these are here considered as derivative consequences of the combined effects of the variables that are listed. Finally, the changes in the stratification systems that are described in the following pages are meant only to be illustrative.

III. Fineness of measurement of role performance
   1. Finely calibrated measures
   2. Gross distinctions between the acceptable and unacceptable
IV. Type of rewards emphasized
   1. External or extrinsic
   2. Intrinsic
   3. Social relational
  V. Availability of rewards
   1. Scarce
   2. Abundant
VI. Mode of distribution of rewards
   1. Unequal (stratified)
   2. Equal, as much as desired, or both
VII. Consequences for other opportunities in life
   1. Greatly ramified and seriously consequential
   2. Restricted to particular area
VIII. Consequences for social rating
   1. Used as basis for differentiated prestige
   2. Used as basis for acceptance as equal
 IX. Consequences for power
   1. Perfect correlation between property and power
   2. Completely random associations

## INDUSTRIALIZATION AND STRATIFICATION

With this outline as our guide, we can specify some of the more general changes in stratification systems that occur *during the movement of a society toward industrialization.*

I. The division of labor grows increasingly complex and, as a corollary, the system of differentiated statuses, i.e., socially recognized and differentially evaluated positions and functions, also grows more complex.

II. Status tends to be allocated on the basis of achievement rather than ascription, or at least the ideal tends to shift from a socially approved award of status on the basis of membership in groups such as kin, to that of achievement such as is implied by the term "skilled worker."

III. Since the occupational structure and the attendant structure of rewards become specialized and elaborated, accurate and satisfactory measurement of performance becomes central to both the labor and the managerial sectors of the productive system.

IV. The traditional rewards for work that flow from the character of the social relations enjoyed at work give way to rewards that may be considered extrinsic to the work itself, in that they are rewards *for* the performance, rather than rewards *in* performance. The same change is noticeable in the attrition suffered by the "meaning" of work, in that gratifications formerly derived from the craftsman's relation to his work, or from the fact that one's work certified one as an acceptable human being, also tend to vanish. In short, work tends to become dominantly instrumental rather than consummatory in its gratifications. Orientation toward and motivation in work thus come to depend much more on marginal differentiations in extrinsic rewards, e.g. wages, than was traditionally true.

V. Ordinarily we associate the process of industrialization with the economic development of a society, marked by an increase in its gross national product and, in general, by greater production of desired goods and services. From the point of view of stratification theory, this change is seen as increasing the rewards to be distributed.

VI. We also tend to associate the process of industrialization with some general movement toward greater *equality* of rewards among the various sectors of the society. At the least, our visual image of the structure of rewards shifts from one with a large base rising to a very narrow apex to one with both a narrow base and a narrow apex, and a middle bulge indicating the greater homogenization of rewards.

VII. One important aspect of stratification has to do with the extent to which an individual's position on any of the hierarchies of rewards is determined by or determines the range of life chances to which he is exposed. Thus, we ask, in what social circumstances do the poor die at younger ages than the rich, and under what social arrangements do death rates among various income groups tend to approach equality? The evidence on this issue, as between agricultural and industrial societies, is mixed. On the one hand, we have reports on the ever-normal granaries which are maintained in various forms in numerous primitive and peasant societies, so that no one ever goes hungry as long as food is available. On the other hand, we know that in well-developed industrial societies a number of auxiliary agencies of social welfare are specifically charged with using public funds to reduce the unequal life chances flowing from differences in income. These are crude and gross contrasts, but they illustrate the variability of the conditions that determine whether, and to what extent, differences in position on the occupational and income hierarchies may be consequential for the whole range of other chances and expectations.

VIII. Among the most important and most desired opportunities in life in any society are those concerned with receiving a favorable evaluation of one's self from one's associates and of having this evaluation symbolized publicly by whatever criteria are currently recognized by the society. Again the evidence as to what transformations occur in stratification systems under the impact of industrialization is mixed. There are societies in which the relations between income and prestige strain toward a minimum of connection and interdetermination. There are also societies in which income virtually equals prestige. Both these types are found in nonindustrial as well as in industrial societies. There are sharp intersocietal differences in this variable in each major form of productive organization; and it is not easy to say which is empirically more dominant.

IX. The same sorts of observation must be made about the power correlates of a stratified position on the occupational and income hierarchies. The search for power may not be as ubiquitous as the search for prestige. Yet the connections of power with occupation and income are or can be as close as those between occupation and prestige. Moreover, the form of productive organization—whether agricultural or industrial—does not seem surely to determine the extent of the connections between the power, occupations, and income.[4]

In regard to the interconnections of property, power, and prestige, Inkeles has noted that two processes seem to occur most frequently in the transition from agriculture to industry or, better, in the transition from a traditional society to a modern one. He speaks of the three hierarchies as social "orders":

> . . . the modernization of a traditional social system leads to a decrease in the degree of differentiation in each of the . . . subsystems or orders. That is, a process of relative homogenization takes place, reducing the gap or range separating the top and the bottom of the scale in income, status, power, experience (self-expression), and knowledge (skill). More important, in each hierarchy modernization brings about a marked increase in the proportion of the total population that falls in the same or adjacent strata near the middle of the distribution. . . .
>
> . . . under conditions of modernization there is a tendency to equilibration within the stratification system as a whole, . . . that is, for standing on any one of the stratification scales to be the same or similar to the individual's or group's relative standing on the other scales.[5]

---

4. Stratification theory, like any sociological theory, has two equally important purposes: (1) to describe in formal structural terms the possible variant forms; and (2) to account for the major gross empirical regularities of association and compendency among variables that have been found. The evidence suggests that power, property, and prestige are, at least theoretically, independently variable; and that when correlations do exist, they range from strong positive to strong negative relations. In certain circumstances the wealthy man is degraded by the fact of his wealth, and the powerful man suffers loss of prestige precisely because of his great power, etc.

5. Alex Inkeles, "Summary and Review: Social Stratification in the Modernization of Russia," in Cyril E. Black, ed., *The Transformation of*

In brief, Inkeles is here asserting that the evidence is actually much clearer than we have been able to find it.

In applying these propositions to the case of the modernization of the Soviet Union, Inkeles is constrained to recognize that the case, at least for the second proposition, tends to break down when one considers the relative monopolization of power in that country. He contends, however, that the present great centralization there may be simply a "short-term reversal" of a different over-all trend—that the sharing of power has been increasing but has not yet reached its full extent. Even if the power system of the Soviet is exceptional, he thinks this need not impugn the value of the general model of transition, of which the Soviet case may be one distinctive variant.

However mixed the evidence may be, for our purposes it is most important to recognize that these central aspects of stratification theory are also central features of that social change called industrialization or modernization. We are dealing with fundamental aspects of social change when we focus on changes in the various hierarchies of power, property, and prestige. The ways in which the wide assortment of political, economic, and cultural facts can be classified to show their relevance to stratification theory should now be clear.

When we speak of the division of labor and its increasing complexity, we are obviously concerned with those changes usually focused on by economists. By considering these changes as the basis for new status arrangements, we translate the changes into terms relevant to the analysis of stratification. Similarly, when we speak of the systems of reward for work, we are concerned with the data derived from studies, for example, of the change from exchange by barter to wage labor. But we show the relevance of these data for stratification analysis by considering rewards for work in terms of their scarcity, their symbolic status significance, and their capacity to motivate men to conscientious performance, with or without considerable differentiation.

In considering such economic facts as the development of a system of wage labor, we are calling attention to the narrowing bases on which claims to social distinction may come to rest, as against the more diffuse claims to fame made by men in societies where status is primarily ascriptive and depends on membership by birth or lines of kinship. Each shift in the form of reward for work is intimately influenced by and strongly influences the modes and proprieties of inequality as these have been manifested in the society.

---

*Russian Society* (Cambridge: Harvard University Press, 1960), pp. 341–342.

The elements of stratification theory that are most significant for the study of industrialization may serve as convenient categories within which to compare various systems in order to discover major lines of consonance and strain in social forms, and also may be used to ascertain whether certain general evolutionary developments tend to dominate the transformation from a traditional to a modern society. The interconnections of these categories may be studied directly, and any or several of them may be used in analyses of their relations with specifically economic factors. . . . Or an examination of politics and social organization may be attempted by relating certain stratification variables to political organization. Similarly, the cultural anthropologist or historian concerned with integrating disparate facts from various disciplines into more inclusive gestalts may make selections from these facts. . . .

## STRATIFICATION AND COMMITMENT: OBJECTIVE AND SUBJECTIVE ASPECTS

A more difficult problem now confronts us: What can be said about the bearing of these aspects of stratification on the commitment of labor to an industrial way of work and life? To answer this question we must first distinguish between two kinds of statements about commitment; one refers to objective conditions, while the other refers to attitudes and definitions of the situation.

The first type of statement would describe the degree to which the society contains the formal arrangements or structures that are thought to be required for efficient manning of an industrial system—including, for example, the various technologies and the charted numbers of organizational relations which efficient industrial organization is said to demand. Here, too, reference would be made to the quality and quantity of markets, including those for goods, labor, and money. Such descriptions indicate whether, or how well, a society is equipped for the industrial tasks which it assumes, or may wish to assume, but do not necessarily tell anything about the processes by which societies emerge from traditional, agricultural conditions, nor indicate the extent to which the population is subjectively committed to any way of life. Any statement concerning the latter must deal with habits and ways of thinking, feelings of satisfaction and dissatisfaction, reluctances and readinesses, and accepted and unchallenged patterns of social relations.

From at least one point of view, one may say that many persons in the most developed industrial societies do not accept, i.e., are not fully committed to, the industrial way of life. They find themselves seriously at variance with many of the pressures of life in such a society. They feel alien to the major impulses and kinds of behavior that seem to be required for success in the market place. They dislike the criteria of evaluation of the social worth of individuals. They deplore the interpersonal relations that develop when men view each other impersonally and instrumentally.

These objections to and alienations from the industrial way of life on the part of persons already involved in it may be indicative of the principal sources of resistance to moving into such a way of life. We can classify major resistances to industrialization expressed by people in preindustrial or quasi-industrial societies in terms of unwillingness to be subjected to the pressures implicit in industrialization; reluctance to break with forms of social relations that give assurance of security in the traditional societies, hesitancy to yield the comforting ratings and ranks they enjoy as members of their families and communities.

There is evidence in these resistances of the universal effort of normal individuals to maximize the favorableness of their self-images. This effort is of course always relative to perceived resources and perceived limits. Prospective self-images which are theoretically possible and which might, all other things changing appropriately, prove even more psychologically desirable to the individual may be rejected because they are not perceived as such, or because the attendant prospective risks and gains cannot intellectually and emotionally be brought into a satisfying balance.

## ROLE IMAGE AND COMMITMENT

There is also a universal strain to maintain the most favorable image of one's roles. The major guides to behavior acquired by any individual in the process of being socialized, whether as a child or an adult, involve certain images of roles that are related to the major statuses that one expects, and is expected, to occupy at various times in one's life. The normal adult statuses of breadwinner, husband, father, and citizen are examples. We all tend to make our behavior conform to those models of decorum and conduct that were sketched on our social memories, early in life. This is true even though the finer details are acquired only with the actual status, and even though the final manner of comporting ourselves in these roles depends largely on interaction with other persons.

In these images of major roles lie the dynamics of commitment, for the change to any system of behavior from any previous system depends on the ability of the particular individual to see himself as a player of the roles involved in that system. And this in prior turn depends on his ability to see himself as no longer playing the roles attached to the traditional statuses.[6] There are, then, at least two stages in the development of commitment. It is possible for a group of persons to be ready to change *from* certain status and role arrangements, without being ready to adopt and commit themselves to any other particular set of arrangements.

The restraining power of the traditional statuses lies not only in the habitual and customary nature of their requirements, which makes them easier to fulfill, but also in moral certifications implicit in the role images. Role prescriptions, in short, are not only descriptive; they are evaluative and normative. A father habitually or traditionally does this or that, but there are specific things a *good* father *should do*. And we all know what a *good* citizen *should* be like. Moreover, these general normative role prescriptions are frequently concretized, and their moral aspects introjected. The general statement is translated into a set of personal commandments in the form, "I am the kind of father who . . ."; the very *identity* of the person is thus defined by the personalization of the general role prescriptions. The importance of this identification of self with role lies in the fact that this is the self with which the individual actor confronts the world and, in that confrontation, measures out his own personal esteem for himself. He is encouraged to do so by the reactions to his role image on the part of those with whom he interacts.

The crucial resistance to industrialization found in peasant and primitive societies may come from the tendency of various major role images to be reasonably well-integrated with each other, although no one formula or pattern alone suffices as a model of such integration. There is integration in the sense that individuals in such societies generally have formulated a stable composite role image that includes the chief aspects of each of the component roles, even though their interconnections may involve the stressing of one as *compensation* for another. Thus, the utterly devalued untouchable in a caste system may be resistant to change of any considerable kind, even though one of his major roles may be a source of pain and deprivation.

The breaking of any aspect of a traditional society, then, immediately tends to involve much more change than that in the aspect where the impetus to change first appeared. This is why a peasant society frequently seems to recoil from the beckonings and bemusements with which it is confronted when it comes into contact with a culture of another world

---

6. For some of the dynamics of this process of change in one particular case, see Melvin M. Tumin and Arnold S. Feldman, "Status, Perspective and Achievement: A Study of Education and the Class Structure in Puerto Rico," *American Sociological Review*, 21:464–472 (August 1956).

of understandings. It is not metaphorical to say that the total society is threatened by a change in any one of its major aspects, for such a statement tends to be true in a literal sense. Morals, habits, forms of community interaction, patterns of power and prestige, bases of self-esteem, as well as the general and impersonal arrangement of the society's institutions come into question when any *one* of these aspects is questioned.

The essence of the foregoing observations is that the way of work and the rewards for work in traditional societies are most frequently central to their way of life. To attempt to change the way of work is therefore to attempt to change the way of life. Naturally the resistance is much stronger than it is when a change in occupation implies little more than a change in the bus that one has to take every morning, or even such relatively large changes as moving from one city to another, changing one's community of peers, or acquiring new skills and attitudes essential for efficient performance.

The interaction of work with the total way of life in traditional societies has been discussed in several preceding papers. Thus, Elkan and Fallers have noted that wage work in town tends to be a phase rather than a way of life for the Baganda, many of whom commute daily from rural holdings where their wives cultivate food and cash crops, while others return to rural homes every weekend. Attention is focused throughout their paper on the tension between the attractions of town work and its level of pay, and the retentive forces of the traditional social system. We are led to understand why the Baganda maintain a strong affiliation with the traditional social structure, at the same time that they make some considerable ventures into the new labor market.

We also note that there is considerable difference between age groups in the frequency and depth of involvement in town life, as we should expect. One would assume that younger men, not yet integrated in their adult roles, and not yet privileged to receive the full rewards of participation in the traditional society, typically would be much more footloose and susceptible to the marginal attractions of the town. This is especially likely to be true when the prevailing definition of the worth of town work, provided by the words and actions of older men, tells the younger men to view such work as a temporary arrangement.

In the same vein, Singer points out that the problem of gaining the craftsman's acceptance for technical improvements is not one of changing his character and values, but of assuring him of continued opportunities for their expression under changing forms of social and economic organizations. This formulation underestimates some of the difficulties that rise because at least some aspects of character and some values have to be changed if individuals are to adjust to the new system. But the more important truth is that, except where sharp breaks with former traditions are *forcefully* required, any population will tend to move into new work ambiences and to commit itself to the new ways only as it sees itself able to fulfill its traditional image of itself within the new. And this image is a configuration of a variety of separate but connected role images, which include prescriptions about how to think and feel, how to react to others, what to want from life, what is good and bad, and the proper course of life.

# *Thomas W. Shea, Jr.*

# *Barriers to Economic Development in Traditional Societies: Malabar, a Case Study*

THE DISTRICT of Malabar on the Southwest coast of India has been a major exporter of a wide variety of agricultural products to Europe for more than two thousand years. Despite the two millenia of sustained contact between agricultural producers and merchants, however, social relationships in land are, even today, of a predominantly feudal character; cultivation techniques are generally primitive, and the rural portion of the district, notwithstanding the great commercial importance of its produce, appears to be surprising impoverished. How could the social and economic organization of a people so long exposed to the influence of world market activity remain so little affected by the currents of economic change and development in the outside world? The purpose of this article is to explore, by the study of this extreme example, the reasons for the apparent failure of a pattern of sustained economic growth to become established in a rural area exposed to continuing commercial influences.

\*      \*      \*      \*      \*

The important barriers to economic growth in Malabar are:
1. Immobility of the caste structure.

2. The traditional occupational distribution of the elite.
3. Absence of systematic government in the pre-British period.
4. The pattern of land tenures.
5. The structure of family property laws and
6. The pattern of population growth during the nineteenth and twentieth centuries.

Although, as we shall see, these barriers to growth have long obstructed the efficient utilization of agricultural resources in Malabar, it would be quite wrong to base our thesis upon the assertion that the agricultural economy has been entirely static. A commercial society existed side by side for two thousand years with a pronouncedly "feudal," "non-economic" rural society; much change in cultivation techniques, in crop patterns, and in the distribution of the proceeds from agriculture among the different social classes did take place as a result of this juxtaposition. However, these changes were not associated with increases in per capita income or wealth. We shall therefore use the term "stagnant" to mean simply the absence of economic growth, the term "economic growth" meaning simply increase in per-capita income and wealth.

The Hindu caste structure in Malabar was, until the past decade or so, unusually rigid, with caste segregation practiced to an extent extreme even for India. Untouchability was carried to grotesque lengths, with differential distances of polluting contact defined for each caste, in the most extreme cases extending even to shouting distance. Mobility of labor was severely restricted. A low-caste person, outside his village, could, if he were a Hindu, pursue no occupation; within his village he was restricted to work spurned by the higher castes. Conversely, the guardians of local mores viewed cultivation as degrading work precluding higher castes from engaging in it. Among the most serious effects of these barriers were the lack of effective social communications which they engendered, and their discouraging influence on entrepreneurial morale. Where social and economic resources necessary to economic development are scattered among numerous non-competing social groups, the opportunity for exchange of ideas, techniques, and material resources is curtailed, reducing both the scope and incentive for development. In Malabar, rent-receiving landlords could not, as a rule, effectively reinvest their income in agricultural operations because of taboos discouraging both their personal participation in cultivation and close physical contact with cultivating castes. Since the pursuit of agriculture as a calling was deprecated, no incentives stimulating the resource-owning classes to make systematic studies of the technical needs of their cultivators existed, and cultivators had no motivation to work toward systematic improvements in cultivation techniques.

The Hindu cultivating classes were inhibited by lack of authority, lack of physical resources, and the apathy-inducing effects of social oppression from engaging in the experimentation and risk-taking steps necessary to the initiation of systematic economic development. A large proportion of agricultural workers were, in the Southern part of the district until the mid 1800's, slaves, subject to purchase, sale, and transfer with or separate from the land they tilled. Others, including mainly the cultivating leaseholders, were subject to various types of behavior restraints limiting both the acquisition and display of wealth. For most cultivating tenants, increased yields merely invited the imposition of higher rents, or even ejection from their holdings by landlords seeking to appropriate the enlarged surplus.

Although caste barriers were differential in their intensity—social intercourse among the higher castes was extensive—contact between the non-cultivating classes and the cultivators, and apparently between successively lower castes of cultivators such as the Tiyyas and the untouchable Cherumar, was extremely circumscribed, each lower caste tending to discriminate more strongly against those castes which it regarded as inferior, in perverse imitation of the behavior-practices of the elite toward them.

The Hindu ruling castes—those who held superior title to land and possessed wealth and authority—took little or no direct interest in the cultivation process. The Nambudri Brahmans, a priestly caste constituting until recent times the dominant landholders in the district, were, and to a large extent still are, the least commercially-oriented and most tradition-bound of Malayali castes. For generations subsequent to British rule, they firmly rejected exposure to Western education in any form. They took, until very recently, no active part in commerce, industry, or the civil service. Their consumption habits were, and still are, meagre and rigidly circumscribed by tradition. They systematically avoided social contact with all other castes, with the exception of the ruling Nayars. They were, in short, the least endowed of Malayali castes with social attitudes regarded as essential to the development of an investment mentality.

The various sub-castes of Nayars which furnished Malabar with its soldiers, statesmen, and administrators were, in pre-British times almost exclusively engaged in activities directly or indirectly connected with warfare. The district was, in pre-British times, divided into over thirty virtually independent principalities with fluid, uncertain boundaries. These petty kingdoms appear to have been almost perpetually at war with one another prior to the arrival of the British. Their administrative structures and even the family organization pattern of the ruling Nayars were geared to war. Younger members of the Nayar families typically spent years in rigorous gymnastic training designed to fit them for guerrilla warfare, and the Nayars, like the Nambudris, were extremely frugal in their consumption habits.

Such commercial activity as did exist appears to have been carried on by Moslems and by foreign Hindus (chiefly Gujeratis), both of whom were predominantly urban residents. Although the Moslems were largely indigenous Malayalis, their dress, food, religion, and social attitudes set them apart so completely from the caste Hindus that their contact with them was confined to specific commercial or administrative transactions. Yet, particularly in the south, they were liberally interspersed among the rural Hindu population, some as predominant landlords, others as peasants and agricultural laborers. The monopoly of the Moslems and foreign Hindus over the lucrative spice trade enabled these groups to siphon off virtually all of the profits realized from foreign sales. This probably explains the failure of the traditional landowners, during the pre-British period, to share in the resultant accumulation of tangible wealth. It also may explain a great deal of the subsequent Hindu-Moslem strife following the British conquest of the district.

The pronounced division of labor into a predominantly Hindu agrarian section and a chiefly Moslem and foreign mercantile sector has, with certain modifications, persisted to the present day. Most Nambudris remain rustic, traditional landlords; Nayars of prominent families who have not remained in agriculture follow careers analogous to those in which they were dominant in traditional times—the civil service, teaching, and the legal profession. Moslems and foreign Hindus dominate business activity. Although census figures on the occupational distribution of castes are dated and notoriously unreliable, an analysis of the occupational distribution of caste leaders can be made from a study of the nearly 400 entries in a recent Malabar Who's Who.[1] Of the 136 listings which I could identify unmistakeably as Nayars and Nambudris, only 26, or 19 per cent were engaged in commercial or industrial activity. On the other hand, 49 out of 69, or 72 per cent of the Moslems listed were in some form of business activity, and 53 of the 76 Parsis, Christians, and foreign (that is, non-Malayali) Hindus, (70 per cent) were businessmen. The 23 non-businessmen from this latter group were almost all lawyers from East Coast (Tamil) Brahman families domiciled for generations in Malabar. Of the 146 persons of identifiable

---

1. N. Ahmed Koya, *The Year Book and Who's Who in Malabar, 1954* (Kozhikode: Adna Co. 1954).

caste who cited their occupation as merchants or businessmen, only 3 were Nambudris, 17 were Nayars, and 24, Tiyyas. Non-Hindu and foreign merchants formed 70 per cent of the business listings.

The most noticeable change in the caste-composition of the mercantile community in the past half-century is the rise in the importance of the lower caste Tiyyas, whose traditional occupation was the cultivation of the coconut palm. Since this caste is numerous (comprising about a fourth of the total population of the district) and has been engaged principally in the cultivation of a commercial crop, it is perhaps not surprising that it should come to occupy an important role in commercial activity. It is notable that the Tiyyas were the one community in Malabar whose leading families readily assimilated Western mores and consumption habits and even extensively (for a time) inter-married with Europeans. The eagerness with which they acculturated may perhaps be attributed to the fact that they were excluded from association with the traditional elite, yet (following the British conquest) attained a sufficient measure of independence and mobility to make a decisive break with tradition when such a break became possible.

Although each of the petty rulers of Malabar's more than two dozen principalities appears to have maintained something resembling an administrative staff, there is much evidence to indicate that institutionalized administration, with systematic record-keeping, such as that found in many Oriental countries in pre-capitalist times, was absent from Malabar. There was no land revenue levy, and no record of land rights; only the customs offices in the ports functioned effectively, and they were largely run by non-Hindus.[2] The extremely rugged terrain probably inhibited the development of large, well organized administrative units because of the communication problems which it engendered. The topography of the countryside was, moreover, unsuited to the introduction of such large-scale enterprises as the vast state-maintained irrigation works found in great river valleys in ancient China, Egypt, or Northern India, and the extremely rigid caste divisions would, in any case, probably have hampered the development of economic or social activities dependent upon synchronized, coordinated group activities on a large scale. Finally, the very living patterns of the villagers—their preference for residence in scattered individual houses rather than in the dense house-clusters so typical of

---

2. A more detailed account of the political structure of pre-British Malabar is contained in the author's unpublished paper Agrarian Politics and Land Reform in India—Malabar District, A Case Study (Philadelphia: 1956), pp. 15–42.

other parts of India—helped to sustain a social predisposition to anarchy. Absence of formal legal codes, as well as a general lack of such paraphernalia of modern administration as organized civil and criminal law courts, regular law-enforcement procedures, systematically maintained state archives, or rational tax structures, engendered in their turn an atmosphere highly unfavorable to capital investment in agriculture.

Accounts dating to pre-British times indicate that a highly differentiated set of land rights, closely linked to status-relationships, existed in traditional Malabar.[3] Although the different tenures themselves appear to have been defined with precision, the extremely chaotic and disorganized state of public administration seems to have precluded the existence of consistent and dependable means of evaluating or enforcing claims to rights over land. Ability to enforce contractual agreements relating to land appears to have depended upon one's strength in the community. Low-caste cultivators were at the mercy of the whims of their landlords. On the other hand, the apparently powerful political status of the Moslem and foreign mercantile community (resulting no doubt in part from their monopoly of the spice trade) probably sufficed to ensure that the terms which they reached with landholders relating to delivery of agricultural produce were enforceable.[4]

An analysis of pre-British land tenure relationships is severely hampered by the fact that the British conquest of the country in 1792 followed 30 years of prolonged and destructive guerrilla warfare between the Hindu rulers of Malabar and Moslem conquerors of the district from Mysore. This struggle had thoroughly shredded the flimsy administrative fabrics of the individual principalities and produced abnormally strained relations between the ruling Hindu castes and the Moslems.

---

3. The role of land tenure in the historical evolution of agriculture in Malabar forms the subject matter of the author's The Land Tenure Structure of Malabar and its Influence upon Capital Formation in Agriculture (Unpublished Ph.D. thesis, University of Pennsylvania, 1959).

4. Superior rightholders, for example, customarily granted special development leases guaranteeing the cultivator rent-free tenure to undeveloped land for an extended period in order to facilitate the clearing of the jungle and the planting of coconut groves, pepper gardens, and other commercial crops which required long and costly pre-production waiting periods. There were also provisions in customary law for compensatory payments to evicted tenants for improvements made during the period of tenure, although these became hopelessly inadequate following the inflationary pressures built up during British rule. See the author's thesis, ch. iv, for a detailed analysis.

The British undertook the tasks of civil administration in a context of severe Hindu-Moslem communal strife. In the field of land tenure, their administrative and judicial tasks were complicated by the claims and counter-claims of Hindu landlords who were displaced at the time of the Mysorean conquest, and Moslem tenants who had appropriated substantial land rights from their former landlords. Although the intentions of the British administrators were to refrain from tampering with existing land rights, confining their attentions to applying traditional law as impartially as possible, they soon found that basic conflicts existed between their conception of laws of evidence and procedure and those of the traditional ruling castes. By substituting systematic court procedures for the largely chaotic and capricious methods hitherto followed, the British built up, in the decades following their conquest, a body of court decisions which wrought far-reaching changes in the nature of Malabar land law.

The British administrators, basing their conclusions on the verbal testimony of local informants and upon the meagre written records which had survived the Mysore wars, decided that a class of land holders called *janmis* had rights roughly equivalent to free-hold proprietors in English land law. This *janmam* tenure, closely identified in pre-British Malabar with high social position, was held almost exclusively by Nambudri Brahman and Nayar joint families, by temples of which Nambudris or Nayars were managers, and by the entailed estates of former rulers.

Despite the extravagant assertions of the Malayali informants on whose testimony the British based their findings, the *janmam* title appears typically to have been a mere titular claim conveying but nominal rights over land. Much of the *janmam* property of the Nayars and Nambudris had consisted merely of ceremonial title grants made to them by local chieftains as gestures of loyalty or piety. The land over which these *janmam* rights extended was often held by two or more layers of subordinate right-holders who had enjoyed undisturbed tenure for long periods of time.

Most of the large *janmam* holders had been impoverished both by their long and costly struggle with the Mysorean conquerors and by the loss of important sources of revenue following the displacement of their temporal authority by the British. Therefore, once British rule was consolidated and the views of the British administration with regard to the nature of the *janmam* tenure were made clear, many *janmis* made serious efforts to augment the income from their remaining landholdings. They first sought to raise the rents from the low customary levels which had hitherto been prevalent; when they encountered opposition from their tenants, they filed eviction suits in the courts. Favorable decisions were easily obtained. Courts in the early 19th century tended toward the view that tenure contracts conveyed no rights except those which were explicitly stated, and that all rights to land were derived from the *janmam* tenure. Since most subordinate tenures were ill-defined, with many of the terms of tenure implicit and unsupported by documents, plaintiffs who could successfully establish their claims to *janman* title found little difficulty in obtaining eviction decrees against unwanted tenants.

The history of the 19th century in Malabar was primarily one of continuous and occasionally violent conflict between high-caste Hindu landlords who sought to augment their rent-income, and their Moslem and Hindu tenants (many of the latter of whom were descendants of the administrative staffs of former rulers), who resisted encroachments on their tenures. By 1880, the eviction rate had climbed so high that roughly one tenant in five had been thrown off his holdings.[5]

Although it is difficult to determine to what extent the agrarian discontent of the 19th century acted as a barrier to economic development in agriculture, certain generalizations seem pertinent. Court decisions conferred substantial *net* rights on *janmis*. *Janmis* were mostly from traditionalist, non-investing castes. Court decisions abridged the land rights of communities actively engaged either in cultivation or in the financing of cultivation.[6] These comprised Moslem and low-caste Hindu cultivators, and intermediaries of all castes and communities. The widespread presence of communal strife and agrarian discontent reduced the area of cooperation between the various claimants to agricultural income and minimized the incentives of tenants to make productive investments. These developments probably curtailed opportunities for systematic expansion of agricultural operations. On the other hand, it must be remembered that typologies represent central tendencies. Considerable dispersion in attitudes existed;

---

5. T. W. Shea, unpublished thesis, p. 157.

6. Two offsetting mechanisms were at work:

a) The long run effect of British rule was to reduce caste discrimination and occupational immobility; these were byproducts of improvements in communications and an increase in mass-media participation.

b) The immediate effects of court decisions giving *janmis* freehold title were to reduce all or nearly all leases with vague or unspecified time periods to tenures at will. Since the effects of court decisions on tenure were more immediate than the gradual weakening of caste, the Moslem and low-caste Hindu cultivators were the net losers. Also, the *janmis* acquired a net increment of rights over their prime rivals, the assertive Moslem commercial outgroups, who, when landholders, were usually intermediaries rather than *janmis*.

not all *janmis* were Nambudris and Nayars; not all Nambudris and Nayars were equally rigorous in their aloofness from other castes; not all Nayars were uninterested in commercial advantages to be derived from seeing to it that their lands were efficiently tilled; and not all Hindu-Moslem or landlord-tenant relations were acrimonious. The restrictive influences of tenure on over-all economic development were thus consistent with considerable differences in individual economic opportunity. . . .

The pattern of inheritance laws in Malabar tended to perpetuate certain features of the land tenure structure which have acted as barriers to economic development. The properties of Nayar and Nambudri joint families, who held *janmam* rights to a large portion of the land in Malabar, were, until 20 years ago, virtually all entailed. Since these families could not readily sell their *janmam* rights, granting of leases was the customary method of land alienation. Although leases were made to persons of all castes, the customary way in which the individual sub-families held property rights was as sub-lessees of their joint families. The Nayar joint families, in particular, were large, heterogeneous, fissiparous, and administratively unwieldy. The Nayars followed a matrilineal system of inheritance according to which a person's property rights descended not to the sons and daughters of his natural family, but rather to his own sisters' children. The Nayar family system, a creature of economic necessity in time of war when the Nayar population was a floating population, had little to justify its existence in the patrilocal, largely monogamous society which arose following British rule. A growing number of court cases led to decisions which awarded the manager of the joint family property progressively stronger legal rights, leaving the younger members finally with little more than rights to subsistence. Although the confirmation of the joint family manager as the sole contracting authority made it easier for enforceable contracts to be made between landholders and businessmen, the internal structure of the Nayar family made effective estate administration extremely difficult. When a Nayar *tarwad* (matrilocal joint family) member became, usually late in life, the manager of his joint family property, growing loyalties to his natural family (which legally had no rights to his joint family property) tended to outweigh his loyalty to his *tarwad*. This encouraged him to abuse his position as manager by siphoning off estate income and resorting to surreptitious transfers of property rights to his own sons. More ambitious younger family members, frustrated by the mismanagement and dissension within the *tarwad* and unable to compel partition of family property, sought employment outside their villages. For the most part, they entered the civil service or the professions, and although they usually leased their land rights to tenants rather than sold them outright, they ceased to take any active interest in cultivation. Thus the energies of the ablest, most enterprising Nayars were usually lost to agriculture. The Nambudris, on the other hand, followed a modified form of primogeniture whereby only children of the firstborn male remained within the family; others consorted with the matrilineal Nayars and the children of such unions were considered Nayars. This tended to lead to concentration of Nambudri family property as family lines with no male heirs died out. . . .

The rapid growth of population which followed the British conquest provided a short-term stimulus to agriculture in the sense that it led to the clearing of more forest land for cultivation purposes. Most of this newly cleared land was put under commercial crops. British planters leased large areas of land in the hitherto virtually unpopulated foothills of the Western Ghats, which they transformed into coffee, tea, and to a lesser extent rubber and pepper plantations.

However, the expansion of the land area under cultivation and the introduction of new opportunities for employment outside agriculture which accompanied the slow but gradual development of commerce and light industry in the district were both insufficient to offset the rapid growth of population during the nineteenth and twentieth centuries. Neither the state apparatus, nor the social structure of the rural inhabitants was well adapted to accommodate the increase in population. State aid to agriculture was negligible and the dispersed residents of Malabar's caste-ridden villages were little inclined to initiate cooperative schemes for economic development.

The continued rapid growth in the absolute number of persons dependent on earnings from agriculture absorbed progressively more of the surplus produce of agriculture. The proliferation of the families of the large estate owners, the increase in the number of intermediaries, and the rapid increase in the ranks of agricultural laborers and cultivators led to so dispersed a scattering of the surplus as to make concerted investment planning, even were it contemplated, virtually impossible. Most cultivators (as distinct from landowners) belonged to castes which traditionally permitted property subdivision on the death of the family head. As a result of prevailing customs whereby each heir received prorated portions of land of different quality, subdivision and fragmentation of holdings increased with the rise in population, eventually reaching the point where a typical family holding of less than an acre of land would frequently be scattered in a dozen or more separate plots. Thus in Malabar those inheritance laws which permitted partition of family property had economic effects as adverse and undesirable as the laws which prevented partition.

The adverse economic effects of rapid population growth were felt by landholders of all types. On a superior tenure level, repeated subletting of land, litigation over title, prolonged partition suits, and the rapid growth in the number of persons dependent upon agricultural rent for a living have acted as barriers to new investment and have hampered the accumulation of an investible surplus. On the cultivators' level, subdivision and fragmentation of holdings have tended to reduce the income of most cultivating families to the subsistence level, and to narrow the scope and reduce the efficiency of agricultural operations.[7] The proportion of destitute agricultural laborers continues to increase as progressively larger numbers of cultivators are obliged to supplement the income from their diminutive holdings by seeking employment on the lands of others.[8]

---

7. One adverse effect of increased subdivision of cultivators' holdings in the absence of a growth of a cooperative movement is a tendency toward wasteful duplication of agricultural equipment and livestock. The effects of this duplication is well illustrated by the case of cattle. Each cultivating family seeks to own its work and milch cattle, partly for prestige reasons, and partly because of the absence of effective channels for sharing of livestock resources. As the average size of holding per family diminishes, the availability of fodder declines. Yet the demand for cattle continues to rise, calling forth an increased supply of progressively less efficient and less productive cattle; this in turn increases the number of cattle required to perform a given volume of work. A vicious circle ensues with no downward limit, save an exhaustion of subsistence requirements.

8. As concentration of *cultivated* holdings in Malabar appears to be low and the acreage of cultivatible but uncultivated land is apparently small, the scope for employment of additional numbers of laborers in agriculture in the future seems appallingly dim.

# Cities and Savings

Two SIGNIFICANT difficulties of the transition from the traditional to the industrialized societies are over-urbanization and the inadequate savings available for investment purposes. Both raise sociological as well as economic issues. The rapid growth of cities, is, of course, a partial reflection of the world population explosion under way since the eighteenth century. But urban population has increased more rapidly than population as a whole, particularly in the underdeveloped areas. The first stages of industrialization are accompanied by massive migration from the farm to the city, bringing in its wake economic and social problems.

Philip M. Hauser's article is a careful analysis of this theme. After exploring the quantitative aspects of urbanization, he examines the imperfect expansion of urban employment opportunities to accommodate the newcomers and the physical difficulties of inadequate housing. These specific problems are seen against a background of social tensions generated by the conflict of urban and rural values.

A somewhat different approach is taken by the anthropologist Oscar Lewis, who underscores the basic similarity in the life styles of the urban poor in different countries. His moving case study (consisting in part of the actual words of an inhabitant of a Mexico City slum) stresses the alienation and cynicism characteristic of incomplete integration into the industrialized society.

Richard D. Lambert examines the problem of the inadequate level of savings in the nations of southern Asia. He argues that the chief barriers to the accumulation of liquid savings lie in the persistence of traditional values, religious and secular, of a conservative peasant culture, which impede the development of a money profit motive. Religious derogation of wealth, an ethos of fatalism, the high esteem associated with acquisition of land, and the distrust of the mercantile community are some of the inhibiting factors.

# Philip M. Hauser

## The Social, Economic, and Technological Problems of Rapid Urbanization

A WORLD DEMOGRAPHIC REVOLUTION has been under way since at least the middle of the seventeenth century. Accompanying the observed explosive increased rates of population growth have been profound changes in the distribution of population. Perhaps the most dramatic of these during the modern era is the increasing concentration of population represented by the huge and still growing urban agglomerations. In fact, urban population has increased more rapidly than world population for as far back as reliable data are available, i.e., at least since 1800. Moreover, the rate of world urbanization has been accelerating and this acceleration is undoubtedly still going on.

TABLE 1.

*Comparison of World's Urban Population Growth Rates and World's Total Population Growth Rates, 1800—1950**

| Period | Total world population | World population in cities | | |
|---|---|---|---|---|
| | | Percentage increase in | | |
| | | 5,000 and over | 20,000 and over | 100,000 and over |
| 1800—1850 | 29.2 | 175.4 | 132.3 | 76.3 |
| 1850—1900 | 37.3 | 192.0 | 193.5 | 222.2 |
| 1900—1950 | 49.3 | 227.7 | 239.6 | 254.1 |

* Source: Kingsley Davis and Hilda Hertz, "Patterns of World Urbanization" to be published by Macmillan & Co.

245

During the nineteenth century, world urbanization was largely the result of the large concentration of population in the cities of Europe and North America. In the twentieth century, however, the rate of world urbanization has been sustained by the rapid growth of urban populations in the economically underdeveloped areas of the world, particularly in Asia, Latin America, and Africa. During the course of this century, the economically advanced areas of the world had already reached near-saturation points of urbanization; the economically underdeveloped areas were still experiencing the flow of people from the rural countryside to the cities. Despite the present relatively rapid rate of urbanization in the economically underdeveloped areas of the world, they still have comparatively small proportions of their populations living in cities. In 1950, for example, the world average showed twenty-one per cent resident in cities of twenty thousand or more; but only nine per cent of Africa's population lived in such cities, and only thirteen per cent of Asia's. Twenty-one per cent of Central America's population, and twenty-six per cent of South America's, lived in cities of twenty thousand or more. In contrast, forty-seven per cent of the population in Oceania, forty-two per cent in North America, thirty-five per cent in Europe (excluding the U.S.S.R.), and thirty-one per cent in the U.S.S.R., lived in cities of this size.

TABLE 2.
*Percentages of Urban Population in Major World Areas, 1950*[*]

|  | Percentage of total population in cities of 20,000 and more | Percentage of population in cities of 100,000 and more |
|---|---|---|
| World | 21 | 13 |
| Oceania | 47 | 41 |
| North America[†] | 42 | 29 |
| Europe[‡] | 35 | 21 |
| U.S.S.R. | 31 | 18 |
| South America | 26 | 18 |
| Central America[§] | 21 | 12 |
| Asia | 13 | 8 |
| Africa | 9 | 5 |

[*] Source: Kingsley Davis and Hilda Hertz, "The World Distribution of Urbanization," *Bulletin of the International Statistical Institute*, XXXIII, Part 4, 227-42.
[†] Includes U.S.A. and Canada.
[‡] Without U.S.S.R.
[§] Includes Mexico, countries of Central America, and Caribbean Islands.

A large urban population is appropriately identified as characteristic of an economically advanced area, the advent of industrialization, and the development of Western civilization in general. Yet, despite the relatively low rate of urbanization in the economically less advanced areas, they have more people living in cities of twenty thousand or more, or cities of one hundred thousand or more, than do Europe and North America combined. In 1950, forty-one per cent of world population living in cities of twenty thousand or more was in Europe (excluding the U.S.S.R.) and North America; whereas Asia, Latin America, and Africa combined contained over forty-five per cent of the world's residents in cities of this size. The U.S.S.R. contained about twelve per cent of the world's urban population, and Oceania the remaining one or two per cent.

The rate of world urbanization, and particularly that of the areas with low proportions of urban populations at the present time, may be expected to continue to accelerate. In 1950, about 502 million persons lived in cities of twenty thousand and over. By 1975, should the rate of urbanization as observed between 1900 and 1950 continue and total world population increase in accordance with United Nations projections, urban population in places of this size will have more than doubled, to reach a level of 1.2 billions. Similarly, under the same conditions, population in cities of one hundred thousand and over—314 million, in 1950—could reach a level of 745 million, i.e., also more than double, by 1975. Even if the proportion of the world's urban population remained fixed from 1950 to 1975, the population in places of twenty-thousand and over would increase by about fifty-five per cent simply because of total population increase alone. If the trend continues, by 1975 thirty per cent of the world's peoples will live in cities of twenty thousand and over, and nineteen per cent will live in cities of one hundred thousand and over. The large share of the increase in the world's urban population will occur in the economically underdeveloped areas. Asia, alone, will account for over half of the increase during the 1950–75 period.

Urban problems and the problems of rapid urbanization are quite different in the economically advanced and the economically underdeveloped areas of the world respectively. In the economically advanced nations, urbanization is both an antecedent and a consequence of high levels of living. It both makes possible and is a manifestation of great increases in division of labor and specialization, in technology, in skill, and in productivity. In the economically underdeveloped areas, it does not usually have these properties. There, large concentrations of urban population are only to a minor degree symbols of man's mastery over nature—they represent more the transfer of underemployment and poverty from an overpopulated rural countryside to an urban setting. In consequence, the social, economic, and technological problems of rapid urbanization must be considered separately for the underdeveloped and the developed areas of the globe respectively.

\* \* \* \* \*

## SOCIAL PROBLEMS

The city represents not only a new form of economic organization and a changed physical environment. It also is a profoundly modified social order affecting man's conduct and thought. Urbanization produces the city as a physical and economic artifact, and also produces "urbanism as a way of life." The size, density, and heterogeneity of population—aspects of "social morphology"—affect the nature, intensity, and frequency of contact, and, therefore, influence the nature of the process of socialization and human nature itself. The city is a type of mutation in culture that has far-reaching effects on social structure and process and on social institutions, including the structure and function of government. The transition from pre-urban to urban living necessarily involves frictions, which are manifested in social and personal problems. Rapid urbanization exacerbates these frictions.

The effects of living in large urban agglomerations have frequently been treated in the sociological literature. A number of frameworks for the analysis of the impact of urbanization on the social order and on the person have emerged. Among these are the distinction between "organic" and "mechanical" solidarity (Durkheim, 1893); between "community" and "society" (Toennies, 1897); and between "folk" and "urban" ways of life (Redfield, 1930; Wirth, 1938). The chief effects of urban living on the personal level are, probably, discernible in the changed nature of interpersonal relations and in the relative flexibility of personal patterns of behavior. On the cultural and social level, they are to be found in the changed nature of the forces making for cohesion, in the changed genesis and function of social institutions, and in the changed structure and role of government.

On the personal level, contacts in the urban setting become secondary, segmental, and utilitarian, rather than primary, integral, and sentimental as in the traditional social order. Personality tends to change from a relatively rigid structure molded by the traditional social heritage to more fluid flexible patterns, arising from the necessity to exercise choice and from rationalism in behavior, as the hold of tradition loosens and new urban problems emerge. On the social level, cohesion in the urban social order becomes a function of interdependence engendered by increased specialization and division of labor; it is no longer the product of the constraint of convention in a relatively homogeneous and closed traditional order. Social institutions in the urban setting become "enacted" rather than "crescive" as older functions become attenuated or disappear and new instrumentalities arise to cope with unprecedented situations and problems. Even the basic social institutions—the family and the church —are subjected to forces which modify their structure, their role, and their hold on the behavior of the person.

In the urban setting, the role of government is one of increasing interventionism as organizational complexity and interdependence increase. In the West, the transition from a feudal to an industrialized and urbanized order has been characterized by the emergence of complex formal organization—bureaucracy—not only in government, but also in business, labor, voluntary associations, and virtually all organized aspects of the mass society.

In this macrocosmic consideration of the impact of urbanization, we must emphasize that the transition from the traditional to the urban society does not proceed in an orderly and synchronized manner. The process of urbanization and its impact proceed with different tempos in different sectors of the society and among the several nations. In fact, one of the basic social problems of urbanization is to be found in the coexistence, at any one time, of different stages and of differential impacts of urbanization on the social order. Moreover, the more rapid the rate of urbanization, the greater becomes the probability that divers sectors of the social order will be characterized by anachronistic relationships.

These general elements provide a framework for more specific manifestations of the social problems associated with rapid urbanization. The acute as well as chronic aspects of social problems that result from rapid urbanization are, perhaps, most discernible in the adjustment of in-migrants to urban living. The rural in-migrant to the city is typically from a relatively homogeneous origin. In the city, he is confronted with a bewildering and almost incomprehensible vastness and heterogeneity. He usually lives for some time with his fellow villagers or relatives and only gradually becomes accommodated to city life. He must adapt to new and unfamiliar ways of making a living; a money economy; regular working hours; the absence of warm family living; large numbers of impersonal contacts with other human beings; new forms of recreation; and a quite different physical setting, often involving new kinds of housing, sanitation, traffic congestion, and noise. One of the greatest adjustment problems centers around the transition from a subsistence to a monetary economy, and dependence on a job for subsistence.

Furthermore, the in-migrant often finds his area of first settlement is the shanty town, in which the decadence of the underdeveloped urban environment is manifest in its most extreme form. Consequently, superimposed on problems of adjustment there may be severe problems of health and nutrition, and of extreme poverty and squalor in living conditions. In such a setting, the in-migrant frequently displays personal disorganization as the subjective aspect of social disorganization. It is in the in-migrant family that the greatest incidences of personal and social pathology are found—delinquency, crime, prostitution, mental illness, alcoholism, drug addiction, etc.

Another element contributes to the social problems and is a source of severe problems for the economy as well. This is the fact that rural in-migrant workers often lack rudimentary skills for industrial work, possess high rates of illiteracy, and are otherwise ill-prepared for city living. Throughout the underdeveloped countries, the need to increase literacy and to provide minimum vocational training for urban employment is acute. In fact, the provision of adequate educational and vocational training, both to the in-migrant and to the more permanent inhabitant of urban places, is among the most critical social problems which confront the underdeveloped areas.

Rapid urbanization is accompanied by increasing tempos of cultural, social, and personal change. A number of scholars have maintained that underdeveloped areas with non-Western cultures possess ideologies and value systems that tend to resist change in general and, therefore, changes of the type induced by urbanization. A rapid rate of urbanization, as contrasted with a slow one, conceivably increases the frictions of transition from non-Western to urban (and presumably Western) value systems. It is, of course, disputable whether Western values identified with urbanism as a way of life are an antecedent or a consequence of industrialization and urbanization; and whether they are the only values consonant with urban living. Conceivably, the difference between non-Western outlooks produces different kinds of "urban mentality" and interpersonal and social relations in the urban setting. Whatever the answer to this question may be, it *is* true that rapid urbanization increases the tensions and frictions of adjustment in value systems from pre-urban ways of life.

Also among the more pressing social problems in the urban setting are the series constituting "the population problem." As dramatically demonstrated in Ceylon, contemporary public health methods permit startlingly rapid decreases in mortality to be effected in short periods of time, while fertility rates and aggregate product remain relatively unchanged. In consequence, the underdeveloped areas of the world are just beginning the type of "population explosion" which the economically advanced nations have undergone over the past three centuries. Since the capacity to decrease mortality rates is growing more rapidly, the population-explosion potential of the underdeveloped areas is of considerably greater magnitude. Urban growth rates are fed by immigration from rural areas, as well as by the natural increase resulting from lower death rates; but the large streams of migration from rural to urban areas are a function of the national explosions in the underdeveloped nations. Rapid rates of urbanization could, in the longer run, contribute to the solution of the population problem in so far as urbanization can accelerate literacy, change value systems, and prepare the populace for limiting fertility.

Another group of serious problems created or augmented by rapid rates of urbanization are those of internal disorder, political unrest, and governmental instability fed by mass misery and frustration in the urban setting. The facts that the differences between the "have" and "have not" nations, and between the "have" and "have not" peoples within nations, have become "felt differences," and that we are experiencing a "revolution in expectations," have given huge urban population agglomerations an especially incendiary and explosive character. In the domestic and international settings in which many underdeveloped areas find themselves, huge and rapidly swelling urban populations constitute supersensitive tinderboxes with explosive potential. Newspaper headlines of the last few months provide adequate documentation of this observation.

Another major social problem that is precipitated by rapidly increasing urbanization is the task of planning and devising programs designed to deal with urban social problems. Planning agencies, health and welfare services, educational, vocational training, and recreational facilities, etc. are either inadequate or non-existent in many of the underdeveloped nations. In particular, agencies for receiving and dealing with the problems of the in-migrant are inadequate or non-existent. Planning and programming the solution of social problems entail difficult decisions involving national planning, in general. They involve, among other things, the complex task of maximizing the participation of the urban dwellers themselves by motivating them to play a major role in helping to solve their own problems.

## Oscar Lewis

# The Culture of Poverty

THE CULTURE of poverty, as here defined, does not include primitive peoples whose backwardness is the result of their isolation and un-developed technology and whose society for the most part is not class stratified. Such peoples have a relatively integrated, satisfying, and self-sufficient culture. Nor is the culture of poverty synonymous with the working class, the proletariat, or the peasantry, all three of which vary a good deal in economic status throughout the world. In the United States, for example, the working class lives like an elite compared to the lower class of the less developed countries. The culture of poverty would apply only to those people who are at the very bottom of the socio-economic scale, the poorest workers, the poorest peasants, plantation laborers, and that large heterogenous mass of small artisans and tradesmen usually referred to as the lumpen proletariat.

The culture or subculture of poverty comes into being in a variety of historical contexts. Most commonly it develops when a stratified social and economic system is breaking down or is being replaced by another, as in the case of the transition from feudalism to capitalism or during the industrial revolution. Sometimes it results from imperial conquest in which the conquered are maintained in a servile status which may continue for many generations. It can also occur in the process of detribalization such as is now going on in Africa where, for example, the tribal migrants to the cities are developing "courtyard cultures" remarkably similar to the Mexico City *vecindades*. We are prone to view such slum conditions as transitional or temporary phases of drastic culture change. But this is not necessarily the case, for the culture of poverty is often a persisting condition even in stable social systems. Certainly in Mexico it has been a more or less permanent phenomenon since the Spanish conquest of 1519, when the process of detribalization and the movement of peasants to the cities began. Only the size, location, and composition of the slums have been in flux. I suspect that similar processes have been going on in many other countries of the world.

It seems to me that the culture of poverty has some universal characteristics which transcend regional, rural-urban, and even national differences. In my earlier book, *Five Families* (Basic Books, 1959), I suggested that there were remarkable similarities in family structure, interpersonal relations, time orientations, value systems, spending patterns, and the sense of community in lower-class settlements in London, Glasgow, Paris, Harlem, and Mexico City. Although this is not the place for an extensive comparative analysis of the culture of poverty, I should like to elaborate upon some of these and other traits in order to present a provisional conceptual model of this culture based mainly upon my Mexican materials.

In Mexico, the culture of poverty includes at least the lower third of the rural and urban population. This population is characterized by a relatively higher death rate, a lower life expectancy, a higher proportion of individuals in the younger age groups, and, because of child labor and working women, a higher proportion of gainfully employed. Some of these indices are higher in the poor *colonias* or sections of Mexico City than in rural Mexico as a whole.

The culture of poverty in Mexico is a provincial and locally oriented culture. Its members are only partially integrated into national institutions and are marginal people even when they live in the heart of a great city. In Mexico City, for example, most of the poor have a very low level of education and literacy, do not belong to labor unions, are not members of a political party, do not participate in the medical care, maternity, and old-age benefits of the national welfare agency known as *Seguro Social,* and make very little use of the city's banks, hospitals, department stores, museums, art galleries and airports.

The economic traits which are most characteristic of the culture of poverty include the constant struggle for survival, unemployment and underemployment, low wages, a miscellany of unskilled occupations, child labor, the absence of savings, a chronic shortage of cash, the absence of food reserves in the home, the pattern of frequent buying of small quantities of food many times a day as the need arises, the pawning of personal goods, borrowing from local money lenders at usurious rates of interest, spontaneous informal credit devices (*tandas*) organized by neighbors, and the use of second-hand clothing and furniture.

Some of the social and psychological characteristics include living in crowded quarters, a lack of privacy, gregariousness, a high incidence of alcoholism, frequent resort to violence in the settlement of quarrels, frequent use of physical violence in the training of children, wife beating, early initiation into sex, free unions or consensual marriages, a relatively high incidence of the abandonment of mothers and children, a trend toward mother-centered families and a much greater knowledge of maternal relatives, the predominance of the nuclear family, a strong predisposition to authoritarianism, and a great emphasis upon family solidarity—an ideal only rarely achieved. Other traits include a strong present time orientation with relatively little ability to defer gratification and plan for the future, a sense of resignation and fatalism based upon the realities of their difficult life situation, a belief in male superiority which reaches its crystalization in *machismo* or the cult of masculinity, a corresponding martyr complex among women, and finally, a high tolerance for psychological pathology of all sorts.

Some of the above traits are not limited to the culture of poverty in Mexico but are also found in the middle and upper classes. However, it is the peculiar patterning of these traits which defines the culture of poverty. For example, in the middle class, *machismo* is expressed in terms of sexual exploits and the Don Juan complex whereas in the lower class it is expressed in terms of heroism and lack of physical fear. Similarly, drinking in the middle class is a social amenity whereas in the lower class getting drunk has different and multiple functions—to forget one's troubles, to prove one's ability to drink, and to build up sufficient confidence to meet difficult life situations.

Many of the traits of the subculture of poverty can be viewed as attempts at local solutions for problems not met by existing institutions and agencies because the people are not eligible for them, cannot afford them, or are suspicious of them. For example, unable to obtain credit from banks, they are thrown upon their own resources and organize informal credit devices without interest. Unable to afford doctors, who are used only in dire emergencies, and suspicious of hospitals "where one goes only to die," they rely upon herbs or other home remedies and upon local curers and midwives. Critical of priests "who are human and therefore sinners like all of us," they rarely go to confession or Mass and rely upon prayer to the images of saints in their own homes and upon pilgrimages to popular shrines.

A critical attitude toward some of the values and institutions of the dominant classes, hatred of the police, mistrust of government and those in high position, and a cynicism which extends even to the church gives the culture of poverty a counter quality and a potential for being used in political movements aimed against the existing social order. Finally, the sub-culture of poverty also has a residual quality in the sense that its members are attempting to utilize and integrate into a workable way of life the remnants of beliefs and customs of diverse origins.

I should like to emphasize that the Sánchez family is by no means at the lowest level of poverty in Mexico. About a million and a half people out of a total population of approximately four million in Mexico City live in similar or worse conditions. The persistence of poverty in the first city of the nation fifty years after the great Mexican Revolution raises serious questions about the extent to which the Revolution has achieved its social objectives. Judging from the Sánchez family, their friends, neighbors, and relatives, the essential promise of the Revolution has yet to be fulfilled.

This assertion is made in the full knowledge of the impressive and far-reaching changes which have been brought about by the Mexican Revolution—the transformation of a semifeudal economy, the distribution of land to the peasants, the emancipation of the Indian, the strengthening of labor's position, the spread of public education, the nationalization of oil and the railroads, and the emergence of a new middle class. Since 1940 the economy has been expanding and the country has become acutely production conscious. Leading newspapers report daily in their headlines record-breaking achievements in agriculture and industry and proudly announce huge gold reserves in the national treasury. A boom spirit has been created which is reminiscent of the great expansion in the United States at the turn of the century. Since 1940 the population has increased by over thirteen million, to reach a high of thirty-four million in 1960. The growth of Mexico City has been phenomenal, from one and a half million in 1940 to over four million in 1960. Mexico City is now the largest city in Latin America and the third or fourth largest city on the American continent.

One of the most significant trends in Mexico since 1940 has been the increasing influence of the United States on Mexican life. Never before in the long history of U.S.-Mexican relations has there been such a varied and intense interaction between the two countries. The close co-operation during World War II, the rapid tempo of U.S. investment, which has reached almost a billion dollars as of 1960, the remarkable influx of U.S. tourists into Mexico and of Mexican visitors to the United States, the annual migration of several hundred thousand Mexican agricultural workers to the United States, the exchange of students, technicians and professors, and the increasing number of Mexicans who are becoming U.S. citizens have made for a new type of relationship between the two countries.

The major television programs are sponsored by foreign controlled companies like Nestlé, General Motors, Ford, Procter & Gamble and Colgate. Only the use of the Spanish language and Mexican artists distinguish the commercials from those in the United States. American department-store retail practices have been made popular in most of the large cities by stores like Woolworth's and Sears Roebuck and Co., and self-service supermarkets now package many American brand foods for the growing middle class. English has replaced French as a second language in the schools, and the French tradition in medicine is slowly but surely being replaced by U.S. medicine.

Despite the increased production and the apparent prosperity, the uneven distribution of the growing national wealth has made the disparity between the incomes of the rich and the poor more striking than ever before. And despite some rise in the standard of living for the general population, in 1956 over 60 percent of the population were still ill fed, ill housed, and ill clothed, 40 percent were illiterate, and 46 percent of the nation's children were not going to school. A chronic inflation since 1940 has squeezed the real income of the poor, and the cost of living for workers in Mexico City has risen over five times since 1939. According to the census of 1950 (published in 1955), 89 percent of all Mexican families reporting income earned less than 600 *pesos* a month, or $69 at the 1950 rate of exchange and $48 at the 1960 rate. (There are 12.50 *pesos* to the dollar.) A study published in 1960 by a competent Mexican economist, Ifigenia M. de Navarrete, showed that between 1950 and 1957 approximately the lower third of the national population suffered a decrease in real income.

It is common knowledge that the Mexican economy cannot give jobs to all of its people. From 1942 to 1955 about a million and a half Mexicans came to the United States as *braceros* or temporary agricultural laborers, and this figure does not include "wetbacks" or other illegal immigrants. Were the United States suddenly to close its borders to the *braceros*, a major crisis would probably occur in Mexico. Mexico also has become increasingly dependent upon the U.S. tourist trade to stabilize its economy. In 1957 over 700,000 tourists from the United States spent almost six hundred million dollars in Mexico, to make tourism the single largest industry in the country. The income from the tourist trade is about equal to the total Mexican federal budget.

One aspect of the standard of living which has improved very little since 1940 is housing. With the rapidly rising population and urbanization, the crowding and slum conditions in the large cities are actually getting worse. Of the 5.2 million dwellings reported in the Mexican census of 1950, 60 percent had only one room and 25 percent two rooms; 70 percent of all houses were made of adobe, wood, poles and rods, or rubble, and only 18 percent of brick and masonry. Only 17 percent had private, piped water.

In Mexico City conditions are no better. The city is made more beautiful each year for U.S. tourists by building new fountains, planting flowers along the principal streets, building new hygienic markets, and driving the beggars and vendors off the streets. But over a third of the city's population lives in slumlike housing settlements known as *vecindades* where they suffer from a chronic water shortage and lacking elementary sanitary facilities. Usually, *vecindades* consist of one or more rows of single-story dwellings with one or two rooms, facing a common courtyard. The dwellings are constructed of cement, brick, or adobe and form a well-defined unit that has some of the characteristics of a small community. The size and types of the *vecindades* vary enormously. Some consist of only a few dwellings, others of a few hundred. Some are found in the commercial heart of the city, in run-down sixteenth- and seventeenth-century two- and three-story Spanish colonial buildings, while others, on the outskirts of the city, consist of wooden shacks or *jacales* and look like semitropical Hoovervilles.

It seems to me that the material in this book has important implications for our thinking and our policy in regard to the underdeveloped countries of the world and particularly Latin America. It highlights the social, economic, and psychological complexities which have to be faced in any effort to transform and eliminate the culture of poverty from the world. It suggests that basic changes in the attitudes and value systems of the poor must go hand in hand with improvements in the material conditions of living.

Even the best-intentioned governments of the underdeveloped countries face difficult obstacles because of what poverty has done to the poor. Certainly most of the characters in this volume are badly damaged human beings. Yet with all of their inglorious defects and weaknesses, it is the poor who emerge as the true heroes of contemporary Mexico, for they are paying the cost of the industrial progress of the nation. Indeed, the political stability of Mexico is grim testimony to the great capacity for misery and suffering of the ordinary Mexican. But even the Mexican capacity for suffering has its limits, and unless ways are found to achieve a more equitable distribution of the growing national wealth and a greater equality of sacrifice during the difficult period of industrialization, we may expect social upheavals, sooner or later.

*[The remainder of this selection consists of portions of the extended recorded statement made by Jesús Sánchez (the name is fictitious) whose family history provided Professor Lewis with much of the materials for his study of the culture of poverty.]*

## JESÚS SÁNCHEZ

I am a person who bears grudges and I have a lot against three of my children, Manuel, Roberto and Consuelo. My body is becoming half-paralyzed from being so angry with these children of mine. I am ashamed to talk about it. It is hard for a father to have such sons. They turned out bad because of bad surroundings, bad companions. Their friends are doing these boys no good. It is a shame that I cannot do anything about it. In spite of my advice, they go the other way instead of taking the straight path.

There is nothing better in this world than upright work. I am a poor and humble person but I try to do things the best way I can. They can't say their father came home drunk, or abandoned them. An uncle of theirs just died of drink. It seems they take after their uncle more than they do me. I don't understand it.

My sons haven't amounted to anything because they don't like to have anyone order them around. First, they want to be millionaires and then get a job. How can you expect to start from the top? We all have to work our way up from the bottom, isn't that so? But my sons, they want to do it the other way around. So everything they do is a failure.

They don't have any stamina for work. They haven't got common sense. They don't have the will power to get a job and stick to it, an honest job so that they can go out into the street looking decent and feeling proud of themselves. I'd be happy, it would give me the greatest satisfaction, if they could be like that.

The other day I said to Consuelo, I don't want you to be somebody you're not supposed to be or to forget what social class you belong to. When people who've had a little bit of education suddenly start acting uppity, they get slapped down. Now take me as an example," I said to her. "I've always been a simple worker and I'll always be that way and nobody is going to slap me down. Even though you've gone to school a few years, that doesn't mean you should feel you've joined the upper classes. Take a look at yourself in the mirror and tell me what class you belong to, what your place is in society." It's all right for her to improve herself a little, but she shouldn't get swell-headed and look down on her own people, the class she belongs to. I told her the other night, "I'm your father, whether you like it or not. No matter how I go dressed or how poor I am, I'm your father and you can't get away from it."

I admit I've made some mistakes. I am no white dove but I've always taken care of them. There are a lot of men who get rid of their children when they take a woman. Do you know what it's like to have mother-less children on your hands? An orphan has everything against him, no-body wants him. And so what could I do? I've provided everything for them because I like to do things that way. I work like a slave and go on struggling the best I can, moving ahead, as everyone can see. Lots of times you can do more harm to your children by giving them their food and having the table spread for them all the time . . . they don't worry about doing anything for themselves.

I wanted them to go to school, to learn a trade. I didn't ask them to work so they would bring me money, to buy their own clothes or to feed themselves. I have taken care of them for over twenty years and they have never lacked for a plate of soup or a cup of coffee. Why should they have turned out bad? I don't understand.

\*     \*     \*     \*     \*

The biggest mistake we Mexicans make is to marry so young, without money, without savings and even before we have a steady job. We marry and have a houseful of children before we know it, and then we're stuck and can't possibly get ahead. To tell the truth, we Mexicans lack preparation for life.

There are lots of cases of abandonment of children in Mexico. It happens all the time. The government should take a hand in the matter and put a stop to it. I wish we had laws in Mexico, in my country, like you have in the United States. We wouldn't have so many bums . . . all this rotten treatment of people, speaking frankly, all of this is bad for children, for people, for the whole country. All of this freedom is bad for people. They should close up 80 percent of the saloons, build more schools, close up 80 percent of these places that breed vice. There should be more control over youngsters, over youth, rich and poor alike. "O.K., tell me, how many children do you have?" "Well, four." "How old are they? Fifteen and up, right? What do your children do, who supports them, how do they spend their time, where do they work?" "Well, they're not working." "Why aren't they working? You make them go to work and if you don't, you'll get a week in jail to start with." No bribes, a week in jail, and when it happens the second time, then it'll take a year and you'd see how much more orderly everything would be and how the Mexican people would behave more decently if we had stricter laws, because the laws we have here in my country are very loose. The Mexican people are going under, because there's no leadership and no faith, and there's so much lousy corruption, as you can see.

If we ever got a really tough government here, and it called up everyone who had been a president and said, "You go to the Zócalo and pile up all the millions you've robbed from the people," why, there'd be enough to build another capital!

You have to live among our families to see what we suffer from and how it can be cured. They haven't made a thorough study of the problem. Those gentlemen who rule over us have expensive cars and many millions in the bank, but they don't see what's underneath where the poor people live. Why, they won't drive over to look from their cars. They stay down there in the center of town where all the fashionable stores are, but as for the sections where the poor live . . . they just don't know what a miserable life we lead. They disregard this great and deep problem which exists in Mexico today. They disregard the fact that right here in the capital there are lots of people who eat only one or two meals a day.

There is not enough money, not enough work and everything is so expensive; prices went up again today. The cost of living has gone up a great deal within a few days. For example, take a family with eight, or six mouths to feed. How are you going to support them on a wage of eleven *pesos* a day? True, they've raised the minimum wage a *peso* a day. What does a *peso* amount to if the stuff you buy has gone up three or four times? Well, that's the way it is. We need different rulers who can make a better study of Mexico's problem and do something for the people, for the worker and the peasant, because they are the ones who most need help. Take a worker in the capital for example, if he gets two hundred *pesos* on pay day, he'll throw away 150 or 180 in the saloon and take twenty *pesos* home. People don't know how to use the money they earn. Poor mothers, and the kids half naked! You see kids five and ten years old with tuberculosis. What do you think is the reason? Lack of care by the parents in the home, lack of responsibility and lack of money. They spend more out on the street on foolish things than they do for what's needed at home. There are very few fathers who try to meet their obligations. A fellow who is halfway decent and tries to do what he's supposed to, he'll find some way to make out, one way or another, he'll bring some bread home to his family.

I've gone so far as to tell some people I'd like to see us have an American president here in Mexico. Then we'd see how Mexico would change and make progress. He'd pull in all the bums, all the tramps. "You don't like to work? Off you go to the Islas Marías for the rest of your life." None of this passing out a little money and this and the other and back they come. No sir, they stay right there. They're parasites.

Yes, there has been progress and some have benefited, thanks to the governments that have concerned themselves with the workers. But they never helped me! My situation is better because of my pigs and the lottery. I have been very lucky in the lottery. I won my first prize with No. 9878. I never forget the numbers that have given me prizes. With that money I bought the radio. With the same number I won again and I bought the bed. My biggest prize was five thousand *pesos*, which I won with No. 19228. With part of that money I built my house in El Dorado. And with the rest of the money, I bought the wall clock. The little I had, I used well and it helped me get ahead.

But in the thirty years I've been in Mexico City, the life of the poor people has changed very little, very little. Some of them call it a big change when, for example, they used to make one or one and a half *pesos* during the Calles period, which was very little, right? But then sugar and beans cost fifteen *centavos*. Now take beans; you make eleven *pesos* and beans cost from three to four *pesos*. That's a fact! So where is the improvement? Now, for example, you have things which cost twenty *pesos* yesterday and they've gone up to thirty-five. All right, so for one reason or another they reduce it two *pesos*. So you say something, and they tell you, "Why, no, sir, if it was thirty-five yesterday and it's thirty-three today, we've reduced the price." Reduced the price . . . with an increase of thirteen *pesos!* That's the way they reduce prices here today. So what's the advantage for the people, for the worker, for the peasant? None at all, the way I see it. On the contrary, every day they're squeezing us more. So what?

\*　　\*　　\*　　\*　　\*

I struggled and worked day and night to establish my home, a poor home, as you can see, but I have my happy moments with my grandchildren. It is first for God and then for my grandchildren that I'm on my feet, plugging away. When I'm downtown, I'm careful about traffic. At my age, it isn't myself I have to watch out for, but the kids. I won't be able to give them very much but at least they go on living and growing and I hope God will allow me to be with them until they can earn their own living.

I want to leave them a room, that's my ambition; to build that little house, one or two rooms or three so that each child will have a home and so they can live there together. But they don't want to help me. I asked God to give me the strength to keep struggling so I won't go under soon and maybe finish that little house. Just a modest place that they can't be thrown out of. I'll put a fence around it and no one will bother them. It will be a protection for them when I fall down and don't get up again.

Richard D. Lambert

---

# The Social and Psychological Determinants of Savings and Investments in Developing Societies

THE FUNDAMENTAL QUESTION posed by this paper[1] is: To what extent do attitudes and values intrinsic to the cultures of the countries from Pakistan to the Philippines determine the amount, the components, the demand for, and the use of savings? It seems clear that differences among countries in their current level and pace of economic development are imperfectly correlated with the rate of savings alone.

Kuznets[2] reports that the range of differences among nations in the proportion of their national product they devote to capital formation is fairly narrow, much narrower than either differences in per capita income or in gross national product.

1. This paper grows out of a project sponsored by UNESCO and the Conference on Economic and Cultural Affairs. Participants in the project were Professor Bert Hoselitz of the University of Chicago, Professor A. F. A. Husain of Dacca University in East Pakistan, Professor Agaton Pal of Silliman University in the Philippines, Professor Michael Swift of the University of Malaya, Professor S. J. Tambiah of the University of Ceylon, Professor V. Q. Thuc of the University of Saigon in Viet Nam, Professor Marjorie Topley of Hong Kong, Professor T. K. N. Unnithan of the School of Town and County Planning in New Delhi. I have drawn heavily upon their work for these comments. The Asian countries covered, as indicated by the participants, are those in South and South East Asia (what used to be called Southern Asia), from Pakistan to the Philippines and excluding China and Japan.

2. Simon Kuznets, "Capital Formation Proportions: International Comparisons for Recent Years," *Economic Development and Cultural Change*, VIII, No. 4, Part 2 (July, 1960).

Throughout South Asia, an annual national savings rate of eight to nine per cent is common. A recent estimate[3] for India's savings from 1951–57 found them to range from 7.6 to 5.9 per cent of the national income. This was accompanied by a capital formation rate of 5.1 per cent of the net domestic product, compared with 10.2 per cent for the United States, 8.3 per cent for the United Kingdom, and a massive 23.2 per cent for Japan.[4] Latest reports indicate that India may have reached eleven per cent. However, these rates of savings and capital formation can be misleading. In the first place, they are based on aggregate data in which as much as forty per cent of the value of the national output must be imputed, since it never reaches the market. In the second place, a large part of the savings, perhaps twenty to twenty-five per cent in India, is in non-monetized form; and this part is expended on direct investment, particularly in agriculture and small-scale enterprise, where replacement consumes an indeterminate, but sizable, amount of investment. Malenbaum[5] estimates that seventy-five per cent of investment in the private sector in India may have been directly invested, that is, expended by the individual saver on his own assets. Two-thirds of the private investment went into agriculture and housing, where such difficulties are greatest.

For these reasons, I shall not be primarily concerned with the volume of total national savings, i.e., income less consumption. I shall concentrate on other variables, both qualitative and quantitative, that influence the degree of effectiveness with which savings create the greatest possible additions to the national product. These variables comprise, in part, the factors relating to the separate schedules for savings and investment. They also include both structural features and attitudes relating to the demand side and to the effective utilization of savings. I shall omit consideration of a whole host of variables, such as interest rates, inflation, and other financial covariables of savings and investment,[6] even though these may be the primary implements available to government policy-makers seeking to manipulate the over-all rates. I shall examine ideologies and broad cultural features, some of them outside of the economic sphere proper, that are not so subject to short-run fluctuations or easy manipulation. As one consequence of the emphasis on cultural abstractions, the discussion will have more relevance to the private household sector of savings, where

---

3. V. V. Bhatt, "Savings and Capital Formation," *Economic Development and Cultural Change*, VII, No. 3, Part I (April, 1959), 318-42.

4. Kuznets, *op. cit.*

5. Wilfred Malenbaum, *East and West in India's Development* (1959).

6. For a review of current findings, see Irwin Friend, "Determinants of the Volume and Composition of Saving with Special Reference to the Influence of Monetary Policy" (to be published).

individual decisions are more directly influenced by cultural norms. I shall direct most of my remarks to the interaction between governmental development strategies and the attitudes and values in the rural areas where the greatest need for change occurs.

This emphasis is given in spite of the fact that aggregate national savings include, in addition, a sizable contribution provided by business corporations, where the ratio of savings to income is about the same in most countries whether developed or underdeveloped. These limitations, however, while they must be explicitly stated, do not undermine the importance of the attitudes and values of which I am writing.

In the countries of southern Asia, a high proportion of saving comes from the household sector—about eighty-seven per cent in India in 1956-57. Then, too, it is the scarcity of household savings that sets a limit to the domestic capital formation proportion.[7] In addition, one of the most important problems in underdeveloped countries is the conversion of household savings into corporate investment, particularly in the manufacturing sector, whose relative contribution to the gross national product can serve as a good index of domestic capital formation proportions. This problem involves the discouragement of direct investment in the household sector, greater monetization of savings, and the transfer of savings to the corporate sector, where the marginal propensity to save and invest is highest and where savings will be allocated to producer goods rather than to inventory or housing.

There is a tendency to use the experience of Western Europe and the United States as a model against which to contrast and measure the progress of developmental efforts in the underdeveloped countries. In some ways, the situation facing the underdeveloped countries—in particular the southern Asian countries—is very different from that which the West confronted at the outset of its period of rapid growth.

For instance, there was no parallel in the West to present Asian subsistence levels and rural population densities; and these factors make savings and accumulation for industrial investment more difficult for Asian countries. Also, at the important stage in the development of Western industrialism, wealth became concentrated in fewer and fewer hands. Today, in Asia, this would be politically dangerous in democratic countries, at least. Moreover, while Western capitalism and industrialization were based on the great trade of the eighteenth century and its accompanying capital accumulation, no similar virgin markets and favorable terms of trade await the developing countries today.

These and similar contrasts are essentially situational and more or less

7. Kuznets, *op. cit.*

directly related to economic affairs. Most observers would admit their relevance to economic growth. We are on much more treacherous ground when we include the attitudinal and non-economic variables.

Max Weber's venture into the relationship between religion and economics provoked a fulsome and sometimes acrimonious controversy. The dispute involved not only his attempt to attribute the rise of capitalism to the tenets of the Protestant ethic, but also similar efforts to show that non-economic factors lay behind economic phenomena. The attempts to find non-economic causes for economic events have graced the development of economics as an art and have permitted scholars from other disciplines to work happily in the economists' vineyards; but within the field of economics itself, the battle lines are still drawn. In the report of a recent set of conferences sponsored by the National Bureau of Economic Research on the comparative study of economic growth and structure, the editor remarked:

> The exact nature of the relationship between economic and non-economic factors in economic growth, and in particular the best method of studying this interrelationship, turned out to be possibly the most controversial point in our conferences and in comments on a preliminary draft of this report.[8]

Most economists would, I suspect, agree with an additional statement in the report that said, in effect, that non-economic factors should be given second priority, since most of them cannot be quantified, their connection with economic aspects is uncertain, and there is enough work to go around just with the economic factors without including others.

In spite of these arguments, this paper is on the attitudinal and valuational side of the line. Taking full cognizance of the Bureau's considered judgment, however, we must say that we too can argue only plausibility for the discussion to follow. One of the intentions of the UNESCO study is to generate the careful research necessary to test the propositions arising from this exploratory stage.

The classic way to study the problem is to match the elements that contrast in our own society before and after its period of rapid growth with contrasts between the West and the Orient today. This method rests upon the assumption, most clearly stated by Max Weber, that the development of "the rational capitalistic organization of free labour" in the West was a unique historical emergent, and that other countries wishing to emulate the rapid economic advance which accompanied that historical

---

8. Wilfred Malenbaum, *The Comparative Study of Economic Growth and Structure* (New York, 1959), p. 31.

process must supply the same cultural ingredients which produced it. Bert Hoselitz and I, in another paper,[9] have argued that the broad changes described below were crucial to the growth process in the West.

First, the domain of economic decisions became greatly enlarged so that, when an economic and a familial or religious value are in disagreement, the economic value wins out. To put it another way, the institutional limits of the economy, vis-à-vis the state, the family, and religion, were greatly extended. The second major factor was the evolution of a particular economic ideology of rational profit maximization. This, of course, follows Max Weber. The words *rational, profit,* and *maximization* should each be emphasized. The search for gain is ubiquitous in all societies; but rational profit maximization involves the principles that whatever brings the greatest monetary gains will be engaged in, and that science and technology will be used to the utmost in the reckoning and pursuit of this end. The third element crucial to the growth of the advanced economies of the West was the legitimation of the pursuit of maximum profits for all segments of society and not for just a limited few. In medieval Europe, subsistence was the fundamental motive for economic activity for the vast bulk of the populace. Traders who sought gain and accumulation were generally ethnically separate—Syrians, Greeks, Jews, Italians, Provençals, etc.; for others, this was not a worth-while endeavor. In the economic transformation of the West, profit became a generalized motive, legitimately sought by all members of the society. The fourth factor was the transformation of labor into a commodity, subject to the same market mechanisms as goods, however circumscribed the operation of the market.

If Weber's conception of the unique historical emergent is adopted, to what extent do the contrasts distinguishing the period before from the period after rapid economic growth in the West also distinguish the societies of the Orient from those in the West today? Weber chose the impact of religion on economic behavior as the starting point for his analysis. We are not interested in the specific validity of the Weber-Troeltsch theory[10] about the role of Protestantism in the West; but Weber's characterization of the Asian religions as lacking the attributes

9. Hoselitz and Lambert, "The Acquisition and Uses of Wealth in Western Societies," to be published in forthcoming UNESCO symposium.
10. For a good summary of the controversy see Ephraim Fischoff, "The Protestant Ethic and the Spirit of Capitalism: the History of a Controversy," *Social Research,* 11 (1944), 61-77. For a sampling of excerpts in the dispute, see Robert W. Green, *Protestantism and Capitalism: The Weber Thesis and its Critics* (Boston, 1959).

which had induced the rise of rational capitalism in the West is relevant to our purpose. He wrote of Asian religions:

> The unrestricted lust for gain of the Asiatics in large and in small is notoriously unequalled in the rest of the world. However, it is precisely a "drive for gain" pursued with every possible means including universal magic. It was lacking in precisely that which was decisive for the economics of the Occident: the refraction and rational immersion of the drive character of economic striving and its accompaniments in a system of rational, inner-worldly ethic of behavior, e.g., the "inner-worldly asceticism" of Protestantism in the West. Asiatic religion could not supply the presuppositions of inner-worldly asceticism.[11]

Weber's concern was primarily historical. He maintained that the religious philosophies of the East made unlikely the *indigenous* development and ascendance to power of an elite like the Western bourgeois class. The problem with which we are concerned is somewhat different. The countries of southern Asia are currently governed by elites who are committed to rational profit maximization, albeit for national rather than for private units; and the important question is whether the religions present an obstacle to such development. The most common assumption in this regard is that priority's being given to spiritual rather than material ends presents a major handicap. This thesis, like the story of Mark Twain's death, is highly exaggerated.

The two most extreme cases of "other-worldly" religions, Hinduism and Buddhism, consider personal salvation as the highest goal, but conceive of it as attainable only by a limited few. The doctrines of self-denial or the cessation of desire were applicable only to religious professionals or, for the ordinary man, confined to a stage in life in which worldly obligations had already been met. Among the Hindus, most of the traditional literature concerns the soul and is a glorification of the practice of religion; but some of it is highly secular. For instance, Kautalya's *Arthashastra* is explicitly a primer on means of maximizing wealth and power. An entire stream of literature, sometimes called the *banya* or merchant literature, which was most highly developed among the Jains, gives religious sanction to what would elsewhere be called secular ends. Laxmi, the goddess of wealth and good fortune, is a favorite in the Hindu pantheon. Even in the most sacrosanct of all Hindu literature, the *Rig-Veda*, the patronage of the sacred ritual was intended to advance the wealth and power of the kings. Later, the particularistic

---

11. Max Weber, *The Religion of India*, trans. Hans H. Gerth and Don Martindale (Glencoe, Ill., 1958), p. 337.

nature of duty included in the concept of *dharma* meant that each man carried out his *vrata*, his function—which, for all but the ascetic few, meant the pursuit of secular goals. Thus, while the search for wealth was not the highest of purposes, it was a perfectly respectable one. There is, moreover, a great gap between the religion sponsored by this priestly literature and popular Hinduism, which is full of magic, deities, devils, and spirits both benign and malevolent; and the extent to which the Brahmans historically enjoyed the ascendancy they depict in their literature is an open question.

The same is true for Buddhism, where the denial of worldly pleasures is even more marked. Salvation and release from the pain of worldly existences and cycle of rebirths is a possibility only for *bhikkus*, or monks. For the rest of the populace, the emphasis rests upon the accumulation of merit through good deeds, *Karma*, which, for the laity, are in the main socially visible forms of piety and dedication to the Buddhist *Sangha*. For many of these deeds it was useful, even imperative to be wealthy. For instance, merit derives from supporting monks, constructing monasteries, wells, and ponds. The rewards for good deeds were secular riches, a good caste in the next life, good name, good friends. Nirvana was pictured as a land of splendor, wealth and happiness. In popular Buddhism, asceticism is not associated with the laity. The rewards for the deeds of the *upasaka*, or lay disciple, were not release but mundane pleasure in this life and the next.

The esoteric doctrines of Taoism contained no injunctions against trying to acquire wealth, and Confucianism is most secular in its orientation. Islam is not an other-worldly religion, and the *Koran* and *Hadith* do not depreciate the pursuit of wealth. In fact, Muslim law lays down a definite code for business activity, regulating purchases, sales, contracts, partnerships, loans, deposits, etc. But Islam does prohibit certain means of attaining wealth. Unlike Hinduism, in which the defiling occupations are largely menial, Islam prohibits the taking of usury, which is distinguished from permissible interest in that the latter involves risk-bearing or return on capital for productive activity. There are, in fact, some professional Muslim moneylenders in South Asia, like the Pathans, the Memons and the Khojas, but they either operate outside of their home regions or are descendants of Hindu trading castes. One of the most powerful incentives for the creation of Pakistan was that trading and credit facilities were monopolized by Hindus and Jains in areas where the populace was overwhelmingly Muslim; but Pakistan is still having difficulty in filling the gap created by their departure.[12] The recent expulsion of the Chinese minority from rural Indonesia is another case in point.

---

12. See Richard D. Lambert, "Religion, Economics and Violence in Bengal," *Middle East Journal*, IV (July, 1950), 307-28.

While the major religions of Asia do not denigrate wealth, they do tend to place the responsibility for the acquisition or lack of wealth on forces other than the individual's own efforts. In the Philippines, success is attributed to "swerte," or luck. In Islam, each man is apportioned at birth a certain *risq,* or share in life. True, he must work for it; but the amount is not set by his own efforts. In Viet Nam, the astrological rules of Tu Vi and the astral cycle determine one's destiny. In all the Asian societies where one's chances in life depend upon ascriptive characteristics,[13] the cultures bear a heavy burden of fatalism. I do not argue that fatalism destroys either the aspirations or the striving. It does provide an explanation for success and a consolation for the lack of it. It removes the necessity of seeking rational means for manipulating one's fate.

The removal from rationality is reinforced by the ubiquitous dependence in popular religion upon the intercession of minor deities and spirits who must be pleased—or, in the case of lesser ones, even magically manipulated. In fact, the behavior of villagers throughout southern Asia clearly shows that to them the only form of investment likely to produce the spectacular change in their fortunes that is necessary to bring them to a surplus standard of living is the investment of money, time, and food in the service of some supernatural power. If this investment is unproductive, the drain upon any small increment in income, particularly monetized income, may be substantial. In general, I would argue that the inhibition to economic growth engendered by religions in Asia lies not in their other-worldly orientation but in their institutional characteristics— especially in their ability to absorb accumulations of wealth that might otherwise be put to more economically productive uses. Even in a Christian country like the Philippines, increments in family wealth call for increased expenditures on religious rituals. Wedding ceremonies, burial ceremonies, and feasts for the dead are sharply graduated by cost. In a wedding, the proximity of the bride and groom to the altar, the use of an embroidered pillow, the celebration of high mass, the prolonged ringing of the bells, are all a function of expenditure. In death ceremonies, the priest's going to the house where the body lies, instead of waiting at the church; an elaborate ceremony at the church, complete with choir and church bells, the priest's going to the cemetery to make offerings for the dead; a choir singing and a band playing at the grave—all these can

13. In a recent study I made of factory labor in Poona, I found that some of the workers seemed to have genuine aspirations to become supervisors—but it soon appeared that these were more expectations than aspirations, and that those workers who had social characteristics similar to the present supervisors expected to reach that post. Their own efforts were to be confined to minimal job performance until the position came to them.

increase the cost of a funeral ten to fifteen times. Graduated ceremonials are common in all countries. What is important in Asia is their priority in allocating expenditures and the high ratio of expenditures to both income and wealth.

Another of the institutional aspects of the religions that impede the transformation of the society to fit Max Weber's model are the support of social structures such as the caste system, the feudal economy, or the heavy family dependency—structures which inhibit incentives, prevent the entrance of many groups into the maximization competition, and make it less likely that concentration of savings will occur in the hands of a single person where rational economic decisions might dispose of it productively.

Religions provide the broad unifying cultural tradition in the countries of southern Asia. However, there are, in each of these countries, more secular ideological streams which also define the proper modes of economic activity. In the different countries, the relative strengths of these streams vary considerably; but in all of them, the friction between the different clusters of attitudes has proved a major obstacle to the successful implementation of development plans.

The first and most important of these competing streams might be described as the "caretaker elites," committed to governmentally induced, planned economic growth. In each of the newly independent countries, the post-World War II years have witnessed the accession to power of these caretaker elites, who are remarkably similar, in their motivations, ideologies, and relationships, to the rest of the people in their countries. I call them "caretakers" because their legitimating principle is an instrumental ideology in which the material benefits of their efforts are to accrue to all members of their society. An ancillary, and in part contradictory, aim is to diminish the inequalities in the societies by letting the state champion the rights of the less powerful and less wealthy. Such a principle of legitimacy can operate as strictly in defining membership in the elite as blood kinship, lineage, or piety did in earlier eras. It provides the means for denying membership to such groups as business leaders or the landed aristocracy, who presumably operate in their own interests. In general, its goal is modernization—those elements of Westernization that suit indigenous valuational tastes. In particular, this includes: national unification, i.e., the supersession of all secondary, non-economic sources of power; nation building, i.e., acquiring the format and the hardware of an industrialized economy; equalitarianism, i.e., reducing the power of non-governmental economic organizations and individuals, and removing the more visible signs of poverty among the masses; and mass participation, i.e., legitimating centrally conceived and adopted plans by involving the largest number of people in their implementation. Briefly characterized, the economic ideology of the caretaker elite is a sort of *ad hoc* Fabianism. Their general attitudes toward wealth and savings include the notion that wealth is best when it is most evenly distributed. They consider that both wealth and savings in the economy as a whole will be most effectively increased and best utilized for national growth to the extent that they are controlled by government. The history of the private sector in their economies, and what they consider the anti-social acquisitiveness of both foreign and indigenous business groups, do nothing to dissuade them from this viewpoint.

The economic ethic of this elite, in a way, fits our concept of rational profit maximization. The fact that planners in "socialistic" societies seek their profits in national income totals, rather than in the assets and liabilities of an individual concern, does not weaken the fact that their action is predicated above all on a rational calculation of achieving a final surplus, measured in terms of money, and those actions are chosen which presumably will maximize the return. There are, of course, many other factors which intrude in policy decisions—political favoritism, broad social welfare considerations, equalitarianism, etc.—but these are competing streams of thought that engender imperfections in, not negations of, the orientation toward rational gain-producing activities. The emphasis in the plans on the distribution of capital outlay, and the reckoning of the rewards in terms of per capita income, confirm our point.

Partly in agreement with, and partly in juxtaposition to, the caretaker elite are the Western-based or Western-oriented industrial and commercial houses. While they share the ethic of rational profit maximization, the unit to be benefited is more limited. To the extent that they are joint-stock companies, their ideology is also instrumental. However, it has none of the egalitarian, welfare-state motif, although the best do tend to exercise a paternalism toward their workers. They are less committed than the caretaker elite to the process of altering the traditional society at large, being interested primarily only in those segments which directly affect them—their market and labor force.

The caretaker elite, on the other hand, is committed to making sweeping changes in their efforts to increase the economic well-being of the populace. Hence, to them, almost all elements of the traditional society appear to be obstacles to modernization and economic growth. At the same time, the difficulty of effecting the desired changes is underestimated. In connection with agriculture, Charles E. Kellog writes:

> Perhaps the greatest handicap to agricultural improvement in many
> underdeveloped areas is the false notion that this improvement is a

relatively simple matter. This unhappy idea has even been supported by some American and European advisors. The notion implies, firstly, that improved farming results from emphasizing a few simple practices; secondly, that "someone" knows what these should be; and thirdly, that it is necessary to find this "someone" and have him pass the "good word" on to the cultivators. None of this is approximately true for the most underdeveloped parts of the world.[14]

The reasoning of the caretaker elites about the alteration of the traditional society is much the same as that Kellogg criticizes. Often, the economic motivations and organization necessary to implement plans do not exist or are contravened in the culture. All too frequently, planners expect cultural attitudes and values which might impede progress to (1) disappear as a consequence of changes in the economic structure; (2) be altered by the universal solvents of education and enthusiasm; or (3) be changed by multi-faceted community-development projects at the local level. It is by no means inevitable that these desired results will obtain; and one might hazard a guess that the most important obstacle to development programs has been the slippage in which programmatic inputs are dissipated as they filter through the traditional agrarian society.

Just as the caretaker elites in the various countries of southern Asia seem to share a remarkably similar ideology, so too the agrarian societies are remarkably similar in the broad outlines of their economically relevant attitudes and values. Considerable variations of detail occur, but the complex in each country is very much the same. The conceptions of what constitutes wealth and property, and of the priorities of most valued possessions, are strikingly alike. There is general agreement about the desirable and undesirable methods of acquiring wealth, about the appropriate means for transforming wealth into status, and about the responsibilities of the wealthy man. Taken together, these attributes form an interlocking system which provides a pattern of motivation for gain. Its touchstone is a particular form of property, land; but its rewards lie within a much more complex framework of mutual obligations and legitimation of status.

In all of the countries of the area, land heads the list of approved possessions. Where tenancy forms are simple, as in the Philippines and parts of South-East Asia, land rights may approximate our own conception of private property. Elsewhere, tenancy practices are an intricate system of graduated rights and privileges, as in India, Pakistan, or Ceylon. In the latter case, the drive for more land takes the form of maneuvering

14. Charles E. Kellog, "Transfer of Basic Skills of Food Production," *Annals of the American Academy of Political and Social Science,* September, 1960.

upward in the complicated labyrinth, enhancing one's security of tenure and share of the harvest, and diminishing the onerousness of the duties and services owed to the landlord. Recent tenancy legislation has had the effect of foreshortening the hierarchy, but it has by no means abolished it. Status and power differentials within rural areas are dependent upon land rights, and even wealth earned in non-agricultural pursuits must be converted into landholding to be fully legitimate. This overwhelming emphasis on acquiring land is partly understandable, since it is the primary agricultural producers' goods; but often it is pursued even when the return from it is marginal and alternative investments are demonstrably more rewarding. This is also true of the peasant's preference for growing food crops, particularly the staples like paddy or wheat. Even in areas of the highest commercialization of agriculture, peasants want to keep enough land in food staples so that they can avoid the whimsies of the market mechanisms. From Ceylon to Viet Nam, paddy land is sold last, and has a special significance for family prestige beyond that of land in other crops. One result of this emphasis is that, with increasing densities and general inflationary trends, the price of land rises rapidly. In the Philippines, the Japanese occupation and the guerrilla opposition during World War II exhausted most forms of portable wealth; land values spiralled; and today even uncultivated lands are held as investments by speculators. In 1960, the price of land is eight to ten times more than in 1939, and its costs more than can normally be earned on it in fifteen to twenty years. The conception of land as the primary form of wealth is also enhanced by the growing proletarianization of agricultural labor in many countries.

The demand for other forms of producers' goods in agriculture is essentially inelastic, in that the relatively crude implements, the small sizes of the holdings, and the commitment of agriculturists to traditional methods of cultivation, leave little scope for expansion. One can increase the number of buffaloes or oxen or implements when the amount of land increases; aside from that, there is little status-giving wealth in agricultural producers' goods. Improvements in agriculture, such as the digging of wells and canals for irrigation, are heavily labor-intensive, and tend to take the form of direct investment with payment in kind or reciprocal services rather than monetary rewards.

The same inelasticity is discernible in most rural consumption items, particularly the necessities like housing and clothing. Except for the very wealthy, who are usually absentee owners, the range of expenditures on housing and clothing is relatively narrow. The peasant is prepared to consume luxury items, like bicycles, flashlights, radios, and clocks; but these are not considered normal wants and come far down the list in wealth. In some places, sumptuary laws or customs limit the consumption of certain luxury goods to individuals whose high status is ascriptive rather than achieved.

If accumulation takes a form other than landholding, it is in currency or coins hidden in trunks or buried in a corner of the house, in jewelry and precious metals—the lower classes' insurance—and in stores of grain. The last may be used not only to safeguard a supply for consumption, but also to speculate on mid-seasonal fluctuations in prices.

In Viet Nam, an interesting distinction is made that confirms the general point. Hidden goods (*cua chim*) are distinguished from goods on display (*cua noi*). The former include houses, rice fields, cattle, rice in storage, money at the bottom of a trunk, and money on loan. The latter include clothing, jewelry which is worn, furniture, vehicles, etc. Items in the first category are highly valued; those in the latter are not.

Various permanent crops are important in rural wealth—coconuts, rubber, coffee and tea, fruit. In general, however, lands devoted to these are supplemental to, rather than in place of, land sown with food staples. After annual cash-crop land, they are the first to be sold in times of economic distress.

As a rule, the status dividends of rural wealth vary in ways which are directly opposed to the principles of rational profit maximization. This is not to say that the peasant is insensitive to economic incentives, nor that wealth in and of itself is not status-enhancing. However, differentiations are made among forms of wealth that are based on traditional hierarchical relationships where the holding of property was only part of the stratification principle, where the isolation of consumers from producers' goods was at a minimum, and where the incentive to place gain above the other obligations was weak.

The primary bases for the legitimation of wealth in the rural areas are (1) how it is made and (2) how it is spent. In the first category, there is a distinct preference for wealth accumulated in the agricultural sphere rather than in commerce or moneylending. In the second category, each culture establishes a set of traditional philanthropies and dependencies which become part of behavior required of the wealthy man.

The preference for the landed aristocrat over the wealthy trader is deep. This is partly due to the special status value of land, which in South Asia is correlated highly with caste rankings. It is also due to the fact that the landholders are bound, by a set of traditional obligations, to their economic dependents. They should lend work animals, money, or seed free or at reduced costs; they should support the village festivals, assist in court cases, allow free grazing on their lands, help in times of family crisis, etc. At the same time, economic transactions between them and their inferiors in status are hedged about with non-economic controls which limit the permissible degree of exploitation—controls which grow out of the whole network of customary relationships in the village.

The paternalistic role described above is most clearly applicable to inherited landed wealth. As in all cultures, the *nouveaux riches* are on trial. An interesting illustration of this was the public pressure on war widows in the Philippines, who were suddenly wealthy with insurance payments, to invest the money in land, and the criticism of any conspicuous consumption. The conversion of wealth into status is an expensive process. In an extreme form, it may provide for the circulation of fortunes within three generations.

The example of a newly rich man in Viet Nam in trying to "wash his face" is instructive. He begins by giving help, chiefly financial, to his relatives and friends. He must own rice fields and a comfortable home in his native village; he must "purchase" a place of honor in the community hierarchy; he must organize a major banquet to which all villagers are invited; and his sons must be trained for a job higher in the social hierarchy, that of a scholar or a government official. By this time, any surplus has been dissipated and his children are in no position to renew it.

Moneylenders, storekeepers, and traders who mediate between the village and the outside world are considered to be parasitical, since, in the view of the peasants, their work does not contribute to the agricultural process. Moreover, they represent the point at which assets are monetized; and the peasant's general expectation in monetary transactions is that he will be swindled. Peasants are, of course, encouraged to find the best selling price for their grain. However, attempts made by merchants and traders to maximize their return or to respond to market considerations are considered to be cheating and exploitation of the agriculturists. This attitude is partly due to the fact that the peasant usually has dealings with the trader and moneylender at a time when he is at a disadvantage in bargaining. Merchants are doubly suspect; since they are not bound by the customary code of inferior-superior relations, their rapacity, as the villagers see it, is uncontrolled. Where rapid accumulation occurs, violation of the economic norms is assumed to have preceded it.

The hostility toward the presumed exploiter in most societies results in the insulation of the non-agriculturist profit maximizers. Consequently, when this function is a full-time occupation, it is usually performed by groups outside of or immune to the normal system of sanctions and status gradations of the society. Their isolation is also necessary to them because it enables them to raise their children with a set of norms in direct contrast to those of the rest of the society. This is easy in a society like India's, where the distinctiveness of the ethics and style of life of each group is encouraged; but in other countries, it requires those with the motivation of gain to be ethically separate from the rest of the society—in fact, traders and merchants are often alien in origin. Good illustrations are provided by the South Indian Chettiars and the overseas Chinese in South-East Asia; and by the diffusion of Marwaris and western Indian *banya* castes in India. The trading groups, thus insulated, develop a strong cohesion within their own community, and evolve their own traditions, which are highly resistant to change. The ethnic discreteness of the trading community also induces low permeability; i.e., it inhibits the entry of newcomers into trading activities.

What are the consequences of this peasant complex for savings and investment?

The primary economic motivation in the village is the provision of security and status for the family—what Sombart would have called the principle of subsistence rather than the principle of gain. Economic activity is carried on to supply consumption needs. It is true that when a family is living close to or below the subsistence level, the two motivating principles are indistinguishable in actual behavior. The important differences are in the preference for production of one's own consumption goods, especially food; in the low marginal propensity to save when the subsistence level has been reached; in the unwillingness to forego present consumption for future gain; in the lack of motivation to invest more effort once the comfort level has been reached; and in the low degree of responsiveness to rapidly changing rates of return on investment of effort and money. Savings which do occur are drained off—into the inflationary pressure on land; into enhanced consumption of better quality, if not more, foodstuffs and consumers, goods; into economically unproductive investments in status; into own-account expenditures on housing that are entered in the investment and capital formation column by courtesy only; and into hoarding of foodstuffs and currency. To a great extent, savings remain in non-monetized form. This is partly because the most common outlets for them do not require monetization, and partly because the peasant expects that he loses every time his assets are turned into cash. This expectation is reinforced by his thorough distrust of the personnel through whom he monetizes his product. Not the least of those whom he distrusts are the government's tax assessors. One of the major problems confronting the planners is the fact that, the more they try to reach some of the incremental income accruing to the rural sector as a result of national development efforts, the more it is likely to recede into non-monetized own-account expenditures on marginally productive investments like housing.

The chief savers and accumulators in the rural areas are the traders, brokers, moneylenders, and shopkeepers. Their savings do somewhat enhance the rural economy, in that they provide credit in the traditionally money-short countryside. Generally, however, only a small part of this credit is used for capital investment in agriculture, and even less for improvement of production techniques. Some traders and moneylenders become involved in the peasant complex in trying to legitimate their wealth by traditional means, a process which is rarely completely successful. One of the most explosive issues in southern Asia is the progressive alienation of land into the hands of non-agriculturists.

It might be asked why these groups have not spurred the kind of economic growth that occurred in the West; why petty capitalism has not taken the next step toward rationalizing the organization of production. These questions take us far afield, into the origins and role of entrepreneurs in these societies—a topic much too extensive to be considered here. It is relevant, however, to comment that custom defined the horizons of their activities, just as it did those of other groups in the traditional society. Their urban counterparts were, in fact, productive of highly developed commercial and handicraft economies; but the conservative nature of tradition within these insulated groups kept them in commerce and finance and out of manufacture.

With a few exceptions, the modern sectors of the economy were built by foreigners or "new men" not drawn from the traditional mercantile houses. Currently, as the new generation is increasingly educated in a Westernized fashion, some of its members are passing over into the Western-oriented business and industrial elites. This entails a consequent loss in the solidarity of the traditional communities. Their status and role in the rural areas make it unlikely that they would exercise much influence on the techniques of production, even if they cared to.

Leverage, if it is to come, must come from the caretaker elites. Apparently, at least in the rural areas—and it is there that the basic changes in the society must be made—the task of creating the characteristics of the "unique historical emergent" that spurred economic development in the West is a gigantic one. Too many other demands take precedence over economic ones. Rational profit maximization is laid very lightly on top of traditional economic attitudes and values. The pursuit of profit maximization is highly circumscribed. A large part of mutual rights and obligations lies outside of the market mechanism. Perhaps southern Asia will develop a unique historical emergent of its own.

# Making Social
# Change Possible

THESE TWO SELECTIONS represent a summary of as well as logical conclusion to the previous articles in Part Two. Both deal with prescriptions for feasible social transformation.

Drawing upon a wealth of anthropological and sociological information, Melville Herskovits urges that the core concept of successful development is appropriate cultural manipulation. By this he means maximum integration of pre-existing social patterns into the industrialization process. Whenever possible, for example, the traditional patterns of work rhythm, labor recruitment, and labor incentive should be incorporated into the developmental scheme. He reminds us that "developmental projects must build in ways that make sense to the people involved in them."

This theme of preservation of cultural integrity is developed in the UNESCO article from a different perspective. Recognizing that technological change often results in the disintegration of cultural values, the authors of this report focus on individual psychological well-being rather than developmental success. If the desired economic change is to be accomplished, it should be introduced with explicit safeguards to mental tranquillity. A list of recommendations to reduce the psychic cost of cultural change focuses on lessening the conflicts of technical innovation. Like the Herskovits essay, the recommendations have a common theme in the adjuration to maintain continuity of cultural patterns rather than wholesale dismissal for entirely new social configurations.

# Melville J. Herskovits

## The Problem of Adapting Societies to New Tasks

In the rapidly growing vocabulary of American social science a new term has come to be heard with increasing frequency in recent years—one might almost say in recent months. This is the term "manipulation." In this new use it applies where an individual or a group, working with the tools research has provided, moves into a social situation with the aim of altering patterns of thought and action so as to achieve a given practical end. It represents the logical working out of those aims of physical science, prediction *and* control, which for so many years have been accepted by the students of human behavior and human institutions as the ends toward which they, as scientists, should strive.

In a general, prescientific sense, the process of manipulating human behavior and thus, to varied degrees, the course of human history is nothing very new. The action of the democratic process itself, in terms of argumentation and persuasion, represents an attempt to manipulate behavior and thought for given ends. The rule of the manifold historical autocracies, or the ways of diplomacy, bring to mind countless examples of manipulation of peoples and their political and social destinies. Cross-culturally, colonization, commerce, the slave trade to the New World, the missionary activities of the eighteenth and nineteenth centuries—all served as conscious or fortuitous instruments of induced change in belief systems, social organizations, and many other phases of the lives of those on whom these forces impinged.

What distinguishes the prescientific procedures in bringing about change from the methods which the disciplines that study man, whether as an individual or as a member of a society, employ today is the new dimension that has been given all programs of action, the dimension of scientific method. On its most ubiquitous level we have applied scientific method to the manipulation of preferences for one product as against another through advertising. It can be seen in such other varied aspects of our life as labor-management relations, town-planning, public administration, fund-raising campaigns, the development of new industries, and education and child welfare.

These random examples of the application of science to problems of directed ends have been drawn from our own society. Certainly in such areas of public concern as education, child welfare, or public administration, they represent attempts to solve problems of importance. Or, where manipulation of one group by another within the same population is undertaken, it is still a process which operates within the conventions of our society as a whole. Common cues to behavior, a common historical background, and common language are shared by both groups. The basic motivating drives can be taken for granted; the area of agreement as to the values that shape ends is large. To put the matter in technical terms, this is intracultural manipulation, in which only such differences as exist between subcultural groups need be taken into account.

When we approach the problem of influencing peoples other than ourselves, the matter becomes vastly complicated. The area of prediction is narrowed by factors that do not enter where concern is with one's own culture, where the task is to predict behavior on the basis of reactions that fall within a reasonably well-recognized framework of total response patterns. For to adapt another society to new ways of living involves the formidable process of reshaping basic habits that are manifest both in belief and in behavior. It calls for an induced shift in pre-established ends and a directed reorientation of value systems. It requires, consequently, an intensive analysis of the existing relationships among the various aspects of culture—technological, economic, social, educational, political, religious, and aesthetic—before any kind of prediction can be made of the results that will follow the disturbance of the balance between them.

Here, then, we come on a primary factor. "In the areas of technical aid to underdeveloped countries," states the call for these meetings, "most attention has been paid so far to certain theoretical economic problems, whereas the relations between cultural changes and economic growth, as well as the aspects of the impact of the sociopolitical structure of underdeveloped countries on modernization, has received less attention." What kind of adjustments seem to be indicated when the technological and economic patterns of Europe and America are introduced into nonindustrialized areas? What are the psychocultural mechanisms that cause peoples having different ways of life to hold tenaciously to their established modes of behavior, especially in terms of the sanctions which give these ways of life meaning and value? With these propositions examined, we can consider some of the assumptions of the same order in our own culture that underlie programs aimed at benefiting other peoples. In this manner we will move beyond the unilateral position customarily taken in planning and implementing technical aid programs and lay a conceptual basis of a process of mutual helpfulness that is a prerequisite to their effective functioning.

Let us take a recurring situation under programs of economic development all over the world that has had to be faced by those in charge of operations calculated to bring the benefits of the technical proficiency of our industrialized economy to underdeveloped areas. This situation rarely, if ever, figures in discussions of those "theoretical economic problems" where considerations of large scope, such as basic resources, national income, labor pool, or location, determine the answers that set the goals for the operating missions. It concerns one of those elements in the total problem that has to do with the human factor in the equation, the element which, because of the operation of culturally prescribed motivations that lie outside the patterns of our own pecuniary economy, introduces unknowns that make for the gap between theoretically based prediction and actual achievement.

We here consider the problem of labor turnover. It is a commonplace that one of the greatest difficulties faced in the development of enterprises of any sort in underdeveloped areas, whether extractive, agricultural, or industrial, is that of holding workers to the job. Typically, what occurs is that men will take employment for a period of time and then, when money to meet certain specific wants is in hand, leave. Among numerous illustrations, that of the attempt to establish a textile plant near the native reserves of South Africa may be cited. Erected under the auspices of the South African Social and Economic Planning Commission, its purpose is to bring industry to the African and thus avoid some of the evils that have marked the migration of workers to the cities or that have followed their segregation in the mine compounds of the Rand. It is to be manned by Africans who are to be trained not only to operate the machines but eventually to assume managerial and technical posts.

The experiment is a continuing one, but it is recognized by those concerned with it that labor turnover is one of its most serious problems. Even though it is near the reserves, so that a native need not face the long separation from his wife and family that the man who goes to the cities or to the mines must contemplate, workers come and go. It is the same story—a man will work long enough to meet the limited goal set by the needs of his family unit. When he has earned enough for this, he leaves, to return to a mode of life that is in harmony with an economic system that existed before industrialization was introduced into the area, whereby subsistence and prestige wants are satisfied without reference to pecuniary considerations.

The problem of how to cope with this unstable labor market has had various answers. The imposition of taxes, payable only in currency, was attempted as an early solution. This method got roads built but could scarcely provide labor for large-scale, continuing undertakings. There has been wide recourse to contract labor, which permits the employer to compel a worker to stay on the job for a specified time. On the Firestone plantations in Liberia a policy of paying wage differential incentives to workers who remain on the job beyond a specified time has been instituted. First-class hospital facilities, good schools for the children of the laborers, and the attraction of well-built houses are additional incentives to facilitate a dependable labor supply. It is argued that the incentive of a larger wage would only increase the difficulty, since, the more the worker earned in a given time, the sooner he would attain his objective, and consequently the sooner he would leave his job. The encouragement of a wider range of wants, in terms of an induced goal of a higher standard of living, is another longer-range solution that has been suggested. Yet, in the final analysis, despite the many methods formulated of inducing change in economic attitudes and behavior on the part of the existing and potential labor supply, the factor of pre-established custom dominates the labor scene, and the problem remains essentially unsolved.

What, then, are some of the special aspects of tradition that, rarely taken into account, may be considered as operative in these situations, rendering it difficult to achieve what would, on the face of it, seem to be a simple task of utilizing available labor power for the development of underdeveloped areas? We may turn to Africa for some insight into this perplexing problem. This is not because the problem as such is in any way peculiar to Africa but because the examples to be drawn point the difficulties encountered here, as elsewhere, in the development of a rich continent, so dynamic in its present-day political and economic orientations, yet about which so little is known in the United States.

The instance of an indigenous manufacturing system will give us something of the type of background against which proposals for economic development must be projected. It should be stressed that the instance is a regional example and is not to be taken as representative of Africa as a whole. No single instance could subsume the vast range of institutions, lying in all aspects of culture, that mark the many bodies of tradition found there. But if it is not to be taken as typical, neither is it to be thought of as atypical. It is useful, and it is here used because it highlights a problem.

Ironworking has, from very early times, been known throughout Negro Africa. There is good though not conclusive evidence that the technique was developed on that continent. Ironworkers are almost invariably members of a guild, membership in which is customarily based on family relationship, with the craft validated by supernatural sanctions.

This is the pattern among the peoples of the Upper Volta River in French West Africa, where knives, hoes, and other iron implements are manufactured by members of such guilds. Yet because here, as in nonindustrial societies the world over, the lines of specialization are blurred, these men are not the full-time specialists they would be in our society. They are, as a matter of fact, primarily agriculturalists, earning their living only partially by the sale of their products and working their forges principally during that part of the year, the dry season, when the fields are not cultivated. . . .

One does not have to pursue the matter further to perceive that motivations quite different from those obtaining in the economies of Europe and America are operative here. The question that would occur to one conditioned to the patterns of business enterprise in the Western world would be why these ironworkers do not take advantage of the obvious market at hand. Why do they not supply it by complete, full-time specialization and the training of more apprentices to enlarge their operations so that, as entrepreneurs in the strict sense, they could then hire these trained workers to increase further their production? And this is a fair question—fair, that is, for those who approach the problem in terms of current economic theory. All the conditions for the expansion of production are present, yet they are ignored. It is apparent that the answer lies outside the scope of economics as envisaged for our culture; that to reach a satisfactory explanation would require probing deep into what we know concerning the psychology of culture, as applicable to this particular situation. And since, in this case, we have nothing more to go on than the facts that have been provided us and are presented here, we can only have recourse to generalizations about the reasons why a people hold to such customary modes of behavior in the face of a patent economic opportunity—modes of behavior that seem logical, rational, and of self-evident worth to them, while to the outsider they seem so illogical and so irrational. . . .

If we examine the indigenous productive systems of the continent in more general terms—and much of what will be indicated is applicable to nonindustrialized societies outside Africa as well as to the peoples of that continent—we find that they present certain consistent characteristics that are highly relevant to the question we are considering. One of these has to do with the rhythm of work, a second with the way in which the available supply of labor is mobilized so that the economy can function, while a third concerns the motivations for labor, the factor of incentives. There are still other significant characteristics whose analysis must await more detailed presentation: the role of kinship groupings and sex division of labor in organizing and orienting the economics of production; the importance of supernatural sanctions governing ritual cycles for the service of deities or ancestors, when customary tasks are not performed; the influence of class stratification and native political structure on attempts to introduce new economic concepts and technical procedures.

Especially in the tropics, the zone where the greatest portion of technical aid to underdeveloped countries will be made available, the rhythm of work in indigenous societies is the rhythm of the seasons. This does not mean that there are no daily rhythms, but these do not dictate changes in economic activity as do the longer fluctuations of seasonal change. . . .

The daily rhythm that continues irrespective of seasonal change dictates the allocation of time during a given day to the tasks immediately at hand. The day may be thought of as broken into segments delimiting the hours between rising and retiring. The limits of these segments are set by the time of the day at which meals are eaten. In West Africa, and to a degree over all the continent south of the Sahara, the breaks come at about ten in the morning and at midafternoon. At times the large meal is eaten late in the day, often shortly before going to sleep. It must be recalled that night falls early. The day comes without a prolonged dawn. There is no time for the preparation of a large meal at waking. At night, cooking in the dark is not favored. Thus, arising with the dawn, the African takes but a bite before occupying himself with his other concerns; at the other end of the day, when the principal meal is consumed, he rests.

The contrast between this seasonal and daily work rhythm and the work pattern of the industrial laborer will be at once apparent. Except in the case of large-scale agricultural undertakings, the seasonal factor does not enter. The routine of work in extractive and industrial enterprises moves around the calendar with a schedule of operations fixed not by natural conditions but through decisions reached far from any contact the worker may experience and as much beyond his control as are the seasons. He is thus caught up in a system that goes contrary to his prior experience. The variety of economic activities in which he engages under his own economic system is, furthermore, entirely lacking. His task remains the same from one day to the next and his time is apportioned for him, so that he is not free to vary the monotony of his work by moving from one aspect of a job to another. This is a commonplace for the industrial worker in a mechanized society. But in our Western economy a rhythm of life has been developed to afford some outlet to compensate for this monotony. The African sees no adequate reward in forms of his system of values to make this acceptable to him.

There is some tendency to define the industrial routine as disciplined, in contrast to an assumed carefree round held to characterize "primitive" man. Yet it takes but cursory analysis of the economic organization of nonindustrialized societies to recognize that, if we approach this from a human point of view, what we are really contrasting is different types of discipline that derive their validation from different sources. It soon becomes apparent that no question of the presence or absence of discipline, as such, enters in either type of economy. The discipline of the worker in nonindustrialized societies is self-imposed, while that of the industrial operative is imposed from outside. To the worker born in an industrial society, as well as to others who live in terms of the cultural orientations existing there, this outer source of discipline is taken for granted, as is any other culturally sanctioned mode of behavior. But to the worker who has been accustomed to different patterns, especially patterns under which the allocation of time and energy are self-determined, and who is newly brought into an industrial scene, the problem of reorientation necessitates a far-reaching process of adjustment. The degree of social no less than of personal disorganization that has resulted from many such attempts to make an adjustment of this sort needs only mention; when we consider how far-reaching it must be, we may take it as a measure of the plasticity of the human organism that the amount of demoralization is not greater.

Adjustment to the daily rhythm imposed by industrial work presents problems of an equivalent order of difficulty. Here it is not the question of a fixed as against a self-determined routine but of a difference in the cultural patterning of primary, biological drives. One of the most severe adjustments that is required here arises from the operation of a factor in the daily life of all of us, so taken for granted that it would be surprising if it entered in planning and executing technical aid programs. This factor concerns the schedule of mealtimes, whose importance in setting the daily rhythm of native labor has been indicated.

*     *     *     *     *

The second problem that we will consider arises out of the changes that occur in the manner in which the labor force is mobilized when indigenous societies of underdeveloped areas are brought under the canons of employment prevailing in the industrial communities of Europe and America. While the generalization is not without exception, in the main it is true that the economy of the West differs strikingly from that of most other societies in that it is based on individual effort, whereas these other peoples are communally oriented. In terms of these canons, the worker in this country and in Europe acts as an individual, and, if he organizes trade-unions to protect his position, such organizations still remain aggregates of individuals. In the economies of nonindustrial societies, on the other hand, the individual acts primarily as the member of a group, whether this group is based on kinship or residence or both. In Africa the factor of co-operative effort well exemplifies this. The problem of cultivating considerable tracts of land in West Africa during the short period at the beginning of the rainy season is met quite effectively by group labor of this sort. The hoe, in the hands of one man, is not too efficient an instrument; but many hoes in the hands of many men will in a day ready a large field for planting. Or, again, in the eastern part of the continent and other cattle-keeping regions, where herds must be taken daily to pasture, it is the small boys of the village who together care for the animals belonging to all their elders.

Another aspect of this tradition of group labor has to do with the direction of work. Europeans and Americans who come to Africa soon discover how deeply the concept of the responsible leader lodges in the customary work patterns of the Africans. One who wishes a given task performed does not hire workers as individuals, or, if he is under the illusion that he does, he finds that he soon is negotiating the problems that arise with the head of the group, who may alone be held to account for the quality and amount of work done. To reprimand an individual worker invites difficulties; it is the responsible head alone who must see to it that those in his group do their work, and it is he alone who may call his men to task. . . .

Gang labor has been one response to the recognition of the tradition of co-operative work among workers in underdeveloped areas by those charged with the operation of large-scale projects in industry or agriculture or mining. Yet, again, the perception of this institution of co-operative effort as something that can be built on in effectively utilizing labor power has proved to be only a half-measure, owing to the superficial nature of the percept. For in the African pattern the accountability of the leader of a work group is only secondarily to the employer and not as is the case in industry. His primary responsibility is to the members of the group he directs and of which he himself is a member. The system whereby a group of men working as individuals for a common employer is directed by a leader who is also hired as an individual by the same employer is the most casual of resemblances to the democratically controlled indigenous cooperative work group.

In short, then, the problem resolves itself into one in which the worker, who comes from a culture where the pattern is one of collective effort based on inner control, is to adapt himself to a system where individualism is the dominant motif. From the point of view of programs aiming at the development of underdeveloped areas, it constitutes an aspect of first importance, in terms not only of the impact of these programs on the worker himself, but also on the societies where they are instituted. It is not too much to say that these differences in approach to the problem of mobilizing labor is at the base of much of the social disorganization and individual demoralization that has too often been the concomitant of even the best-planned schemes of development.

Some attention has already been given to the third point to be considered —that of labor incentives. As may be gathered from the preceding discussion of it, this has been recognized as crucial by all those concerned with projects in the underdeveloped areas. Because it strikes to the very heart of the question of the impact of one economy on another, it is closely tied in with the two problems we have just sketched—the rhythm of work and the democratic pattern of co-operative labor—and can profitably be considered further.

One of the complaints most frequently heard in many of these operations, especially in Africa, is that when a native has become integrated into the system of Euro-American economic procedures, and his earnings, in terms of local standards become steady, his "family"— that is, the members of his wider kinship group—feel free to descend on him to share what he earns. In terms of accepted modes of conduct among these peoples, he must care for them or in other ways make his contributions to their joint undertakings. This not only holds true for the wage-worker. The small native shopkeeper and the European-trained professional man are similarly called on to conform to these traditional patterns. In cultural terms such a man as an earner works in accordance with the patterns of an economy based on individual initiative, but his consumption patterns are dictated by the traditions of a collective system. The conflicts that arise from this, as regards both the earner and the group out of which he has come, can be serious. Equally pertinent is the fact that individual initiative, essential to any success in an economy of free enterprise, is scarcely encouraged by the necessity of continuously meeting such obligations, made the more imperative by the fact that they arise out of some of the deepest ties that an individual can experience. . . .

One of the most striking examples of an area that has brought this type of economic agriculture into the world economy, making its potential resources generally available and raising the standards of living of its inhabitants, is to be found in the history of the cacao-growing industry of the Gold Coast. Long antedating present-day developmental schemes, and initially quite without benefit of Western economic planning, it has in large measure achieved many of the ends envisaged in the technical aid programs of this and other countries and of the United Nations agencies concerned with these matters. The native standard of living in the Gold Coast is the highest of any dependency in Africa; its political growth has been steady and today represents the closest approach to self-government of any African colony; its educational system has far wider ramifications into the villages than elsewhere on the continent. All this has been achieved not without stress and tensions, but in essence it represents the results of inner developments based on pre-existing patterns rather than development induced by the direct application of forces impinging from outside and cast in terms foreign to native practices.

Here there is no lack of incentive to expand production. Moreover, Africans, using the capital they accumulated through raising cacao, have moved into areas of commerce and minor industry with a minimum of dislocation of established institutions. There are no extremes of what has been termed "detribalization," but the claims of relatives have, in many cases, been resolved by opening opportunities rather than by merely sharing wages or profits with them. This is not unlike a situation found in eastern Nigeria, among the Ibo, where resources of large family groupings are being pooled to permit certain of their members to take advantage of opportunities that will accrue to the benefit of all. A promising young man is in this way aided to obtain the higher education that will allow him to function to the credit of his family unit in the changing economic and political scene. A good trader is helped to expand his operation and thus contribute to the resources of the group as a whole. This, as in the Gold Coast cacao industry, is an extension of pre-existing patterns to fit the new scene.

Admittedly, to move from this type of development, motivated from within, to planned programs brought from outside is not simple. Yet the African cultures, at least, are receptive to the modern scene, and, if the motivation exists, Africans show appreciable plasticity. In terms of existing orientations it is plain that it is less difficult to provide incentives in agricultural projects than in industrial developments. . . .

Factors such as these, which come into play to further or impede the success of projects looking toward the economic development of under-developed areas, constitute only a part of the whole problem. We have still to consider how what is brought to a people is integrated into their ways of living, as against the manner in which their established patterns of behavior are adapted to the requirements of a new economic and technological system. Here we are confronted with the question of the meaning of a way of life for those who live in accordance with it. This, in turn, can be understood only in the light of the findings of that phase of psychoethnography that has to do with the mechanisms of learning and conditioning which shape the characteristic motor habits, reaction patterns, and accepted modes of thinking of a people. . . .

As individuals, we learn our cultures by a process termed "enculturation." This is subtle and all-prevading and so thoroughly absorbed that for the most part we live our lives in terms of reactions that lodge below the level of our consciousness. Only when some alternative is presented to us do we become aware of the assumptions which otherwise we take as given or of the overt forms of behavior that we manifest so spontaneously. Then we must consider, judge, evaluate, choose. We relearn the new alternative; or, in terms of cultural theory, we undergo a process of re-enculturation.

It is in the area of values that enculturation strikes to its greatest depths. Here we learn the sanctions that give meaning to behavior, the rationale for living. Evaluations of this character, in the last analysis, maximize the satisfactions that culture affords man. Hence, when we put into force programs aimed at changing the modes of living of peoples so that they may enjoy satisfactions outside the purview of the system of values of their culture, we are saying, in effect, that the ends we envisage are so superior to those already in force that their desirability is beyond challenge. It is thus assumed that, when these new values are presented to peoples having other traditionally approved ends, they must ultimately displace the values to which these people were originally enciltured. But this is a proposition that calls for the closest testing in the light of our knowledge of cultural dynamics.

East Africa affords us an instance precisely in the field of those economic goals which are primarily under discussion here; that is, of the problems that arise when attempts to develop resources of underdeveloped areas involve the reconciliation of two diffierent systems of evaluating ends. This instance has to do with the utilization of the rich possibilities presented by the high grassy plateaus of the area for the production of cattle for the world market. This region has long been noted for its excellence as pasture land. Here is where the great herds of wild animals roam, taking advantage of the same pasturage that has provided sustenance for the cattle owned by the natives.

One of the drawbacks to the utilization of this area for the purpose of producing beef for export has been the presence of the tsetse fly in various districts, since the sting of the tsetse is fatal to cattle. A few years ago the discovery of a vaccine against tsetse was announced. East Africa, it was stressed, now rid of its handicap, would become a new Argentina and would supply the meat-hungry parts of the world with beef. Potentially, all the favorable elements for development programs seemed to be present. An existing resource was to be utilized; an expansion of the pre-existing economy would raise indigenous standards of living by increasing cash income, while at the same time meeting a pressing world need; this could be accomplished without the evils consequent on detribalization and urbanization. Yet nothing seems to have happened.

We may leave to one side questions of a technical order that have been raised, such as the actual efficacy of the vaccine or whether the tsetse can be expected to breed a strain whose virulence will in effect nullify the immunization this new discovery was intended to provide. Here we will consider the problem of the value system of the indigenous peoples as it bears on the question of substituting new ends for those in existence. We may first describe the role of cattle in the indigenous cultures, in order to make clear the problems involved in attempts to utilize this resource as a profitable commercial venture.

In all East Africa wealth has traditionally taken the form of cattle. These animals, however, constitute a special kind of wealth, being essentially the depositaries of value in a system of prestige economics and not figuring appreciably in the subsistence economy, since only their milk is consumed. The subsistence economy, as a matter of fact, is simple. Each family is self-supporting to such a degree that, unlike many other parts of Africa, markets were found rarely, if at all, and, except for the ironworkers, there were no specialists. The subsistence economy, therefore, is taken for granted; it is an aspect of life to which a minimum of attention is paid.

Nothing could contrast more sharply to this than the attitude of these peoples toward cattle. Their herds literally give meaning and purpose to life. Ownership dictates social status; the passage of cattle alone validates marriage and gives children the stamp of legitimacy. Cattle, to the people of this area, have the sentimental value of our pets. They are thematic materials for poetry and songs. These animals are never slaughtered for food, so that beef is eaten only when a cow dies or when an ox is sacrificed at the funeral of the owner of a herd. Some of the languages of the area have fifty or more words which we can only translate by the term "cow" plus a qualifying phrase. By the use of this rich and specialized descriptive vocabulary, color, size, shape of horns, even temperamental characteristics, can be denoted by a single term. . . .

It is significant to observe that one value introduced from outside these cultures by those who exercise control over cattle-owning peoples meets with no resistance—the value laid on improving the quality of the breed and preventing disease in the animals. This means longer-lived and better cattle and, as an end result, more cattle. This in turn increases the wealth of an individual and the prestige that accrues to him. The fact that this improvement has raised serious problems involving overgrazing the restricted reserve areas allotted to the natives, and thus has intensified soil erosion as the area of white settlement spread, is here aside from the point. What concerns us in our present discussion is that the resulting increase of cattle yielded no marketable surplus. The end of raising cattle in the native mind being to have more and more of them, any program which necessitated disposing of animals, in terms of the established patterns of value, induced social disutility. . . .

Examples from Africa and the rest of the underdeveloped portions of the world could be multiplied to show how complex is the matrix of custom and sanction to be taken into account when the spread of technological knowledge and economic development to peoples living under differing conditions of life, and in terms of different goals, is contemplated. The fragmentation of knowledge in our society, as represented, for instance, by the specialized academic disciplines, has carried us so far that it is easy for us to forget that a culture is a functioning unit. We do not often take full cognizance of the fact that the aspects into which we divide custom for purposes of study are a fiction of science. By the same token, we overlook the principle that a change effected in any one of these aspects has repercussions over the total way of life on the culture as a whole. . . .

Because our know-how has raised our standard of living and by extending the frontiers of our knowledge has given us benefits that we prize, we assume it can be applied in other societies with equal profit. We implement our good will with projects designed to bring our skills to those who do not possess them. As we move into the area of technical aid programs, however, we discover that even the know-how on which we pride ourselves is not always transferable or even applicable. The knowledge possessed by indigenous peoples concerning the utilization of their land is not scientifically derived, but it is the result of a long process of adaptation to their natural setting, and much of it meets the pragmatic test. Large-scale planting by the use of mechanical agricultural implements has been introduced in many parts of the tropical world. In some instances, however, the land, unprotected by the forest growth, is exposed to the rains that leech out its chemical content and render it less productive than when worked in small patches with the hoe. Benefits anticipated on the basis of the returns these methods yield in temperate climates did not materialize. . . .

When the industrialized people of the world bring their knowledge to those living in what we term "underdeveloped"—that is, nonindustrialized—areas, the assumption is made that our ways are those which hold the answers to problems which have, in actuality, been answered in many ways. The fact that we speak of these peoples as "primitive," the territories they inhabit as "backward," or our continuous use of the word "progress" as a general over-all desideratum, when we really mean moving toward the attainment of goals we determine as good on the basis of our experience is an index of our attitude. This has not escaped the attention of the growing numbers of those who, enculturated to the ways of the native societies from which they derive, through Western education have come to know the deficiencies as well as the good points of our culture. They read what we write about them and with time and repetition come to resent the implications of the inferiority of their cultures so often expressed in what they read. The growing nationalisms in the far parts of the world, in a very real sense, represent in no negligible measure a reaction that has as its driving force the refusal to accept our evaluations of their traditional way of life. Indeed, the student of culture cannot escape the conclusion that the movements called nativistic are highly keyed reaffirmations of the values in the cultures we term "backward." If we but take the example of China and Africa, where the cultures are deeply rooted in traditions of the continuity of ancestral generations, it is not difficult to see how the derogation of established ways, even by implication, can arouse both latent and manifest hostilities.

In a world where increasing rapidity of communication makes for increasingly close contact between peoples, programs of any sort that cut across cultures must take into account the intangibles of established custom if there is to be any positive, lasting gain. It must be recognized, first of all, that there is no single answer to the problems that are faced by mankind. What we term technological and economic "progress" cannot be achieved without integrating the new into the old; moreover, this integration can only be suggested, not forced. The peoples to whom technical aid is brought will, in the final analysis, decide what they will accept and what they will reject. Even where they do not control their own political destinies, the force of cultural inertia prevents their being manipulated like pawns on a chessboard. We know today too well that they are imponderables in the world scene, not pawns.

This is why it must be understood, above all, that the diffusion of ideas, and even of technology, is more than a unilateral process. If we keep firmly in mind the force of our own enculturation, we will be able to understand how the ways of others are similarly valued by those who live in terms of them.

# UNESCO

---

# *Mental Health and Technological Change*

IT IS RECOGNIZED that during technical change, difficulties and conflicts are inevitable. This survey does not offer "solutions" to these problems, but rather indicates how these problems can be approached so as to minimize the difficulties or conflicts creating problems of adjustment, preserve, and where possible promote, mental health.

We may summarize the general principles which can be derived from the type of materials which have been examined for this survey:

1.  The culture of each people is a living unity in the sense that a change in any one aspect will have repercussions in other aspects. This is true even in those cultures which, while in the process of very rapid change, are torn by conflicts and contradictions.

2.  As each human individual embodies the culture through which he lives, discrepancies, inconsistencies, different rates of change of parts of culture, will have their expression in the personality organization of the individuals who live within changing cultures.

3.  An active concern for the mental health of the peoples of the world includes an active concern for the ways in which technical change is taking place. When the introduction of technical change is purposively initiated, or promoted by individuals or responsible bodies, such purposiveness involves responsibility for the effects not only in improved living-conditions, but also upon the total way of life of the people, for reintegration as well as a defence against disintegration.

4.  As each culture is unique, and as each particular situation within which a change is occurring or is to be made is unique, it is not possible to lay down prescriptions for what is to be done in any particular case. It is only possible so to identify and describe the process which occurs that each particular individual or team charged with responsibility for planning, or executing, or adjusting to some type of change, may be able to act in terms of this process. For example, it is possible to point out that in any programme involving popular educa-

tion in public health, the problem of language is a serious one—exact meanings must be explored, questions of adapting old words to new ideas, as opposed to coining new words, must be weighed, choice must be made among rival dialects, issues such as the use of a world-language or the elevation of a local language to a level at which the literature of the world may be expected to be translated into it—all must be taken into consideration. But after such details have been pointed out, whether all the public-health teaching in Sumatra is to be couched in the new national language of Indonesia (Bahasa Indonesia, an adaptation of Malay) would have to be worked out in active co-operation with members of the Indonesian health and education services who have an immediate knowledge of the local conditions in Sumatra. There is no possible prescription except this insistence upon taking into account the culture and the situation and the individual involved.

5. All changes should be introduced with the fullest possible consent and participation of those whose daily lives will be affected by the changes.

6. Every change, even such apparently conspicuous modifications of the external environment as building a dam or a railroad, occurs through the mediation and for the benefit of living individuals, and it is with these living human beings, their aspirations and hopes, their historically given and environmentally limited capabilities, that this survey is concerned.

7. In the light of these general principles, we may consider in somewhat more detail a set of recommendations which should make it possible to observe these principles in any given case.

## RECOMMENDATIONS

### First

It is important to take into account the degree of congruence between different levels of planning, from the international or national level to the final expression of any change in the daily lives of some identified group of people in some part of the world. If there are serious discrepancies in the practices involved or in the goals sought at higher levels, these will be reflected in the way the changes are made which affect the lives of the people whose farming practices, methods of earning a living, or health attitudes are to be changed. For example, if a government is promoting a given change for purposes of prestige, as a way of establishing itself in the minds of the people as progressive, modern, with an active concern for the welfare of the population, while the technical experts who are involved in the next step of the planning are themselves out of sympathy with these governmental aspirations, and are only concerned with better nutrition, or more education for the people—so that what is a sub-goal for one group is a major goal for the second group—a type of internal sabotage and friction may be set up which will be reflected in discordant practices at a more local level, in literature produced, or plans which are drawn up. If, however, the several groups involved can agree on a particular sub-goal, such as increasing the agricultural production or the proportion of a marketable crop, or the lowering of the infant death-rate, so that each interest group is able to focus on a common problem, many of these discrepancies and disharmonies can be avoided. (This is, of course, only a sub-head of the general principle of the interrelatedness of culture: all those who become involved in purposive change share together a sort of temporary sub-culture within which inconsistencies become a hazard.)

As there are bound to be great differences between main goals at different levels and in different sorts of planning—international, national, scientific, humanitarian, educational, engineering, etc.—the identification of a common sub-goal—such as universal vaccination—may prove impracticable. Those concerned with population growth may well point out that reduction in the infant death-rate before adequate changes have been made in agricultural and industrial practice to support the increased population, or before educational practices have been introduced to raise the standard of living and reduce the desire for large families, may only bring more misery. At the same time, those concerned with the immediate welfare of each child born today may feel that to withhold or to fail to promote measures now available for saving human lives would violate those very principles of concern for human welfare on which the whole programme of purposive change is based. Such a conflict, serious though it seems, may be minor compared with the conflict between modern Western values—in which each individual is seen as unique and with but one life to live, so that every effort must be made to promote the survival and health of each individual born—and the values of religious systems which, while affirming the value of individual human souls, disallow this tremendous emphasis upon the human life-span of each individual. Issues such as these lie back of discussions about industrialization, immigration, immunization, etc.—often inexplicit and inarticulate —troubling to the exponents of each point of view just to the degree that they are unrecognized and unadmitted. Attempts to resolve such issues, in which the leading political and religious ideologies of the world of the twentieth century are involved, will inevitably colour decisions which are made to build a giant irrigation project in one country, to build factories in some agricultural area, to start the modernization programme with schools or with public-health clinics.

In this manual we are considering not the resolving of such issues as they relate to the most fundamental concerns of human beings in the world today, but with making recommendations which will protect and preserve individual men, women and children whose whole way of life is being affected and altered, from the ill effects of such conflicts. The only way we now know of in which planning on high levels—involving conflicts of the most fundamental sort—can be handled so as to protect the individual lives affected is to be sure that as much of the implementing action as possible is put into effect by members of the same culture and of the same locality.

For example, in the 1940s there was a series of discussions, in which members of different nationalities participated, on child welfare and nutrition in China. Working from Western assumptions about the need to preserve each individual Chinese infant, the conference emphasized the need in China for cow's milk, canned if necessary. Chinese participants were able to oppose these demands from two points of view, whether the economic or the nutritional emphasis was given. Chinese nutritionists —unencumbered by the Western insistence that if infants are not fed human milk, they must be fed animal milk—had experimented successfully with diets based on vegetables and eggs; Chinese economists were wary of a plan which, while nominally promoting nutritional goals, was economically unrealistic. Those who are themselves members of a culture within which a change is being introduced will be able, often unwittingly, to block suggestions which proceed from quite different value systems than their own, and which would eventuate in destructive changes.

It may be asked how such blockings by the members of a culture, or by the members of a local community or of a particular professional group, are to be distinguished from the type of resistance to change which is offered by those groups who have a vested interest—economic or psychological—in the preservation of the *status quo*, or in the promotion of conditions which are antithetical to the best mental health of the members of the society. Here again the question of sub-goals comes in. If the entire group involved in making a plan is committed to the particular sub-goal, the alteration of the plans in the direction of genuine cultural considerations may more safely be relied upon. Thus in a conference on nutrition, while one cannot with safety rely upon a representative of a manufacturer of synthetic baby foods, or advocate of a change in the agricultural production pattern of a country to a crop of which he is the principal exporter, or the representative of a group whose particular services will disappear if any action is taken, one can rely upon *nutritionists* of different cultural backgrounds to introduce the necessary precautions into any nutritional plan made.

As a general recommendation, then, it is possible to say that it is dangerous ever to make any plan, or to try to execute any plan, without the active participation of members of the culture, of the particular professions, and of the administrative apparatus concerned; as soon as any planned change has a specific population group as its object, members of that group—through demonstration villages, pilot projects, etc.—must be brought into the planning.

Whether we focus on the need for homogeneity in type of practice or on the need for reconciling widely different basic ideologies and values, this procedure is necessary. The arrogant self-assurance which makes more industrialized countries force their methods on the less industrialized, the touchy eagerness to prove themselves that characterizes young nations, the missionary zeal of the apostles of the scientific point of view, and the defensive measures of the religiously orthodox, may all be welded into a working whole if exponents of each position plan together.

Certain other recommendations follow. It is desirable that all groups involved with planning the introduction of technical change—either in its technological aspects or in making those necessary changes in education, social organization, and family life which will protect and promote the mental health of those among whom the change is being introduced —should consist of members of more than two cultures. Such a group would include, of course, the members of the culture in which the change is being made, members of the culture whose developed professional skills or economic know-how and resources are being drawn upon, and members of a third culture, who can maintain a certain objectivity and prevent the consuming group and the resource group from becoming dead-locked or developing an isolated bit of behaviour in which the conflicts—between, for example, Indonesian and American, or Burmese and Dutch, value systems—may become frozen. The same recommendation applies to the composition of every type of team within a country; if the national level and rural communities are the focus of the planning, the inclusion as a third participant of someone who has worked in cities will similarly help maintain a certain measure of objectivity.

What applies to the involvement of members of different cultures and different levels of organization applies equally to the inclusion of different professions; having more than two professions and including one with less involvement again will provide steadiness of team-work.

Such measures are a protection against the organization of bias, and a certain guarantee that the programmes developed and the steps taken can both embody and be to a degree unhampered by the vested interests and old and new, conscious and unconscious, prejudices of all those concerned.

It will be recognized that this recommendation is again based on the principle that culture is mediated through persons, and that a culture, or a profession, or a level of administration, or a point of view, cannot be represented by a charter, a diagram, or a printed description, but only by living human beings who themselves embody the position which is to be taken into account.

## Second

Where specific technical practices are to be introduced into a culture or a part of a society which has not hitherto used them, it is desirable to strip these technical practices of as many extraneous cultural accretions (from the lands of origin) as possible. This recommendation applies to such varied matters as mass production, methods of immunization, development of alphabets for unwritten languages, methods of antisepsis or of sanitation, etc. It is realized that the technologies and inventions of modern science are themselves the outgrowth of a very particular historically limited type of culture—a culture in which the focus of interest has been upon the observable, the repeatable, the measurable, upon using the external world as a model even when processes within the body were concerned. Without this focus of modern science—this discontent with any except the "scientific" explanation, this attempt to investigate all types of phenomena so that lawfulness in nature could be identified—the particular benefits of modern medicine and of modern industrial processes, which are coveted by and for all the peoples of the world, could not have developed in the way they have. However, once invented, a particular device may be used effectively by peoples within whose culture that particular invention might never have been made. It is also probable that too much emphasis upon the whole complex of cultural attitudes surrounding such inventions as clocks, thermometers, shock therapy, printing, caloric food-counts, assembly-line production, Diesel engines, or electronic self-corrective devices, may slow down the possibility of invention in the world, because the members of the new cultures who import and adopt the invention are prevented from making a contribution to its further development. If in order to use a certain type of machine it is necessary to adopt all the attitudes towards punctuality of Western factories and school systems, absorbing this alien type of education may act selectively within the new culture, so that only the deviant or only the obedient and frightened learn, and the gifted and creative may turn away. An alien technology, supported by forms of education and inter-personal relations which are also alien, is likely to separate the practitioner of the new skill from his cultural roots, prevent the new practice from becoming integrated in the living-habits of the mass of the people, and produce populations who are confused and disoriented because they do not participate meaningfully in the new forms of their society. We see this happening every day in workers who emigrate from country to city, from a peasant to an industrial country, who learn to comply with the alien ritual of factory or clinic, but who are themselves lost and disoriented.

Western-trained professionals carry about with them an enormous amount of cultural baggage which could very well be discarded. We may illustrate this again from the field of nutrition, where, instead of taking the basic principles of nutrition and examining a given local dietary pattern for the actual nutrients, the caloric content, in relation to the growth and work patterns of the population, there is instead an insistence upon ideas like three meals a day, balance of the diet within 24 hours, the importance of animal milk for infants, and so the use of the findings of nutritional science is compromised and confused in other parts of the world. Sanitarians may impose the ideas of their own culture on the proprieties of age and sex standards of privacy, or even introduce systems of behaviour which involve culturally special ideas about the whole process of digestion, or which violate the trust of a particular culture in the goodness of human nature. Extraneous and culturally destructive effects can be avoided by stripping each scientific technique to the bone, to the absolute essentials which will make it possible for other people to learn to use it, and to handle it in a living, participating, creative way.

This recommendation applies not only to stripping scientific practices bare of the particular habits of the members of the Western society within which a practice was developed, but also to the advisability of leaving behind the particular rationalizations and sanctions, both religious and scientific, with which a specific practice may have been associated in a given Western country. For example, the insistence that individual will-power should be invoked in teaching good nutritional usage is the result of a blend of Protestant Christian conceptions of the human will and scientific findings as to the best way to utilize a given set of food resources. In another culture, pleasure in eating, or customary compliance with ritual arrangements of food, may be invoked instead.

To carry out this recommendation, reliance must again be placed on mature human beings. Instead of saying that in order to train a public-health nurse we must first have an elementary-school system patterned on the school system of the West—in which children will be rebuked and rewarded for the same sort or mistakes, learn to read the same kinds of directions, learn to fear the same kinds of errors in arithmetic and to hate the same kinds of tasks—we may experiment with how to teach particular practices to the most educated young adults we can find.

Instead of bringing beginners from the countries wishing to introduce new public-health practices, to learn a pattern in a country with more developed practice, we can bring more mature students who will participate —sometimes with the help of seniors who have worked as foreigners in their country and with representatives from other countries with different types of practice—in making a new pattern which is congenial and meaningful to them, as representatives of their own culture.

The model for such a procedure, by which the end product of modern technology is reinterpreted in terms of particular cultures, was established in the United States during World War II, when the question was raised how recipes were to be developed for using new dried-food products which resembled no known kind of food. As long as recognized food staples were distributed by the nationals of a country carrying out a food-relief programme, a question like this was seldom raised, and the result was the kind of misery and ill feeling which came from assuming that European populations would eat maize. But these new synthetic foods were as strange to Americans as they would be to Greeks or Japanese. Because they were relatively unencumbered with traditional sentiments, were in fact stripped down to the barest essentials, the question of what to do with them could be asked. Experimental groups were set up among women from different countries for whom these were designed as relief foods, to explore the range of different ways in which the same synthetic food might be used as hot soup or cold dessert, or simply as an ingredient in a made dish. Once this exploration was completed, although it did yield suggestive recipes and insights about differences in cultural practice, it seemed clear that the best advice was: (a) Do not set up any fixed way of using the new foods which will inevitably be special to American food-habits and; (b) in each country get local cooks, who may be trusted, if given support and latitude, to work out ways of adopting the new strange materials, of turning what was food only in the scientific sense—in that it had been demonstrated to contain the necessary nutrients for human beings—into food in the cultural sense, something that people would eat and be nourished by.

In this instance, the synthetic food, because it was new, had as yet little weight of cultural meaning, except in matters like colour. But for most of the technological change which is introduced from one part of the world to another, the burden of the habits and beliefs of the people who developed a particular technique is heavy. It will be necessary to set about stripping each practice down, as well as building up training and development methods which permit each new culture which takes over a particular technique to contribute new patterns of use. This means a style of analysis which asks of each procedure: What is the scientifically essential, the minimum core, of this operation? In regard to a thermometer questions would be asked about size, shape, colour, the use of the particular system of measurement, the way "normal" was marked; the preference for a mouth or a rectal thermometer; the phrasing of high and low temperatures; the phrasing of the meaning of temperature deviations as showing that an individual was sick, or that an individual was putting up a fight against disease, etc.

In building a factory questions would be asked about such matters as size and shape—Does a factory have to have walls? Should the assembly line move the object or should a moving platform move the men along with the objects? How long is a shift? What should control the tempo of the operation?—as well as the more obvious question of how an operation of a factory type should be set up in a society with entirely different patterns of human relations.

But one of the great advantages of first stripping each technological change to the core, of querying the most time-honoured accretions and practices, is that the experts then genuinely need constructive thinking by members of the culture where they are going to work. Because the situation is new, no one can give them a recipe, and usually the culturally workable answer can only be arrived at by experiment—with living human beings from the culture in question. If a thermometer is not even to *look* like our thermometer, then what is it to look like? If a factory is not a building with walls, what is it? If dried beans are not bean-soup, what are they? The scene is then set for the participation of the members of the other culture, in which the experts with experience—knowing their helplessness in this area of re-design—will welcome help, and the gifted members of the culture in which the device or process has never been used will be able to contribute imaginatively. By this very contribution they will lay the ground-work for the mental health of all the members of their society who must learn to take temperatures or work in factories.

Obversely, a sensitive attention to the way in which the existing techniques of the country to which change is being brought are interwoven with the local value system is also important. So it may be found that agricultural practices are tied up with an image of the earth as a mother who gives food and is fed, and an image of mutual giving—by man, care and fertilizer; by the earth, food for man—may be used for the new agricultural techniques.

### Third

When the particular values of a given culture are to be used as vehicles for change, such a use should be planned and applied by those members of the culture who share the belief or the aspiration which is to be used. Those who are engaged either in introducing technological change or in providing for a cushioning or muting of the effects of technological change, have become increasingly aware, during the last few years, of the advantages of couching a change in terms which are familiar to a given society, in supporting a new practice by quoting an old sacred text. At the same time, many discussions among experts reveal a deep disquiet about such a procedure, a disquiet which manifests itself in questions, such as whether it is possible to imbed modern scientific practices in age-old systems of religious values. Or is it not necessary, many specialists ask, to plan to introduce a secular, scientific point of view right through a society, if men are to use the inventions and machines of the Western world, with their superior capacity to provide food and shelter, education, and medical care for the masses of the people? These questions reveal a dilemma, in which the secularized expert asks how in fact he— who does not believe in a particular system of values, and shows, by his every act, his adherence to a secularized scientific system of values— can with any integrity use these values, which he believes to be outmoded and wrong, to accomplish such ends as the introduction of literacy and public health.

This problem, however, is also soluble if it is referred to the general principles of cultural integrity. If members of the group of people who are to use the new technology themselves do the planning, then they will be adapting their own beliefs, and quoting their own sacred texts, restructuring their own lives, in accordance with the common sub-goal of infant welfare or universal literacy, which they share with the technical experts from the city, from the modernizing sector of the population, from another country, or from an international agency. For a man who himself believes in no God to search the Koran for an appropriate text to support methods of preventing well-pollution will, at best, limit his efficiency and make his commitment to the effort of guaranteeing a population pure water less whole-hearted. At worst, it introduces an element of manipulation into the operation which reduces the dignity of those whose holy texts are quoted to the level of puppets whose strings are pulled by an arrogant and alien hand. But if the people themselves, steeped in the traditional wisdom of their scriptures, transform the new knowledge into a new expression of an ancient and beloved revelation, then the dangers of lack of spontaneity, falseness, manipulation and degradation are avoided.

Careful attention to this principle of participation will also help to deal with one of the most serious dangers in the purposive introduction of new technologies among peoples who have newly come to trust in and desire the scientifically based achievements and values of the West. Among such peoples a great many of those who acquire an education in medicine, or engineering, or agriculture, will have had to make a considerable break with their own traditions, and will have compensated for this by embracing—with the self-protective zeal and blindness of the convert—the beliefs and practices which they associate with the new knowledge. Their willingness to assume a whole series of symbols—from fountain-pens, rain-coats and brief-cases to an insistence upon marriage for love, and the disregard of traditional patterns of inter-personal relations —is often an essential step in the particular path of modernization or Westernization on which they have determined, or for which their own society has selected them. But they are, for this very reason, seldom the appropriate persons to adapt the new practices to the traditions which are still shared by the masses of the people. To the extent that they are committed to the new form of their society, they will wish to bring their fellow-nationals with them, to use some new public-health practice or method of transportation as a device to wean them from all their old beliefs.

For example, a critical observer, watching from a distance, may be impressed with the way in which local officials in the Indonesian Republic have adapted the traditional shadow-play to their programmes of keeping the people of the villages informed about the changes which are being vigorously pursued throughout Indonesia. This new shadow-play has ordinary human characters and has been stripped of supernatural elements. But this use of the shadow-play is viewed with deep and genuine scepticism by young political leaders, who feel that the shadow-play itself should be eradicated as lending inevitably an inappropriate aura of religious awe to the modern national leadership. For an educator who felt this way to plan to use the shadow-play would mean either a compromise with his principles or an expression of pessimism and contempt for the villagers who, from his point of view, are steeped in age-old mysticism. If, however, some programme of information is entrusted to village leaders, who entertain no such scepticism and who themselves feel the shadow-play to be a most appropriate way of educating the people to take part in the work of developing their country, then there is no such question as compromise or insincerity. The play will be furnished with new lines, and, in time, as the characters explain to the people the advantages of new agricultural practices and new health measures, in the mind of the script-writer and in the minds of his audiences, a new synthesis will take place, which is organic because it has occurred within the same human organisms, which is harmonious because it is an expression of individual human beings' efforts to make sense of their own lives.

*Fourth*

As each culture is a whole, however sorely torn at the moment—whole in the sense that it is the system by which and through which its members live—in all relationships between cultures, each must be accorded dignity and value. Much of the present phrasing of technical-assistance planning, and much of the present evaluation of change within a country, is conducted with explicit or implicit denial of the dignity of members of those countries which, while often the inheritors of much older traditions, have not been in the vanguard of those aspects of culture which stem from modern science. This is self-defeating, in that it arouses violent resistances and attempts at compensation and retaliation from those whose feelings of self-esteem have been violated; it is also contrary to the findings of modern psychiatric practice, which insist on the recognition of the patient's validity as a human being. Phrases which divide the world into the "haves" and the "have-nots" overvalue bread and plumbing and devalue music and architecture. Those whose status is defined as a "have-not" may come to repudiate the possibility of learning anything at all, or of sharing anything at all except "bread" with those who have so denigrated their cherished ways of life. Phrases like "under-developed," "backward," "simple"—to the extent that they cover a whole culture—are equally defeating. If, instead, we draw on an image in which two adults—one experienced in one skill, another in a different skill—pool their knowledge so that each can use the skill of the other for a particular task, as when foreign explorer and local guide venture together into a forest, much more viable relationships can be set up. Leaders of the newest countries, only recently established by revolution or mandate or negotiation, are young adults, not children—less experienced but not less adult than those upon whose skills and resources they need to draw. Indeed, it is possible to contrast the often childlike dependence of members of old societies towards their governments, which they feel ought to look after them, protect them and provide for them, and the responsible adulthood of the members of some new nations who regard their young governments as institutions which must be protected and cherished by the citizenry. A very little scrutiny, if the whole culture is taken into account, is enough to do away with assumptions of superiority, and to permit the establishment of working partnerships in which engineer and architect, scientist and sage, pool their different but not incompatible wisdoms. The most complex invention of the Western world—radar or psychoanalytic therapy—is still only part of a way of life, to which others who are skilled in ways of life which have developed differently may be expected to contribute new insights. The sensitive application of a gadget, or the rejection of some use to which it has callously been put, may be as great or even greater a contribution than the invention of the gadget itself.

## Fifth

Every effort should be made to design the introduction of measures to facilitate or compensate for or provide for benefits from technical change in such a way that the process is circular, and all those involved at every level are able to participate and experience the changes as they occur.

One of the serious difficulties experienced by human beings who attempt to change the culture within which they live is that the very fact of planning itself makes it possible to force through a single-line change in disregard of the hundreds of side-effects which are taken care of in unplanned change which occurs within a society unsupported by disproportionate governmental or industrial pressure. Where a system of piped-in water is gradually spread through a country, with each village taking responsibility for its own water-supply, the changes may be very slow, but problems of landownership, of where the clothes are to be washed, of combining watering cattle and arranging business transactions, etc., will be thrashed out slowly, and the disruption of old ways of life will be less serious. When a new impulse towards better water, or better roads, or better land-use sweeps the country, implemented by funds and personnel from outside the community, its effective progress is rapid, but fewer such adjustments can take place.

This was vividly illustrated by an episode in which housing was planned at the national level, and the architects, anxious to conserve labour and materials (which meant massive savings when thousands of dwelling units were concerned in the plans), reduced the traditional space allotted to stairways only to find that they had built houses in which a coffin could not be carried down the stairs. Harassed housing-managers had to send mildly sick people off to already over-crowded hospitals, afraid of the effects of a death in which traditional burial ritual would be violated. When houses are built within a community on a normal scale, the architects do not take coffins into account, but long experience in human living has brought about an accommodation between the dimensions of the houses and the traditional ceremonials which take place within them. The porte-cochère disappears with the open carriage and the closed motor car stands, itself roofed, before an unroofed doorway.

It is possible to say that in all old and habitual enterprises, with slow and traditional introduction of small changes, the side-effects of a change can be felt and responded to by the members of that society. When change is introduced by external forces, however beneficent in intent, these protective behaviours cannot operate, and changes may go much too far in some given direction before compensatory measures can be taken.

Two inventions which have been made in the last century attempt to deal with these problems: the model or the pilot project, and provision for "feed-back" from an area where any new activity is introduced. In the model, or pilot, or demonstration project, a desired change is introduced on a small scale and meticulous observations are made of the process. These observations can be used as the basis for modifications of the original plan, new provisions for flexibility, and compensatory measures which are necessary. This method is now becoming a commonplace over much of the world, part of the equipment of administrators, educators and planners; but one element is still neglected—the recognition that the experts who inaugurate a given change are so much a part of the project, that they themselves should be observed, and their behaviour should be recorded and analysed. A next step in the use of demonstration, model and pilot projects is the introduction of recorders, and the use of the records of the roles of experts, or representatives of higher administrative levels on the local scene. Thus those who are charged with making innovations—in addition to the observations which they themselves make —can learn what they themselves are doing. Their own behaviour is "fed back" to them and becomes part of the planning process.

There are a variety of other ways in which the "feed-back" process can be elaborated, so that, for example, no planning conference is held without provision for the planners later being fully informed of the outcome of their plans. Modern methods of sound-recording and moving pictures can be tried to increase the insight of practitioners, and function in lieu of the older, slower methods by which the practitioner—educator or physician or engineer—who failed to respond to the needs of a local situation was disciplined and educated by "experience."

In brief, if there is to be purposive change, directed by those with power and resources, to introduce programmes of vast scope with unprecedented speed, so as to add 20 years to the expectation of life within a single generation, or alter the level of literacy from 10 per cent to 90 per cent within a decade, it is necessary to develop substitutes for "experience," so that people may learn in a few weeks what they once learned in a lifetime, and yet learn it with all of the complexity of genuine human experience. Failure to provide such corrections carries automatic penalties, for either the desired changes cannot be carried out at all, or methods of force and manipulation have to be used which, while introducing a particular technology, decrease the well-being of the people as a whole.

### Sixth

In the choice of methods to be used for introducing change, whether technical or compensatory, the criteria of involvement of the whole personality should be used. A great deal of discussion is wasted over the relative desirability of using print or radio, films or discussion groups, cartoons or dramas, practice or demonstration or illustration, as ways of teaching new procedures and attitudes. These discussions tend to ignore the fact that all media for dissemination of new knowledge are to be judged in terms of effectiveness, and effectiveness in turn is a function of the extent to which the new practice becomes part of the way of life of the people among whom the change is to be introduced. Any reliance on a method which is purely intellectual or purely aesthetic, purely emotion, or purely moralistic, purely social or purely individual, will necessarily restrict the area of involvement. Whether, in a given culture, films or group discussions will evoke a more whole participation in adults or children, in the educated or the uneducated, on weekdays or on a holy day, are matters which have to be decided by experiment, with the full participation of the particular population on the spot. If this is recognized, preparation of teaching and demonstration materials will take the form of suggestions of ways of developing materials rather than the provision of ready-made, rigid, untranslatable devices. In the preparation precautions may be undertaken which make local adaptation inescapable—as in a film which has a sound-track which must be translated into a local idiom, or an exhibit with gaps in it which must be filled in with local materials.

### Seventh

In order to preserve the process of change in each culture as a living one through which each generation of human beings increasingly is able to use the knowledge of every part of the human race to solve their emerging problems and advance towards a realization of their highest aspirations, efforts should be directed towards the establishment within each country—and often within each locality—of institutions which will make it possible to assay this ongoing process. Instead of working out blue prints for health and welfare, nutrition and longevity, towards the fulfillment of which populations are relentlessly propelled, it is possible to establish patterns of social evaluation, so that communities and countries may take stock of themselves, assess the present state of nutrition against the present state of agricultural resources and present state of community facilities, match the projected population curve against the present rate of building elementary schools or homes for the aged, project needs for new kinds of personnel and begin to train them 10 years before the need develops.

To preserve and promote mental health in the midst of technical change then emerges as a way of stating a goal of cultural renewal as each group of people undertakes to utilize technical advances for the purpose of creating and maintaining institutions which will cherish and protect the lives of men in world-wide community.

# Part Three

---

# The Politics
# of Development

IN THE COURSE of his celebrated lecture on *The Two Cultures and the Scientific Revolution*, C. P. Snow noted that "technology is rather easy." In the sense that the uneducated can quickly master the operations of the factory and that engineers and technicians can soon be trained, this statement is obviously true. Western notions of natural superiority were nastily jarred by the speed with which the Egyptians learned to operate the Suez Canal and the Chinese Communists mastered military technology. Technology's easy extension to nations in all stages of development is a comparatively new fact of human experience, a matter of a century at most. Indeed, in this new circumstance is a major hope for economic development among the poorer nations of the world.

Unfortunately, there has been no parallel breakthrough in the quality of the arrangements that men make to get along with each other in organized societies. Human politics are a larger obstacle to successful economic development than lagging technology, scanty economic resources, inconvenient geography, or even soaring birth rates. It is easy for an American to assume that the political inadequacies are concentrated among the underdeveloped countries; the headlines of revolution, military coup, and insurrection encourage such an assumption. The selections in this section demonstrate that many of the underdeveloped nations do suffer from the wrong political traditions, histories of political violence, and shortages of trained administrators. But the developed countries themselves have by no means completed their political and social integration, as the history of American race relations adequately indicates. Nor have the developed countries even approached a political consensus about the goals and methods of their policies toward their poorer brethren.

United States policy has been plagued by a host of unresolved questions of objective, strategy, and technique. Consider only a few of them. Should our aid represent simply a generous attempt to decrease the scale of human misery? As Gunnar Myrdal noted recently, Americans are reluctant to own up to their generous impulses. It may be, therefore, that more assistance than we admit springs from altruism rather than calculation. When we do calculate, what items should we weigh? Should aid be a reward to our political allies, as Pakistan's Ayub Khan insists it should be? In Taiwan, Spain, and South Korea this criterion has had major relevance, for no other principle explains the heavy aid allocations these countries have received. Alternatively, should aid be allocated primarily by the standard of efficiency? Maximum use of aid by its recipient implies grants to countries which now show the greatest promise of success through their own efforts and denial of such aid to precisely those countries whose need is greatest. Again, should our national attachment to the ideology if not the fact of free enterprise guide foreign aid policy? In 1963 Congress vetoed a proposed Agency for International Development grant to India for the construction of a state-owned steel mill essentially on the ground that American funds should not promote socialism. What should an American administrator do in Latin America when his choice is between supporting reactionary, anti-Communist governments and encouraging dissident groups which may turn out to be unpleasantly revolutionary, possibly on the Cuban model? Of such political dilemmas there is no end.

Economic aid is not exclusively an American problem. The capital requirements of the developing countries demand the participation of the rich countries of Western Europe. These countries have barely begun to recognize their responsibilities. Indeed, as Gunnar Myrdal has written, what is badly needed is the creation of some redistributive mechanism between the rich and the poor nations. But this achievement in turn is dependent on the willingness of the rich to recognize some community of interest with the poor. In the advanced nations the Welfare State is the institutional embodiment of this sense of shared interest. We are a long distance from a similar recognition by entire nations of their obligations to poorer people. Thus it is dangerous error to conclude that economic development is impeded only by the defective politics of the poorer nations or even to contrast too sharply the politics of the rich nations with the politics of the poor countries.

One final word. There is a hierarchy of complexity and difficulty in the relation of the developed with the underdeveloped countries. Industrial and agricultural techniques are the most easily exported and they encounter the most enthusiastic receptions. Technicians and engineers speak in clear, comprehensible tones. Sometimes the economist when he serves as adviser and planner can approximate this clarity but only by ignoring the institutional limitations upon his activity. For neither the engineer nor the economist has much to say about the political and social conditions which impede or facilitate the deployment of his skills. Hence the economist must either turn political scientist or listen to the political scientists. Both groups speak in the following section and the perceptive reader will discover that we have only begun to grasp the elements of political and social organization that distinguish successful from unsuccessful efforts at development. The essays we have included represent some of the most acute attempts to define these elements and to prepare the way for a more general theory of the development process.

# The Rich and
# the Poor

THESE FIVE ARTICLES center upon a common theme: the desirable relationships between advanced, economically progressive countries in the West and the developing countries of Asia, Africa, and Latin America. In one fashion or another, each writer is engaged in identifying the means by which a country like the United States can best assist economic development.

The first two articles offer contrasting opinions of the general issue. Gunnar Myrdal, author of *An American Dilemma* and Executive Secretary of the United States Economic Commission for Europe from 1947 to 1957, states the case for special treatment and special concessions by the rich to the poor. He is convinced that only a substantial degree of national economic planning will enable development to occur satisfactorily. Professor Bauer argues, on the contrary, that capitalistic forms of development stand better prospects of success and that the situation of the underdeveloped countries presents no essential contrast to that of the West at similar stages of economic life. His article is a direct attack on Myrdal's methodology, emphases, and conclusions.

The next group of three essays concentrates directly upon foreign aid. Professor Morgenthau of the University of Chicago, a political scientist and historian of wide reputation, endeavors to classify the objectives of foreign aid and argues from this classification that the efficacy of such programs is necessarily limited. E. F. Schumacher, an English economist of wide experience in India, warns against the automatic assumption that the introduction of Western patterns of economic organization will necessarily benefit underdeveloped nations. Professor Seers, an economist familiar with the problems of the economic adviser, provides a thoughtful account of what the economist engaged as a technical adviser can and cannot expect to achieve in this role. In its way it is a plea for a broad conception of the place of economics in development.

# Gunnar Myrdal

## The Conditions of Economic
## Integration

"ECONOMIC INTEGRATION" is one of the many learned terms which emerged after the Second World War as new popular banners in the political discussion of international questions. From there the slogans have been sent back to the economists as indicating important problems for scientific study. "Economic development of underdeveloped countries" is another and closely related species of the same genus. Their appearance as banners in popular debate reflects a changed world situation to which we have to adjust our scientific exertions. They symbolize interests, ideals, aspirations, and visions which on the international scene are new, at least in their present political significance.

### ECONOMIC INTEGRATION

Literally, integration means nothing more than that parts are brought together into a whole. Up till the Second World War the term was used most frequently in the social sciences by sociologists and cultural anthropologists. They were still working under a stronger static bias than the economists, and the term, having then as now a positive value connotation, was usually employed to characterize the stable social relations within a stationary community: most typically an isolated primitive community in Malthusian population balance, with fixed mores and an established division of functions and responsibilities. When exogenous influences caused changes in the social relations within such a closed community, these changes—which at least in the shorter view could be considered as detrimental disturbances to the functioning norms of the community—were characterized as "disintegration," with a meaning very similar to the other statically conceived sociological concepts: "disequilibrium," "disorganization," "maladjustment," and "crisis."

The new term "economic integration," particularly when applied to the international scene, obviously means something different. The world situation, in response to which the term has acquired popularity and political significance, has its very essence in a violent and radical breaking down of cultural isolation; and so the term economic integration comes now to be employed as signifying an ideal for the mutual adjustment of national communities rapidly brought into much closer relationship. The specific sociological problem hinted at also receives a new dynamic and practical setting in the question how to forge and direct economic development and all other social changes so that institutions, patterns, and mores are adjusted in such a way as to avoid cultural impoverishment and social breakdowns.

To the economist, however, integration must mean primarily incorporation in the same "market." The ultimate and from a valuation point of view most important equalization is that of the remuneration paid to the factors of production. An economy is integrated when labor of a given kind commands the same price, when there is one market for capital, with a single price for comparable risks, and when the price of the same kind of land has been equalized (with appropriate amplifications for noncompeting groups and location of land, among other considerations).

The realization of these conditions would in human terms mean the achievement of that old ideal in Western democratic thinking, equality of opportunity. In recent times the concept of economic integration has increasingly incorporated more and more of another old Western ideal, closely related to but not identical with the former one, namely the equalization of incomes and wealth.

Economic integration can mean a process or an achievement; on this score clarity can be preserved by careful wording. But the concept of economic integration is vague for a more fundamental reason: people mean different things when they express their allegiance to that ideal, depending on differences both in their basic moral and political valuations and in their beliefs about reality and in particular about the possibility of changing reality by means of policy. That the concept is nonetheless not without logical content is an indication of the degree to which the same valuations and beliefs about policy are held in common in Western civilization. The content of the concept can be studied in the advanced democratic national communities, where integration is in fact being gradually achieved as a consequence of the fact that there is an effective political technique by which people can voluntarily organize their living together through the development of appropriate policies.

*International integration is the main value premise of the present study.* Reality is studied from the viewpoint of the ideal. The practical problem is how or by what policy means reality can be made to approach the ideal. The primary task of scientific inquiry in this field is to ascertain the actual trends: whether and to what extent they really imply a process towards closer international economic integration or whether, on the contrary, the world economy is continuously disintegrating. Closely connected with this is the other question of the probability of integrative policies actually being pursued and their likely effects, and consequently whether and to what extent the trends are likely to be changed into a process of integration. The title of this chapter should be understood to formulate a query, not to express an assertion.

The use of the general social-science concept of integration in relation to some of the old and familiar problems of economic analysis along the classical lines implies an invitation that the study be undertaken in such a way that it embraces a broader vista than that of economic science. After considerable hesitation, this challenge will, to the best of the author's ability, be accepted in the preparation of this chapter. It will mean that the problem itself will be allowed to determine the discussion, without regard to the limitations of specific methods of a particular discipline. It is more difficult to do this competently than to keep within one of our established social-science disciplines; the difficulty may warrant a greater degree of indulgence to shortcomings.

The wider scope of the study will naturally result in a more general approach. At the same time, matters will be treated in full as they appear in actual political life. The study will therefore inevitably concern valuations and opinions to a far greater extent than a partial and therefore abstract treatment within a particular discipline, and this is another reason why it makes greater demands for tolerance.

This convergence on a broader view of the problems has indeed very sound logical justifications. As a matter of fact, social integration is an essential requisite for economic integration if the latter is to be achieved. When for instance we economists approach the most important single issue within the general international integration problem, that of the economic development of underdeveloped countries, failure to give due regard to the broader social and political viewpoints implies the danger that our analysis remains a sort of humble econometrics of limited interest outside our own craft.

## NATIONAL INTEGRATION

\*    \*    \*    \*    \*

### Conditions of Integration

The development towards a highly integrated state, the growth of the complex public and quasi-public institutions by which this development takes its form, and the putting into effect of the economic and fiscal policies which such a state employs and which interfere very harshly with the citizen's disposal of his own person and his property must all have a firm foundation on the psychological level. The citizens of the country must have such a strong feeling of belonging to the nation that they are prepared willingly to bear their share of common sacrifices when these are decided upon by due political process.

The feeling of a national community of interests and aspirations, the common willingness to make sacrifices for purposes other than immediate economic return, and the development of institutions and rules appropriate to these ends are the historical result of living for a long time closely together under a united policy and of actively participating in the political process of determining this policy. Should this psychological basis falter, the state would disintegrate. But in the progress towards economic integration and in conditions of continuous economic growth, it is apt to become ever firmer.

National solidarity is naturally quite heavily tested by the highly redistributional tax system in these countries. The unstable basis for national integration in countries like France, Italy, or Greece is reflected in their inability to stamp out large scale tax evasion and to give effect to progressive direct taxation. The fact that the United States, on the contrary, in spite of all its peculiar centrifugal problem situations, succeeded in the last generation in giving effect to its ever increasingly progressive direct taxation is a confirmation that the psychological basis of solidarity was becoming firm and that the country was successfully reaching national integration.

But the gradual conditioning of the citizens to pay taxes even when they constitute a heavy burden is not the only test of national solidarity. If strikes, instead of serving as rarely used safety valves, socially sanctioned and institutionally controlled in a highly organized process of collective bargaining in the labor market, develop as in France and Italy into recurring and aimless mass demonstrations of general dissatisfaction on the part of all the lower-income groups—workers, farmers, clerks, teachers, and government officials—then we are confronted in fact with the open reappearance of the "class struggle."

In the other countries there are differences in interest, too. But the different interests evolve within the specialized institutional forms developed for this purpose—the parliament and all other machinery for collective bargaining—and they manage to merge into continuously altered *modi vivendi*. The participating groups feel the institutions to be "theirs," they think about the organized community in terms of "we," whereas the striking masses in France and Italy are dissatisfied with the "system" and do not identify themselves with the organized social forms for the settlement of conflicting interests. Rather, they look on organized society as if it were outside their control by normal means; it is the community of "the others," who do them wrong.

The most significant difference between Western countries where the "price system" is accepted and those where it is openly challenged in group actions outside the established and sanctioned social forms is, of course, that the former countries are progressing economically and the others are not. Undoubtedly, part of the explanation why the former countries are progressing is that there the "class struggle" has been successfully held in leash (and, in the ideal case, tamed) by being harnessed to collective bargaining, where all interest groups act upon the agreed assumption that a settlement shall be reached and that it shall be respected. But even more important is the recognition that it is economic progress which provides room for the expansion of legitimate group interests and permits the element of mutual generosity which is the condition for successful collective bargaining—successful in the sense that a settlement is reached and that the parties to it feel that they are, for the time being, satisfied or will anyhow obey its terms.

Very clearly the necessity of reaching collective agreement is continuously exercising pressure on the limits of possible expansion. The postwar tendency to inflation in the northwestern countries of Europe is undoubtedly in part a consequence of the fact that the interest groups in these countries did not succeed in reaching a settlement in their collective bargaining on wages and farmers' prices without overstepping the limits of expansion and so causing a modicum (and sometimes more than a modicum) of wage and price inflation.

The above summary analysis of the economically highly integrated countries is offered as a factual account of their process of national integration in the historically given institutional and ideological setting and under the influence of the forces that were then operating. It is not a valuation, except that the total result of many elements—of which many are repugnant to many participating citizens in different respects and different degrees—namely, integration, is assumed to be an ideal.

You as Americans and I as a Swede recognize the realism of this outline of the main characteristics of the existing highly integrated national communities to which we belong. As a general and therefore vague characterization of the trend of social and economic relations in our type of countries, the term "economic integration" makes sense: the essential idea it emphasizes is the relatively wide range and the equality of opportunities these countries have gradually succeeded in offering the individual. Countries which have not reached so far as ours may likewise in a manner which makes sense characterize their effective national goals as "closer economic integration."

It must be emphasized, however, that even in relation to a single national state the concept is vague; in every country ideas on how to move towards the more integrated state have differed and do differ as among individuals, social classes, and political parties. Most people see short-comings in those national communities where they live and whose rules they observe.

Nevertheless, viewed from a distance, the differing political attitudes to the community as it is functioning become relegated to ripples on the surface of fundamental similarities, variations built around a main theme. From this distance the common features in our national communities can be abstracted and fitted into a coherent image. This fact testifies to the wider community of ideals in our Western civilization at which we hinted, and shows that when these ideals can work themselves out under exceptionally favorable conditions, they tend to result in a type of national community, the rather firm contours of which can be ascertained.

## INTERNATIONAL INTEGRATION

The disintegration of the world today compared with the world of 1913 is partly, but not entirely, more apparent than real. The more closely integrated world community before the First World War was a very partial one, excluding in the main, peoples of color, colonial lands, and backward countries in general.

### The Limits of Integration

International migration, capital movements, and trade functioned on the whole rather effectively within the small group of the advanced countries which were developing towards national integration as described in the previous section, and between them and tiny enclaves cut out of the submerged world about it. The world of 1913 was, like Athens in the days of Pericles, in many respects a model civilization, if one forgets the fact that it excluded from its benefits the larger part of mankind. Any new international system involving economic stability, broadly shared progress, and arising therefrom, a commonly felt confidence in the future must be attained on different terms, since the peoples which were then excluded are unwilling to resume their earlier passive role.

There is still a tendency to discuss the world economic problem from the narrow point of view of the small minority of mankind in the nationally highly integrated and prosperous countries, and to do so in terms all too exclusively of their trade and payments problems. By far the most glaring evidence, however, of the failure of international integration, according to our definition of this ideal, is the relatively great poverty of so many countries, with such large populations. As a matter of fact, the world trend seems to be towards even greater inequality.

It is in fact the richer countries which are advancing while the poorer countries with the large populations are stagnating or progressing very much more slowly. This has been the case for several generations. In the richer countries we are very conscious of being part of an economic civilization which has given us, and promises to continue giving us, rapidly rising economic standards, but for mankind as a whole there has actually been no progress at all. As H. W. Singer has rightly pointed out, world real income per capita, and with it the standard of living of the average human being, is probably lower now than in 1913 and perhaps lower than in 1900 and even earlier, because the nations which have rapidly raised their economic standards have been a shrinking proportion of the total world population.

## Reasons for Lagging Integration

In a sense, the awakening of those large, barely subsistence-level sectors of the world previously ignored implies the enlargement of the international economy, which in itself is a step towards closer economic integration. But the enormous and steadily increasing differences in factor prices and factor proportions which are thus revealed within our sphere of attention and which cannot possibly be overcome rapidly, perhaps not for generations and centuries, signify a glaring lack of international integration, which dramatically enlarges the scope of our problem precisely because of the extension of the international economy.

This is the problem. Migration has ceased to function as a factor of integration even between the advanced countries. Capital movements have shrunk generally, and with the breaking down of the colonial structure, they can even less be depended upon to provide the underdeveloped countries with capital for development. International aid has within limits effectively come to the rescue of those national economies in difficulties which belong to the old partial world of fairly advanced countries, but it has barely begun to face the bigger task of integrating the world as a whole. Trade has limits as a substitute for factor movements in effecting integration, even in a partial world. In any case, no liberalization of international trade can be expected *by itself* to change radically this situation of open international disintegration or this trend towards an increasingly widening gap in levels of production and consumption and of living standards. *By itself* "freer trade" may even tend to perpetuate stagnation in the underdeveloped regions.

Migration, capital movements, and international aid and trade are not the primary means of achieving this wider integration. In a real sense these are the products of integration, not the cause. They can help, but they cannot be relied upon to do the job. The major task is to force economic development in the underdeveloped countries to the point where a more unified system can be solidly built.

In the poor and backward countries efforts for economic development will have to take the form of measures to start the process towards national integration; for their main weakness is undoubtedly that they are badly integrated even nationally. This will certainly mean taking a number of steps which in the short term are not directly calculated to promote closer international integration. But without national integration the present enormous differences in standards and developments will be maintained and probably further increased. These countries also need national integration and, if possible, regional cooperation in order to win bargaining power, a very necessary condition for the achievement of some political balance in the world. It would be a poor international integration of a democratic world which left so little bargaining power in the hands of the great majority of its peoples.

The practical problem is to find a steadily progressive *modus vivendi*. A short-term solution in more absolute terms is out of the question.

Meanwhile, and mainly for independent reasons, the advanced countries themselves have not yet found a new and viable international balance between their national economies. In the world setting this is the smaller, and also the vastly simpler, problem to solve practically; but much the greater part of current international discussion is presently devoted to it. Unfortunately there are no valid reasons to expect an early solution even of this simpler problem. There is one thing, however, that we do know about any system of better international relations among the advanced countries which in time might come into existence, and this is that it will bear little resemblance to the old, pre-1914 system with its gold standard, free labor and capital movements, and multilateral trade. As an element in the greater complex of world problems, the problem of the advanced countries is not unimportant, particularly in the sense and to the degree that a solution would create a climate where we could tackle with more zeal and vigor the much bigger problem of the development of the underdeveloped countries.

Over this whole complex of world problems there looms ominously the East-West split. The division of the world into two hostile camps represents in itself the biggest single element of acute international disintegration. As such it falls outside the scope of this chapter, which is entirely focused on the limited problem of international economic relations in the non-Soviet world. Yet it has direct and indirect effects for the economy of every single country. It would be entirely unrealistic to discuss the development of economic relations in the non-Soviet world and not take into account these effects.

These are the problems which should be studied under the norm of closer economic integration. Economic integration has been defined in terms of the old ideals in Western social thinking of equality of opportunity and equalization of economic standards. In recent decades a few countries have come quite a long way towards *internal* economic integration in this sense. It has increasingly been a process of social organization in the course of which social and economic barriers could be abolished. In this process a complex system of interferences with the functioning of the price mechanism has played an important role. The principle of sharing risks and of equalizing income and wealth has been applied with ever sterner methods, and the whole process has been proceeding upon the psychological basis of attitudes of national belongingness and solidarity. This basis has continuously been strengthened as a result of the integration process itself and the sharing in the political responsibility for its direction.

* * * * *

## CONCLUSIONS

A study of trends and problems in the field of international integration should instill humility. This is, indeed, the effect which the marshaling of the data and the inferences under the various section headings has had upon the present author. The problems facing us are momentous, and if we take a general look at present world trends, it is not possible to answer affirmatively the question implied in the title of this paper. On balance the picture is almost everywhere one of increased national economic integration, but continued disintegration internationally. Very big policy changes would have to be effected to change this trend.

The economically advanced nations are in the continued throes of economic progress. The industrialization which is going on in the world is concentrated in the countries which are already highly industrialized. Some of the advanced countries, mostly those which were not so advanced before, are lagging behind, while those which were furthest advanced have forged ahead. Income gaps are increasing, not only between advanced and backward countries in general, but also within the advanced group. Western Europe, cut off from its eastern hinterland, and having lost most of its profitable dependencies in the backward regions as well as its investments in the new continents, is shrinking in economic importance, while North America continues to rise as the giant, dominating more and more the Western world.

During this process, which has been going on since before the First World War, international migration has been reduced to small proportions; even neighboring countries have virtually sealed their national labor markets against any intruders. The international capital market has almost ceased to function, except for capital going to the imperial outlands where investments are closely controlled as auxiliaries to the economy of the home country. Government credits, mostly granted by the

United States, and the operations of the International Bank have not to any material extent been a substitute for the defunct capital market.

The vigorously expanding economy of America and the, by comparison, contracting economies of Western Europe, have not yet been able to establish equilibrium in their trade and payments relations, in spite of the large amount of Marshall aid, not to mention much other aid in various forms before and after. Recently the intensification of cold war and the rising burden of rearmament have introduced new elements of uncertainty into these trading relations, even if the increased defense efforts have been successfully absorbed in the economic expansion. It might be—though we do not and cannot know for certain—that these defense expenditures have assured the continuation up till now of the postwar wave of expansion.

The years after the Second World War have seen the emergence of a new phenomenon, international aid, again given mostly by the United States. It is an interesting innovation, but, except for Marshall aid and other assistance to Western Europe, it has as yet been insignificant and haphazard from a broader economic point of view. The bigger problem of international integration, that of the economic development of the underdeveloped countries, is as yet hardly more than a vision and a challenge.

In the underdeveloped countries a considerable number of new approaches, the breaking down of stale social traditions, and a new realignment of human efforts have been made possible by the war and its aftermath. New independent nations have come into existence and older ones have embraced new aspirations. The backward and stagnant populations in Asia, Africa, Latin America, and Southern Europe are seething. In the advanced countries there is increasing awareness of these untold masses of new active participants in the international political concert of nations, seeking their destiny.

The difficulties facing the underdeveloped countries in their efforts to further economic development are so stupendous that a sober study can hardly end with any other conclusion than that short of a number of near miracles, they will not succeed in attaining their goal. The alternative to reasonable success is catastrophe. But near miracles do occur in the history of nations. The unexpected can always happen. When the need was greatest, inspiration and leadership have often changed trends. History is never determined in advance.

### Danger of Generalization

One general conclusion may be drawn from the analysis in the preceding sections. It should discourage the habit we have, and often display, of pretending to say something important about a complicated international problem and to contribute essentially to the solution of it by dealing with it under a conceptual system or a general theory from which emerges a glib formula for solution. The world problem is far too serious and too complicated for ready-made theories. Moreover, new constellations of facts and problems require fresh thinking. Many of our old pet theories represent today nothing more than cultural lag and intellectual inhibition. The only reason why they are not recognized as panaceas (which for good reasons we have come to disparage) is that they are old and therefore appear "sound" and respectable.

On the ethical level another conclusion emerges, closely related to that just expressed on the intellectual one. We have to guard ourselves against the comfortable habit of building up our own morale by stimulating our congenital optimism. Some problems are too heavily laden with difficulty to have an easy, happy ending. The courage which we need is not the cheap and in the end unreliable kind of optimism and the forced belief that everything will finally turn out to be going our way. We need instead the courage of desperation, which all the time seeks and exposes the cold truth and is strong enough to accept calmly serious reverses and long retreats and which urges us to work on nevertheless, even against all odds.

The forces of disintegration in the world are now so powerful that we must take much bolder measures than can ever be inspired by the cheap courage of optimism. We should be clear that a turn of the tide would require not only a greater degree of social cohesion than now exists among and within the advanced, nationally highly integrated countries, but also much greater solidarity with the poorer countries outside our circle. We are constantly deluding ourselves, and we are paying for widespread organized publicity to do it, with policies—convertibility, moderate cuts in tariffs, emphasis on getting private capital to move where it does not want to go, very partial and largely unreal efforts towards integration among a few Western European countries—which, even when they are laudable in themselves, only nibble at the fringes of the big problems. Yet at the same time we are often closing our eyes to what we do not want to see. This is, indeed, the essence of our courage of optimism, and its effect is that we are not preparing the ground among our peoples for the great change of attitudes on their side which the bolder integration measures would require.

## Effects of Cold War

All our intellectual exertions have been taking place for several years in the strange climate of the Cold War. Anyone who is in a position to make firsthand observations in a limited area of international events soon be-

comes very much aware of the powerful bias in the selection and evaluation of news for the general public, not only in the Soviet orbit, but
increasingly also in the non-Soviet world. It is especially our most general
ideas, our implicit assumptions, and our way of facing and stating problems that are apt to be sensitive to this continued and systematic bias in
the reporting of recorded events and in their interpretation. The Cold
War also has a more direct impact on our thinking, as certain beliefs
become commonly recognized as the right and respectable ones and certain others as wrong or deviously dangerous.

If the world ever returns to sanity, it will soon stand out a mile that
much of our so-called scientific thinking on international problems during
recent years has been illusory. This is a matter which comes within the
broad realm of the still undeveloped sociology of science; its crucial importance, not only for social science but also for political development,
would warrant penetrating and pitiless study. Here I shall confine myself
to stating the general premise upon which I would base the study, if I
were myself to undertake it: In a democracy it is in the common interest
that the truths—not least the uncomfortable ones—be established and dis-
seminated as widely as possible among the citizens; illusions, and particularly the opportunist ones are a public danger. This value premise is
implied in the great motto, "Man's right to knowledge and the free use
thereof," with which Columbia University enters the celebration of its
two centuries of existence as a force for rationality in America and in the
whole world of learning.

To these general conclusions I shall only add a few selected and specific
ones which are strategic in the sense that it would be of great importance
if attitudes were accordingly changed in the advanced countries, which
naturally play the leading roles in the international concert of nations.

### Flow of Capital

As to the flow of fresh capital to the underdeveloped countries, it is
beyond dispute that both creditor and debtor countries should do what is
within their power to enlarge it. It is, however, becoming apparent that in
any foreseeable circumstances little private capital will be available for a
flow in this direction. Governments should therefore empower the International Bank to go as far in its lending for development purposes as its
laudable policy of keeping on straight business lines will permit, and
should instruct it to act accordingly. Non-self-liquidating development
projects should be financed by the proposed Special United Nations'
Fund for Economic Development. There are also very good reasons for
setting up the proposed International Finance Corporation.

The peoples of the advanced countries should, further, gradually be educated to make the sacrifice of an increasing amount of international aid to underdeveloped countries. We need particularly to tap more effectively the resources of other countries in this group than the United States. Quite apart from the increase in aid which this would imply, a broader participation in international sharing would also help to keep a semblance of political balance in the international aid schemes. A gradually increasing part of international aid could then be canalized through international agencies. This is probably the only means by which aid to underdeveloped countries can be preserved on any appreciable level. Aid should be kept separate from credit and prevented from deteriorating sound business standards in credit affairs, which form the only basis upon which any volume of increased credit is possible.

## Foreign Aid

An internationalization of international aid would be important also in order to tackle more successfully the thorny question of distinguishing between "good" and "bad" backward states. A stricter adherence to our old-fashioned standards of economic and social rentability, which should be a natural guide in any international undertaking, would go a long way towards correcting the present haphazard and biased distribution of aid. Instead of remaining aloof, we must be more prepared to come to the aid of those governments which prove themselves willing and able to tackle with determination their basic problems. It is recognized, of course, that if international aid is completely swallowed up in the military strategy of the Cold War, none of these reforms in the direction of good economy and fair standards is feasible.

The most hopeful forecast—assuming a much more favorable development than is at present objectively warranted—would have to conclude that foreign credits and aid will only to a small extent fill the real needs of the underdeveloped countries for capital for economic development; if things go less well, foreign credits and aid will continue to be insignificant. On any assumption these countries will have to furnish by far the greater part of development capital themselves; they will have to extract it from their citizens by keeping down consumption, and they will further have to budget their foreign-exchange resources most economically in order to increase their possibilities of importing capital goods from industrially advanced countries.

## Import Controls

Import restrictions are inevitable for underdeveloped countries which want to push ahead their economic development, and these countries have also a very important policy use for these restrictions. We should stop circumventing the plain truth that underdeveloped countries have a rational interest in protecting their struggling industries against our competition, an interest which goes much further than the infant-industry argument or any other of the traditional amplifications of the free trade doctrine. To admit this openly and squarely and to take the consequences in our commercial policy towards these countries is probably the most powerful of the aids to self-aid that we are at present in a position to give them.

The appeals to abolish restrictions on international trade and payments have a legitimate address, and that is to the industrially advanced countries. Very much more fundamental changes in these countries' internal and international policies than are usually envisaged or are politically feasible within the foreseeable future would be called for to reach substantial results in this direction. The advanced countries should, in fact, manage their internal affairs and their international relations so that they can take their proper place in a better integrated world economy as creditor countries; and creditor countries should accept the consequences of their position. When creditor countries liberalize their own trade, they raise the level of world trade in general, and at the same time help specifically the underdeveloped countries, which are interested in maximizing their exports and obtaining freer access to markets.

### Other Economic Policies

Other services which we can render the underdeveloped countries without any cost to ourselves and actually to our own advantage are, first, to perfect our business stabilization policy, nationally and internationally, and second, to take seriously the technically very complicated but not insurmountable problems raised by the underdeveloped countries' request for special international measures to stabilize the prices of staple commodities.

We need to give some thought too to increasing the possibilities for individuals, and not simply for commodities, to move across the frontiers between our countries. Labor should be allowed to flow freely. More generally, we should relax our national restrictions. For four decades now our little part of the world has been busy splitting itself up into isolated national compartments. By limiting the international elbow room for ordinary working people, farmers, and professionals, as well as the small-scale businessmen (big shots and big business will always have their way) we have cast aside a fundamental value in Western civilization of which we are in dire need if we are to have any chance of tackling constructively the formidable international problems that are now facing us.

# P. T. Bauer

## International Economic Development

THE THREE BOOKS that will be discussed in this article[1] mark Dr. Myrdal's entry into the field of the economics of under-developed countries and their development. The entry is massive, not only because the author is a leading social scientist and former international administrator, but also because of the sheer bulk of these volumes. Although they are bound to be influential, albeit in the limited sense of supporting already fashionable and widely held points of view and lines of approach which are rarely examined critically, the books may disappoint not only those who recall his earlier contributions to monetary theory but also many of those who, in the present field, sympathise with his proposals for policy. This disappointment may, I fear, arise because the books provide so little in the way of new knowledge or new insights; and the most substantial, *An International Economy*, seems to me to fall seriously short of its author's expressed objectives "to state [his] premises explicitly, get the facts straight, and think things out stringently" (*Preface*). The books do, however, deserve serious attention as presenting a comprehensive exposition and convenient examples of the most influential and widely held ideas on under-developed countries and economic development. In discussing the following I shall try to keep distinct arguments based on technical economic reasoning or on empirical evidence from those stemming from a political position.

---

1. *An International Economy: problems and prospects*. By Gunnar Myrdal. (London: Routledge & Kegan Paul, 1956, pp. xi + 381. 37s. 6d.) *Development and Under-development: A note on the mechanism of national and international inequality*. By Gunnar Myrdal. National Bank of Egypt 50th Anniversary Commemoration Lectures. (Cairo: National Bank of Egypt, 1956, pp. 88.) *Economic Theory and Under-developed Regions*. By Gunnar Myrdal. (London: Gerald Duckworth, 1957, pp. xii + 168. 18s.) The general argument of these three books is essentially the same. The first (referred to here as *International Economy*) is the more substantial; references to the other two books (quoted as *Cairo Lectures* and *Under-developed Regions*), the presentation of which is somewhat clearer and crisper, help to interpret the author's meaning when the exposition of the larger book is ambiguous.

Since the books cover an immense field and a vast range of topics, a review which attempts to deal with the most important issues inevitably has to wander far afield. I shall begin (Section I) with some comments on Dr. Myrdal's explicit methodological position which underlies the whole treatment. A second section summarises his central argument. The principal elements within the argument are discussed in Sections III–VI, followed in Sections VII–IX by a discussion of his main policy concepts and proposals.

## I

Dr. Myrdal writes in the Methodological Appendix to *An International Economy*:

> There is no way of studying social reality other than from the viewpoint of human ideals. A "disinterested social science" has never existed and, for logical reasons, cannot exist. The value connotation of our main concepts represents our interest in a matter, gives direction to our thoughts and significance to our inferences.
>
> The recognition that our very concepts are value-loaded implies that they cannot be defined except in terms of political valuations. It is, indeed, on account of scientific stringency that these valuations should be made explicit. They represent value premises for the scientific analysis; contrary to widely held opinions, not only the practical conclusions from a scientific analysis, but this analysis itself depends necessarily on value premises.[2]

I find this difficult to accept. The principal concepts of economics are surely not value loaded; for example, concepts of opportunity cost, demand and supply as functions of price, the volume of output or of imports and exports, the consumption function and the multiplier, and the devices of aggregation, general and partial equilibrium analysis and period analysis.[3] This is true also of such positive propositions as the law of demand or the conditions of price discrimination.

Dr. Myrdal's methodology, and with it much of his argument, seems to me to be vitiated by failure to distinguish between positive and normative propositions, a distinction which is essential in discussions on method, analysis and policy. The substantive propositions of positive economics embody the discernment of uniformities underlying the diversity of phenomena. Their validity is entirely independent of political positions.[4] But

---

2. *International Economy*, pp. 336–7.

3. This freedom from value loading does not, of course, in itself establish their usefulness.

4. The same applies to the useful tautologies which serve as an analytical filing system of economic theory.

equally they are insufficient for policy recommendations, since these depend on assessments of the probable results of particular courses of action on the total social situation allowing for administrative and political possibilities; and also in value judgments, notably concerning alternative types of society and social arrangements. Thus, when policies are proposed, value premises and, more generally, bases for recommendation should be set out. But this is very different from the suggestion that the validity of economic propositions depends on value judgments; that they are scientific only if these are stated; and that the statement of value judgments confers scientific status on a proposition; or that their value and significance depends on their contribution to goals of policy.[5]

The significance of a scientific proposition depends primarily on its generality and depth;[6] and in a phenomenal subject its validity depends on conformity with observed phenomena. Of course, there is often disagreement in the interpretation of phenomena which may or may not stem from a political position. Further, the field of study selected may be much affected by a political position. But this does not bear either on the significance or on the scientific value of a proposition.

The following appear to be some of the inevitable results and implications of the author's methodological position. It confuses the advancement of knowledge with the promotion of policy. It obscures the meaning of achievement of results: instead of meaning the establishment of successful and illuminating generalisations, it comes to mean the achievement of particular aims of policy. It prevents assessment of the competence of reasoning and of the validity of propositions, and thus also the establishment of minimum standards of technical competence, since criticism can always be ascribed to political differences. It destroys all possibility of reaching agreement even on elementary propositions, and it also prevents definition of the grounds of disagreement. It implies that the logical status of all propositions in economics is equal, because their validity depends on political acceptability or on their political results, and not on internal consistency or on correspondence with empirical evidence. This in turn spuriously justifies in academic and scientific work the emergence of political statements which do not reflect and promote systematic reasoning,

5. On this argument scientific significance would be conferred on the biological theories of the National Socialists if that party returned to power in Germany.

6. That is on the penetration required to discern the uniformities which they embody. It is a valid generalisation that human beings are born with two legs, but this is of no significance because it is obvious. The recognition that Mendel's Law applies to all forms of life is of very great interest and significance, because it is far from immediately obvious that the laws of heredity are the same for all living organisms.

though they may advance the social causes espoused by the author. Such a position destroys economics as a systematic discipline.

Although his position is untenable, Dr. Myrdal has rendered a great service with the statement of his position. Henceforth disregard of these important issues of method will be much more difficult, both because he has had the courage explicitly to state a position which is widely accepted implicitly or even subconsciously; and also because these books reveal the results of its thoroughgoing espousal.

## II

The main theme of these books is world economic integration. An economy is integrated if its members have equal opportunities, which implies substantial equality of wealth and income. But the unchecked operation of social forces, especially of the market mechanism, is towards cumulative disequilibrium and disintegration by a process of circular cumulative causation. The few developed countries have become largely integrated internally through state action helping poor people and depressed industries. Very different is the position of the under-developed countries in which live over two-thirds of humanity. Poverty and colonial rule have prevented their national economic integration, and have set up a wide and widening gap between the developed countries (often termed by Dr. Myrdal the privileged and upper crust, or upper class of nations) and the under-developed countries (often termed the under-privileged nations). This disparity, the result principally of the cumulative tendency towards inequality in the absence of world government, is the outstanding example of disintegration in the world to-day.

Without deliberate large-scale national and international action this gap must widen further until it results in a world political catastrophe. Large-scale government planning is necessary to integrate and develop the stagnant under-developed economies. Internationally the under-developed countries must combine to increase their bargaining power; and developed countries must abandon their unsympathetic attitude, which is a partial cause of the desperate poverty of the under-developed world, and assist it chiefly by capital and income transfers, by raising or stabilising their export prices, by assisting them in their national planning, by refraining from forcing their own exports on the under-developed countries, and by reducing the barriers facing exports and to some extent immigrants from the under-developed world.

## III

The position and prospects of the under-developed world are Dr. Myrdal's overwhelming concern. Two basic arguments underlie and pervade the treatment. One is that all economic propositions are political statements. This follows from the methodological position already examined.

The second proposition, the general operation of circular cumulative causation, is the cornerstone of the whole discussion. The author argues that circular cumulative causation, which he describes as his main hypothesis, is the general rule in social life, and that the vicious circle of poverty and the stagnation it implies constitutes an important example of this phenomenon. However, this is a simple assertion, the general validity of which is readily refuted by observation. Poverty is compatible with even rapid advance if this is of recent origin, and has begun from a low level. This is the position of many, indeed most, under-developed countries and regions which have only in recent decades begun to develop materially. The identification of poverty with stagnation in effect confuses a low economic level with a zero rate of change.

The general validity of the thesis of the vicious circle of poverty is refuted by the experience of individuals and groups throughout the world in rising from poverty to prosperity. It is also refuted by the very existence of developed countries, all of which began in an under-developed state, and also by the more recent experience of many under-developed countries, especially in South-East Asia, Africa and Latin America, which have progressed rapidly. It is also contradicted by the frequent changes in industrial and commercial leadership between different nations, both in general economic attainment and also in the position and performance of particular industries. Indeed, if it applied so generally, there would for centuries past have been only one developed country constantly increasing its lead over the others.

The poverty, stagnation or even retrogression of the under-privileged nations, and the consequent ever-widening economic inequality, are a principal theme of these books.

> The trend is actually towards greater world inequality. It is, in fact, the richer countries that are advancing while the poorer ones, with the large populations, are stagnating or progressing much more slowly . . . for mankind as a whole there has actually been no progress at all.[7]
>
> I have chosen to focus attention on one particular aspect of the international situation, namely the very large and steadily increasing economic inequalities as between developed and under-developed countries . . . these inequalities and their tendency to grow are flagrant realities.[8]

---

7. *International Economy*, pp. 1–2.
8. *Cairo Lectures*, p. 7.

No evidence is offered for this opinion beyond reference to two articles, one by Dr. H. W. Singer, the other by Professor P. N. Rosenstein-Rodan, which, however, do not provide evidence either. This is not surprising. There are no series of national-income figures for any Asian or African country before the First World War, and only a few hazardous estimates for individual years or periods of the inter-war years. Even if they were available, there would be serious difficulties in interpreting the statistics and even greater difficulties in drawing meaningful comparisons because of fundamental changes in the conditions of existence in many under-developed countries over this period. Neither Dr. Myrdal nor these articles discuss either the national income figures in the developed countries or in the under-developed countries over the relevant period (the last half-century), nor any other information on the absolute or relative position of different countries, nor do they mention the extreme heterogeneity of the under-developed world. The references to the ever-widening inequality, retrogression, stagnation and bottomless misery are *obiter dicta,* based on an axiomatic and inadmissible identification of low per capita incomes with stagnation.[9]

Dr. Myrdal suggests that "the economic level at which they [the under-developed countries] start is in most cases very much lower [than the starting point of developed countries]."[10] As it stands, the statement eludes precise interpretation, since the historical starting-point for the now developed countries is not indicated. Other contexts in these books refer

---

9. Dr. Myrdal writes "as Mr. H. W. Singer has rightly pointed out, world real income per capita, and with it the standard of living of the *average* human being, is probably lower than twenty-five years ago, and perhaps lower than in 1900, because the nations that have rapidly raised their economic standards have been a shrinking proportion of the total world population" *International Economy,* p. 2 [my italics]. The relevent passage in Dr. Singer's article reads: "If we define the 'average' world income as that of the median world citizen, the spectacular improvement which has occurred at one extreme and which has fascinated economists and other observers becomes irrelevant" ("Economic Progress in Under-developed Countries," *Social Research,* March 1949, pp. 2 f., quoted in *International Economy,* p. 341). Quite apart from the absence of statistics, these passages rest on an unwarranted use of the concept of the average. The median income could fall even if individual incomes rise everywhere, if population in poorer countries increased much faster than in richer countries.

10. *Under-developed Regions,* p. 98. This is one of many passages referring to initial differences in wealth and income between developed and under-developed countries without specifying either the starting point or the length of the process.

to the industrial revolution of the eighteenth century as the starting-point for these comparisons. This approach neglects the long period of progress of Western Europe, including Great Britain, before the eighteenth century, a process which extended over many centuries. At times (indeed usually) Dr. Myrdal ignores this long process altogether, while at other times he greatly underestimates its significance. The present under-developed countries, most of which began to develop only recently, cannot be expected to reach the level of developed countries in the space of decades; and there is nothing abnormal or paradoxical or inherently cumulative in the disparity between them and the developed world. There is no prescriptive right or general law that all communities must develop simultaneously and equally.[11]

While the author stresses cumulative processes, it is odd that the discussion is nevertheless static, because it is so often timeless, in that it ignores the relevance and importance of differences in starting-points on the road of progress, or in the length of period over which certain proc-esses have occurred. Yet consideration of the period of certain processes, and the dating of turning-points, are essential to dynamic treatment.

Dr. Myrdal applies the thesis of increasing inequality to the different regions of the same country in the absence of deliberate government action; this is premised chiefly on differences in capital, transport facilities and education. This again, however, is contradicted by much historical evidence. The unsubsidised development of manufacturing industry in the North of England, away from the established centres of industry and commerce, is only one example. The decline of industry in South Italy following the removal of tariffs with the unification of Italy, is instanced as a particularly well-documented example of the damage to a backward region through unification with a more advanced area. The simple ques-tion is not asked how the South has been able to pay for the industrial products of the North. The decline of particular activities previously subsidised by the rest of the region does not in the least indicate that the region as a whole has been affected adversely by a particular change. The removal of tariffs and of other barriers to mobility following the uni-fication of Italy, widened the range of alternatives open to the people of Southern Italy; and the extension of the range of choice normally benefits rather than harms a population. Besides identifying an historical change with a functional relationship, this treatment identifies one sector in a

11. The remarks in the text do not imply acceptance of the state of under-development of large parts of the world, nor are they a plea for *laissez-faire* or any other particular type of policy. These are matters quite different from the criticisms of Dr. Myrdal's treatment of the process of development.

region with the economy of the region as a whole, that is, it ignores the transfer of resources between sectors. There are also other instances in these books of an unwarranted identification of the performance of one sector with that of the whole economy, which are likely to mislead the unwary reader.

## IV

In Dr. Myrdal's view the developed countries have contributed to the plight of the under-developed countries, especially through the effects of colonialism and the operation of the international demonstration effect.

The treatment of the economic results of colonialism seems to me at times ambiguous. On occasions the author implies[12] that it has raised material standards in the colonies. But more often he suggests that it has retarded progress by discouraging wider economic contacts, by promoting economic activities benefiting the metropolitan countries and especially by preventing the pursuit of policies designed to promote the general economic development of the colonies.[13] Yet politically independent countries in Asia and Africa are among the most backward, usually much more so than the neighbouring colonies. Again, some of the former colonies became prosperous while they were colonies, and this indeed paved the way for their political independence. Further, the developed countries were already far ahead of the under-developed countries before the Industrial Revolution, and the differences had become even more marked by the time large parts of the under-developed world came to be colonised in the nineteenth century. Dr. Myrdal is—I cannot help feeling—prepared to strain language to be able to suggest that extraneous powers are in part responsible for the poverty of the under-developed world. This is exemplified by his frequent use of the term colonial economies to refer to independent sovereign countries whose policies are not controlled by other governments. This usage identifies poverty with colonialism, and thereby empties the latter term of all meaning.

Dr. Myrdal argues that colonialism has prevented the governments of under-developed countries from pursuing deliberate policies of economic development. This argument seems to me to be built on the assumption, explicit in the discussions on policy, and implicit throughout these books, that economic progress is largely a matter of government policy. Whatever is thought about the general validity of this assumption, it is not clear what sort of intervention by efficient independent governments

---

12. For instance, *Under-developed Regions*, p. 56.

13. For instance, *Cairo Lectures*, pp. 53–5, 75, 76; *International Economy*, pp. 100–2, 168, 225; *Under-developed Regions*, pp. 57–9, 74.

would have accelerated development in eighteenth- and nineteenth-century Africa and Asia. But it is certain that no conscious development policies would have been pursued by the rulers of the remains of the Mogul empire and of its successor states, by the local sultans of South-East Asia, or by African chiefs.

The mere presence of developed countries is thought by Dr. Myrdal to have damaged the under-developed world through the international demonstration effect, which discourages the small amount of saving which might otherwise take place. But is it not the case that now, as in the past, the most advanced of the under-developed regions and sectors are those in contact with developed countries? Contact with more advanced economies may indeed suggest new wants, but these can be satisfied only if incomes are first earned to purchase the consumer goods, and this usually requires saving and investment, invariably so when it requires the replacement of subsistence cultivation by production for exchange. Moreover, these contacts generally suggest new methods and the introduction of new crops, and also provide markets. Thus they induce higher economic performance, especially by encouraging agriculturalists to produce for sale. Dr. Myrdal's treatment appears to ignore the influence of the real reward in the exchange sector and of consumption prospects on the supply of effort and saving. This is surely unwarranted, especially in under-developed countries, where subsistence production is large, and the extension of the exchange sector an important factor in development. These contacts also often result in the import of capital, and in the import of entrepreneurial, technical, and administrative skills, or their acquisition by the local population. There are also other objections to the suggestion that under-developed countries are harmed by contact with more advanced economies. Thus the population of these countries can imitate the saving and investing habits as well as the consumption habits of the more advanced countries. Further, there are generally some rich people in under-developed countries, so that the demonstration effect can operate even in the absence of international contacts.

Dr. Myrdal recognises, albeit reluctantly, the presence of advanced and advancing (in fact often rapidly advancing) countries, regions, sectors and activities in the under-developed world. Following other influential writers, he refers to these as enclaves carved out of the local economies by the advanced countries, as colonial types of economic activity, which do not serve to improve the economic position or prospects of the local population.[14] Thus the thesis of the vicious circle and stagnation appears to remain intact. But the thesis of the alien enclave is no more securely based

14. For instance, *International Economy*, pp. 100–2, 107, 168, 225; and *Cairo Lectures* and *Under-developed Regions*, passim.

than the main argument. First, the fact that foreign personnel, enterprise and capital played a large part in the development of these advancing sectors does not mean that the process has not benefited the local population. The suggested contrast or incompatibility of interest is spurious, and ignores the complementarity of resources. Again, there has generally been no single centralised force acting in this sphere as a representative or agent of the interests of the developed countries. Moreover, in many instances the progressive sectors are largely, or wholly, owned and operated by members of the local community. For instance, all West African agricultural exports, including such world staples as cocoa, groundnuts and oil-palm products, are produced entirely by Africans on their own lands, and the same applies to the bulk of South-East Asian and South American exports. In all these areas the local population also has a large share in the transport, distribution and simple processing of these exports, and in the distribution of imports. The same holds also for the often appreciable commercial, transport and industrial activity for sale locally or even for export, as in Hong Kong, Puerto Rico, India and Pakistan. But even when the enterprises in the advanced sectors are foreign, they usually still assist development by contributing to government revenues, by spreading skills and generally by promoting the exchange economy.

These sectors are not enclaves cut off from the rest of the economy, but focal points, the points of first impact, of development, a process which always affects certain activities and regions first, from which it spreads to the rest of the economy. The time this requires depends, among other factors, on the qualities of the population, on institutional factors and on physical communications. There is nothing unusual or abnormal in the uneven regional or sectoral incidence of economic progress.[15] There are countless examples in the most highly developed countries.

The practice of regarding the more rapidly advancing regions and sectors (at times even to entire countries) as enclaves has now become general in the literature on under-developed countries. The appeal of this catch-phrase seems to stem in part from the spurious reconciliation it offers between the manifest evidence of progress in many under-developed countries and the thesis of the vicious circle of poverty, which is both the cornerstone of the current orthodoxy on development of which Dr. Myrdal is now a leading exponent, and a basis for far-reaching proposals

---

15. In this context also Dr. Myrdal seems to regard as reprehensible any difference in rates of development or levels of attainment. Though it is not disputed that in Latin America the advancing sectors are largely locally owned and administered, he notes with disapproval that progress (in fact rapid progress) has been uneven, and that certain areas have advanced much further than others. For instance, *International Economy*, p. 152.

for policy. The sharp and clear-cut contrast between a progressive but alien enclave and the stagnant local economy is also more readily intelligible and more congenial to current intellectual habits than that of a varied economic landscape, of differing levels of attainment and rates of advance. The habitual reference to advancing sectors in under-developed economies as alien enclaves serves to obscure the process by which developed economies made their initial advances, and it is also likely to prevent us from encouraging this process in the contemporary under-developed world.

## V

In describing the social landscape of the under-developed world, Dr. Myrdal presents a picture of rigid, highly stratified societies, with groups privileged in wealth, power and status lording it over under-privileged masses; and the more backward the country, the wider the inequalities.[16] This deep disintegration is, again, as he pictures it, evidence of circular cumulative causation, since the stagnant and impoverished countries do not have the resources necessary to achieve the integration required for economic progress.

In fact, economic inequality is by no means general in under-developed countries; much of what inequality exists does not reflect privilege; nor is economic equality necessarily evidence or instrument of economic development, or inequality an obstacle to its achievement. Over large parts of the under-developed world, and especially in the most backward areas of Africa, and South-East Asia, the social landscape is not that of wide inequality, but rather one of masses of undifferentiated people. Moreover, some of the most striking examples of inequality do not reflect privilege in the accepted sense of the term. Originally penniless immigrants or their sons are the richest people in South-East Asia, and the wealth of Indians in East Africa and Lebanese in West Africa has been accumulated by poor unprivileged immigrants or their descendants in one or two generations. Throughout the under-developed world there are often rich indigenous merchants, industrialists, executives, professional men and even agriculturalists, who were not beneficiaries of inherited wealth or official favours. These inequalities are thus bound up with differences in economic qualities, such as perception of economic opportunity, industry, thrift, persistence, unrelated to special privileges or institutional or monopolistic restrictions; and, of course, in some cases they result from sheer luck.

16. Especially *International Economy*, Chapter XII: cf. *Cairo Lectures*, p. 48: "In a rather close correlation to their poverty they are ridden by internal economic inequalities . . ."

Such differences in aptitudes are just as real as, say, those in physical appearance. These may or may not be regarded as justification of differences in wealth, but they are certainly not the result of privilege. Though at times his treatment is ambiguous, Dr. Myrdal seems to suggest generally that people's capacities and qualities are fundamentally equal, and that differences in attainment and prosperity reflect the operation of external factors.[17] Complex and debatable issues are raised by such questions as the different grounds on which different types of material inequality, or different policies for reducing inequality, may be justified; and again the concept of responsibility for one's fortune is not simple. It could, of course, be argued legitimately that those less intelligent, able and enterprising should be comforted and compensated for their disabilities by redistribution. But at any moment of time there are real and wide differences between individuals and groups in relevant economic capacities. These differences are almost certainly not fixed for all time, but they are real and relevant over decades or even centuries.[18] The treatment here reflects, and is likely to reinforce, two related opinions, which are difficult to substantiate but are widely held and influentially advocated. These are that there is no significant difference in economic qualities between individuals and groups, even at any given time or over any given period; and that differences in economic attainment and progress are abnormal and reprehensible, calling for special explanations of their presence and for far-reaching policies for their removal.

---

17. Thus he writes: "As we know, modern research has in the last half century gone a long way to prove scientifically the correctness of this essential kernel of the naturalistic doctrine of human equality with respect to natural endowments and thereby justified the environmental approach in the social sciences which lays the basis for rational radicalism in social reform." *Under-developed Regions*, p. 108. And later, p. 113, he adds that recent research has confirmed "that as a general rule men are equally endowed by nature."

18. In the general context of material inequality an important problem of measurement may be noted. The meaning of a given measure of inequality is very different if the composition of the different social groups is stable or is changing rapidly. Even a large measure of apparent material inequality is compatible with a high degree of equality over a period of time if the composition of the different groups is very unstable. The composition of, say, the upper 5% of wealth owners and income receivers is likely to change much more rapidly in South-East Asia than, say, in India. This is usually neglected in discussions on inequality, necessarily by Dr. Myrdal, who believes in the well-nigh universal operation of circular cumulative causation. Besides the political implications of its recognition, this would also throw into relief some of the conceptual and statistical problems of inequality and its measurement.

Inequality of wealth need not be an obstacle to economic advance. For example, the accumulated wealth of the Chinese immigrants of South-East Asia, which implies a high degree of economic inequality conventionally measured, has obviously not retarded economic advance. It reflects largely the result of the performance of economic services, and the fruits of saving and of re-investment of profits. The prospects of higher incomes and of the possibility of accumulating wealth have attracted enterprising people of various races to South-East Asia, and elicited a supply of productive effort, enterprise, saving and investment.

Moreover, a differentiated social structure may be both a reflection and an instrument of economic development, particularly where social intercourse and mobility are reasonably free. Such a social structure, which emerges only after a long period of social and economic progress, is congenial to further and accelerated development. It conduces to long views in economic decisions, since in such a society people are apt to consider their descendants; and at the same time such a society is compatible with mobility and flexibility, and with a spirit of experimentation and curiosity, which is indeed encouraged by the perception of differences.

## VI

The treatment of a number of more specific topics deserves closer examination. They are selected on two grounds. First, they treat of issues in which the author's discussion is more clear-cut. Second, the selected issues will be recognised as being prominent in current discussions of under-developed countries, both in academic discussion and in proposals for policy.

(a) Dr. Myrdal subscribes to the familiar view that savings are unproductive if the proceeds are used for the purchase of land.[19] But if some people consume less than their incomes, they make available resources to the economy. Their contribution may be offset by the dis-saving of others, but this is unaffected by the nature of the assets bought by the savers, except on peculiar assumptions (which would need to be specified), especially of general unemployment of all types of productive resources which is clearly inapplicable to under-developed countries.

(b) Fluctuations in the export proceeds of primary producing countries are said to lend an inflationary bias to these economies.[20] In fact, both in Africa and Asia deflationary forces were prominent throughout the inter-war period, as well as in earlier times. The frequent inflations in Latin America over this period can be attributed more properly to a failure to

---

19. *International Economy*, pp. 183, 203.
20. Especially *International Economy*, pp. 240–2.

control the supply of money rather than to the composition of their exports. The discussion of this subject seems to me confused. For instance, he argues that an increase in export proceeds sets up inflationary forces. But this does not happen when the supply of imports is elastic.[21]

(c) Balance-of-payments difficulties are regarded by Dr. Myrdal as chronic and indeed necessary in progressing under-developed economies, especially primary producing countries. This view is widely held at present. Yet it disregards the infrequency, or even absence, of such differences, both in the early history of the developed countries, and also in the comparatively recent history of rapidly developing under-developed economies or primary producing countries, including North America, Australasia, South-East Asia, West Africa, Hong Kong and many others.[22] Neither in this context, nor in his discussion of the dollar shortage, does Dr. Myrdal consider or even mention the rate of exchange; and he mentions only most perfunctorily the relevance of monetary policy. Again, Dr. Myrdal urges priority in the national plan for exporting and for import-saving activities, without stating that this is economic only if the exchange rate is over-valued in some defined sense. Only then will the proceeds of exports (or the saving in imports) yielded by a given volume of resources and expressed at the official rate of exchange under-state their contribution to the national income compared to the other uses. Characteristically, the principal discussion of this range of issues is entitled "The Foreign Exchange Front";[23] once more, the rate of exchange is not mentioned, and the discussion is essentially in terms of physical quantities.

(d) The discussion of the balance-of-payments and of foreign-exchange problems seems to provide an example of what one might term "price-less economics," that is of the treatment of supply and demand as physical quantities unaffected by price. In spite of general references to the value of the price mechanism as an efficient instrument of economic control, Dr. Myrdal frequently ignores the effects of prices and real rewards on supply and demand, or on the extension of the exchange economy, even where they are essentially relevant, notably in fiscal policy.[24] An example

---

21. With a fixed rate of exchange, an improvement in the terms of trade postulates a rise in local prices and incomes relative to import prices at that rate. But this is simply the monetary counterpart of a rise in real income and is not inflationary.

22. ". . . there must be something wrong with an under-developed country that does not have foreign exchange difficulties." *International Economy*, p. 270.

23. *International Economy*, pp. 273-5.

24. These remarks are not intended to suggest that the price mechanism brings about an ideal allocation of resources. The very concept of a mechan-

is the reference to the low level of investment in public utilities in Latin America, instanced by Dr. Myrdal as characteristic of unbalanced private investment, without mentioning that statutory rate fixing at uneconomic levels in inflationary periods has removed both the wherewithal and the incentive for it.[25]

(e) Dr. Myrdal repeatedly refers to the inelastic demands confronting the exports of under-developed countries. But the essential distinction is not drawn clearly between the elasticity of demand for a particular product and the elasticity of foreign demand for that product from a particular country.[26] The elasticity of demand for a country's exports depends not only on the underlying elasticity of demand for the commodity, but also on the share of this country's exports in total exports of the commodity and the elasticity of supply of the commodity from all other resources. Many primary producers have lost heavily by overlooking the distinction.

(f) In the lengthy discussion of commodity stabilisation,[27] the cardinal problem of distinguishing between fluctuation and a change in the trend is not discussed. This is fundamental, because neither private individuals nor Civil Servants can tell in advance whether a particular change is a fluctuation or a change in the trend. Moreover, at times Dr. Myrdal uses stabilisation interchangeably with monopolistic raising of prices, which is a familiar and possibly excusable practice of the spokesmen of primary producers, but is not easy to justify in serious discussion.

(g) The author insists that under-developed economies are very rigid.[28] In support of this proposition he instances their reliance on agriculture in spite of low incomes and of unfavourable terms of trade. But there is no evidence that alternative forms of activity would have yielded higher returns. Moreover, producers in many under-developed countries respond readily to change, as is shown, for example, by the rapid growth of the output of certain crops, the changes in the relative importance of different

---

ism implies that it is neutral, and what comes out of it depends on what is put into it, which in this context depends among other factors on institutional arrangements, market structure, distribution of wealth, and government policies. Dr. Myrdal is right when he stresses the essential neutrality of the price mechanism, but this does not warrant the frequent neglect of its operation.

25. *International Economy*, pp. 168 and 343. He also notes (p. 64) the absence of foreign investment in recent years in Greece, where capital imports are badly needed. But he does not mention the relevance of the record of Greek governments in defaulting on their external obligations.

26. For instance, *Cairo Lectures*, p. 71.

27. *International Economy*, pp. 244–53.

28. Especially *International Economy*, Chapter XIII.

types of crop over periods of a few years and the pronounced response of smallholders' production to price changes and differentials in India, Pakistan, South-East Asia and West Africa.

(*h*) The author suggests that ". . . all history shows that the cheap and often docile labour of under-developed regions does not usually attract industry."[29] This is truistic if it means that labour is not the only factor of production, and untrue (an example of price-less or cost-less economics) if it means that labour costs are irrelevant. Low labour costs have been a major factor in the rapid growth of manufacturing in Japan and Hong Kong; and in many western countries manufacturing interests are protesting against the exports produced by cheap labour.

(*i*) Dr. Myrdal asserts that all under-developed countries are over-populated, and that regularly (*sic*) about one-third to one-half of their agricultural population could be removed without affecting agricultural output, even without any special labour-saving devices.[30] This is unsubstantiated, and would be untrue for practically all African countries and many Latin American and some Asian countries.

These are only a few examples out of many; the preceding list could be extended greatly.

## VII

The two major value premises of these books, equality of opportunity and of political democracy, are notoriously imprecise, and his discussion does nothing to give them precision. As a result, the chosen instruments of policy, the nature of which is less imprecise, can be used in pursuit of widely different, and indeed contradictory, directions and ends.

At times the discussion suggests that absence of discrimination, and substantial equality of income and wealth, are the essence of equality of opportunity, called integration.[31] There is a fundamental difficulty here which needs to be made explicit. People differ widely in their capacities, inclinations and aims, they live in different climatic and geographical conditions, they are brought up by parents of widely different attitudes and values, and they are subject to different religious, social and customary obligations. Thus absence of discrimination will not automatically bring about substantial equality of income and wealth. In fact, the two elements in integration, *i.e.*, absence of discrimination and substantial equality of income and wealth, can be reconciled only if the sources of differentiation are removed by compulsory standardisation. This can be

29. *Under-developed Regions*, p. 31.
30. *International Economy*, p. 193.
31. For instance, *International Economy*, Chapters III and XI.

achieved only by the over-riding powers of the state. The exercise of these powers over large areas of social life, or indeed social life as a whole, involves great inequality in power between the governors and the governed; and the wider the differences in capacities and circumstances, the more extensive and intensive is the compulsion necessary for the required standardisation. This necessary corollary of the author's interpretation of integration seems to me to be ignored in these books.[32] This is the more surprising because he is largely concerned with world economic integration, and differences in capacities and conditions are very much wider on a global than on a national scale.

Political democracy, the other major value premise, is interpreted in these books as majority rule under universal suffrage.[33] But this condition is compatible not only with the over-riding of the wishes of a large minority but also with extreme tyranny, as is explicit in the title of J. L. Talmon's *The Origins of Totalitarian Democracy*. This is only one of several reasons why the inequality of power discussed in the preceding paragraph—the necessary corollary of equality of opportunity as generally interpreted in these books—cannot be rendered innocuous by the democratic process.

The national interest, the promotion of which Dr. Myrdal wishes under-developed countries to pursue, is another vague concept which he treats as if it were unambiguous and simple to interpret. Thus he frequently implies a simple cleavage of interest between the country and the rest of the world, or between the local population and foreigners. In fact, the relationship between groups is far more complex, and in the economic sphere it is often more nearly complementary than opposite or rival. He also suggests that in countries in which all are allowed to participate in the political process, the governments and the Civil Servants can both unambiguously discern the national interest, and unlike private individuals, will conform to it. This obscures both the vagueness of the concept and the reality of the possible cleavage of interest between administrators and their constituents.[34]

---

32. Dr. Myrdal frequently states that the unchecked working of market forces leads cumulatively to growing inequalities; indeed he greatly overstresses this influence. But he does not recognise that his proposals to deal with this involve more serious inequalities of power.

33. For example, *International Economy*, p. 176; *Cairo Lectures*, p. 65; *Under-developed Regions*, p. 83. In one aside he refers to the maintenance of civil rights, but these would be defined by the political majority.

34. There are many other instances in these books of the use of imprecise general terms as if they unambiguously described specific analytical categories, types of situations, or aims of policy. They include usury, exploita-

## VIII

The main instruments of development policy envisaged by the author are clear. He considers comprehensive development planning, in the sense of government determination and control of the direction of economic activity, including large-scale compulsory saving, as indispensable and presumably sufficient for the increase in output, which is the essence of economic improvement for the masses.[35] However, it is not stated why the particular pattern of productive resources envisaged by this proposal should break the vicious circle or otherwise accelerate economic growth. The discussion simply presumes what requires to be established.

Dr. Myrdal emphasises the benefits, made possible by development planning, of the disregard of market prices and costs, which he regards as fictitious.[36] He stresses the importance, especially in the context of industrialisation, of external economies, which he regards as a major ground for subsidisation of particular activities and enterprises, or for the estab-

---

tion, land reform, economic colonialism, fair and equitable prices, and stabilisation. Again, general rejection of discrimination is meaningless, since all social and human intercourse is based on it, though different people may and do discriminate for different purposes and on the basis of different criteria. Such usage is misleading, and especially unwarranted in a book such as *An International Economy,* for which the author explicitly claims scientific objectivity.

35. For instance he writes: "All special advisers to under-developed countries who have taken the time and trouble to acquaint themselves with the problems, no matter who they are . . . all recommend central planning as the first condition for progress." *International Economy,* p. 201.

"However difficult the task, one thing stands out: the hope for economic development of under-developed countries depends very much on the state's being able to plan and to direct, and even to invest and to produce." *Ibid.,* p. 210.

36. "The national plans cannot be made in terms of costs and profits for the individual enterprises; they can, in fact, not be made in terms of the prices in the markets . . . the whole meaning of the national plan is to give such shelter from the market forces to investment, enterprise and production that they become undertaken in spite of the fact that they are not remunerative according to private business calculations."

"It is here that the national state comes in as representing the common and long-term interests of the community at large. It senses the fictitiousness of the private business calculations in terms of costs and profits." *Cairo Lectures,* pp. 66 and 67. It will be noted that the actions of the government are here axiomatically assumed to represent the national interest.

These passages are almost identical with similar passages in *Underdeveloped Regions,* pp. 86–7.

lishment of state enterprise. But these measures imply a transfer of resources, and a corresponding diminution of activity and of external economies elsewhere. They promote economy of resources and growth only if the subsidised activities or the state enterprises yield goods or services and external economies exceeding in value those lost through the contraction of the taxed activities, allowing also for the announcement effects of taxation and the administrative cost. In spite of general admonitions on the importance of economy of resources, the author treats the assisted or officially sponsored activities as straightforward additions to total activity, without asking where the resources come from.[37] This vitiates much of the discussion of compulsory saving for development. Moreover, a policy of compulsory saving cannot be framed sensibly if the repercussions on the private sector of both the collection and the expenditure of the funds are ignored, and if it is conceived in a framework of price-less economics.

The insistence on the rejection of market prices and costs goes much beyond the recognition of differences between money and real costs, or the importance of external economies, or the emphasis on growth compared to the allocation of resources. The author generally regards individual choice and valuation as irrelevant: the decisions of planning governments

---

37. Dr. Myrdal frequently gives the impression that he wants the state to increase the supply of almost everything without indicating the provenance of the resources. To quote two instances:

"If, as is assumed to be an urgent necessity in the under-developed countries, the movement towards industrialisation is to be pushed ahead, the state will have to intervene in the field of manufacturing industry too [as well as in agriculture, transport and public utilities] not only creating the external economies and supplying transport and power, but often also organising the marketing of the produce of the expanding industrial sector, providing facilities for training workers, foremen, and technicians on all levels, as well as business executives, giving managerial advice, making capital available, often subsidising or protecting new industrial enterprises, and sometimes actually establishing and operating them." *International Economy*, p. 209.

"The plan must determine this overall amount [investment] and must, in addition, determine the proportions of the capital to allocated in different directions: to increasing overall facilities in transport and power production; to constructing new plants and acquiring the machinery for heavy industries, and for light industries of various types; to raising the level of productivity in agriculture by long-run investment in irrigation schemes and short-term investment in tools, machinery and fertilisers; to improving the levels of health, education and training of the working people, and so on." *Under-developed Regions*, p. 81.

are the *criteria* as well as the *instruments* of development. For instance he writes:

> The plan and its targets, in other words, have to render the basis for deciding the criteria; the decisions themselves are political decisions reached in terms of national welfare, as this is determined by the political process.[38]

On this argument again the actions of the government by definition accord with the national interest. Moreover, the criteria of development need not be related to peoples' wants, and can be set in terms of the growth of output deemed important by the government, or in terms of the output of particular industries or sectors only. Development so defined or measured can be wholly unrelated to living standards, especially those of the masses.[39] Both in the discussion of more specific economic issues and of broader social and political issues, Dr. Myrdal largely ignores the wishes of individuals and groups other than those of government, their executives and of political spokesmen.

## IX

Although he is not sanguine about its early prospects, Dr. Myrdal envisages substantial international redistribution by means of inter-governmental transfers. He notes that an irreversible step in this direction has already been taken under United Nations auspices, especially by the Technical Assistance Programme. He regards such transfers as both moral duty and political wisdom on the part of the developed countries; and he argues that they should take place through international agencies to assure their allocation in accordance with rational economic and moral criteria, rather than on political grounds. This exposition again misses the central problems:

(*a*) The transfer of such funds is essentially a political matter, because they represent resources compulsorily collected from the citizens of the transferor country. The funds are not the result of voluntary acts by individuals impoverishing themselves in order to assist their less fortunate fellow men. They can thus be reasonably required to be used to promote the interest of the donor countries.

---

38. *Cairo Lectures,* p. 73.

39. A specific example of this attitude, which pervades these books, may be mentioned. Dr. Myrdal enjoins the developed countries to abstain from forcing the under-developed countries to accept imports which they do not want. *International Economy,* p. 292. But if the consumers did not want them the commodities would not be imported. There is here (as in many other places) an unwarranted axiomatic identification of the government with the population.

(b) Dr. Myrdal implies that there is a moral obligation on the governments of advanced countries to tax their citizens for the benefit of the governments of the under-developed countries, regardless of the use of the funds and of the policies pursued, and regardless also of the attitudes, qualities, efforts and institutions of the recipients. Even if these policies and influences are wholly unsuitable to economic development, the moral obligations of the developed countries apparently remain unaffected.

(c) It is regarded as self-evident that no conditions should be attached to inter-governmental grants or loans. This is not obvious, since they represent funds in urgent demand throughout the world. Amounts made available to one country diminish those available to others. Moreover, the policies pursued by the recipients are among the factors (indeed the principal factor, in Dr. Myrdal's scheme of things) affecting their rate of development, and thus their need for further aid. Thus the policies pursued by the recipients are clearly relevant to eligibility for assistance.

(d) Though emphasising their importance, Dr. Myrdal nowhere specifies the moral and economic criteria in the allocation of funds. Should they go to the poorest countries, or those poorest in natural resources, or those which have progressed least or most over a specified period, or should some other tests be adopted from among dozens of possible criteria?

(e) The exposition assumes that the international agencies and their Civil Servants are completely disinterested. In fact, they have considerable interest in terms of prestige, position and power. Dr. Myrdal expressly refers to the need to keep technical assistance agencies free from the influence of private business interests. He does not recognise, or at least does not admit, the reality of the interests of those in charge of the agencies.

(f) Inter-governmental transfers affected through the international agencies are likely to be wasteful. The interest of the suppliers of capital is generally a major factor assuring its productive use. It is for this reason that direct investment, espcially by individuals or partnerships, in which there is close correspondence between the supplier of the capital and its user, is least likely to be wasteful. At the other end of the spectrum are the inter-governmental transfers through the international agencies under which the suppliers have little knowledge and no control of the use of the funds.

## X

These books are, as I have shown, concerned with the promotion of policy rather than with the promotion of knowledge. It is not easy to reconcile either their argument or their presentation with the author's explicit objective, already noted, of getting "the facts straight and think things out stringently," or with his advice that an international agency should act as "a free and independent scientific agent, which approaches the problems and reaches and states its findings guided only by the inherited and established standards of the profession, without sideward glances at what would be politically opportune."[40]

Although the books abound in sympathetic references to the plight of the under-developed countries, there is nevertheless a distinct ambiguity about the beneficiaries of Dr. Myrdal's proposals. He writes:

> Not merely to save the world, but primarily to save our own souls, there should again be dreamers, planners, and fighters, in the midst of our nations, who would take upon themselves the important social function in democracy of raising our sights—so far ahead that their proponents again form a definite minority in their nations and avoid the unbearable discomfort for reformers of a climate of substantial agreement.[41]

But the price to be paid by others may be too high for the salvation of even the most ardent souls, if inter-personal comparisons of utility and cost may be permitted for the moment.

# Hans Morgenthau

## A Political Theory of Foreign Aid

OF THE SEEMING and real innovations which the modern age has introduced into the practice of foreign policy, none has proven more baffling to both understanding and action than foreign aid. The very assumption that foreign aid is an instrument of foreign policy is a subject of controversy. For, on the one hand, the opinion is widely held that foreign aid is an end in itself, carrying its own justification, both transcending, and independent of, foreign policy. In this view, foreign aid is the fulfill-

---

40. Quoted from "Economic Essays in Honour of Erik Lindahl," ECONOMIC JOURNAL, March 1958, p. 119.

41. *International Economy*, p. 322. This attitude is the opposite of the scientific which seeks to discern uniformities and to reach agreed generalisations.

ment of an obligation of the few rich nations toward the many poor ones. On the other hand, many see no justification for a policy of foreign aid at all. They look at it as a gigantic boondoggle, a wasteful and indefensible operation which serves neither the interests of the United States nor those of the recipient nations.

The public debate on foreign aid has contributed little to understanding. In the spring of every year the nation engages in such a debate, carried on almost exclusively in terms of the amount of money to be spent for purposes of foreign aid rather than of the substantive purposes which a policy of foreign aid is supposed to serve. The Administration tries, as it were, to sell a certain amount of foreign aid to Congress, and Congress refuses to buy that amount. Congress generally appropriates about ten per cent less than what the Administration has requested, and the Administration spends what is appropriated as it sees fit within the general categories authorized. Only when glaring abuses and inefficiencies are uncovered, as for instance in our foreign aid to Laos, is the question of the substance of our foreign aid policy raised in public, and even then it is put in the negative terms of remedying the abuses and inefficiencies rather than in the positive terms of the purposes our foreign aid policy may be supposed to advance and the kinds of measures best calculated to serve these aims.

It is in fact pointless even to raise the question whether the United States ought to have a policy of foreign aid—as much so as to ask whether the United States ought to have a foreign political or military policy. For the United States has interests abroad which cannot be secured by military means and for the support of which the traditional methods of diplomacy are only in part appropriate. If foreign aid is not available they will not be supported at all.

The question, what kind of policy of foreign aid we ought to have, can then not be evaded. As it has developed in recent years, the kind we have is fundamentally weak. It has been conceived as a self-sufficient technical enterprise, covering a multitude of disparate objectives and activities, responding haphazardly to all sorts of demands, sound and unsound, unrelated or only by accident related to the political purposes of our foreign policy. The United States, in short, has been in the business of foreign aid for more than two decades, but it has yet to develop an intelligible theory of foreign aid that could provide standards of judgment for both the supporters and opponents of a particular measure.

## SIX TYPES OF FOREIGN AID

The first prerequisite for the development of a viable foreign aid policy is the recognition of the diversity of policies that go by that name. Six such can be distinguished which have only one thing in common: the transfer of money, goods and services from one nation to another. They are humanitarian foreign aid, subsistence foreign aid, military foreign aid, bribery, prestige foreign aid, and foreign aid for economic development.

Of these distinct types, only humanitarian foreign aid is *per se* nonpolitical. The aid which governments have traditionally extended to nations which are victims of natural disasters, such as floods, famines and epidemics falls in that category. So do the services, especially in the fields of medicine and agriculture, which private organizations, such as churches and foundations, have traditionally provided in Asia, Africa, and Latin America.

While humanitarian aid is *per se* nonpolitical, it can indeed perform a political function when it operates within a political context. The foreign aid that private organizations provide will be attributed for better or worse to their respective governments insofar as humanitarian aid emanating from a foreign country is recognized by the recipient country or its inhabitants to perform a political function. Thus the agricultural aid which the Rockefeller Foundation has provided for many years to certain Latin American countries is likely to take on under contemporary conditions a political function which it did not perform previously. The same has from the beginning been true of the work the Ford Foundation has been doing in India. By the same token, humanitarian aid extended by a government may have political effects.

Subsistence foreign aid is extended to governments, such as those of Jordan and Nigeria, which do not command the resources to maintain minimal public services. The giving nation makes up the deficit in the budget of the recipient nation. Subsistence foreign aid is akin to the humanitarian type in that it seeks to prevent the breakdown of order and the disintegration of organized society. But it also performs the political function of maintaining the *status quo,* without, however, as a rule, increasing its viability. Where a political alternative to a nonviable regime may exist, subsistence foreign aid diminishes the chances of its materializing.

Bribes proffered by one government to another for political advantage were until the beginning of the nineteenth century an integral part of the armory of diplomacy. No statesman hesitated to acknowledge the general practice of giving and accepting bribes, however anxious he might be to hide a particular transaction. Thus it was proper and common for a government to pay the foreign minister or ambassador of another country a pension, that is, a bribe. Lord Robert Cecil, the Minister of Elizabeth, received one from Spain. Sir Henry Wotton, British Ambassador to Venice in the seventeenth century, accepted one from Savoy while applying for one from Spain. The documents which the French revolutionary government published in 1793 show that France subsidized Austrian statesmen between 1757 and 1769 to the tune of 82,652,479 livres, the Austrian Chancellor Kaunitz receiving 100,000.

The Prussian Ambassador in Paris summed up well the main rule of this game when he reported to his government in 1802: "Experience has taught everybody who is here on diplomatic business that one ought never to give anything before the deal is definitely closed, but it has only proved that the allurement of gain will often work wonders." It is worthy of note that the first appropriation act adopted by the first Congress of the United States in 1789 included a modest contingent fund for such purposes.

Much of what goes by the name of foreign aid today is in the nature of bribes. The transfer of money and services from one government to another performs here the function of a price paid for political services rendered or to be rendered. These bribes differ from the traditional ones exemplified above in two respects: they are justified primarily in terms of foreign aid for economic development, and money and services are transferred through elaborate machinery fashioned for genuine economic aid. In consequence, these bribes are a less effective means for the purpose of purchasing political favors than were the traditional ones.

The compulsion of substituting for the traditional businesslike transmission of bribes the pretense and elaborate machinery of foreign aid for economic development results from a climate of opinion which accepts as universally valid the proposition that the highly developed industrial nations have an obligation to transfer money and services to underdeveloped nations for the purpose of economic development. Thus, aside from humanitarian and military foreign aid, the only kind of transfer of money and services which seems to be legitimate is one ostensibly made for the purpose of economic development. Economic development has become an ideology by which the transfer of money and services from one government to another in peace time is rationalized and justified.

The present climate of opinion embraces another assumption as universally valid: that economic development can actually be promoted through such transfers of money and services. Thus economic development as an ideology requires machinery that makes plausible the postulated efficacy of the transfer for the stated purpose of economic development. In contrast to most political ideologies, which operate only on the verbal level and whose effects remain within the realm of ideas, this political ideology, in order to be plausible, requires an elaborate administrative apparatus serving as an instrument for a policy of make-believe. The government of nation A, trying to buy political advantage from the government of nation B for, say, the price of 20 million dollars, must not only pretend, but also act out in elaborate fashion the pretense, that what it is actually doing is giving aid for economic development to the government of nation B.

This practice of giving bribes as though they were contributions to economic development inevitably creates, in the giver and the recipient, expectations which are bound to be disappointed. Old-fashioned bribery was a relatively straightforward transaction; services were to be rendered at a price, and both sides knew what to expect. Bribery disguised as foreign aid for economic development makes of giver and recipient actors in a play which in the end they may no longer be able to distinguish from reality. In consequence, both may come to expect results in terms of economic development which in the nature of things may not be forthcoming. Thus both are likely to be disappointed, the giver blaming the recipient for his inefficiency and the recipient accusing the giver of stinginess and asking for more. The ideology, if taken for reality, gets in the way of the original purpose of the transaction, and neither side believes that it has received what it is entitled to.

For the past decade, military aid took the lion's share of the foreign aid programs of the United States. A shift in favor of nonmilitary aid occurred during the 1961 session when Congress appropriated somewhat over 2 billion dollars for military aid, while the total voted for all the other foreign aid programs ran in excess of 3 billion dollars. To the latter amount must be added the equivalent of approximately 1 billion dollars in foreign currencies, the proceeds of the sale of agricultural commodities abroad, to be used for economic grants and loans to purchasing governments.

Foreign aid for military purposes is a traditional way by which nations buttress their alliances. Rome used to receive tribute from its allies for the military protections it provided. The seventeenth and eighteenth centuries are the classic period of military subsidies, by which nations, and especially Great Britain, endeavored to increase the military strength of their allies. Glancing through the treaties of alliance of that period, one is struck by the meticulous precision with which obligations to furnish troops, equipment, logistic support, food, money, and the like were defined. The loans which France extended to Russia after the conclusion of the alliance between the two nations in 1894 fall in the same category. This traditional military aid can be understood as a division of labor between two allies who pool their resources, one supplying money, matériel, and training, the other providing primarily manpower.

In contrast to traditional practice, military aid today is extended not only to allies but also to certain uncommitted nations. The military aid the United States has been giving to Yugoslavia is a case in point. The purpose is here not so much military as political. It seeks political advantage in exchange for military aid. It obligates by implication, the recipient toward the giver. The latter expects the former to abstain from a political course which might put in jeopardy the continuation of military aid. Military aid is here really in the nature of a bribe.

What appears as military aid may also be actually in the nature of prestige aid, to be discussed below. The provision of jet fighters and other modern weapons for certain underdeveloped nations can obviously perform no genuine military function. It increases the prestige of the recipient nation both at home and abroad. Being in the possession of some of the more spectacular instruments of modern warfare, a nation can at least enjoy the illusion of having become a modern military power.

As bribery appears today in the guise of aid for economic development, so does aid for economic development appear in the guise of military assistance. In the session of 1961, for instance, Congress appropriated 425 million dollars for economic aid to strategic areas, and it is likely that in the total appropriations of over 2 billion dollars for military aid other items of economic aid are hidden. This mode of operation results from the reluctance of Congress to vote large amounts for economic aid in contrast to its readiness to vote virtually any amount requested for military purposes. Yet the purposes of aid for economic development are likely to suffer when they are disguised as military assistance, as we saw the purposes of bribery suffer when disguised as aid for economic development. The military context within which such aid is bound to operate, even though its direct administration be in the hands of the civilian authorities, is likely to deflect such aid from its genuine purposes. More particularly, it strengthens the ever-present tendency to subordinate the requirements of aid for economic development to military considerations.

Prestige aid has in common with modern bribes the fact that its true purpose, too, is concealed by the ostensible purpose of economic development or military aid. The unprofitable or idle steel mill, the highway without traffic and leading nowhere, the airline operating with foreign personnel and at a loss but under the flag of the recipient country—all ostensibly serve the purposes of economic development and under different circumstances might do so. Actually, however, they perform no positive economic function. They owe their existence to the penchant, prevalent in many underdeveloped nations, for what might be called "conspicuous industrialization," spectacular symbols of, and monuments to, industrial advancement rather than investments satisfying any objective economic needs of the country.

This tendency sheds an illuminating light upon the nature of what is.

generally referred to as the "revolution of rising expectations." We are inclined to assume that the urgent desire to improve one's lot by means of modern technology and industry is a well-nigh universal trend in Asia, Africa, and Latin America. Actually, however, this trend is universal only in the sense that virtually all underdeveloped nations want to appear as having achieved industrialization, while only a fraction of the population, and frequently only small elite groups within it, seek the social and economic benefits of industrialization and are willing to take the measures necessary to achieve them. For many of the underdeveloped nations the steel mill, the highway, the airline, the modern weapons, perform a function that is not primarily economic or military, but psychological and political. They are sought as the outward show of modernity and power. They peform a function similar to that which the cathedral performed for the medieval city and the feudal castle or the monarch's palace for the absolute state. Nehru is reported to have said, when he showed Chou-En-Lai a new dam: "It is in these temples that I worship." And the more underdeveloped and less viable a nation is, the greater is likely to be its urge to prove to itself and to the world through the results of prestige aid that it, too, has arrived in the mid-twentieth century.

The advantage for the giver of prestige aid is threefold. He may receive a specific political advantage in return for the aid, very much like the advantage received for a bribe. Also, the spectacular character of prestige aid establishes a patent relationship between the generosity of the giver and the increased prestige of the recipient. The giver's prestige is enhanced, as it were, by the increase of the recipient's prestige. Finally, prestige aid comes relatively cheap. A limited commitment of resources in the form of a spectacular but economically useless symbol of modernity may bring disproportionate political dividends.

The giver of foreign aid is therefore well advised to distinguish between prestige aid and aid for economic development, though both are justified by the prospective recipient in terms of genuine economic development. The prospective giver, if unaware of the distinction, is likely to fall into one of two errors. By mistaking prestige aid for aid for economic development, he may waste human and material resources in support of the latter when the purpose of prestige aid could have been achieved much more simply and cheaply. Or else he may reject out of hand a request for prestige aid because he cannot justify it in terms of economic development, and may thereby forgo available political advantages. The classic example of this error is the American rejection of the Afghan request for the paving of the streets of Kabul as economically unsound. The Soviet Union, pursuing a politically oriented policy of foreign aid, did pave the streets of Kabul.

## FOREIGN AID FOR ECONOMIC DEVELOPMENT IN PARTICULAR

None of the types of foreign aid discussed thus far poses theoretical questions of great magnitude; rather they raise issues for practical manipulation which can be successfully met by common sense tested by experience. Foreign aid for economic development has been the primary area for theoretical analysis and speculation, and these have been primarily of an economic nature. Economic thought, true to its prevailing academic tradition, tends to look at foreign aid as though it were a self-sufficient technical enterprise to be achieved with the instruments, and judged by the standards, of pure economics. And since Western economic development, from the first industrial revolution onwards, has been due to the formation of capital and the accumulation of technical knowledge, we have tended to assume that these two factors would by themselves provide the impetus for the economic development of the underdeveloped nations of Asia, Africa, and Latin America. This tendency has been powerfully supported by the spectacular success of the Marshall Plan, the political origins and motivations of which were easily forgotten in its justification as a strictly economic measure for the provision of capital and technological know-how. Yet it is not always recognized that this success was made possible only by the fact that, in contrast to the underdeveloped nations of Asia, Africa, and Latin America, the recipients of Marshall aid were among the leading industrial nations of the world, whose economic systems were but temporarily in disarray.

The popular mind, on the other hand, and, through it, much of the practice of foreign aid have proceeded from certain unexamined assumptions, no less doubtful for being deeply embedded in the American folklore of politics. Thus the popular mind has established correlations between the infusion of capital and technology into a primitive society and its economic development, between economic development and social stability, between social stability and democratic institutions, between democratic institutions and a peaceful foreign policy. However attractive and reassuring these correlations may sound to American ears, they are borne out neither by the experiences we have had with our policies of foreign aid nor by general historic experience.

The first of these assumptions implies that underdevelopment is at least primarily the result of lack of capital and technological know-how. Underdevelopment is regarded as a kind of accident or at worst as a kind of deficiency disease, which can be taken care of through subcutaneous injections of the missing ingredients. Yet a nation may suffer from deficiencies, some natural and insuperable, others social and remediable, which no amount of capital and technological know-how supplied from the outside can cure. The poverty of natural resources may be such as to make economic development impossible. Nations such as Jordan and Somalia are in all likelihood permanently incapable of economic development for that reason. Many of the nations which are the perennial recipients of subsistence aid are likely to fall in the same category.

A nation may also suffer from human deficiencies which preclude economic development. As there are individuals whose qualities of character and level of intelligence make it impossible for them to take advantage of economic opportunities, so are there nations similarly handicapped. To put it bluntly: as there are bums and beggars, so are there bum and beggar nations. They may be the recipients of charity, but short of a miraculous transformation of their collective intelligence and character, what they receive from the outside is not likely to be used for economic development.

Other nations are presently deficient in the specific qualities of character and intelligence that go into the making of a modern economic system, even though their general or inherent capabilities qualify them potentially for the necessary transformation sometime in the future. They are, to use a rough analogy, in a medieval stage of cultural development, still awaiting the equivalent of the moral and intellectual revolutions which in the sixteenth and seventeenth centuries created the cultural preconditions for the economic development of the West. Yet we tend to take the existence of these preconditions for granted, forgetting that without the secularization and rationalization of Western thought and society the industrialization of the West would not have been possible.

A civilization, such as the Burmese, which deprecates success in this world because it stands in the way of success in the other world, puts a cultural obstacle in the path of industrial development, which foreign aid by itself cannot overcome. Saving, that is, the preservation of capital or goods for investment or future use, has become so integral a part of our economic thought and action that it is hard for us to realize that there are hundreds of millions of people in the underdeveloped areas of the world who are oblivious of this mode of operation, indispensable to economic development. We have come to consider the productive enterprise as a continuum in the betterment of which the individual owner or manager has a personal stake. Yet in many underdeveloped areas the productive enterprise is regarded primarily as an object for financial exploitation, to be discarded when it has performed its function of bringing the temporary owner the largest financial return in the shortest possible time. Foreign aid poured into such a precapitalistic and even prerational mould is less likely to transform the mould than to be forced by it, in ways hardly predictable in advance, into channels serving the interests of a precapitalistic or prerational society.

The economic interests which tend to prevent foreign aid from being used for economic development are typically identified with the ruling groups in underdeveloped societies, which derive their political power in good measure from the economic *status quo*. The ownership and control of arable land, in particular, is in many of the underdeveloped societies the foundation of political power. Land reform and industrializiation are in consequence an attack upon the political *status quo*. In the measure that they succeed, they are bound to affect drastically the distribution of economic and political power alike. Yet the beneficiaries of both the economic and political *status quo* are the typical recipients of foreign aid given for the purpose of changing the *status quo*. To ask them to use foreign aid for this purpose is to require a readiness for self-sacrifice and a sense of social responsibility which few ruling groups have shown throughout history. Foreign aid proffered under such circumstances is likely to fail in its ostensible purpose and, performing the function of a bribe to the ruling group, to strengthen the economic and political *status quo*. It is more likely to accentuate unsolved social and political problems than to bring them closer to solution. A team of efficiency experts and public accountants might well have improved the operations of the Al Capone gang; yet by doing so, it would have aggravated the social and political evils which the operations of that gang brought forth.

Given this likely resistance of the ruling group to economic development, foreign aid requires drastic political change as a necessary condition for its success. Foreign aid must go hand in hand with political change, either voluntarily induced from within or brought about through pressure from without. The latter alternative faces the giving nation with a dilemma. On the one hand, to give foreign aid for economic development without stipulating conditions that maximize the chances for success will surely maximize the chances for failure. On the other hand, to give aid "with strings" arouses xenophobic suspicions and nationalistic resentments, to be exploited both by the defenders of the *status quo* and the promoters of Communist revolution.

Furthermore, once one has decided to bring about political change in opposition to the ruling group, one must identify some alternative group as the instrument of political change. Sometimes, the only choice is among alternative groups which are equally unattractive. Sometimes, and not infrequently, the absence of any available alternative group leaves only the choice between creating one or doing nothing.

Finally, the promotion of drastic social change on the part of the giving nation may create the indispensable condition for economic development, but it also conjures up the spectre of uncontrollable revolution. In many of the underdeveloped nations peace and order are maintained only through the ruthless use of the monopoly of force by the ruling group. Determined and skillful foreign intervention may find little difficulty in weakening or even removing altogether the power of the ruling group. It is not so easy to finish what has thereby been started. While the interventionist nation may be able to control events up to the point of instigating drastic reform and revolution, it may well prove unable to control the course of the revolution itself. More particularly, a democratic nation, such as the United States, is greatly handicapped in competing with Communists in the control of a revolution. The revolution may start, as it did in Cuba, under the democratic auspices of unorganized masses dedicated to social reform and supported by the United States, and may in the course of its development be taken over by the highly organized and disciplined Communist minority, the only organized and disciplined revolutionary group on the scene.

Successful foreign aid for economic development may have similarly unsettling political results. Economic development, especially by way of industrialization, is bound to disrupt the social fabric of the underdeveloped nation. By creating an urban industrial proletariat, it loosens and destroys the social nexus of family, village and tribe, in which the individual had found himself secure. And it will not be able, at least not soon, to provide a substitute for this lost social world. The vacuum so created will be filled by social unrest and political agitation. Furthermore, it is not the downtrodden peoples living in a static world of unrelieved misery who are the likely protagonists of revolution, but rather those groups that have begun to rise in the social and economic scale have not enough to satisfy their aroused expectations. Thus, economic development is bound to disturb not only the economic *status quo* but, through it, the political *status quo* as well. If the change is drastic enough, the social and political effects of economic development may well bring about a prerevolutionary or revolutionary situation. And while the United States may have started the revolutionary process, it will again be uncertain under whose auspices it will be ended.

The United States faces a number of formidable handicaps in trying to control social and political change in the underdeveloped nations either as a prerequisite for, or a result of, foreign aid for economic development. First of all, as a Western capitalistic nation, the United States is a conservative power both domestically and internationally, and must appear particularly so to the underdeveloped nations. Both in its civilization and its social and economic structure, it belongs to that complex of nations which until recently were able to hold Africa, Latin America, and the outlying areas of Asia in a condition of colonial or semicolonial dependency. It has military alliances with these nations, and while it has generally shunned and even opposed outright colonial policies, it has actively and successfully participated in the semicolonial exploitation of backward nations. Thus the resentment against the former colonial powers attaches also, to it and its policies of foreign aid are frequently suspect, as serving in disguise the traditional ends of colonialism.

Furthermore, the United States, by dint of its pluralistic political philosophy and social system, cannot bring to the backward nations of the world a simple message of salvation, supported first by dedicated and disciplined revolutionary minorities and then by totalitarian control. In the nature of things, the advantage lies here with the Communist powers. They are, as it were, specialists in exploiting a revolutionary situation, which is bound to cause us embarrassment. For while the Communists are able to direct a revolution into the desired channels through their use of a disciplined minority, we, even if we are convinced that revolution is inevitable and therefore do not oppose it, tend to look on it with misgivings since we cannot control the direction it will take.

The Communist powers have still another advantage over the United States in that, at least on the surface, their problems and achievements are more meaningful to the underdeveloped nations than ours. The Soviet Union has achieved, and Communist China attempts to achieve, what the more enlightened underdeveloped nations seek: a drastic increase in national output through rapid industrialization. The Communist powers use totalitarian control as their instrument and Communist doctrine as rationalization. Seeking the same results, the underdeveloped nations cannot help being attracted by the methods which brought about these results elsewhere. In contrast, the slow process, stretching over centuries, through which the nations of the West achieved a high standard of living through industrialization must appeal much less to them. That appeal is further lessened by the economic processes of the free market and the political processes of liberal democracy through which in large measure Western industrialization was achieved. For these processes require a degree of moral restraint and economic and political sophistication which are largely absent in the underdeveloped nations. The simple and crude methods of totalitarianism must appear to them much more congenial.

Thus we arrive at the disconcerting conclusion that successful foreign aid for economic development can be counterproductive if the social and political goal of the giving nation is the recipient's social and political stability. In some cases at least, the failure of American aid for economic development may have been a blessing in disguise in that it did not disturb a stable *status quo* whose continuance was in our interest. Such aid, intended for economic development, actually performs the function either of a bribe or of prestige aid. Here again, however, these functions are likely to be impaired by disappointed expectations of economic development on the part of the giving and the recipient nation.

It is equally a moot question whether successful foreign aid for economic development is conducive to the development of democratic institutions and practices. Without stopping here to examine the complexities of the relationship between democracy and economic development, it is enough to observe, as recent history has made clear, that no necessary causal relationships exists between the two. The most impressive example is the Soviet Union. Its rapid economic development has gone hand in hand with totalitarian government, and a case could well be made for the proposition that the former would have been impossible without the latter. It is more likely than not that where the intellectual and moral preconditions for economic development are lacking in the population at large and are present only in a small elite, as is true in many of the underdeveloped nations, the imposition of the will of that small minority upon the majority of the population is a prerequisite not only for the start of economic development but also for sustained economic growth.

As concerns the promotion of a peaceful foreign policy, economic development is likely to be counterproductive if a political incentive for a belligerent foreign policy is present. The contrary conclusion derives from the popular, yet totally unfounded assumption that "poor" nations make war on "rich" nations for economic advantage and that "rich" nations are by definition peaceful because they have what they want. In truth, of course, most wars have been fought not for economic but political advantage, and, particularly under modern technological conditions, only economically advanced nations are capable of waging modern war. We did not consider the Soviet Union a military threat as long as it was economically underdeveloped; it became one when its economic development had transformed it into a modern industrial power. Similarly, Communist China today, except to its immediate neighbors, is only a potential military threat by virtue of its economic potential, both likely to be activated by economic development.

Foreign aid for economic development, then, has a very much smaller range of potentially successful operation than is generally believed. Its success depends in good measure not so much upon its soundness in strictly economic terms as upon intellectual, moral, and political preconditions, which are not susceptible to economic manipulation, if they are susceptible to manipulation from the outside at all. Furthermore, the political results of successful foreign aid for economic development may be either unpredictable or counterproductive in terms of the political goals of the giving nation. In any event, they are in large measure uncontrollable. Foreign aid proffered and accepted for purposes of economic development may turn out to be something different from what it was intended to be, unless it is oriented toward the political conditions within which it must operate. Most likely, it will turn out to be a bribe or prestige aid, or else a total waste. To do too much may here be as great a risk as to do too little, and "masterly inactivity" may sometimes be the better part of wisdom.

## CONCLUSIONS FOR POLICY

The major conclusions for policy to be drawn from this analysis are three: the requirement of identifying each concrete situation in the light of the six different types of foreign aid and of choosing the quantity and quality of foreign aid appropriate to the situation; the requirement of attuning, within the same concrete situation, different types of foreign aid to each other in view of the over-all goals of foreign policy; and the requirement of dealing with foreign aid as an integral part of political policy.

The task of identifying concrete situations with the type of foreign aid appropriate to them is a task for country and area experts to perform. Can country A not survive without foreign aid? Is its government likely to exchange political advantages for economic favors? Would our military interests be served by the strengthening of this nation's military forces? Does this country provide the noneconomic preconditions for economic development to be supported by foreign aid? Are our political interests likely to be served by giving this nation foreign aid for purposes of prestige? Can a case be made for foreign aid in order to alleviate human suffering? What kind and quantity of foreign aid is necessary and sufficient to achieve the desired result?

To answer these questions correctly demands first of all a thorough and intimate knowledge and understanding of the total situation in a particular country. But it also requires political and economic judgment of a very high order, applied to two distinct issues. It is necessary to anticipate the receptivity of the country to different kinds of foreign aid and their effects upon it. When this analysis has been made, it is then necessary to select from a great number of possible measures of foreign aid those which are most appropriate to the situation and hence most likely to succeed.

In most cases, however, the task is not that simple. Typically, an underdeveloped country will present a number of situations indicating the need for different types of foreign aid simultaneously. One type given without regard for its potential effects upon another type risks getting in the way of the latter. One of the most conspicuous weaknesses of our past foreign aid policies has been the disregard of the effect different types of foreign aid have upon each other. Bribes given to the ruling group, for instance, are bound to strengthen the political and economic *status quo*. Military aid is bound to have an impact upon the distribution of political power within the receiving country; it can also have a deleterious effect upon the economic system, for instance, by increasing inflationary pressures. Similarly, the effect of subsistence foreign aid is bound to be the support of the *status quo* in all its aspects. Insofar as the giving nation desires these effects or can afford to be indifferent to them they obviously do not matter in terms of its over-all objectives. But insofar as the giving nation has embarked upon a policy of foreign aid for economic development which requires changes in the political and economic *status quo,* the other types of foreign aid policies are counterproductive in terms of economic development; for they strengthen the very factors which stand in its way.

This problem is particularly acute in the relations between prestige aid and aid for economic development. The giving nation may seek quick political results and use prestige aid for that purpose; yet it may also have an interest in the economic development of the recipient country, the benefits of which are likely to appear only in the more distant future. Prestige aid is at best only by accident favorable to economic development; it may be irrelevant to it, or it may actually impede it. What kind of foreign aid is the giving country to choose? If it chooses a combination of both it should take care to choose an innocuous kind of prestige aid and to promote economic development the benefits of which are not too long in coming. Afghanistan is the classic example of this dilemma. The Soviet Union, by paving the streets of Kabul, chose a kind of prestige aid that is irrelevant to economic development. The United States, by building a hydroelectric dam in a remote part of the country, chose economic development, the very existence of which is unknown to most Afghans and the benefits of which will not appear for years to come.

It follows, then, from the very political orientation of foreign aid that its effect upon the prestige of the giving nation must always be in the minds of the formulators and executors of foreign aid policies. Foreign aid for economic development, in particular, which benefits the recipient country immediately and patently is a more potent political weapon than aid promising benefits that are obscure and lie far in the future. Furthermore, the political effects of foreign aid are lost if its foreign source is not obvious to the recipients. For it is not aid as such or its beneficial results that creates political loyalties on the part of the recipient, but the positive relationship that the mind of the recipient establishes between the aid and its beneficial results, on the one hand, and the political philosophy, the political system, and the political objectives of the giver, on the other. That is to say, if the recipient continues to disapprove of the political philosophy, system, and objectives of the giver, despite the aid he has received, the political effects of the aid are lost. The same is true if he remains unconvinced that the aid received is but a natural, if not inevitable, manifestation of the political philosophy, system, and objectives of the giver. Foreign aid remains politically ineffectual—at least for the short term—as long as the recipient says either: "Aid is good, but the politics of the giver are bad"; or "Aid is good, but the politics of the giver —good, bad, or indifferent—have nothing to do with it." In order to be able to establish psychological relationship between giver and recipient, the procedures through which aid is given, and the subject matter to which it is applied, must lend themselves to the creation of a connection between the aid and the politics of the giver which reflects credit upon the latter.

The problem of foreign aid is insoluble if it is considered as a self-sufficient technical enterprise of a primarily economic nature. It is soluble only if it is considered an integral part of the political policies of the giving country—which must be devised in view of the political conditions, and for its effects upon the political situation, in the receiving country. In this respect, a policy of foreign aid is no different from diplomatic or military policy or propaganda. They are all weapons in the political armory of the nation.

As military policy is too important a matter to be left ultimately to the generals, so is foreign aid too important a matter to be left in the end to the economists. The expertise of the economist must analyze certain facts, devise certain means, and perform certain functions of manipulation for foreign aid. Yet the formulation and over-all execution of foreign aid policy is a political function. It is the province of the political expert.

It follows from the political nature of foreign aid that it is not a science but an art. That art requires by way of mental predisposition a political sensitivity to the interrelationship among the facts, present and future, and ends and means. The requirements by way of mental activity are two-fold. The first is a discriminating judgment of facts, ends and means and their effects upon each other. However, an analysis of the situation in the recipient country and, more particularly, its projection into the future and the conclusions from the analysis in terms of policy can only in part be arrived at through rational deduction from ascertainable facts. When all the available facts have been ascertained, duly analyzed, and conclusions drawn from them, the final judgments and decisions can be derived only from subtle and sophisticated hunches. The best the formulator and executor of a policy of foreign aid can do is to maximize the chances that his hunches turn out to be right. Here as elsewhere in the formulation and conduct of foreign policy, the intuition of the statesman, more than the knowledge of the expert, will carry the day.

# E. F. Schumacher

## A Humanistic Guide to Foreign Aid

ECONOMIC MISERY is something altogether different from mere poverty; it is a scandal and signifies a breakdown of the natural order, for it prevents men from being human. It is a fallacy to assume that once men are given an adequate provision of the necessities of life, the further they can go beyond that the better. But it is no fallacy to assert that adequate provision of the necessities of life is the first priority of all—a priority so high that it transcends all divisions of the human race and becomes the collective task and responsibility of the whole of mankind. Yet it seems to be precisely in this task that we tend to fail. The following notes attempt to find out why.

The science of economic development cannot be simply economics. Eugene R. Black, the president of the International Bank for Reconstruction and Development, has rightly emphasized that "We are talking about transforming whole societies." This obviously involves issues far beyond mere economics—as the French political economist, Bertrand de Jouvenel, has pointed out—and economists have no right when discussing economic development to appraise "every form of change occurring or capable of being brought about in a society . . . solely on the grounds of its contribution to the rate of economic growth." When it is a matter of transforming whole societies and of destroying ancient traditions, it is illegitimate—even theoretically—for economists to consider that economic development is the end and that "social, psychological, moral, and political change, are means to that end." It is illegitimate and—as I shall try to demonstrate—a barrier to worthwhile progress.

It is fashionable today to treat all noneconomic considerations with impatient contempt. Even Mr. de Jouvenel appears to share in the general impatience when he writes: "As it is a fact that economic growth is widely and ardently desired, the humanistic critique of economic development is doomed to futility. The best it can achieve is to create disequilibria in economic growth by intruding into a general process checks and regulations which do not change the character of the process but which bring it into disorder." I cannot believe that Mr. de Jouvenel really means this. The humanistic critique of economic development, it seems to me, is today more than ever before necessary, both in the highly developed and in the underdeveloped countries. How can it be said that such a critique must necessarily be doomed to futility or that it would bring disorder into a "general process" which is already in the greatest possible degree disorderly? And, if a critique is called for, is the possibility of futility a valid reason for neglecting one's duty?

In fact, there is no "general process" which free men could not alter if a "humanistic critique" indicated to them the need for a change; that, I believe, is also the opinion of Mr. de Jouvenel when he pleads for a "sense of quality within the framework of a search for quantity." And it is obvious that such a sense of quality can be derived only from an appreciation of spiritual, moral, psychological, and political realities which cannot be treated as subservient to the aims of economics.

It is necessary to insist on these points because, as I indicated above, the neglect of non-economic realities seems to me the principal barrier to worthwhile progress in the very field of economic development with which we are concerned. The science of economics becomes the more exclusively quantitative (and thus a pure abstraction) the more rigorously it is developed. This may be useful for narrowly circumscribed tasks of analysis within a given and stable setting; but it is of extremely limited applicability and, in addition, generally misleading when the task is one of changing the setting itself. Eugene Black, at least, knows this very well. He writes:

It is very easy to forget how exceptional, historically, are the attitudes and institutions necessary for modern economic growth. . . . Just to list a few of the requirements is to illustrate how ambitious is the task of those who would bring modern economic development to an underdeveloped country today. And how uncertain is the outcome in a society which sets out to absorb these very special institutions and attitudes! . . . Man does not come naturally by any of the attitudes and institutions necessary for economic growth; he must be driven—even to hard work—by need, or by the prospect of material gains, or somehow these attitudes must be made politically or religiously inspiring.

Here we have the authentic voice of the modern West. "He must be driven"; some hidden, or not-so-hidden, persuaders must invent political or religious slogans to make "inspiring" those attitudes which are thought to be the precondition of economic development. Here we are not told that the humanistic critique of economic development is doomed to futility because "economic growth is widely and ardently desired," but instead that men must be driven, coerced, enticed, manipulated. Does not this require a "humanistic critique"? Naturally, the resulting economic development generally proves, as Mr. Black admits, "peculiarly fickle": "even now it is creating human desires much faster than it is providing means for their gratification." And Mr. Black's verdict is that "economic development has left tragic problems in its wake in the underdeveloped world which only more economic development can solve."

Now this amounts, to say the least, to a somewhat daring prescription. Normally, when a course of action leaves in its wake "tragic problems," it seems proper to consider whether the course has been set quite correctly and not merely to call for speedier movement in the same direction. The question is not—of course *not*—whether the rich should continue to try and help the poor, or whether a fight against economic misery, wherever it is to be found, should be carried on: the question is simply whether the *type* of economic development currently pursued, and the methods of its pursuit, are the right ones. And that question is neither raised nor susceptible of being answered by Mr. Black and all the other multitude of economic technicians who talk about *driving* men to work and who stimulate desires beyond any practical possibility of satisfaction. To think that the only way to promote economic growth in the so-called underdeveloped countries is to imitate as closely as possible the current practices of the advanced countries (or perhaps to do even better by "jumping" intermediate stages), and to force every time-honored institution into the service of purely material aims of Western inspiration, betrays not only an astounding lack of imagination but also a truly ominous lack of awareness of the dehumanizing deformities of the modern West.

The problem of the right *type* or *pattern* of development is so fundamental and deep that it is highly questionable whether the normal concepts of economics can be applied without tying the mind to the very pattern of living—the pattern of the advanced West—from which they have been abstracted. Mr. Black says that "words like 'savings' and 'investment,' 'efficiency' and 'productivity' are the tools of our trade, and like good artisans, we try to develop proper standards for their use." And Mr. de Jouvenel says that "there are *some* necessary conditions to *any* economic growth, such as the accumulation of capital, the acquisition of new techniques, and, above all, the capacity to conceive and to carry out new combinations of productive resources." Both statements are, of course, impregnable at the formal level. But I suggest that—not necessarily, but in actual practice—they turn the mind in the wrong direction; they produce associations of thought that lead almost inevitably to the tacit assumption that economic development is a synonym for Westernization. While it is formally true to say that economic development depends on "the accumulation of capital," on "savings" and "investment," what really matters is their material source, which is labor, and which, realistically speaking, must be primarily indigenous labor. The labor power of the indigenous populations is the great potential source of "capital," "savings," "investment," and so forth, as it is the source of income. How can it be mobilized and usefully applied?—that is the crux of the question of "savings" and "investment." When indigenous labor power is directly applied to the creation of durable consumers' goods like houses, or to capital goods like roads, land improvements, implements, and the like, then "savings" and "investment" come in one act, without any of the monetary associations which these terms normally produce.

Or take Mr. Black's concepts of "efficiency" and "productivity," or Mr. de Jouvenel's "acquisition of new techniques" and "capacity to conceive and to carry out new combinations." These terms almost inevitably turn the mind toward Western methods, toward ways of doing things that are foreign to the local populations, that overawe or even frighten them, and thus do not help in doing the "one thing needful," which is to mobilize as fully as possible the indigenous labor power. Such a mobilization can be effected on the required scale only if the people are encouraged to use the methods they know—to improve upon them; to develop them by all means; even to marry them in some cases with methods imported from abroad (if that can be done easily and organically); even occasionally to drop them in favor of something foreign (if that happens naturally and spontaneously). But no such mobilization will be possible if the all-pervading notion is that everything that is different from its Western counterpart is inferior; that the people's own "know-how" is worthless, that their own traditions must be done away with, that their religion must be modified or abandoned wherever it stands in the way of "economic development." It is, I suggest, this attitude itself that stands in the way of economic development, because it produces an unconquerable apathy, an atmosphere of hopeless resignation that can do nothing and will do do nothing but wait for aid from afar.

Economic development—and again I stress that this means the transformation of whole societies—is a very big thing and, like all big things, depends primarily on movements that take place on the unconscious, rather than the conscious, level. In an Indian journal I find an article titled "A Surfeit of Planning—Where Are the People?" The author— himself an Indian—begins by saying that "the people for whom we plan and weave our dreams are seldom in the picture. More often they are just laborers, wage earners with little sense of participation or adventure in the India we plan to reconstruct. The reasons for such apathy are perhaps very deep, somewhere very near the soul of India." The author pleads then for a "movement of reconstruction" rather than a plan con- trived by economists, in the abstract jargon of economics, because only such a movement, "deciding its aims and targets according to local need and desire from area to area, could gather the people, make them partners in plans which, if not very grandiose, are at least after their hearts."

These words, in my opinion, are more closely in touch with reality than the language of Western economics; they point to the living source of wealth, which is the labor power of "the people"; they indicate what I believe to be the one decisive criterion for judging the value of any development measures: whether they will encourage or discourage the spontaneous mobilization of this labor power. To quote again from Eugene Black, who after all is the most prominent representative of present-day orthodoxy in matters of economic development: "Even the most enthusiastic supporters of economic aid recognize that the outside world cannot provide more than a small margin of the resources needed; the really crucial economic and human resources must come from within." But what if the manner in which the "small margin" is injected causes the "really crucial economic and human resources"—namely those that ought to be forthcoming from within—to sink deeper and deeper into the kind of apathy to which the Indian author refers above? This is a question which Mr. Black has not considered because it does not at all fit into his official ideology, which he explains as follows:

> In the World Bank we concentrate on economic development as if its only end were higher consumption and greater comfort. We try to remove the taint of ideology from the language of economics and then relate that language solely to the end of promoting higher material liv- ing standards.

Is it surprising, then, that this does not reach down to anything that lies near to the soul of the people? That it fails to awaken the soul, but merely makes apathy more fearful and sullen?

Or take another famous prescription for economic development, W. W. Rostow's "take-off into self-sustained growth":

For the present purposes the take-off is defined as requiring all three of the following related conditions:

(a) a rise in the rate of productive investment from (say) 5 per cent or less to over 10 per cent of national income (or net national product);

(b) the development of one or more substantial manufacturing sectors, with a high rate of growth;

(c) the existence or quick emergence of a political, social, and institutional framework which exploits the impulses to expansion in the modern sector and the potential external economy effects of the take-off and gives growth an on-going character.

Now I do not wish to quarrel with these sentences as a piece of analysis of past events. But I become very uneasy when (a), (b), and (c) are described as "conditions," thus turning the analysis into a prescription. These three so-called conditions are, after all, mere abstractions, useful for assisting our understanding *ex post facto*, but, being abstractions, they cannot be "done" (except possibly by totalitarian methods). They do not touch the people's heart; they induce the imagination to turn to the actual —that which exists already, and exists most conspicuously in the rich countries—whereas it should be turned to the potential: the unused labor power and creativity of the indigenous population.

As these things are not easily understood, nor easily expressed, I may perhaps give one further example. Bertrand de Jouvenel says this:

> It is desirable to examine the means whereby farm income is supplemented by industrial income without any migration of workers. This can of course be achieved if, in areas where there obtains a considerable density of agricultural population, factories can be set up, occupying some members of the family without any need for rehousing.

This statement, again, is perfectly correct in what it says; but is it also correct in what it suggests? It would be if we were speaking in the context of a modern Western country. But in an underdeveloped country full of grinding poverty? ". . . if factories can be set up," yes, and obviously the poor ignorant villagers could never, by themselves, set up a factory— they have no "savings"; they cannot "accumulate capital"; they lack the "capacity to conceive and carry out new combinations"; their methods, like their traditions, as Mr. Black would say, "have been rendered tragically inadequate by the passing of time." Yet all this is generally quite untrue. All these gross and insulting errors are conjured up by the use of the words "if factories can be set up"—words which can only serve to confirm the feeling of impotence and despair and apathy of the people who ought to be providing "the really crucial economic and human resources." We should not be talking in this language at all—about factories and about supplementing farm income by industrial income. We should be talking about getting the people to use their own labor power, with their own intelligence (which is not incapable of picking up improved methods from outsiders), and their own local resources and materials to provide, in the first place, for their own fundamental needs, which are food, clothing, and shelter, and certain communal assets like roads, wells, and public buildings.

I can, frankly, see no value in discussing such questions—very interesting from an academic point of view—as the ideal size of towns, the ideal location of industry, or the ideal transport system, because even the most brilliant answers to them will do nothing to mobilize the creative power of the people. Instead, I think, we should ask the much simpler and much more profound question: Why is it that the people are not helping themselves? What has come over them? On the whole, throughout history, all healthy societies have managed to solve their problem of existence, and always with something to spare for culture. Grinding poverty, with malnutrition and degradation, with apathy and despair, as a permanent condition of millions of people, not as a result of war or natural catastrophe—this is a most abnormal and, historically speaking, an unheard of phenomenon. All peoples—with exceptions that merely prove the rule—have always known how to help themselves; they have always discovered a pattern of living which fitted their peculiar natural surroundings. Societies and cultures have collapsed when they deserted their own pattern and fell into decadence, but even then, unless devastated by war, the people normally continued to be able to provide for themselves, with something to spare for higher things. Why not now, in so many parts of the world?

I am not speaking of ordinary poverty, but of actual and acute misery; not of the poor, who, according to the universal tradition of mankind, are in a special way blessed, but of the miserable and degraded ones who, by the same tradition, should not exist at all and should be helped by all. Poverty may have been the rule in the past, but misery was not. Poor peasants and artisans have existed from time immemorial; but the existence of miserable and destitute villages in the thousands and urban pavement dwellers in the hundreds of thousands—not in wartime or as an aftermath of war, but in the midst of peace and as a seemingly permanent feature—is a monstrous and scandalous thing which is altogether abnormal in the history of mankind. We cannot be satisfied with the snap answer that this is due to population pressure. Since every mouth that comes into the world is also endowed with a pair of hands, population pressure could serve as an explanation only if it meant an absolute shortage of land—and although that situation may arise in the future, it decidedly has not arrived today (a few islands excepted). It cannot be argued that the population increase as such must produce increasing poverty because the additional pairs of hands lack capital. Millions of people have started without capital and have shown that a pair of hands can provide not only the income but also the durable goods—i.e., capital— for civilized existence. So the question stands and demands an answer: What has gone wrong? Why cannot these people help themselves?

I believe that the cause lies in the impact of the modern West upon these societies and populations. The paralysis or apathy—"somewhere very near the soul of India," as the Indian author said—is similar to the paralysis of the Aztecs when they met Cortes and his men sitting on the backs of horses and equipped with firearms. It was not the power of the Spaniards that destroyed the Aztec empire, but the disbelief of the Aztecs in themselves. I suggest that the cause of economic misery in a country like India is not the adherence to her own traditions[1] (which Eugene Black presumes to call "tragically inadequate"), but the turning away from these traditions, and that the cause of this turning away is the mere existence, in India and elsewhere, of the modern Western methods of production, distribution, administration, and so forth. Mr. de Jouvenel says that it is more difficult for Asian countries to achieve a "take-off" than it was for the West. This is probably true, but hardly because "the industrial revolution in the West coincided with the demographic explosion, while this explosion occurred in Asia without an attending industrial revolution." A population determined to help itself is never at a loss for productive tasks to employ all hands. What seems to me of infinitely greater importance is that the West abandoned its own traditions only as it developed and applied the modern methods itself, while the Asian countries—partly owing to European domination—lost (not all, but still too much of) their own traditions, as a result of something that had arisen not among themselves but in the West.

To talk in purely economic terms, probably the greatest cause of poverty in an underdeveloped country today is the existence of a modern transport system. None of the Western countries ever had to achieve development at a time when transport was fast and cheap. It was only *after* extensive and broadly based development had taken place that transport became fast and cheap in those countries. To start with, every town and every village enjoyed the protection of high transport costs—a kind of natural tariff to shield it against competition from all other towns

---

1. Needless to say, there are some usages that are not true traditions but decadent bad habits. The sooner these are abandoned, the better.

and villages. Hence it was obvious and normal that each locality should attempt to provide for its own needs through its own labor, intelligence, and natural resources. And hence there arose a multitude of skills in a multitude of localities, and out of the ground thus prepared grew a middle class among which could be found the adventurers and entrepreneurs for more ambitious enterprises. All this was an organic process of growth, carried forward by individuals coming from "the people," not by small groups of intellectuals, educated in foreign lands, who took it upon themselves to transform whole societies and create new traditions.

All these possibiities, however, are destroyed by cheap and fast transport. Village industries—thousands upon thousands of small workshops—wither away because there is somewhere an "efficient" modern factory which can deliver similar (though often vastly inferior) goods at a lower price. But is not this the essence of "progress"—the substitution of superior methods of production for inferior ones? Does not the lower price benefit the villagers, raising their standard of living, enabling them to save and to invest and finally to accomplish the "take-off"? Many economists argue this way, but the truth is otherwise. Because they themselves no longer produce, the villagers are poorer than ever before; they may be unable to pay for any of the factory goods, except by getting into debt. It has happened even that the factory itself, having accomplished its frightful work of destruction in the villages, has had to close down for lack of a market.

It was his intuitive understanding of these fatal mechanisms which led Gandhi to say in 1912 that "India is being ground down, not under the English heel, but under that of modern civilization." On another occasion he said: "Much of the deep poverty of India is due to the departure from Swadeshi in the economic life. If not a single article of commerce had been brought from outside India, she would be today a land flowing with milk and honey."

Gandhi also proposed that a small part of India ought to be set aside and protected against all goods from outside the area except for necessary commodities not locally producible. The inhabitants of the chosen area would then extricate themselves from their misery by their own efforts and within a very short time.

Economists have assumed too easily that what works best in an advanced country must be best for economic development. Gandhi never made this mistake. "England has sinned against India by forcing free trade upon her. It may have been food for England, but it has been poison for this country." The problem posed by free trade, however, exists equally *within* a country when such a country possesses a modern transport system and a fringe of Western-type industries. Efficient and fast communications, like free trade, are food for an advanced country and poison for an underdeveloped country. Modern economists have generally seen the "potential" of an underdeveloped country mainly in terms of its raw material exports to the rich countries; and as such exports are obviously cheapened and facilitated by efficient transportation, the economists have concluded that investment in transport facilities deserves a high priority. This is a tragic error; it must spell ruin unless counteracted by deliberate measures of what might be called "controlled isolation" for a great number of relatively small communities, so that local labor will be used primarily to cover local needs.

It is here also that the institution of money, if handled in a manner which is "food" for advanced countries, may become poison for the underdeveloped. Today there is fairly general agreement that a country struggling for development cannot do so on the basis of free convertibility of its currency—in other words, that there must be some "controlled isolation." But that the same need arises *within* the country, particularly a large country like India, is usually overlooked. If no provision is made for this, then there will be innumerable occasions when useful economic activity will only be possible on a barter basis (i.e. without money) or not at all. Barter, however, is clumsy and inflexible; what is really needed is local money or scrip issued in accordance with local needs, such as the American colonies possessed before the Revolutionary War.

These suggestions will appear reactionary and retrogressive to economists who imagine that the experience of advanced countries, where "development" is self-generating and may even be excessive, can be applied to underdeveloped countries, where "development" is not only urgently needed but also exceedingly difficult to get started. From so unrealistic a point of view my suggestions must of course look retrogressive, because it is in fact necessary to go back in the experience of the advanced countries to the early stages of their own development to find useful analogies.

Mr. de Jouvenel rightly insists that "there are degrees of freedom in the processes" of economic development. This is perfectly true and constitutes a very necessary corrective to certain schools of economic determinism. But it is also necessary to recognize that in a given situation some things are possible and others are not. What is decidedly impossible is to achieve economic development on a wide scale when every budding activity is automatically exposed to the icy blast of competition from production units employing advanced Western techniques of high capital intensity, whether such units are situated at home or abroad. Equally, it is impossible to mobilize and utilize "the really crucial economic and human resources" which "must come from within" if the ideology of the "planners" mocks and denies the ideology of the people. For instance, Mr. Black expressed his own ideology in the words: "There is real hope that people will take ideology less seriously simply because they will be too busy." Man does not live by bread alone, and the poor, having little bread, are more dependent for their life and happiness on immaterial things than are the rich. And if they are robbed of them, they lose their self-respect, their will to live, and their will to help themselves. How can they then be mobilized?

It is the impact of the West, now intensified by Westernized native ruling groups, which tends to produce this paralysis. And so, too, it produces the phenomenon which Mr. de Jouvenel refers to as "technological dualism," but which also represents an irreconcilable division far beyond the field of technology, that splits society into "two nations," each leading a totally different life from the other. Mr. de Jouvenel himself says: "In fact there is no difference between the situation thus arising and the situation arising in a colony with a 'colonial' and a 'native' sector"— surely the most unfortunate and destructive disease to befall the body of any nation that has only recently gained its independence. This is not, as is sometimes suggested, merely a problem of the location of industry, for even the widest possible scatter of an alien industry over the entire country could not reunite the "two nations," but would only spread the disease.

All the most decisive problems of development may be summed up, it seems to me, in the question: "How can the impact of the West be canalized in such a way that it does not continue to throw the people into apathy and paralysis?" It is only when this question has been satisfactorily answered that we can be certain that Western aid—to render which we are in honor bound—will do more good than harm. More or better economic planning from the center provides no answer. It is only for the purposes of analysis that one can isolate the economic factor from the rest of human life. For fruitful action, the whole of man has to be recognized. If this is not done and action is based solely on economic calculations as laid down in elaborate central plans, the only possible result can be coercion from the top. But what shall it profit? If coercion succeeds, freedom is lost; stultified by apathy and sullen disdain, the people sink ever deeper into misery.

The alternative to coercion cannot be found when spiritual realities are dismissed as being of no account or treated as merely subservient to economic aims. It cannot be found when the people are considered as objects to be driven, cajoled, or manipulated. Perhaps the best—perhaps even the only—effective slogan for aid is: "Find out what the people are trying to do and help them to do it better."

# Dudley Seers

---

# Why Visiting Economists Fail

Economics is a very serious subject when the economist assumes the role of counsellor to nations.—A. F. Burns, *The Frontiers of Economic Knowledge.*

A LARGE and growing number of economists are working for foreign governments, as direct employees, as invited visitors, or more commonly as experts supplied under national or international technical assistance programs. It would be invidious to cite examples, but there is little doubt that many of us have been, in some degree, failures. In the ministries of almost any underdeveloped country you can find cupboards full of the reports of economists, reports which have been talked about for a week or two, then put away and forgotten. Scores of "missions" and individual advisers are now overseas writing reports, many of which, it can safely be predicted, will suffer the same fate, and others are making plane reservations in happy ignorance of what awaits them.

It is perhaps worthwhile to ask ourselves why failure is so common, and whether there is any way in which we can guard against this fate. Let me say at the outset that the fault often lies rather with the "host" government than with the visitor. The terms of reference of a job may be vague, or they may reflect a mistaken view on what needs to be done; it may not be feasible to carry them out because of lack of material or of secretarial or research assistance. Sometimes the authorities are quite uninterested in the whole matter—the visit may have been set up by someone with little power, or by a minister of a regime which has fallen by the time the expert arrives, or it may be the result of a zealous agency pressing technical aid on a government which is not enthusiastic. Some invitations to foreign experts are simply political maneuvers to distract attention, at home or overseas, or to obtain a well-known foreign name as a cachet on a policy already decided.

But what are at least as frequent, and more our concern, are failures due to mistakes committed by the visitors. This paper has four parts. The first deals very briefly with some personal reasons why economists fail when they work as foreigners in underdeveloped countries; the second discusses common mistakes in professional technique; the third draws attention to the dangers of either too little or too much involvement in the local political scene; and the fourth contains some practical conclusions.[1]

## PERSONAL DEFICIENCIES

There are scores of ways in which economists fail through personal mistakes; a few examples will suffice. Some visitors are rather lacking in *savoir-faire*. They may never discover who is the real decision-maker or the right way to influence him. They may be insufficiently sociable to establish rapport with their hosts or, alternatively, lacking in discretion. Even to be seen drinking in the "wrong" company may cause someone to be written off at once; visitors are watched more closely than they realize, especially in a small or multiracial society. Certain of our colleagues cannot easily bring themselves to make criticisms, and some lack the judgment to know how and when it is appropriate to do so. Others do not have the stamina to keep going in the face of the inevitable frustrations and rebuffs, which often appear highly unreasonable. (Missed appointments have to be accepted as almost normal practice in a number of countries.) Others again lack any interest or ability in speaking the language in common use.

Another category comprises economists who remain fundamentally loyal to their own country or organization, instead of to the government they are advising. It requires an unusual detachment to jeopardize, or even forget, one's career for the sake of a country one is merely visiting, and some would not, even for a moment, consider doing so. Less obvious pressures also operate. An economist is by no means immune to chauvinistic or ideological influences, and these are strong today, precisely in this type of work. His local compatriots, such as businessmen and embassy staff, who may constitute most of his friends, are unlikely to look very favorably on a person who puts the interests of the local government above theirs, when the interests conflict. But a politician in an underdeveloped country, even if he is most sympathetic to "the West," quickly

---

1. "Underdeveloped" is admittedly an imprecise term. A good deal of what follows applies to those who advise any government (even their own), but the most serious difficulties, as well as the formally most interesting problems, arise in cases where economists from North America or Western Europe try to advise a government in Asia, Africa, or Latin America. I include under "economists" anyone working on economic problems, including bankers, administrators, and industrial experts whose professional education has been zero, scanty, or archaic. In fact some of these remarks apply with special force to such quasi-economists.

sizes up those economists whose advice somehow always coincides with, or is at least compatible with, the view of (say) the State Department, or an international financial organization, or a foreign petroleum company. Thenceforward they are treated as agents rather than as advisers with professional objectivity, and their advice is discounted accordingly.

There are those whose work includes the administration of a staff, and who are either just bad administrators or at least incapable of the more delicate tasks of supervising foreigners. (Xenophobia is *always* present, either actually or potentially.) Some even show contempt, prob-ably unconsciously, for the people with whom they are working. Others fail to organize and train staff members against the day of their depar-ture.

By no means least serious are the cases of those who are professionally unqualified or unprepared. The narrow specialist is not much good, since even technical questions cannot be separated from general issues or even from sociology or politics (see below). Nor is the economist with little theoretical or (more important) practical experience in the field of economic development. Up to a few years ago, such experience was not essential, but a great deal of knowledge has been accumulated, and the visitor is expected to be familiar with it. The group of local economists is by no means lightweight in many countries; they will be quite critical of a visitor who is completely "green."

The various processes by which economists are recruited for work over-seas are at times a trifle indiscriminate, and these examples are not at all uncommon. The required combination of qualities is very unusual; it is a matter of common observation that there is a marked negative cor-relation between professional ability and administrative capacity. More-over, the field for recruitment is limited. Nearly all economists are engaged on jobs which keep them continually in their own countries, or else limit them to an occasional sabbatical year abroad. Those available for posts in underdeveloped countries are often people who have not succeeded in finding satisfactory niches at home.

## TECHNICAL ERRORS

For one or other of the above reasons, a large proportion of visiting economists is doomed to failure from the beginning. But this paper is concerned primarily with those who are welcome guests, who are at least not entirely disqualified on various personal grounds, but who fail nevertheless.

The explanation is usually that the advice does not seem very useful to those who are being advised. To see the technical reasons why this is so, let us look at the various stages of work involved in reaching conclusions on policy.[2] It will be useful to follow here the framework of analysis in the theory of policy, as it has been worked out, primarily for developed countries, by J. Tinbergen[3] and others. In the conventions of this field, the steps are as follows: first, stating the objectives; second, specifying the structural relations of the economy; and third, choosing values for the instruments of policy. We can ask ourselves what special pitfalls there are, under each of these headings for an economist from a developed country.

### Objectives

The person the economist is advising, whom I shall assume to be a politician of an underdeveloped country, has certain basic political objectives.[4] One might be the strengthening of the country vis-à-vis some actual or potential enemy. Other possibilities are to eliminate unemployment, to raise levels of consumption, and to change the distribution of income. There are always dozens of components in the welfare function of anyone with political power.

The first problem for the visiting economist is to find out what the targets are. Targets which are taken for granted by all local citizens may not appear in any published document, and even if they do, it is often a problem to see which of several stated objectives, perhaps mutually inconsistent, really count. This is especially true if what are means (for example, retail price stabilization) are presented as if they were ends. A second problem is that the task of quantifying targets may be even more difficult than in the developed countries. Few politicans are accustomed to thinking in these terms, while the visiting economist is hardly in a position to estimate the quantitative implications of a set of rather vague objectives.

---

2. The discussion that follows refers to the formulation of *general* policy (as opposed to policy in particular fields). In underdeveloped economies, what is always of central importance is the rate and nature of economic growth.

3. Esp. in *Economic Policies: Principles and Design* (Amsterdam: North-Holland Publishing Co., 1956). See also W. A. Jöhr and H. W. Singer, *The Role of the Economist as Official Adviser* (London: George Allen & Unwin, 1955), which contains, *inter alia,* an interesting critique of an earlier version of Tinbergen's system (*On the Theory of Economic Policy*). It will be clear from what follows that, although the framework of analysis is useful, the methods proposed by Tinbergen cannot easily be applied in underdeveloped economies.

4. The distinction between politicians and civil servants is not as sharp as it is in developed economies. In practice, one can substitute a senior civil servant for a politician in the whole of this discussion, and one often does have to treat them as if they were identical.

## Structure

Still there is nearly always someone, such as an experienced civil servant, who will help by discussing these problems. The general aim of maximizing real per capita income may suffice as a first approximation. A much harder problem is to find out how the economy works. There are several steps here—first, one has to discover the data, all the geographical, social, economic, and political elements of a problem. Examples are climate and soils; land tenure and racial composition; the organization of the world market for the leading exports; the distribution of income; the relation between local and central authorities; the political power of the trade unions. The visiting economist has to be sufficient of an all-rounder to be able to build up a complete picture of a society that is quite novel to him.

Normally, there are not many sociological or other technical studies that he can use. A visitor can, it is true, pick up a certain amount of information just by looking around for himself and by talking to people, but he soon finds that he has to choose between irreconcilable statements even on matters of fact. Acquiring a really reliable picture of the socio-economic structure is a long business, especially for someone who lives in the very sheltered and atypical environment of a luxury hotel. The politician he is advising knows a great deal that would be helpful, but it may be difficult for this knowledge to be communicated. There are nearly always linguistic barriers, even when politician and economist both apparently speak the same language. This is partly because the same words have different overtones in different countries (for example, compare the various versions of English spoken in America, Britain, and India) and partly because those with an academic background always have some difficulty in communicating with politicians. (If economist and politician share the same background, the politician may be almost as ignorant of the local social structure as the economist.)

Most economists are, in any case, rather incompetent at assessing and allowing for the non-economic elements of the picture. Professional training inculcates distrust of the sort of intuitive appreciation that has to be made. (This is one reason why economists are in general unsuccessful as politicians.) The whole business may indeed seem to them slightly disreputable.

More important, and still more difficult, is to find out what happens when this socio-economic structure is set in motion. The task can be described as one of building up a model—of course, the model may not be specified, but this is what the economist is actually doing. He selects certain variables as significant, identifies those which are "exogenous" and arranges them all in production functions, consumption functions, and so forth. It is clearly rather optimistic to expect someone to be able to do this for a foreign country. The training economists receive does not prepare them for the task and, in some ways, makes it more difficult. What usually happens is that the model the economist consciously or unconsciously uses turns out to be the sort of model suitable for a developed country. This common mistake of transference, which is encouraged by most economic textbooks, raises too many issues to discuss exhaustively here.[5] Suffice it to pose certain questions: does it make much difference to the model whether or not there is a capital-goods industry? Whether or not population growth is rapid? Whether or not supply conditions are generally elastic? Whether or not the level of activity depends (at least in the short run) mainly on the export industry? These questions point to essential features of analytical models in underdeveloped economies.

One of the mistakes due to transference must be mentioned—underestimating the importance of qualitative factors, which appear in the guise of short-period constraints. For example, the rate of industrial expansion depends in large degree on the supply of various types of skilled and supervisory labor. As another example, the transport system may have at some point a "bottleneck" (limited port capacity or a single-track railway) which imposes a ceiling on freight movement. Tinbergen has an ingenious device in his system to cope with this difficulty. He uses "boundary conditions" to specify limits outside of which the structural relations do not apply. It is possible, though often unwise, to ignore such contraints when working on the problems of developed economies, but to do so in underdeveloped economies is a serious error. The trouble is that the limiting values of simple structural relations (for example, linear relations connecting two variables) typically lie very close together, and outside these limits the functions change drastically.

In principle, one could develop the model by including more variables (say, by constructing functions for the supplies of different kinds of labor) and by allowing for all the boundary conditions, but I think it would be impossible in practice to choose the right functions and to quantify all the coefficients.

A fundamental difficulty is that historical evidence will be difficult to interpret due to institutional changes; for example, the import regime may have varied greatly in the period studied. What is more relevant here, the boundary conditions change as labor is trained, bridges are built, and the economy develops. In fact a developing economy alters

---

5. Some of them are discussed in my "An Approach to the Short-Period Analysis of Primary-Producing Economies," *Oxford Economic Papers* (February, 1959).

beyond recognition in a few years, so that average coefficients derived from figures for a decade or more may have little meaning. On the other hand, if one derives coefficients from *less* than a decade's experience, there is a danger of being seriously misled, unless the economy is very simple—for example, a petroleum economy. Short statistical series are affected by "irrelevant" influences, such as inventory changes, and it is analytically hard to separate trends in these series from cycles.

Another problem is the weakness of the statistics likely to be available. Among the commonest errors made by economists working abroad is to attempt to construct an elaborate model (for example, one incorporating multiple regressions), using statistical information which is poor, perhaps poorer than they can imagine, especially in the case of derived statistics.[6] Thus an increase of 5 per cent shown in the figure for real gross national product may be best interpreted in many countries as an indication that the product is rather more likely to have risen by a figure in the range from o to 10 per cent than either to have fallen, or to have risen by more than 10 per cent. The estimated rate of population growth, to take another fundamental variable, will reflect the varying degrees of efficiency of enumeration in different censuses. In fact, many of the more elegant models that have been devised for various underdeveloped countries are little better than fantasy.

It is also a mistake, however, to go to the other extreme and conclude that, when statistics are poor, quantitative analysis is impossible. In practice, one first looks closely at the methods of obtaining the statistics one uses (at the worksheets, if possible), assessing their worth and making any adjustments that will improve them (for example, dropping bad indicators from an index).[7] One then judges the shape of structural relations as best one can, supplementing what one can learn from official statistics with personal observation and study of the past history of the country concerned. This is not an easy professional task, but the end result can hardly be less useful as a guide to action than pure intuition.

### Policy Instruments

It is perhaps obvious that policy instruments will not have the same significance as in developed countries, because of the different institutions

---

6. Sir Robert Hall, formerly Chief Economic Adviser to the British government, pointed out in a discussion of the work of advisers that "it is extremely difficult to get the facts needed for economic analysis" and that economists, among others, were accustomed to generalize on insufficient evidence (*Oxford Economic Papers* [June, 1955], p. 127). This applies much more strongly in the case of underdeveloped economies.

7. The visitor therefore needs still another personal qualification, practical experience as a statistician.

to be found overseas. For instance, monetary policy will have a different content and a different degree of influence, if there is no organized bond market, if banks in the area are foreign owned and outside the scope of local monetary regulation, and if a large proportion of the national output is in the hands of foreign companies that raise their funds overseas.

What is more easily overlooked, qualitative policies and reforms of one kind or another are likely to be immediately feasible possibilities—for example, reform of the banking system, expansion of educational opportunities, or changes in the structure of land ownership. If existing institutions have to be taken as given, as they normally do in developed countries, problems may seem almost insoluble, in the sense that no policies can be devised for the known political objectives. However, the roots of institutions go less deep in underdeveloped economies, and institutional change is often on the agenda of current policy.

A third special consideration is that in a foreign country it is very hard to assess *all* the consequences of changes in both exogenous variables and policies. This appears to be merely restating the point that it is hard to construct satisfactory models; but the difficulty is particularly severe when projections are attempted, because growth will by definition take the economy into new areas, where income levels will be higher than before, and the socio-economic structure will certainly be changed, if not transformed. (The economist may have to refer, if he knows of it, to the experience of other countries at later stages of development.) Moreover, the total appraisal of all the likely effects of policy also poses once more the problem of weighting the aims of the government, and with greater sharpness, because some of the likely side-effects may not even have been considered by the political leadership.

Fourth, there is a common tendency to concentrate one's attention on requirements in the field of one's own specialty.[8] Thus an agricultural economist may put forward an irrigation program, the scale of which implies devoting an excessive share of available finance to the agricultural sector. Essentially, resources are very scarce, and it is not really relevant to say that it is worthwhile to spend $X millions in one sector, let alone one project. What one has to show is that the *total* yield (social and economic) of the last million in that sector would be at least as great as in any other. If one is not prepared to make a general analysis, therefore, one can only draw highly qualified conclusions.

Last, what is very often overlooked, particularly by those of the Left, is that instruments of policy are also subject to boundary conditions, and

---

8. I am grateful to Thomas Balogh for drawing my attention to this point.

that these conditions are rigorous in underdeveloped areas because of weaknesses in administration. To attempt strict import controls, for example, may only increase smuggling or corruption and demoralize the whole public service, reducing its total capacity to administer an economic program. Even if such limits do not hamper particular policies, they may restrict the combinations of policies that can be followed in various fields. Typically, there are two or three really good and selfless top administrators, and a score or so of capable young men, and these cannot be deployed on all fronts at the same time. It may be possible to tighten up income tax collection, *or* reorganize education, *or* operate import quotas, *or* expand public investment, *or* reform land tenure, *or* set up a statistical office, *or* nationalize the railways; one may even be able to do two or three of these things at the same time. But any economic program that implies doing them all simultaneously may prove to be just as unrealistic as one that requires, for example, more imports than can possibly be financed.

Then again certain values for policy instruments are just not politically practical (there is more discussion of this point below). These limits are very difficult for an outsider to judge.

It will readily be seen that the visitor who stays for only a few weeks (a fortiori, the person who works on a country's problems without visiting it) will be unable to make the necessary appraisal of the socio-economic structure and the capacity of the administration. Short-period visitors, therefore, however experienced and eminent, are very unlikely to be a success. They may even make the rather grotesque error of handing out quite sweeping recommendations that derive rather from ideological bias than from study of the local problem, recommendations such as "balance the budget," "control imports," or "unify the exchange rates." Some peripatetic economists prescribe the same medicine for all countries, whatever the symptoms. (In the medical profession, to do this is considered quackery.)

## POLITICAL MISTAKES

Economists who avoid all these errors, by dint of great skill and much careful study, may still be less than successful, and this for a reason which is perhaps less widely appreciated, namely, the failure to select the right role and to make this known to all concerned, including himself. An economist has to decide whether he will speak qua independent technician, qua political economist, qua supporter of a political party or regime, or qua active politician himself. These distinctions depend, as I shall try to show, on what types of consideration he takes into account.

To characterize oneself in this way may seem somewhat pedantic, and it may well be superfluous for an economist working at home. We all take up positions with more or less political involvement, according to temperament and according to the competence we feel in dealing with issues of policy. A man's colleagues know in time roughly what non-economic factors he considers relevant, and how much his remarks rest on unstated value judgments. They can, therefore, without conscious effort assess what he is saying. If he speaks from a political platform, it is generally supposed that he accepts the basic aims of the organization concerned and shares its views on what social factors are to be considered data and what are open to change by policy. It would not be very difficult for a fellow countryman to spot his general outlook even without such clues. The ability to "place" someone, not merely from what he says, including his accent and vocabulary, but also from his clothes and bearing, is one of the hallmarks of experience in public affairs.

There are several reasons why it is dangerous to ignore this question, even in work at home. In the first place, not everyone is in a position to classify the economist in this way; undergraduates find it especially difficult to do so. More important is the danger that the economist will make wrong assumptions about the social content of policy and not even realize what these assumptions are.

Be that as it may, there can be no doubt that the conscious and public definition of one's role is essential in work overseas. The audience, whether it is private or public, may lack the experience needed to interpret such clues, particularly in the case of a foreigner. Unless the visitor makes his position clear beyond doubt, people will not know how to interpret what he says, and they may attribute to him a political position he does not hold. Moreover, he may unconsciously fall into a number of procedural traps.

## The Four Types of Advisers

The best way of indicating what some of these traps are is to describe the roles open to an economist and then to look at the dangers involved in each of them.

There are broadly four possibilities. One method is to limit advice to specific technical questions. This means manipulating a single structural relation, or very few of them, and confining attention to narrow ranges of changes in the variables—for example, one could conclude that a rise in GNP of cap X per cent (X not being a large number) might be expected to induce various increases in the consumption of food, textiles, or petroleum, which imply certain predictable consequences for home production and imports. The economist working in this way could be called a "technical adviser."

Suppose he goes further than this and tries to indicate how the aims of the government could be achieved by using certain policy instruments, having made intelligent guesses about the more important characteristics of the economic and social structure and about the likely response of a number of variables to exogenous influences. He is then acting in a different capacity, which might be described as that of the "statesman adviser."

So far I have been talking of general policy aims in terms of the needs of the country; a politician will also be very much concerned about whether his party stays in office or, more generally, about the party's long-term future. There is no need for us to be cynical about this: power is, after all, seen by a politician as a necessary condition for achieving the objectives he considers important, and politicians in every country try to retain it. The importance of spending money in politically doubtful areas, the implications of reducing unemployment in the short period, the question of which industrialists in which industries are supporting the government—all are highly relevant for the party in power. These party-political factors are linked, by what might be considered additional structural relations, to social and economic factors. Even a dictatorship, or a government elected on a limited franchise, or a nominated colonial administration, has to concern itself with the degree of public consent to its policies and therefore has to ask itself the same questions or similar ones. (Power is never absolutely absolute.) Economists who align themselves so closely with the authorities that they take account of considerations of this type form a third category, which I shall call "party advisers." It is obvious that those who do this, consciously or otherwise, will give very different advice on economic problems from those who have accepted one of the two more restricted positions discussed previously.

Finally, any individual politician takes account not only of the party's interests but also of his own, such as preserving alliances within the party and protecting his own sphere of influence from other ministers, not to speak of more remote considerations like the friendships that he cultivates with leading citizens outside the government and even possibly in some cases his own financial stake in certain contracts. Very occasionally, one finds an economist who becomes in time the alter ego of a particular politician, able to indicate what the politician himself would think if he had some economic training. This role, of "personal adviser," is interesting mainly because it is the extreme case. All considerations relevant to the decision in the mind of the politician—whether "properly" so or not—are taken into account. The other possible roles that have been described limit the scope of the adviser's work in some way.

In practice, of course, the possibilities are not so easily distinguished as I have suggested. There are all sorts of intermediate positions. One, which is not uncommon, is that of working for a certain section of the government—economists may gravitate to this role when the government party is more or less permanently in power and covers a wide political range, like the administrations of Ghana, India, and Mexico. Nevertheless, to classify the four major possibilities in this way does help us to see the implications of the economist's decision on this issue, which is a fundamental one for his work.

### The Problem of Choosing a Role

The description of the possible roles makes it look as if the economist can simply choose whichever suits his own talents and interests, on the one hand, and the requirements of the problem, on the other. But the choice is in fact far from easy. It is naturally least difficult for a specialist, such as a transport economist, who has to deal with problems like whether a railway or a road should be built between two points. Even then, questions such as the adequacy of labor supply and how various areas will be affected make it necessary for him to take account of additional factors, both outside and within the field of economics. But the quandary is really severe for the general economist, including the specialist (such as those in public finance or banking), whose work demands, even if it does not always receive, analysis of the economy as a whole.

Many of these try to keep to a technical level of analysis too, leaving the reader to make his own assumptions on social aspects of the problem and to draw his own conclusions on policy. Although there is a great deal to be said for such restraint, one of its limitations is that a report has little effect in an economically backward country, especially a small country, unless the politicians pay attention to it. Unfortunately, a government that asks for an economic adviser often hopes to receive a *deus ex machina,* who will alight from an airplane and produce sweeping and painless remedies (just as a patient may have the same hopes from consulting a medical specialist). In newly independent countries, what the politicians sometimes want is not so much an economist as another, more experienced, politician. Even those with lower expectations will probably find a purely technical report on matters of general policy disappointing. In any case, an economist who insists he is only a technician may be disbelieved, possibly not without reason; the government may come to the conclusion, especially if they dislike the report's implications, that this is just a pose to cover what is really opposition, or even foreign intervention.

But a more weighty reason for eschewing this role is that it is really not a satisfactory way of working. As was pointed out in the previous section, even apparently technical questions such as choosing variables considered significant, deciding what ranges for these variables are plausible, and assessing the scope for policy, raise issues which are fundamentally social and political. To leave out of one's analysis the distribution of income say, or the degree of urbanization is equivalent to a statement that they are irrelevant. To assume a constant savings ratio in a projection is tantamont to saying that one despairs of changing it. To omit from the range of possible policies a capital gains tax, or a land reform, or the nationalization of electricity companies, almost comes to the same thing as recommending against their adoption.

In this respect, we cannot, at least without specifically defending our procedure, use the same way of working as we would in developed countries. There is some general agreement in the United Kingdom or the United States on what variables are relevant for a particular discussion, and what policy alternatives are worth exploring. Overseas, there is much more latitude, and as soon as one selects, one introduces nontechnical considerations.

Although a visiting economist can hardly hope to maintain a strictly "technical" role, any other is certainly difficult, because a person working in a foreign country is in a very weak position to assess the socio-economic structure, for reasons given above. It is hard for him to avoid making the same social and political assumptions as he does at home.

One problem for those who do look beyond purely technical considerations is that they may decide that the government's whole approach is wrong. It is, for example, not much use for an economist to spend a large portion of his time making proposals which implicitly or explicitly run counter to an industrialization policy, if that policy is something on which the government is determined. Nor is it much good to insist continually on the need for social reforms which a government is evidently unwilling or unable to carry out. In many parts of the world expatriate economists are brooding in bitter isolation for this reason, unconsulted, and even in some cases denied the use of an office. Former colonial administrators who have taken to working in independent countries (not a small class) are sometimes in this position. It requires a big adjustment for someone who has helped impose policy to work in an environment where he has to accept other people's objectives. Jöhr and Singer argue, I thing rightly, that an economist must be able to identify himself, at least reasonably closely, with the aims of the political leader he is advising, and that it is unprincipled to accept, even hypothetically, objectives of which one fundamentally disapproves. The corollary is that it is better to pack up and go than to work in a completely uncongenial environment.

Most economists, however, find they can accept, at least for the sake of argument, the economic philosophy of the host government—after all, they go to a country knowing more or less what to expect. Some go precisely because they are attracted by this philosophy. Yet there are also problems, though different ones, for those who are more committed, politically speaking. They are not always completely trusted by their host, and on their side all sorts of personal reasons discourage too close an association. Those employed by national or international organizations may fear the effect on their careers, and they may worry whether it will harm their employers if they get involved in local politics. What will happen if there is a change of regime, or even a major change of policy? So they often hover between the positions I have called "statesman adviser" and "party adviser."

But an ambivalent status is not a comfortable one. A foreign adviser may be the named target of part of the press, yet the government may not feel any responsibility for defending him or helping him preserve an independent status. Sometimes, in fact, economists in this position are thrown to the wolves to appease the opposition; those with little experience of public affairs rarely survive the cut-and-thrust of party politics.

The difficulties of fully accepting the role of party adviser are by no means insignificant either. In the first place, once an economist has identified himself to a certain degree with the party in power, there is a tendency for others to suspect everything he says. But more important are the basic problems of political involvement. The economist who attends cabinet meetings, or even just speaks regularly to the politicians, is in one way or another continually saying what policy *ought* to be. Those who adopt the roles of technical adviser or statesman adviser may do this too, but they are not compelled to. They can simply point out the likely consequences of various courses of action.

Not everyone will feel that it is fundamentally wrong to make value judgments—this is itself a value judgment. Jöhr and Singer think it is not merely the right but the duty of an economist to recommend certain policies. It is "the completion of his task."[9] Das Gupta is of the same opinion: "It is not enough for the economic adviser to suggest means to attain given ends. He has not merely to diagnose; he has also to prescribe."[10] This is perhaps a matter of personal disposition when an economist is talking about his own country's problems (the case these writers have in mind). But there is a radical difference if he is working abroad, as is assumed here.

---

9. *Op. cit.*, p. 71.
10. *Economic Weekly*, July, 1961.

The above discussion, cursory though it is, indicates how hard it is to grasp the whole social and economic process of a foreign country, and to acquire a "feel" for local politics. In any case, to make value judgments about policy in a foreign country seems to me particularly questionable. One reason is that many of the major issues of policy involve deciding how "pro-Western" or "anti-Western" to be—for example, which countries to approach for loans, whether to limit remittances of profits out of a country, and whether to nationalize foreign assets. It is hardly possible to maintain true professional objectivity when such issues arise, and quite impossible to avoid the suspicion of bias.

Another reason is that weighting political objectives is an inescapable necessity, for the reasons given above. It is often argued that to choose which of various means will best achieve a given end, or a given set of ends, does not in itself imply making a value judgment. In practice, however, to choose between means is to make value judgments, apart from those implied in the ends themselves.[11]

Let us take the case where the end specified is to maximize agricultural production; expropriation of large landowners has quite different implications (for income distribution, for the balance of political power, and so on) than land taxation, or an extension of agricultural credit, or the provision of educational facilities in rural areas. This is especially true if one allows for possible long-run consequences—once social change is set in motion, it acquires its own momentum. Similarly, to adopt a policy of monetary stabilization implies a willingness to accept not only a short-term sacrifice of potential output, but also possibly a greater inequality in income distribution and a strengthening of political opposition, with all *its* implications. The final decision on which is the best out of the various sets of expected economic and political consequences is a matter for a politician, not an economist, particularly a foreign economist.[12]

These various difficulties are even more noticeable in the case of the personal adviser I mentioned above. Only rarely is the economist acting in this capacity successful. When he does succeed, he may achieve more than someone who strictly avoids political associations. But he is more

11. Cf. E. A. G. Robinson, in his foreword to the work of Jöhr and Singer: "There is one problem of the establishment of aims that I would stress rather more than Professor Jöhr has done: the extreme difficulty of distinguishing aims or ends from means" (*op. cit.*, p. vii).

12. These considerations imply that, even if it is not improper for foreign governments and international agencies to require certain policies to be adopted, as a condition for financial assistance, it is very difficult for them to decide what the policies should be, and it may well prove unwise to impose such conditions.

vulnerable, and if he has been provided under an assistance program, his position is still more equivocal vis-à-vis the organization that employs him. It is true that he can be withdrawn by his employers if the balance of political power alters, but this still leaves them associated to some extent with a political regime, and one which has lost office.

## CONCLUSIONS

There is no general solution to this problem. The foreign adviser may well find that there is no role that is professionally reputable and at the same time politically satisfactory to the host government. The inescapable dilemma is that governments normally expect a visiting economist to do what he simply cannot manage, namely, to provide recommendations that take account of a social and economic environment which is quite strange to him.

The above analysis does, however, suggest one or two ways in which the risk of failure can be reduced. First, it is helpful if the "host" government and the visitor check up on each other before any contract is signed. (It is surprising how rarely this is done.) Second, the visitor is more likely to find technical and political success mutually compatible if he fully grasps that he is working in a completely different environment and if he faces the need to take account of factors outside the scope of his usual work. In the third place, it is surely best in the long run to make quite clear one's status *and its limitations* whatever the temptations to do otherwise (it may seem quite intoxicating to be near to the center of power). This means stating and restating (at least in a general way) one's assumptions.

The discussion above also suggests that the real and permanent solution of this problem requires something more far-reaching. Economists would be in a stronger position to work overseas if professional training provided a better preparation for such work. They particularly need to be taught to appraise and use statistical material (not just "statistical methods") and to recognize the geographical limitations of the models described or assumed in textbooks and lectures. It would also help if some system could be devised by which those who worked in universities could spend large portions of their professional careers overseas, more than just sabbatical leave and vacation journeys. A corps of professional economists with international experience would thus be built up—and incidentally this would help to improve university teaching along the lines indicated above.

To close on a more encouraging note, I should add that the visiting economist can still achieve a great deal by showing what is involved in various lines of policy that interest the authorities, by pointing out obvious errors in economic arguments, and by indicating what kinds of choices have to be faced if economic policies in various fields are to be mutually consistent. He can make statements relevant to policy decisions, and these statements are of a type that can only be made by an economist and that usually badly need making, particularly in big economies.[13]

In fact, a visitor can achieve a great deal merely by asking the right sort of question. Even if he is, for one of the several reasons mentioned above, a failure, in the sense that his report has no effect and his advice is ignored, an economist has a considerable impact on the people he works with. Conversations with politicians and officials, especially informal ones, can show them new ways of looking at economic affairs. I have known cases where the main achievement of an economist, but not a negligible one, has been simply to let a minister think aloud about his problems and bring to the surface his real motives and his judgments on social and economic policy; the economist can carry out the function of a psychotherapist. Stimulation of younger officials may be even more important in the long run; and merely by requesting data a visitor can help to bring about a big improvement in official statistics. Add to this the effects of contacts with local university teachers and students and the broadening of the economist's own outlook (not to speak of the respite from his usual duties), and his journey may be thoroughly justified whatever happens to his report and to his recommendations.

---

13. In very small economies, such as those with a gross national product of less than $100 million, the economist's contribution is smaller, because such interconnections are obvious to anyone.

# Elites and Development

THE FINAL ARTICLES in this section, and in this volume, ask a crucial question: from which social group will emerge the leadership to evoke and organize the latent energies of a population? It is almost tautological to say that underdeveloped countries are short of dedicated political leaders, risk-taking businessmen, and efficient administrators. This is but another way of saying that a characteristic of backwardness is the absence of strong elite groups both within and outside government. When these groups begin to emerge, economic development becomes feasible. It is by no means clear how these elites can be fostered and indeed in which social or occupational group they are most likely to be located.

The distinguished sociologist, Edward Shils, finds one such elite group in the military. His essay is a careful evaluation of their influence and potential as agents of economic development. The military career, it emerges from his analysis, is one of the more promising avenues of social mobility for the ambitious poor boy, much as the Church offered in the Middle Ages the promise of power and influence even to the boy of lowly birth. Professor Benda's discussion of the intellectuals identifies another key group and explains why intellectuals frequently fail as administrators and political leaders. Professor Eckstein's essay is an analysis of the relative roles of state and private entrepreneurs in economic advance. He reaches the somewhat paradoxical conclusion that a larger role for the state at the beginning of accelerated economic growth will permit private entrepreneurs to operate more confidently and more effectively in the subsequent phases of economic development. Professor Eckstein thus identifies two rival sources of economic entrepreneurship: the state and the private capitalist. He assigns more importance to the private capitalist than does Myrdal and less than does Bauer.

# Edward Shils

## The Military in the Political
## Development of the New States

OF THE MORE than thirty states acquiring sovereignty since the end of
the Second World War, the military forces have played an important
political role in at least ten. In only a few of the new states did the
armed forces, mostly as guerrilla formations, play a significant role in
attaining independence. In Israel, Cyprus, and the successor states of
Indo-China, guerrilla armies were very important in leading the British
and the French to grant independence to these countries. In Indonesia
and Burma, the guerrilla forces created during the Japanese occupation
played a modest and by no means decisive part in the liberation of their
countries from foreign rule. In at least six of the new states, the military,
although of no great moment in the attainment of sovereignty, has taken
a central position in the political life of the country. Pakistan, Iraq,
Sudan, the United Arab Republic, and the Republic of Korea are now
under military rule. In Jordan, such security as the monarchy enjoys rests
on the army. In Burma, the army insisted on its right to govern for
many months; in Indonesia, the army and the President are balanced
in a relationship of mutual distrust and dependence; in Lebanon, the
army deliberately refrained from participation in the fitful civil war, and
ultimately the care of the public weal was taken over by a general. In
India, notable among all the new states for the stable subordination of
the military to the civil power, one of the major political crises of recent
years broke out over the alleged efforts of the Defense Minister to
politicize the army. In the Congo, the mutiny in the ranks of the Force
Publique shattered the regime, and such international support as the
feeble government of M. Adoula has possessed rests on the tolerance of
the fragmentarily reconstituted army.

In Latin America, the armed forces historically have played a role
similar to that of the military in many of the new states of Asia and
Africa. The older, better-established states of the West and the Communist states disclose a rather different relationship between the military
and the civil sectors of the elite. In most of these countries, the military
has considerable influence over foreign and defense policy, but it plays

393

very little part in domestic policy or its administration. In the United States and France, respectively, General Eisenhower has held and General de Gaulle now holds the highest position of state, but neither their incumbency nor their administration was the intended result of actions of the armed forces. Even Germany, where the glory of the warrior was more prized than in other Western countries and where the army contributed to the downfall of the Weimar Republic, was never ruled by the army in the way that so many of the new states have been ruled during their brief existence.

How are we to account for this prominence of the military in Asian and African societies where, on the whole, martial accomplishments have not headed the list of public virtues and where, with a few exceptions, the military has not distinguished itself on the battlefield? The ascendancy of the military in the domestic life of these states has been a response to the difficulties which the new states have encountered in their efforts to establish themselves as modern sovereignties. Yet a newly autonomous regime need not inevitably yield, sooner or later, to rule by the military. The fact that it has in the new states is evidence that there are weaknesses in them which are not compensated by those political institutions which were inherited or established at the moment of independence. These political institutions were mainly parliamentary, more or less democratic, and liberal. Military rule is one of several practicable and apparently stable alternatives when parliamentary, democratic regimes falter. The inherited and the newly engendered obstacles over which these regimes have been stumbling are more determinative than the aspirations of the military elites of these states, although the latter are not unimportant. We shall, therefore, focus our inquiry on the political and intellectual elites of the new states, examining their political skills as well as the inherited culture and social structure which they attempt to govern and transform in their pursuit of modernity.

There are very few states today which do not aspire to modernity. Not all of them, and not all the sectors of their elites, pursue each of the constituent elements of modernity with equal vigor and zeal. Nonetheless, in practically every new state, the drive toward modernity is a major factor in the country's public life. The leaders of both old and new states feel a pressing necessity to espouse policies that will modernize their nations.

Among the elites of the new states, to be "modern" means to be dynamic, concerned with the people, democratic and egalitarian, scientific, economically advanced, sovereign, and influential. The elites must range themselves against the *ancien régime* of landlords, sheikhs, chiefs, rajahs, and grand viziers in both the old and the constitutional forms. Even when they affirm the past of their country, they must stress its adaptability to present needs.

Modernity entails democracy, and democracy in the new states, even where it is not representative, must above all be egalitarian. To the elites of the new states, modernity therefore entails the dethronement of the rich and the traditionally privileged. It involves breaking up large private estates, especially those which are owned by absentee landlords. It involves universal suffrage, even where the suffrage is exercised through the acclamation of a single-party ticket. It requires breaking the power of traditional interests of chiefs, sultans, and priests; and replacing monarchies by republics, which often maintain a similar concentration of authority. Modernity demands universal public education and equality of access to opportunities for entering into the more influential and better-rewarded positions with which even an egalitarian regime cannot dispense. To be a "modern" democracy implies, according to the prevailing conception in the new states, that the rulers should be answerable to the people for their actions. Where the rulers are not in fact so answerable, through a legislature which is popularly and periodically elected, then they allege that they exercise a stewardship on behalf of the people, and that they are answerable to the collective will—that higher will which is more real than the empirical will of their people.

To be modern is to be scientific. This means, in principle, that a modern state sets its face against such superstitious practices as divination, magic, and astrology as guides in policy-making. The elites usually claim to believe that progress rests on rational technology, and ultimately on scientific knowledge. Hence, progress involves the promotion of scientific research and the utilization of its results for the common good. Education is commonly regarded as one way of diffusing the scientific outlook among the new generation, of breaking the hold of traditional beliefs and of the traditional privileges associated with them.

The proponents of modernity—elites and counterelites—assert that no country is modern unless it is economically advanced or progressive. To be advanced economically means to be industrialized and to have a high standard of living. No country can aspire to modernity and ignore its economic improvement. All this requires planning, employing economists and statisticians, conducting surveys, controlling the rates of saving and investment, controlling imports and foreign exchange, constructing new factories, building roads and harbors, developing railways, irrigation schemes, fertilizer production, agricultural research, forestry research, etc. These call for modern techniques of administration. To the elites of the new states, modernity seems often to call for the primacy of technology, of a technological outlook, and of persons with technological training. Technology is associated with efficiency in administration and, above all, with honesty. Corruption in administration is a constant preoccupation of counterelites, to whom it is the hallmark of both the old regime and its heirs.

Modernity requires national sovereignty, which, in the minds of its supporters, presupposes the existence of a nation which rules itself through indigenous organs and persons. With or without representative institutions, the modern sovereign state is held to embody the essence of its society. National sovereignty means not only autonomy, but also an influential and respected place as a modern nation on the world stage. The elites are extremely sensitive to their country's status among their neighbors and in the world at large, and particularly to any slights or humiliations.

"Modern" means being Western without depending on the West. The model of modernity is a picture of the West detached in some way from its geographical setting; it permits Soviet Russia and China to affirm ideals with a Western content while they remain politically and emotionally anti-Western.

The new states are not yet modern. The states of Western Europe and of North America (and the English-speaking dominions of the British Commonwealth) need not *aspire* to modernity. They *are* modern. Modernity is part of their very nature. The image of the Western countries and the partial incorporation and transformation of that image in the Soviet Union provide the standards and models in whose light the elites of the new states of Asia and Africa seek to reshape themselves.

The new states are "non-Western." They are Asian and African states. Not all the states of Asia and Africa are new: Japan is not, nor are China, Liberia, Iran, Afghanistan, Ethiopia, and Thailand. These states have enjoyed sovereignty for a long time. The South American states are not new; they too have had their sovereignty for a long time, although for the most part they have not become modern. They exist in an intermediate zone between the modern, longer-established states and the unmodern new states.

Indonesia, Malaya, Burma, India, Ceylon, Pakistan, Iraq, the United Arab Republic, Lebanon, Jordan, Israel, Cyprus, Saudi Arabia, Sudan, Somalia, Morocco, Tunisia, Libya, Cambodia, Laos, Viet-Nam, Ghana, Guinea, the Philippines, the Republic of Korea, Mali, Senegal, the Republic of the Congo and the Congo Republic, Chad, Upper Volta, Ivory Coast, Niger and Nigeria, Madagascar, Mauritania, Gabon, Kuwait, and Tanganyika are all new states. Their acquisition of sovereignty is either relatively recent or just now occurring. Their societies are old and governed by tradition. The states which rule them, however, are more or less recent creations, even in those areas where independent sovereign status once existed. They are the results of the recession of Western imperialism.

The new states of Asia and Africa have the following properties in common:

a) They have recently acquired independent sovereignty after a substantial period of foreign, predominantly Western rule; their indigenous machinery of government is of fairly recent origin.

b) Their social structure, economy, and culture are, on the whole, highly traditional. Above all, their central political traditions do not include those of democratic, representative constitutional government.

c) Significant sections of their elites are concerned to transform the society, the culture, and the political life and outlook of these societies; they aspire to modernity.

The confluence of these three properties defines the new states as a significant category.[1]

## THE DETERMINANTS OF POLITICAL DEVELOPMENT

The institutions of government, central and auxiliary, with which the new states have begun their sovereign careers are being resisted by the old societies which they must govern and they are being pulled by the ideal of modernity. In this process, the old societies and the ideal of modernity are both changing, but in so doing they are pressing hard against governmental institutions.

The resultant political order interests us here. Thus, we shall survey the stock of available resources in social structure, cultural tradition, and human qualities and skills with which this journey toward modernity is being undertaken. We shall also try to estimate the influence that these resources exert on the survival of the political regime which commences the journey and on the form which the regime might assume as the journey advances, hesitates, or stops. More particularly, we shall

---

1. New states are not alone in most of their problems. For example, long-established states, such as Ethiopia or Thailand, are characterized by the traditionality of their social structure; and many states with a long history of continuous sovereignty are the scene of conflict between attachment to tradition and the drive toward modernity. Almost all countries outside Western Europe and possibly the United States experience the culture tension between metropolis and province. Numerous problems in the new states are instances of more general classes of problems which are shared by many states, Western and non-Western, new and old, advanced and underdeveloped, sovereign and colonial. The new states present, however, a unique *constellation* of problems.

attempt to estimate their influence on the emergence and subsequent fortunes of a militarily dominated regime.

## SOCIAL STRUCTURE

### Kinship, Territory, and Community

In the societies of the new states, although to very unequal degrees, the status of a human being is very much a function of his kinship and—in certain societies—of his caste and his linguistic community. These things stand in the way of the ordinary man's becoming a citizen and of the elite's ruling on behalf of the whole community. The rural kinship system and, where it exists, the caste system obstruct the entry of the rural mass into the citizenry of the modern nation, for they confine the loyalties of the ordinary man to a narrow, locally circumscribed range. By the same token, they favor the emergence of leaders who serve these parochial interests.

Parochial loyalties hinder the workings of the rule of law; deviations from the rule of law in favor of one related to the official or judge by kinship or locality cause the lower classes to feel that the government is corrupt. As a result, the "political gap" between rulers and ruled becomes a major fact of life and a challenge to every modern type of polity.

The parochialism of kinship, caste, and locality makes it difficult to create stable and coherent nation-wide parties. Parties tend to become cliques or aggregations of bosses and their clients. Insofar as the regime operates within a more or less democratic constitution and is not dominated by the one great party of national independence, the government tends to be an uneasy coalition of sectional interests. Even the Congress-like party of independence shows signs of parochial interest once the goal of independence has been attained and particularly when nationalist enthusiasm begins to fade.

When a government is considered to represent particular kinship, caste, or local interests, each section of society is fearful of being exploited and suppressed by others. The effectiveness of government is thereby weakened. Yet to accredit themselves, the governments of the new states must be effective and strong enough to satisfy some of the demands made of them. If they fumble or seem to favor their own caste or community, they alienate the politically sensitive section of the society and thus accentuate the gap between government and governed.

### Class Structure

The economic and social "underdevelopment" of the new states of Asia and Africa is manifested in the size and structure of the urban middle classes. The small retail traders are largely illiterate, with little modern culture and few modern economic skills. In many new states, the larger enterprisers in commerce and finance are ethnically distinct from the rest of the population: e.g., the Chinese in Southeast Asia; the Indians in East Africa; the Syrians and Lebanese in West Africa; the Scotsmen, Englishmen, and Americans in India, Ceylon, and Pakistan, etc.; and within the Indian population in Calcutta and Bombay, the special communities—such as Marwaris and Parsis—in industry, commerce, and finance. There is an under-representation of modern middle-class professionals, i.e., university teachers, school teachers, physicians, scientists, engineers, nurses, agronomists, chemists, etc. This is a result partly of the economy of the new states, which affords few opportunities in the tertiary occupations, and partly of the long preemption of the best of these posts by Europeans, as well as of the continued dependence on expatriates for many professional services of a more specialized sort. Lower-level civil servants, clerks in commercial firms, and lawyers constitute a disproportionately large share of the more or less educated urban middle classes of the new states. As primarily peasant societies, the new states also lack a stratum of highly skilled industrial workers and of lower-level supervisory workers.

The gulf that separates the most powerful and the most wealthy (foreign businessmen, plutocrats, the wealthier lawyers and doctors, high civil servants, and leading politicians) from the least powerful and the poorest leads the mass of the population, and especially the politically interested middle class—if it is not among the chief beneficiaries of the incumbent government—to believe that the government acts almost exclusively on behalf of the wealthy.

Though occupation and wealth are increasingly significant criteria of status in the societies of the new states, they are by no means the only ones. Kinship, caste, and religious attachment are others, but the new ones are growing in importance in the "modern sectors" of the population. Their growth will intensify still further the differences between the rich and the poor and will supplement caste, linguistic, and ethnic considerations as obstacles to the formation of a comprehensive consensus.

The resentments that these inequalities generate are less overtly expressed than in Western countries. The new states lack the organized infra-structure necessary for their effective expression. Also, there is such a tradition of hierarchy in these societies that the expression of hostility tends to be inhibited much of the time.

Resentments, however, are bound to grow as the new states become more urbanized—as they certainly will become in the course of economic development and administrative expansion. The gap in the newly forming class structure will be transformed into hostility through the "politicization" engendered by universal suffrage. As class consciousness becomes more pronounced, the extreme economic inequality of the societies of the new states is likely to have disruptive consequences. Because there are still few traditions of *disciplined* class conflict in the new states and because the infra-structural institutions through which such conflict can be conducted are still very poorly developed (i.e., the trade-union movement, collective bargaining machinery, etc.), class conflict in the new states might well become more violent than in the older, better established political societies of the West.

How does this type of class structure affect the conduct of the military vis-à-vis the political order? In societies like those of the Middle East, with few opportunities for social mobility, in which the economies are not rapidly expanding and in which there is no corresponding increase in educational opportunities in the posts in the tertiary sector, the army tends to recruit into its officer ranks the brightest and most ambitious young men of the small towns and countryside. These young men often come from the families of petty traders, small craftsmen, and cultivators of small holdings. Like their fathers, they are aware of the distance separating them from the rich and the political elite. Thus there is brought into a potentially powerful position in society a body of intelligent, ambitious young men, equipped with a modicum of modern technical education but with little sense of identity with politicians and big businessmen.

Where, on the contrary, the economy expands rapidly and where there is a corresponding increase in chances for social ascent in the civilian sphere, the military is less likely to attract such a large proportion of the more vigorous and more gifted. Hence, the likelihood of a stratum of young officers, resentful against the established order and isolated from its leading spokesmen, is diminished.

### Educational Structure

*The uneducated:* The gap in the structure of territorial loyalty and in the class structure is paralleled by a wide divergence in the styles of life and the associated outlooks of those with a modern (Western) education and those without it. Nothing is quite comparable to this in Western countries, where the least and best educated share the same language and, to some extent, an attachment to certain important symbols.

It is not so much what education teaches as it is the fact that the experience of having been to school, especially in countries with a steeply graded system of social stratification and a tradition of the superiority of religious education, gives people an enhanced feeling of their own value.

It makes them feel themselves to be closer to the center of the larger society. Correspondingly, those who are not educated tend to feel inferior.

The continuation of the traditional modes of education leaves the ordinary person apathetic to what goes on outside his kinship group and locality. Thus, links which would relate the mind to symbols of the wider world, and unite local and kinship groups with the national society, are prevented from forming. Illiteracy restricts the capacity for rendering thoughtful judgment on national issues. It fortifies the belief that the government at the center is alien to the ordinary man and is interested only in maintaining and enriching itself.

\* \* \* \* \*

## CONCLUDING OBSERVATIONS

No new state can modernize itself, and remain or become liberal and democratic, without an elite possessing force of character, intelligence, and a very complex set of high moral qualities.

The path toward modernization is uncertain; the arrival, uncertain. Nor is it possible to retrace one's steps. Countries may never succeed in becoming modern, but they can never return to a traditional society or polity. A state which, however minimally, advances toward modernity, through organizing a modern army and through establishing modern intermediate and higher educational institutions, has irreversibly turned its back on the traditional oligarchic alternative. Technically trained and professionally formed young officers will be impatient with the slovenliness of the regime of traditional oligarchy, with its combination of indolent oligarchy, mass apathy, and poverty. The students and graduates of modern higher educational institutions, however poor their intellectual quality, are provided with ideas of modernity whose force stems from impulses of adolescent rebellion against a repressive traditional and oligarchic society. If, as is often the case, the economy is too poor to find appropriate posts for them, they dominate "public opinion" and become the agents of an incessant turbulence which no mixture of traditionality and oligarchy can withstand.

It is easier not to go back than to go forward. Going forward requires the closing of the gap. There can be no truly modern society until there is a greater measure of active unity between the mass of the society and its leaders than exists today in any of the new states. At present, the new states are extremely heterogeneous ethnically and culturally. Particularistic religious traditions are powerful among them, and kinship and stratification make for narrow loyalties. Nationalism, on the other hand, tends to be enthusiastic and dynamic rather than civil, leading politicians into demagogy and away from the people. Nearly all the new states confront a vastly preponderant peasant majority which, if it is not apathetic and withdrawn into its own parochial life, is quietly indifferent or actively resistant to efforts to make it conform to the model the politicians hold before it.

The closure of this gap between the modernizing elite and the mass of the population is the prerequisite of the creation of a political society, of a society which is modern not only in its economy and administration but in its moral order as well.

Oligarchic regimes can tolerate the gap more easily than political democracies because they demand little but acclamation from the masses, and much of that can be fabricated on demand. The greater readiness of the oligarchic regimes to use coercion also contributes to this ostensible closure of the gap. The actual closure, however, is probable only in a regime of civilian rule, representative institutions and public liberties. The movement toward its closure can probably occur only in some variant of tutelary democracy, with the external appearance of political democracy, or of a modernizing oligarchy, or of some new form, as yet unknown. The regime of civilian rule, public liberties, and representative government is built around a wide diffusion of initiative and independence of action and judgment. The traditional order entails the concentration or utter absence of these qualities; and in this it is at one with oligarchy. This seems to indicate that the survival or emergence of political democracy is less probable than that of oligarchy. Oligarchy is more compatible with the traditional order because it suffers less than democracy from the reality of the gap. Political democracy is, in many respects, discontinuous with the substantive content of the traditions, i.e., with what these traditions transmit. The much larger amount of voluntary assent and widely dispersed initiative which the regime of representative government and public liberties requires will not be so easily forthcoming in the new states.

The political virtues required for oligarchy are fewer and less demanding on the moral and intellectual powers of a considerable part of the population—including both rulers and ruled. Oligarchy depends, far more than democracy, on the ability of the elite to use organized coercion where necessary; it can tolerate, and even benefit from, apathy in other spheres and at other times. However, a modernizing oligarchy that is nationalistic in outlook requires, for its self-legitimation, a unitary public will which can be activated at the command of the elite. It is doubtful whether this can really be produced by the means available to any known oligarchy.

Totalitarianism depends on organized force at the center and demands enthusiastic conformity in untraditional practices in a large part of the society. There is no reason to believe that a totalitarian oligarchy can create this social unity better than any other type of regime can. It can undoubtedly create the *appearance* of unity better than a more democratic regime can, but it cannot do any better in the creation of the reality.

The present low level of the development of individuality in the new states is more congenial to oligarchic than to democratic regimes. Oligarchic regimes which try to create a unified national might gain the further benefit of the rather uncommon conversion phenomenon of the leap from the preindividual condition of primordiality to the transindividual condition of extreme nationalism. On the other hand, oligarchic regimes which affront the sense of integrity of kinship and local territorial groups by attempting to coerce them simultaneously generate a withdrawal from national symbols, and thus enlarge and stabilize the gap.

Democratic regimes are more likely to arouse individuality and gain more from it than any of the oligarchic alternatives. In the long run, only a regime of representative institutions and public liberties can cure the oppositional mentality while avoiding withdrawal into apathy.

The oppositional mentality, however, is more inimical to the regimes of political and of tutelary democracy than it is to oligarchic regimes. The latter can repress the bearers of the oppositional mentality, whereas democratic regimes cannot do so with the same constitutional ease. The burden of the transformation rests upon the elite. Its chances for success rest on its capacity for self-restraint and its effectiveness in legitimating itself through modernizing achievement, through a due respect for the claims of traditional beliefs, and through its recruitment of intellectuals who can reinterpret traditional beliefs, adapt them to modern needs, and translate them into a modern idiom.

Are such elites now in existence?

Almost every new state except India, Ghana, Nigeria, the Sudan, and perhaps Tunisia is defective in the quality of its civil servants. All except India, and possibly Nigeria, Sierra Leone, and Tanganyika are very short of politicians devoted to parliamentary institutions and skilled in working with them. Of those with substantial indigenous armies, only India has succeeded in inculcating the army with civil loyalty or in maintaining the tradition formed during foreign rule.

India has a large, relatively well-educated middle class and a very competent higher civil service. The civil arm of its government has established an unquestioned ascendancy over the military arm. Its small—perhaps too small—corps of politicians are devoted to parliamentary procedures. Not least important, a rudimentary political society exists. With these qualifications, India has a better chance than any other new state of stabilizing its present regime of civilian rule, representative institutions, and public liberties. It, too, will undoubtedly make some compromise with tutelary democracy.

But even the country with the best chance will probably not succeed in attaining the level set by the model it holds before its eyes. No state ever does. In the new states of Asia and Africa, the chances of realizing any of the models—which took form in other cultures and under different economic and social conditions—seem to be even less.

The likelihood of any oligarchic alternatives fulfilling themselves in the new states is not unqualifiedly good. At the extreme, they demand things most unlikely to be realized, namely, a high degree of mobilization of wills around a single set of symbols, great exertion, and great efficiency. Even if these countries were to be satisfied with the restricted and more realistic program of totalitarian oligarchy—and hence settle for coerced order, the security of their power, and rapid economic development—they would probably be disappointed. The efficiency on which a totalitarian oligarchy prides itself is likely to encounter great obstacles at every level of society, and ruthlessness will be no substitute for it. Ruthlessness might create an impression of discipline, but it does not beget efficient action on behalf of the goals set by the regime.

In a sense, the regime of political and tutelary democracy, which seems to demand so much from men, actually offers a more realistic settlement with the slowly tractable realities of the traditional societies of the new states. If democracy can be understood in a partial sense, in which representative institutions function limpingly—even more limpingly than in the West—and public liberties are maintained, it is entirely possible that, among the alternative models, some form of democracy has, in the long run, the best chance of surviving. But even then, in the coming decades it will have to make significant concessions to the gap. It will survive only if the elite has a very powerful will to be democratic—only if it is willing to be the teacher and parent of democracy in a society which by its nature does not incline in that direction—and if, furthermore, it gets enough of the right kind of assistance from abroad.

The alternatives are oligarchies. The military variety, which promises to maintain order and—as an afterthought—to modernize, does so only by sweeping the disorder temporarily into a box from which it recurrently springs in full strength. The civilian oligarchy, which strives for larger programs, achieves a little in spurts, and between spurts sprawls in disorder and oppressiveness. The totalitarian oligarchy, by the ruthlessness of its elite and by the vigor of its party machine, as well as by the organizational and material aid which it would get from the Soviet Union, would appear to have the best chance of maintaining itself once it has got into power. But it, too, would have to compromise markedly with the human materials which traditional society gives it. It could build industrial monuments and suppress open dissatisfaction, but it could not realize its ideal.

None of the alternatives, as they have been presented here or as their proponents in the new states think of them, has much chance of being fully realized. There is a large realm of disorder between traditionality and modernity, and in this area, in the midst of sloth and squalor, occasional outbursts of progressive action occur. In the compromises which reality will impose on the struggle between tradition and modernity, this third or middle possibility will undoubtedly intrude prominently.

In trying to understand the prospects of the new states, we should not neglect the postindependence experiences of the Latin-American states. However, the new states of Africa and Asia exist in a period of more rapid communications. They also exist at a time when the images of the Western democracies and of the Soviet Union are more forcibly and vividly impressed on the minds of their intellectuals than were the liberal constitutional models of Europe on the minds of those who created the new states of Latin America.

There is no straight and easy road to the city of modernity. Whatever the main road chosen, there will be many tempting and ruinous side roads; there will be many marshes and wastes on either side, and many wrecked aspirations will lie there, rusting and gathering dust. Those who arrive at the city will discover it to be quite different from the destination which they and their ancestors originally sought. Yet, some roads are better than others; some destinations are better than others. Even if none is perfect and none corresponds to the voyagers' hope on starting, some of the destinations will turn out to have been worth the travail, worth the efforts of the voyagers and of their friends who helped them on their way.

*Harry J. Benda*

## Non-Western Intelligentsias as Political Elites

In the course of the past century, the non-western world has experienced a series of revolutionary changes, most, if not all, of them caused by the impact of western civilization on the traditional societies of Asia, Africa and the Middle East (and to some lesser extent also of Latin America). Since 1914, political evolution has proceeded at an accelerated rate, leading in recent times to the creation of new political, national entities, either by internal revolution or by the voluntary or forced withdrawal of western political control. In these states new political élites have come to power in many parts of the non-western world, and a pattern is emerging which allows some preliminary classifications of the new ruling groups.

I

Non-western societies can broadly be divided into two categories, those that have so far remained outside the orbit of westernization or have, at best, barely or only superficially embarked upon it; and those that travelled along the road of westernization to a more or less marked and significant degree. The first group is fairly rapidly dwindling; its hallmarks are a continuation of the old socio-political moulds and *mores,* with political authority continuing to be vested in traditional élite groups. Some Arab sheikdoms, including (for the time being—at least) Saudi Arabia, and the tribal societies in many parts of Negro Africa are the prototypes of this group.

Within the other category, that of westernizing non-western countries, two main types can be discerned. There are, first, those countries in which westernization—to whatever degree it has been or is being achieved—has actually been accomplished by traditional ruling classes, so that the revolutionary changes that have taken place in the process of adaptation have left the pre-revolutionary power pattern more or less intact. One of the outstanding examples of this type was, of course, nineteenth century

Japan, which achieved the fullest degree of westernization attained anywhere in the non-western world through the guidance of the *samurai*,
a military-feudal class that adapted itself, and directed the adaptation of
the rest of the country, to a modern economic and political order without
abdicating its intrinsic control, even though in time it came to share
power with other classes, notably a new economic middle class.[1]

Other examples of this type can be found in more and more isolated
instances in the Middle East, as *e. g.* Iran and (until recently) also Iraq.
But the most numerous instances occur in the areas of the erstwhile
Spanish and Portuguese empires in Latin America and Asia (mainly the
Philippines). Spanish and Portuguese colonialism, an overseas extension
of a feudal, pre-industrial west, through Christianization and cultural
assimilation, called into existence a distinct social pattern whose main
beneficiary was a class of either Spanish or *mestizo* landowners. It was
they who either won independence from the mother countries (as in
Latin America), or who at any rate gained social and economic prominence
(as the *cacique* in the Philippines), where they only assumed political
control under American aegis, after Spain had forfeited political control.
By origin and education westernized, they naturally proceeded to lead in
the further—but, compared to Japan, very slow—process of modernization
while retaining political power in most parts of the former Spanish and
Portuguese realms. The Mexican revolution of 1910 marked the first
successful challenge to this socio-political *status quo*, to be followed by
incidental upheavals in other parts of the area, notably Uruguay, Peru,
and quite recently, in Cuba. As yet, however, the old pattern predom-
inates. The fact that military dictatorships are such a common political
institution in Latin America should not obscure the fact that in most
cases (including Juan Perón until 1945) these military *juntas* are an
offshoot of and tend to govern in the interest of, the traditional ruling
classes of *hacienderos*.

In contrast to this prototype, political power in the second category
is exercised by essentially new ruling groups. These new élites are the
products of revolutionary changes of more profound significance, of social
as well as of political revolutions. This second category consists of western-trained intellectuals and military leaders; for reasons which will presently be discussed, they can be subsumed under the more general, generic
term of "intelligentsia." It is with these élites that the present paper is
primarily concerned.

---

1. In spite of the fact that the Meiji Restoration of 1868 marked a
break with the preceding political order, in terms of élite structure it
signified a change within the *samurai* class rather than a social revolution.

What distinguishes such non-western intelligentsias from most intellectuals in western societies is that they wield political power as it were independently, *i.e.*, they wield it in their own right, *as* intelligentsias, rather than as spokesmen for entrenched social forces. In other words, these intelligentsias are a *ruling class,* or rather *the* ruling class *par excellence,* whereas elsewhere intellectuals do not as a rule constitute a socio-political class of their own so much as an adjunct to other classes or groups in society. Representatives of this group can be easily identified throughout the non-western world. Among intellectuals as rulers are men like Nehru, Bourguiba, Kwame Nkrumah in Ghana and Francisco Madero in Mexico; among the "military intelligentsia" men like Nasser, al-Kassem in Iraq, Ne Win in Burma and also Argentina's Perón in his later years. In several non-western areas there has, moreover, been a tendency—recently demonstrated in Pakistan, Burma, and the Sudan—for the military to take over from civilian leaders within this intelligentsia.

A third category should, perhaps, be added to this list, *viz.* the communist élites in the Soviet Union, China and other non-western countries. To some extent they, in fact, historically fall within the categories listed above, for Lenin and several, if not most, of the early bolshevik leaders belonged to the intellectual prototype. While in the Soviet Union intellectuals as wielders of political power are now an anachronism,[2] the Chinese communist élite and its Asian variants (North Korea and North Viet Nam) are still largely recruited from among the intelligentsia of the early twentieth century; but the Chinese élite (as, for that matter, that of Yugoslavia) is, even by early Soviet standards, a unique intelligentsia in that it combines within itself "ideological" with "military" qualities that, among non-communist élites, tend to be divided into two, often competing, branches of the new non-western ruling classes. In this essay, communist élites will only receive peripheral consideration.

2

To avoid confusion, we should distinguish between two kinds of non-western intellectuals, *viz.* the "old" and the "new" intellectual. The first bears a distinct resemblance to the intellectual of the pre-industrial west, especially—though neither invariably nor exclusively—to the "sacral" intellectual of mediaeval times.[3] For purposes of our present analysis, this group is of relatively minor importance, since it does not furnish the new

---

2. See for example "L," "The Soviet Intelligentsia," *Foreign Affairs,* vol. 36, 1957, pp. 122–30.

3. On "sacral" and "secular" intellectuals see Edward Shils, "The Intellectuals and the Powers: Some Perspectives for Comparative Analysis," *Comparative Studies in Society and History,* vol. 1, 1958–9, pp. 5–22.

political élites of contemporary non-western nation states. This is not to deny that it has played, and in some significant ways continues to play, important political roles. But for one thing, the "old" intellectuals' role, like that of their western counterparts, has almost invariably been limited to an ancillary function, a political task delegated to them, so to speak, by more or less powerful classes in their societies. Not infrequently these intellectuals (in west and non-west) were actually members of the ruling classes themselves and did not exercise independent political power *qua* intellectuals (priests, scholars, etc.) as such.[4] Admittedly there were at all times also members of this "old" intelligentsia—such as Buddhist monks and Muslim *ulama*—who here and there allied themselves with the "outs" rather than the "ins," and who thus attained political significance by resisting the indigenous *staus quo* and, in modern times, western colonialism. On the whole, however, the "old" intellectuals of the non-western world have suffered, and are suffering, a decline in their prestige, great as it may still be in areas hitherto untouched by modernization, especially the countryside, where the "new" intelligentsia's influence is only slowly penetrating.[5]

These "new" intellectuals are a recent phenomenon, for they are for the greater part the product of western education during the past few decades. But though western-trained and therefore in several respects kin of their western counterparts, they also differ from the western intellectuals in some very significant respects. In the first place it is not literacy *per se* but westernization that stamps the non-westerner as the "new" intellectual. To the traditional tasks of manipulating the tools of communication have now been added the tasks of what Toynbee has aptly called the "human transformer." He, so Toynbee says, has "learned the tricks of the intrusive civilization . . . so far as may be necessary to enable their own community, through [his] agency, just to hold its own in a social environment in which life is ceasing to be lived in accordance with the local tradition."[6] Since, then, the criteria of westernization and "trans-

---

4. This is basically true also of the Chinese scholar-gentry, in spite of the fact that entry into that élite group was—in theory and partly also in practice—open to all. To some extent, the scholar-gentry, by representing the state cult of Confucianism, also fulfilled some of the functions of the sacral intellectual, in competition with the Buddhist priesthood.

5. For a fuller discussion, see the present writer's essay, "Revolution and Nationalism in the Non-Western World," in Warren S. Hunsberger (ed.), *New Era in the Non-Western World*, Ithaca, New York, Cornell University Press, 1957, pp. 17–51.

6. Arnold J. Toynbee, *A Study of History*, Abridgement of Volumes I–VI by D. C. Somervell, New York, 1947, p. 394.

forming" are their hallmarks, non-western intelligentsias will tend to include wider categories than has been the case of western intelligentsias.
Westernization—thinking and acting in western, rather than traditionally
indigenous ways—can extend to types of social activity that in the west
have not, as a rule, formed part of intellectual activity as such.

The most common, and historically also most significant, representative
of this category is the new military group, the "Young Turks" so to speak,
of the non-western world.[7] Nor is this at all surprising, since one of the
prime contacts between west and non-west during the past century-and-
a-half has been military in nature. As a result, the desire to attain equality
with the west has often found expression in terms of military equality,
and officers were often the first social group to receive western training.
Thus very frequently military westernizers, or westernized officers, have
played a leading—at times a preponderant—role as independent political
leaders in non-western countries. What distinguishes them as prototypes
from traditional military rulers or dictators is, first, the fact that they are
consciously using the means of coercive, military power for the attainment of essentially non-military, ideologically conceived social ends. And,
second, unlike *e.g.* the military *juntas* of Latin America, the twentieth
century military leaders in Asia and the Middle East are almost invariably
social revolutionaries whose coming to power signals the end of the
*status quo* and the eclipse of the traditional ruling classes. In some isolated
instances of the twentieth century, non-western military leaders can be
found who combine these ideological ends with the qualities of charismatic leadership. The Peróns, the Nassers, and the Castros are thus yet
another phenomenon of the "new" non-western intelligentsia.

Second, to a degree unparalleled in the west, non-western intellectuals are very frequently an isolated social group in indigenous society.
This is largely due to the fact that this "new" intelligentsia is not, as in
the west, a product of organic social growth, but rather a product of alien
education more or less precariously grafted on indigenous non-western
societies.[8] Unlike the "old," predominantly sacral, intellectuals most of
whom represented or spoke for the powers-that-were, and who thus performed the ancillary political roles usually assigned to intellectuals
throughout the world, non-western intelligentsias do not, sociologically
speaking, as a rule represent anyone but themselves. It is the exception
rather than the rule that the young aristocrat, the landowner's son or for

---

7. Toynbee, *ibid.*, p. 395, specifically includes the military leaders in
the category of the intelligentsia.

8. *cf.* E. Shils, "The Culture of the Indian Intellectual," *Sewanee Review,* 1959, pp. 3–46. Shils seeks to minimize the extent of the Indian
intellectuals' "alienation."

that matter even the scion of a newly-established bourgeois class, once he has acquired a western education of any kind, becomes the defender and spokesman of the class of his social origin. In turn, it is equally the exception rather than the rule that these "new" intellectuals will be supported by traditional social classes with a vested socio-economic interest in non-western societies.

In short, non-western intelligentsias, insofar as they are politically active—and, as will be seen, most of them are so to a far higher degree than in the west—tend to be social revolutionaries whose ideological aims as often as not militate against the *status quo*. Since, by definition, most of these aims are western-derived and transplanted to a social environment inherently still far more conservative than is true of the more advanced industrial societies of the west, the task of social engineering becomes far more radical, and its proponents, the only group with a vested ideological interest in change, may find themselves driven to the use of radical reforms in order to hasten the approximation between reality and ideal.

There is, third, an additional reason for the relatively high incidence of radicalism among non-western intelligentsias, and it is connected both with their numbers and employability. As for size, it is on the whole relatively smaller than in industrialized western societies, for the number of persons able to afford western education, at home but particularly abroad, is more limited, and democratization of education has—with the exception of Japan—not yet paralleled that in the west. Yet, in spite of the smallness of non-western intelligentsias, the supply by far exceeds social demand. This unhappy phenomenon of the overproduction and underemployment of intellectuals is in part doubtless conditioned by the social, psychological and ideological traditions of most non-western societies.

Since education, in these predominantly pre-industrial communities, still enjoys great traditional prestige, western education has automatically attracted large numbers of non-westerners; but in spite of the fact that the process of modernization and industrialization would indicate the need for technical, vocational and scientific training, the aristocratic or gentry bias common to pre-industrial societies has, in fact, led non-western students to bypass these fields in favour of humanistic and legal studies. Thus, while a crying shortage exists almost everywhere in Asia, the Middle East, Africa and even Latin America for physicians, engineers and scientists, the bulk of non-western intellectuals can be found in the humanities and the law, both of which appear to promise status satisfaction in traditional terms. In fact, it is predominantly graduates in these fields that compose the present-day political élites of so many non-western states.

The absorptive capacity for this kind of intellectual is, however, severely limited in non-western societies. As a result, intellectual unemployment—a phenomenon by no means unknown in some western countries —has social and political consequences of great importance, for non-western intelligentsias are by and large politicized to a degree unknown in the west. Particularly in areas recently freed from western colonial control, where national liberation has invariably led to a rapid expansion of western-style education, the steady growth of a largely unemployable "intellectual proletariat" presents a very real political threat to stability and social peace.[9] There, the "new" intellectual-rulers are thus, paradoxically enough, threatened by their own kind.

Finally, there is a fourth factor of great importance, that of ideological causation. In opposing the *status quo* of traditional non-western societies, most of the "new" intellectuals also tend to oppose the *status quo* of a world which either directly or indirectly can be held responsible for the internal social and political conditions that form the prime target of the intelligentsia's attack. Thus "feudalism" as well as colonialism—rule by entrenched native classes or rule by foreigners—can be blamed on the political, military and economic preponderance of the western world. It is, therefore, not surprising that socialist and communist teachings have found far more fertile soil among non-western intellectuals than among their western counterparts. If it is symptomatic that the first statues ever erected for Marx and Engels stand on Russian soil, it would be equally fitting to find statues, say of Harold Laski gracing the main squares of New Delhi, Colombo, Rangoon, Accra, and even Baghdad.

Indeed, it is not too surprising that modern socialism has so profoundly attracted intellectuals all over the world. In the most highly industrialized countries of the west, it is, in fact, among intellectuals, rather than among the proletariat itself, that this social philosophy has found its most numerous adherents. This is very likely due to the fact that socialism, especially Marxism, is the most recent, and perhaps also the most coherent and intellectually most respectable version of the philosopher king, the social engineer ruling in the interest of abstract social justice *par excellence*. An intelligentsia thus not only has a vested intellectual interest in socialism, it also has a vested social and political interest in it. In spite of the Marxian theory of the class struggle as the major social determinant of history, in spite even of the quasi-humility at times exhibited by Marx and his later followers in terms of their willingness to be "guided by," and "learn from," the proletariat, programmatic, "scientific" socialism has always, as Lenin himself bluntly stated, been the product of a bourgeois

9. *cf.* Justus M. van de Kroef, "The Educated Unemployed in Southeast Asia," *Journal of Higher Education,* vol. XXXI, 1960, pp. 177–184.

intelligentsia.[10] It is the "vanguard" of the proletariat, not the proletariat itself, that is cast for the crucial role of governing, and for quite obvious reasons: in proclaiming the rule of social justice, the socialist intellectual is proclaiming rule by his own kind.

But whereas in the west the Marxist intellectual's political aspirations have as a rule encountered great difficulties, at least in working class movements dominated by, or at least highly dependent upon, union leaders,[11] the non-western socialist intellectual can in the absence of a sizeable proletariat (as well as of other organized socio-economic forces) actually become ruler in his own right. Socialism, in addition to providing the desired combination of anti-western—*i.e.*, anti-capitalist—westerniza-tion also provides the non-western intellectual with a justification for rule by the intelligentsia. In embracing it, he feels *ipso facto* justified in looking askance at political competition from other segments of society, such as "old" intellectuals, aristocracies, and landowners, but also nascent capitalistic middle classes.[12] Planning in the name of socialism means planning with the intelligentsia as planners, irrespective of whether they be the military intellectuals of Nasser's stamp or the "pure" intellectuals of the Nehru variety.

10. The fact that the intelligentsia is the actual ruling group in the early stages of communism has never been admitted in Marxist analysis. For a recent re-statement, *cf.* Oscar Lange, *Some Problems Relating to the Polish Road to Socialism,* Warsaw, 1957, p. 28: "Wherein lies the specific character of the intelligentsia? In the fact that it is not really a class. Its position comes from the superstructure and not from production rela-tions. . . . Its very essence prevents it from being an independent force; it can only express the opinions and wishes of the working class. . . . It can help, but it is not the social force which by itself can bring about social change. . . ."

11. Lenin encountered such opposition and crushed it after the Kron-stadt revolt, thereby subjugating the workers to the control of the party intelligensia. By contrast, Harold Laski was never able to play a truly decisive role in the British Labour Party.

12. *cf.* the following comment connected with the governing intellectual élite group in Indonesia: "Speaking to the Constituent Assembly on No-vember 10, 1956 [Sukarno] expressed his fears at the recent emergence of a great many prospective Indonesian capitalists. . . . [He] believed that the development on the Indian model would mean, as Sukarno sees it, permit-ting the growth of a group of capitalists; in other words the *oligarchy of the educated* who now control the society would have to share power with a private entrepreneurial group . . . with different interests. To have eco-nomic development on either the Russian or the Chinese model would obviate the need to surrender power." (Italics added.) Leslie H. Palmier, "Sukarno, the Nationalist," *Pacific Affairs,* vol. 30, 1957, pp. 117–18.

3

Up to this point we have drawn no distinction between the military and the civilian, or "pure," intellectual, yet this distinction is of great analytic significance. It is by no means a matter of historic accident whether a non-western country, insofar as it has become westernized and undergone change, is ruled by either one or the other prototype. The existence of a military group of young officers in itself depends on the political status of a country; it depends, that is to say, on the fact of political (though not necessarily economic) independence. It is, therefore, only in non-colonial countries that westernization has been primarily channelled through military leaders. Kemal Ataturk, Yüan Shih-k'ai and the Satsuma and Choshu *samurai* are good examples, as are the many military régimes in Latin America and the newly emerging élite groups in the Middle East.

Wherever, then, the impact of the west did not lead to outright political domination, wherever a non-western society was given a chance of adjusting to the demands of the modern era by internal adaptation without suffering direct political control from the outside, there the officer has almost invariably emerged as the modern political non-western leader. Since he as a rule possesses a monopoly of physical power, he can fairly easily grasp control in a society where he represents the most powerful—even if numerically weak—social group with a vested interest in modernization and change.[13]

Westernization as well as the *status quo* prevailing in these countries, have, as we said, combined to stamp many, if not most of these younger military leaders with an ideological orientation not usually found among the professional soldiers in the west, or for that matter among the older generation of officers in independent non-western states. While this orientation is at times fairly close to the socialism so prevalent among non-western intelligentsias in general, while as a rule little love is lost between them and either the aristocracies, clergies or the nascent capitalist classes in their lands, their political goals tend to centre around the creation of strong, "socially just" régimes rather than around the creation of parliamentary régimes. In their distrust of the professional politician, including the "civilian" intelligentsia, non-western military leaders like the Japanese *samurai* of the nineteenth century and Colonel Nasser of today bear a recognizable similarity to the military prototype of modern societies in the west. Under a military régime "pure" intellectuals play a

13. See *e.g.* Dankwart A. Rustow, *Politics and Westernization in the Near East*, Princeton, N.J., 1956, pp. 26–33.

subordinate role as political leaders, if indeed they are at all tolerated by their military colleagues. In some of the contemporary non-western military dictatorships the intellectual as an independent political actor is politically as ineffectual as he was in, say, Meiji Japan. He has the choice between playing auxiliary to the new powers-that-be and being doomed to political impotence.

If the military intelligentsia has emerged as the most universal revolutionary phenomenon in the non-colonial countries of the non-western world, the "pure" intellectual has made his appearance as political ruler in many areas recently freed from western colonialism. This is an interesting phenomenon, for, unlike the military, the "pure" intellectual does not *a priori* command the means of physical coercion that have, throughout history, made military power so significant a factor. It is, indeed, a phenomenon rooted in modern western colonialism itself. The absence of an indigenous military élite proper is one of the most significant sociological aspects of colonialism of all times. Since military power rests with the alien ruling class, this occupation is closed to the indigenous population.[14] Nineteenth century colonialism had other stultifying effects on social growth as well, particularly in preventing or retarding the development of a sizable bourgeoisie within the populations of many areas. This is particularly true of the plural societies of South-East Asia and parts of Africa, in which the introduction of capitalist economies has tended to benefit foreign rather than indigenous entrepreneurs.

It is this stunted social growth that turned the western-trained intellectuals—the doctors, the lawyers, the engineers, the professors and the students—into the only sizable group with a vested interest in political change. Unlike their military counterparts in non-colonial areas, however, the intellectuals of colonial Asia and Africa remained politically impotent as long as colonialism lasted, *i.e.*, they had no instruments for physically seizing power, and had to content themselves with the weapons of ideological warfare, political organization and nationalist protest within the limits set by their alien overlords. As the westernized leaders of nationalism and anti-colonialism, these non-western intelligentsias formed a numerically very small, and in most cases also very weak, élite group. In some few areas, like British India, where indigenous entrepreneurs had gained a measure of economic strength, they have supported the intel-

---

14. This does not mean that the western colonial powers did not recruit soldiers among the native population. But, for one thing, colonial armies were almost invariably officered by westerners, and, for another, in many instances the soldiers were purposely recruited from among ethnic and/or religious minority groups in the colony.

ligentsia in order to bolster their position *vis-à-vis* foreign competition. In most cases, however, the nationalist leadership did not have such support at its disposal. Smarting under the constant vigilance of colonial masters, it was vociferous rather than politically entrenched. It is doubtless true that these intellectuals—as westernized intelligentsias throughout the non-western world—have sought identification with the rural mass of the population and the "nation" at large, but this identification rests, as we will presently discuss, on slender roots. Partly this is due to the very westernization of these urban élite groups and partly to the fact that in virtually all colonies access to the peasantry was rendered extremely difficult, if not impossible, by the colonial authorities. Only in British India again did the urban intelligentsia—largely through Gandhi—succeed in forging a link with the peasantry.

Thus, whereas military leaders were able to grasp political control in non-colonial areas whenever the opportunity arose from the internal power constellation—as *e.g.* in China after 1911, in Japan after 1867, in Turkey in 1918, in Thailand in 1931, etc.—the "pure" intellectuals had to wait for external liberation from colonial rule to step in to the political arena as actual rulers in their own right. It is not coincidental that the Japanese occupation of South-East Asia performed this act of liberation for the intellectuals of Burma and Indonesia,[15] and that the train of post-war liquidations of colonial possessions has paved the way for the intelligentsia elsewhere, as in India, Ghana, Tunisia and to some extent also in Malaya. In the social and political vacuum created by modern colonialism, the western-trained intellectual was, at the crucial hour, the only politically and ideologically trained élite group on whom political power could devolve.

But if there is historic logic in the emergence of "civilian" intellectuals as rulers in post-colonial non-western areas today, continuation of this fairly unique phenomenon is fairly problematical. The demise of colonialism it-

---

15. In Thailand (a non-colonial country) and the Philippines (where Spanish rule had created a quasi-feudal social system), the Japanese did not vitally affect the pre-war socio-political structure. In the former country the military oligarchy retained power, in the latter the landowning class. Only among the anti-Japanese Filipino underground did potential new leaders, like Ramon Magsaysay and Huk leader Luis Taruc, come to the fore. Magsaysay's presidency in the 1950s constituted the first major breach in the Philippine political scene, in that it temporarily brought to power an intelligentsia, partly military in character, and based on widespread peasant support centred on the charismatic leadership of the president. Since Magsaysay's sudden death, the pre-war *status quo* seems to have been more or less restored.

self has brought with it the breaking down of the artificial barriers to social growth that were, as we said, one of its most significant sociological aspects. In the newly independent countries of Asia and Africa the "pure" intellectual is now free to search for non-intellectual avenues to social status and prestige, and some of them—Aung San of Burma is an excellent example—have rapidly turned towards a military career. In this sense, colonial countries are socially "coming of age," and are demonstrating the adaptability of non-western intelligentsias to new social conditions, an adaptability previously exhibited by Leon Trotsky and some members of the Chinese communist intelligentsia in a non-colonial setting.

Second, quite apart from this incidental transformation of individual "pure" intellectuals, independence, and in particular the revolutionary struggle against colonialism—in South-East Asia, conscious Japanese policies[16]—has given rise to a distinct group of military leaders, who socially, educationally and often also ideologically stand apart from the western-trained academic intellectuals of the colonial era. Having played a significant role in the liberation of their countries and having gained access to military power, they have also created a political following, both among their subordinates and, quite often, among the public at large. The military, in short, have become a competing élite which has increasingly come to challenge the "civilian" intelligentsia's monopoly of political power in formerly colonial non-western countries.

As the struggle between Sun Yat-sen and Yüan Shih-k'ai symbolically showed, the contest between "pure" intellectuals and military leaders is, because of the latter's physical superiority, fraught with grave dangers to the civilian leadership. But the new military élites, it must be remembered, are for the greater part not simply war lords or "strong men" only. To a large extent, they, too, make ideological appeals—if nothing else, appealing for national unity in the face of disunited civilian leadership—that render them truly formidable political opponents.[17] In recent times,

---

16. For Indonesia, see the present writer's *The Crescent and the Rising Sun; Indonesian Islam during the Japanese Occupation,* 1942–1945, The Hague/Bandung/New York, 1958, pp. 138–41, 172–3, 203.

17. As we said earlier, it is so far only among Asian communist élites that a more or less complete merger has apparently been affected between "pure" and military intelligentsias. It was, in fact, Russian advice and aid that had helped to produce a similar merger within the Kuomintang leadership in the 1920s. In the measure that the Kuomintang in later years de-emphasized ideology and political organization it dug, so to speak, its own political grave by yielding supremacy to the Chinese communists who excelled in combining military striking power with organizational and ideological strength.

military leaders have taken over from civilian intelligentsias in the Sudan, in Burma and in Pakistan,[18] while in Indonesia army leaders appear to be gaining increasing political influence.[19]

The apparent ease with which civilian régimes are being replaced by military ones points to the inherent weakness and instability of rule by "pure" intellectuals. The causes of these are not far to seek. In the first place, the "pure" intellectual, however well versed he may have been in the politics of opposition to colonialism, very rarely possesses actual administrative experience that could make him an effective and efficient statesman. Second, the democratic or parliamentary institutions imported by western-trained intellectuals are as a rule operating in a social and political vacuum, with no organizational framework connecting the new edifice at the centre with the country at large. It is true that many non-western intellectuals are stressing the intrinsically democratic nature of traditional village government in their countries; but it may be doubted whether this "village democracy"—whatever its merits—can serve the purpose of providing an adequate underpinning for a modern, viable constitutional state.

Finally, the political parties functioning under most non-western parliamentary systems do not as a rule represent organized social forces so much as factions centred around personalities. The temporary unity exhibited before the attainment of independence thus tends to wane once nationhood has been achieved, and to give way to fierce factional struggles.[20] It is these struggles, accompanied by lack of central purpose and achievement, that leave the intellectual in a precarious position, and thus render the appeal of the military so forceful.

The substitution of a military for a civilian régime does not necessarily involve more than a change within the intelligentsia, and thus a structural change in the façade of government. The short-cut solution of the military *coup* does no more than eradicate the often anaemic institutional forms of a western-style political system; it does not substitute more viable forms in their stead. If the "pure" intellectuals encounter almost insuperable obstacles in realizing their goals, the military

18. Burma and Pakistan are not, strictly speaking, identical cases. The civilian régime displaced in Pakistan was not a régime of intellectuals so much as of landowners. Schematically, Pakistan's case is thus comparable to that of Iraq rather than that of Burma.

19. *cf.* Guy J. Pauker, "The Role of Political Organizations in Indonesia," *Far Eastern Survey*, vol. 27, 1958, pp. 141–2.

20. *cf.* Richard L. Park, "Problems of Political Development," in Philip W. Thayer (ed.), *Nationalism and Prospects in Free Asia*, Baltimore, Md., 1956, pp. 103–104, and Vera M. Dean and others, *The Nature of the Non-Western World*, New York, 1958, pp. 212–13.

leadership, moving into the *terra incognita* of politics, may find it at least equally difficult to translate their long-term aspirations into reality.

If the difficulties besetting non-western intelligentsias as ruling classes of both types appear formidable, they are in many areas partly offset, or at least obscured, by the "countervailing" power of *charisma* embodied in individual members of both the civilian and the military, such as Nehru, Nasser, Nkrumah, Sukarno and Castro, to mention but a few outstanding examples.[21] The simultaneous appearance of charismatic leadership in Asia, Africa, the Middle East and Latin America is perhaps one of the most important phenomena accompanying the political readjustments in the contemporary non-western world.[22] It is the charismatic leader who by force of sheer personality can apparently bridge the gap between the westernized élites and the rural population, and who can serve as the symbolic link between the ruler and the ruled.

It is a moot point whether the presence of such leadership alone can suffice to guarantee a measure of political stability or to extract the cooperation required to set sustained modernization and economic improvement in motion. It is similarly a moot point whether an intelligentsia, bereft of its charismatic leader, will produce adequate cohesion to continue in power.[23] At any rate, there can be little doubt that the charismatic leader is already a deviant from the standard pattern of the western-educated intelligentsia, whether civilian or military: insofar as the charismatic appeal is politically important in the non-western world it is so not because of these leaders' western training and ideological orientation, but perhaps in spite of them. In the eyes of the general population, the charismatic leader may well be *malgré lui,* the reincarnation of the "old," sacral intellectual rather than the modernizer and westernizer he claims to be.

### 4

An intelligentsia ruling in its own right as a ruling class or group is, strictly speaking, not necessarily a specific non-western phenomenon only.

---

21. On charismatic leadership see also George McT. Kahin, Guy J. Pauker, and Lucian W. Pye, "Comparative Politics in Non-Western Countries," *American Political Science Review,* vol. 49, 1955, p. 1025, and Gabriel L. Almond, "Comparative Political Systems," *Journal of Politics,* vol. 18, 1956, p. 401.

22. Charismatic leadership is, nonetheless, not a *sine qua non* of political modernization as witness its absence in Meiji Japan, republican China and in communist countries. Stalin's "cult of the individual" or Mao's all-pervading presence are by no means synonymous with *charisma.*

23. The assassination of Aung San in Burma was followed by gradual dissolution of the party headed by him, until the civilian intelligentsia surrendered power voluntarily to the military.

In the course of western history, there have been brief episodes when intellectuals—sacral, secular and military—have performed similar functions, as for example Calvin, Cromwell, the Jacobins, or the Puritan founders of Massachusetts. This random list indicates that rule by intelligentsias has almost invariably been the hallmark of revolutionary eras in the west. It may thus be suggested that the differences between western and non-western history—leaving aside the specific characteristics of the new non-western élites discussed in the preceding pages—are quantitative rather than qualitative. In other words, since the non-western social and political revolution of the twentieth century is a virtually global phenomenon following the wake of historically well-nigh simultaneous dissolutions of traditional social moulds, what in the west have been chronologically and geographically disparate, local and sporadic incidents, have now assumed the proportions of a world-wide socio-political phenomenon. If, then, western history is to serve as a measuring rod, it could be further argued that rule by contemporary intelligentsias in parts of Asia, Africa, the Middle East and Latin America may represent an interim stage in the political evolution of the non-western world, and that sooner or later it will be superseded by other élites and new forms of political organization.

Suggestive as such a hypothesis may be, it needs to be qualified. The brevity of revolutionary régimes led by intellectuals in western history was intimately connected with the presence of powerful social and economic classes bent on eliminating the "dictatorship of the intellectuals" imposed on their societies. These opponents may have belonged to entrenched social interests (as *e.g.* the Genevan bourgeoisie or the much-discussed English gentry of the 1640s), or more paradoxically, to groups born of, or vastly strengthened by, the very changes inaugurated by the intelligentsia (as *e.g.*, the French bourgeoisie or the *nouveaux riches* landowners and businessmen in Massachusetts). *Mutatis mutandis,* a very similar process led to the elimination of the original core of bolshevik intellectuals by a new generation of party bureaucrats and managers in the 1930s, a process anticipated by Trotsky, and later described by both Milovan Djilas and Arthur Koestler. In the west, intellectuals have only been able to rule in the intervals between the breakdown of an old social and political order and the establishment of a new one (or, as in the *terra nova* of Massachusetts, between the birth of a new order and its normalization, so to speak). Their régimes have usually been ended by "counter-revolutionary" movements instigated by social classes who, in the proper Marxian sense, have commanded wealth and power, as a rule based on control over important sectors of the economy, and who were thus able, sooner rather than later, to displace the intellectual as wielder of independent political power. This done, the intelligentsia invariably found itself reduced to its more "normal" and ancillary role in politics, *i.e.*, it reverted to the task of verbalizing or ideologizing the political interests of other classes or groups, either those in power or those opposing them.

It is not unlikely that intelligentsias represent a similar intermediate stage in the non-western political evolution. But it is probable that their displacement is not a matter of the immediate future, even though, as we have seen, there exists an apparently growing trend for power to devolve upon the military within these non-western intelligentsias. Members of older social groups, such as landowners[24] or sacral intellectuals —as *e.g.* the Muslim Brotherhood in Egypt, the Hindu Mahasabha in India, or the Darul Islam in Indonesia—though they may here and there exert significant political influence, seem as a rule to be lacking in strength or social dynamism to constitute a real threat to the new order. The urban bourgeoisie is numerically and often also economically too weak to challenge the new intelligentsia-rulers. And, finally, the revolutions are of too recent date to have laid the groundwork for the growth of other social groups able and willing to form a viable opposition, in terms of economic strength at least.

For quite some time to come, non-western intelligentsias may there-fore be expected to retain their virtual monopoly of political power. To a large extent this continuity seems to be assured by the fact that the national polities over which they rule are of recent date, and, indeed, of the intelligentsias' own making. Essentially, these are modern govern-mental edifices superimposed on societies which, as yet, do not nourish them by established channels of political communication. The political process in non-western societies is thus, to a far greater extent than is true of most western societies, a superstructure without viable under-pinning.[25] This state of affairs, for sure, cannot but be transitional. But as long as it lasts, intelligentsias are very likely to remain the prime politi-cal actors in many non-western countries. Political changes are likely to take place within these élites rather than to affect their predominance as ruling classes.*

---

24. Their political influence appears to be stronger in formerly Hispanic lands than elsewhere. Moreover, it is very likely that in Latin America they have been able to obtain aid from abroad, as witness the short-lived régime of Col. Arbenz in Guatemala.

25. See also the illuminating essay by Lucian L. Pye, "The Non-West-ern Political Process," *Journal of Politics*, vol. 20, 1958, pp. 469–86.

* A companion article by Harry J. Benda, "Intellectuals and Politics in Western History," appeared in the *Bucknell Review*, X, No. 1 (May 1961), 1–14.

*Alexander Eckstein*

# Individualism and the Role of the State in Economic Growth

ECONOMIC GROWTH can be viewed as a broadening of the range of alternatives open to society. Clearly, technological and resource constraints are likely to be so compelling and overriding in primitive or under-developed economies as to leave comparatively little scope for the exercise of choice—either individual or social. On the other hand the situation is quite different—at least in degree—at more advanced stages of economic development. At these stages, one of the principal manifestations of this broadening in the range of alternatives is precisely the greater opportunity to exercise choice over the form in which choices in the economy become institutionalized. This, in turn, requires a delineation of the spheres of public vs. private choice and a determination of the relative weight of each sphere.

One of the aspects of individualism, and possibly the one most relevant for our purposes, is the scope for individual choice and decentralized decision-making in the economic sphere. In a preponderantly free enter-prise market economy the institutionalization of these ingredients of individualism is more or less automatically assured. This does not, how-ever, mean that this system necessarily assures equal scope for the exercise of choice on the part of all individuals in the economic system, or that it provides a greater scope for individual choice than an alternative system might. In contrast to preponderantly free enterprise market systems, in economies in which the public sector looms quite large, the scope for individual choice and decision making may be more a function of the political rather than the economic system. Thus the mechanism through which economic policy is formulated and the role of the ballot box in economic policy formulation become major conditioning factors.

In essence, what this suggests is that there is a potentially positive correlation between individualism and economic development. The extent to which this potential is translated into reality will depend upon the role played by individual choice and initiative in resource allocation, regardless of whether the choices and decisions are in fact arrived at primarily within the confines of the economic or political process. With this context in mind, let us attempt to spell out some of the factors and variables that are likely to condition the role the state may be expected or forced to play in the process of economic growth and its impact upon the position of the individual.

In analyzing the role of the state in the process of economic growth, the following elements may be considered as essential:

1. *The hierarchy of objectives, goals, and ends of economic development:* This necessarily involves an examination of both the qualitative and quantitative aspects, that is, the character, range, and variety of the ends sought as well as the level to be attained. The interplay of these dimensions of content, range, and level will be one of the principal factors defining the ambitiousness of the particular economic development program. In respect to content, several broad categories of objectives or motivations may be cited, for instance, those revolving around nationalism and those related to a striving for rising standards of living. In a sense, these might be considered as ultimate ends which need to be, and are in fact, broken down into a series of derived and possibly more concrete goals. Thus, at the stage when these objectives are disaggregated and sorted out as to the ranges and levels involved, they inevitably tend to become competitive rather than complementary entities in the sense that under *ceteris paribus* assumptions, the wider the range, the lower will have to be the level, and *vice versa*.

2. *The time horizon in economic development:* This entails a definition of the rate at which the goals are to be attained. In a sense, it is but another aspect of the hierarchy of objectives, since rapid or leisurely growth may be an explicitly stated end in and of itself.

3. *The means available* for attaining—at the desired rate—the content, range, and level of ends explicitly or implicitly formulated. Here one would have to consider such variables as resources and factor endowments and the state of the arts prevailing in the particular economy.

4. *The structure and character of institutions: social, economic, and political:* This is possibly the most complex of all the categories listed here. The considerations most relevant for our purposes revolve around the rigidity of the institutional framework, its capacity to generate, absorb, and adapt itself to economic change and to the disruptive forces of industrialization. This would mean investigating factors such as the prevailing value system, class structure, social mobility, contractual and legal arrangements, degree and character of urbanization, land tenure system, degree of commercialization and monetization, character and

structure of state organization, structure of political power, etc. However, analysis of these variables is greatly complicated by virtue of the fact that some of them are rather intangible, while their particular chemical mix—that is, the nature of combinations and interaction between the different institutional factors—and the reaction produced may be quite unpredictable. In effect, it is much easier to provide *ex post facto* rationalizations or explanations as to why and in what ways certain types of institutional structure were more conducive to industrialization than others, than to assess *ex ante* the height and the tensile strength of institutional barriers and their resistance to economic development.

5. *The relative backwardness of the economy:* From an economic point of view, relative backwardness—and the emphasis should be on relative—involves certain advantages and disadvantages. The disadvantages lie principally in the field of foreign trade, while the so-called "advantages of backwardness" may be found in the realm of technology. Thus industrially advanced countries enjoy certain competitive advantages in world markets, and particularly in the markets of the underdeveloped areas themselves. This in and of itself can under certain conditions become a major handicap in the industrialization of backward countries. On the other hand, as Professor Gerschenkron has pointed out, one of the essential ingredients of relative backwardness is a gap in the levels of technology used and applied. Therefore the backward country can reap large potential gains by importing advanced technology from abroad and thus, in effect, make a technological leap from comparatively primitive to high advanced levels.

At this point another aspect of relative backwardness may be usefully introduced, namely the gap in material welfare or standards of living, and the gap in national power produced by differences in levels of industrialization. All three of these gaps—in consumption, technology, and power—could be viewed as different apects of a "demonstration effect" through which the gulf between a potential and actual state is forcefully brought home. Characteristically, it is in this shape that the pressure for industrialization of backward countries is manifested. Once the disequilibrating and innovating forces of modernization, industrialization, and urbanization have been introduced on an appreciable scale, one could say that, *ceteris paribus,* the greater the relative backwardness, the more acute will tend to be the "tension" arising from this chasm between the potential and the actual, and thus the greater will be the pressure for industrialization.

Given the five categories of elements and variables considered above, we are now in a position to state our hypothesis concerning the conditions under which the state will tend to play a greater or lesser role in the process of economic growth. On this basis then one could say that:

*a.* The greater the range of ends and the higher the level of attainment sought;

*b.* the shorter the time horizon within which the ends are to be attained, that is, the more rapid the rate of economic growth desired;

*c.* the more unfavorable the factor and resource endowments;

*d.* the greater the institutional barriers to economic change and industrialization; and

*e.* the more backward the economy in relative terms

the greater will tend to be the urge, push, and pressure for massive state intervention and initiative in the process of industrialization, and at the same time, the greater will be the need for such intervention if a breakthrough, rather than a breakdown, is to be attained.

Assuming that the state is compelled to make a major commitment on behalf of industrialization, what types of measures may the state be expected to adopt and what effect may these have upon the position of the individual, or more specifically, upon the individual choice and decentralized decision-making in the economic sphere? From this point of view, a sharp distinction needs to be made between the elements and the degree of state power applied in the process of economic growth.

In analyzing the qualitative aspects of state intervention affecting the economic sphere, one could perhaps distinguish between five categories of action: provision of social overhead, provision of economic overhead, application of direct and indirect levers and controls, government operation of enterprises extending beyond the overhead sectors, and central planning.

*Provision of social overhead* might entail maintenance of law and order in the society, provision and enforcement of legal and contractual obligations, supply of educational, health, and social welfare facilities, assumption of military and defense functions, etc. In effect, these are categories of action which to the extent that they are provided at all, are usually furnished by public rather than private agencies.

*Provision of economic overhead* may involve the institution of central banking and monetary and fiscal facilities, the development of a highway and railroad network and of other public utilities.

*Application of direct or indirect levers and controls* may be based on a wide variety of measures, such as introduction of tariffs, railroad rate discrimination, tax privileges and other types of subsidies, rationing of goods and of credit, price controls, etc.

*Government operation of enterprises* extending beyond the overhead sectors may range from management of some industries, or a few firms in different industries, to public ownership of all means of production.

*Central planning* may involve more or less total concentration of economic decision-making in the hands of a national planning board.

Admittedly, this fivefold classification is arbitrary, and the line of demarcation between the different categories is quite blurred. Yet, in terms of their effect upon the exercise of individual choice and initiative, they present qualitatively rather significant differences. Thus, most of the items in the first two categories belong to what, in industrializing societies at least are usually considered as the minimal and essential functions of a state. In contrast, centralized and comprehensive planning combined with total government operation of the economy may be regarded as maximum functions. One of the key questions that needs to be posed in this context is which one, or which combination, of categories will the state use to promote economic development? Whichever means it uses, how massively, to what degree, and with what intensity will it apply its power to the provision of these different categories? Moreover, how will particular kinds and degrees of state intervention affect factor supply, particularly the supply of capital and entrepreneurship?

It may turn out that the more massively and rapidly the state provides what can be considered its minimum functions, the less may be the pressure or the need for it to provide the maximum functions. Therefore, the reliance upon maxima may in effect be a function of past and current failure to provide the minima. In these terms, then, one could say that a necessary precondition for the broadening of opportunities for the exercise of individual choice, individual intitiative, and the growth of individual values in underdeveloped countries, launched on a development program, is a high degree and rapid application of state power for the supply of social and economic overhead, combined with partial controls and planning as circumstances may demand them.

Theoretically one could, of course, visualize a system in which amidst public ownership of the means of production, national planning, and resource allocation was—within wide limits—based upon the operation of free consumer choice and consumer autonomy. Realistically, however, it would be extremely difficult to build sufficient checks and balances into such a Lange-like model to prevent it from slipping into a totalitarian mold. On the other hand, this is much less true in the case of partial planning and partial government operation of enterprises, which in many situations is needed to reinforce the provision of social and economic overheads, if comprehensive government planning and management is to be avoided.

The failure of the state in the minimum fields tends to be more or less directly reflected in capital formation and the growth of entrepreneurship. Thus, in many traditional societies, accumulations of merchant and other forms of capital tend to be dissipated because of: (a) the absence of adequate and contractual arrangements to protect these holdings from the more or less arbitrary ravages of officialdom, and (b) the failure of the state to institute a social security system, so that old age assistance, poor relief, and similar functions must be privately assumed through the family and kinship system. At the same time, condition (a) tends to reinforce the economic risks of various types of business and industrial investments. Moreover, the same condition further encourages the flow of capital into land investment, which in an environment of acute population pressure and agrarian value orientation, represents one of the safest and most profitable forms of holding. However, from the standpoint of the economy, this is merely a transfer payment, ultimately representing a leakage of investment into consumption. In effect, then, this is a milieu in which the state—through sins of commission and omission—tends to undercut actual and potential sources of capital accumulation, while at the same time making its contribution to the narrowing of business opportunities. Under these conditions the scarcities of entrepreneurial and technical talent tend to be further intensified through the neglect of education facilities. Moreover, to the extent that some education is provided, its orientation is frequently inhospitable to the growth of scientific and technical knowledge.

Viewed in these terms, perhaps one of the most important contributions the pre-industrial European city made to the industrialization of the continent was that it provided a legally and more or less militarily protected haven for the accumulation and conservation of capital, and for its investment in fields that were eminently productive from a point of view of economic development.

Amidst such circumstances, the formidable barriers to modernization and industrialization are likely to be perpetuated, while economic, social, and political tensions mount under the impact of innovating influences ushered in—as a rule—through foreign contact. Unless some means are found for alleviating these tensions through a process of change and adaptation, the potentially explosive forces in society may be expected to burst forth, sweeping away the old order, capturing the state, and using it as a total and far-reaching instrument for mounting an industrial revolution.

On this basis, one could argue that if India, for instance, wishes to avoid a totalitarian path to industrialization, her current plans and efforts do not provide for enough, rather than for too much, state intervention.

Thus the large gap in the financial resources available for the implementation of the Second Five Year Plan may be a symptom of the inability and the reluctance of the Indian state to mobilize the means adequate for the implementation of the ends sought. But, even more fundamentally, perhaps, the inadequacy of the government efforts to spread adult education —both basic and technical education—rapidly, may be an important factor in inhibiting the attainment of certain economic objectives, while at the same time it serves to reinforce the great gulf between the small élite and the rural masses—a factor representing marked potential dangers in the political realm.

To sum up this phase of my argument, it may perhaps be useful to attempt to work with the concept of an "optimum level and pattern of state intervention" paralleling other optima—e.g., the optimum propensity to consume—incorporated in different types of economic and social science models. For our present purposes, this optimum would have to be defined in relation to two broad sets of objectives, i.e., striving for rising standards of living combined with an increase and/or preservation of the scope for the exercise of individual choice and initiative. The definition would also have to take account of the specific circumstances in each case, particularly in relation to the qualitative and quantitative aspects of state intervention. . . .

We have discussed thus far the role the state may need to play in the process of economic growth without any reference to the character of the state and its capacity to perform the tasks required of it. Historically, however, particularly in the underdeveloped countries, the state— and the social structure on which it was based—was one of the very agencies hampering economic development. The same conditions that create the need for massive state intervention, in one form or another, also tend to breed a type of state which is singularly unequipped to intervene effectively on behalf of economic development. That is, economic backwardness is usually associated with political and other forms of backwardness.

Thus in China, for instance, the state has played a passive to actively negative role *vis à vis* the economy. The very concept of economic change and economic dynamism was alien to such a society with the nexus between economic growth and national power and/or welfare only very dimly understood, if perceived at all. The function of the economy was a largely static one, being charged with the primary task of supporting the ruling elite. Therefore, the state assumed very few responsibilities in the economy, beyond assuring that it would provide a stable, continuing, and adequate source of revenue for the imperial household and the gentry-bureaucracy.

The continuing failure of the traditional Chinese state to respond to the challenge of modernization, the institutional rigidities permeating the traditional social structure, the incapacity and unwillingness of the ruling classes to come to terms with change, their inability to understand the character of the innovating influences and to follow a policy of enlightened self-interest, have all served to retard the process of industrialization for so long that cumulative tensions of such explosive proportions were generated that they could no longer be contained, while at the same time perhaps nothing short of such an explosive force could have broken the shackles of the old order and swept away the barriers to economic growth. The violent eruption of the Chinese economy into what seems to bear the earmarks of an industrial revolution under totalitarian control can thus be viewed as an illustration of a resort to maximum solutions in the face of repeated and continued failure of the old state to perform and furnish the minimal functions referred to in the preceding section.

This course of development contrasts sharply with that experienced in Japan, where the breakdown of the old order accelerated by innovating influences produced a realignment of elites. The new elite, which bore some continuity with the old, then set out very deliberately to use the state as an instrument for modernization and industrialization. In doing this, the state from the outset paid major attention to developing rapidly the social and economic overhead sectors and to providing a general framework within which all types of enterprises, private and public, large and small, would grow. The state in effect conceived its role as initiator and promoter of the development process, leaving much of the execution to private enterprise.

While this is not intended to suggest that the Japanese experience can necessarily be duplicated in other countries, and in different circumstances, it is worthwhile to note that the state was able to perform this kind of a role amidst conditions which *ex ante* would have seemed exceptionally unfavorable. Not only were factor and resource endowments poor—in many respects poorer, perhaps not only absolutely but relatively, than those of some major underdeveloped areas today—but institutional barriers were formidable too.

However, an analysis of the conditions under which the state would or would not be *capable* of performing the functions required of it would be beyond the scope of this paper. Rather, I have tried to confine myself more specifically to a spelling out of the conditions under which and the ways in which the state may be required to assume a large role in initiating and promoting economic development without jeopardizing the growth of opportunities for the exercise of individual choice and initiative in the economic sphere.

# Selected Bibliography

## Part One: The Economics of Development

### BOOKS

Higgins, Benjamin, *Economic Development*. New York, W. W. Norton & Co., 1959.

Hoselitz, Bert F., and others, *Theories of Economic Growth*. New York, The Free Press, 1963.

Lewis, W. A., *The Theory of Economic Growth*. Homewood, Illinois, Richard D. Irwin, Inc., 1955.

Hirschman, Albert O., *The Strategy of Economic Development*. New Haven, Yale University Press, 1958.

Kuznets, Simon, *Six Lectures on Economic Growth*. New York, The Free Press, 1959.

Nurkse, Ragnar, *Problems of Capital Formation in Underdeveloped Countries*. Oxford, Basil Blackwell and Mott, 1953.

Rostow, W. W., *The Stages of Economic Growth*. Cambridge, Cambridge University Press, 1960.

Staley, Eugene, *The Future of Underedeveloped Countries*. New York, Harper and Brothers, 1957.

### ARTICLES

Galenson, Walter, and Harvey Leibenstein, "Investment Criteria, Productivity, and Economic Development." *Quarterly Journal of Economics,* vol. LXIX, no. 3 (August 1955), pp. 343-370.

Harbison, Frederick, "Entrepreneurial Organization as a Factor In Economic Development." *Quarterly Journal of Economics,* vol. LXX, no. 3 (August 1956), pp. 364-379.

Myint, H., "An Interpretation of Economic Backwardness." *Oxford Economic Papers,* vol. VI, no. 2 (June 1954), pp. 132-163.

Owen, Wilfred, "Transportation and Economic Development." *American Economic Review, Papers and Proceedings,* vol. XLIX, no. 2. (May 1959), pp. 179-187.

Spengler, J. J., "Economic Factors in Economic Development." *American Economic Review, Papers and Proceedings,* vol. XLVII, no. 2. (May 1957), pp. 42-56.

## Part Two: The Social Order

### BOOKS

Hagen, Everett E., *On the Theory of Social Change.* Homewood, Illinois, Dorsey Press, 1962.

Hoselitz, Bert F., ed., *The Progress of Underdeveloped Areas.* Harris Foundation Lectures, Chicago, University of Chicago Press, 1952.

Lerner, Daniel, and Lucille W. Pevsner, *The Passing of Traditional Society.* New York, Free Press, 1958.

Lipset, S. M., and R. Bendix, *Class, Status and Power: A Reader in Social Stratification.* New York, Free Press, 1953.

Malinowski, Bronislaw, *The Dynamics of Culture Change.* New Haven, Yale University Press, 1945.

Mead, Margaret, ed., *Cultural Patterns and Technical Change.* Paris, UNESCO, 1953.

McClelland, David C., and others, *The Achievement Motive.* New York, Appleton-Century-Crofts, 1953.

Shannon, Lyle W., ed., *Underdeveloped Areas.* New York, Harper and Brothers, 1957.

### ARTICLES

Belshaw, C. S., "The Cultural Milieu of the Entrepreneur." *Explorations in Entrepreneurical History,* vol. VII, no. 3. (February 1955), pp. 146-163.

Brozen, Yale, "Social Implications of Technological Change." *Social Science Research Council Items,* vol. 3, No. 3, (September 1949), pp. 31-33.

Gerschenkron, Alexander, "Social Attitudes, Entrepreneurship, and Economic Development." *Explorations in Entrepreneurial History,* vol. VI, no. 1 (October 1953), pp. 1-19.

Hoyt, Elizabeth, "Want Development in Underdeveloped Areas." *Journal of Political Economy,* vol. LIX, no. 3. (June 1951), pp. 194-208.

Levy, Marion, "Contrasting Factors in the Modernization of China and Japan." *Economic Development and Cultural Change,* vol. 11, no. 3 (October 1953), pp. 161-197.

Tax, S., "Selective Culture Change." *American Economic Review, Papers and Proceedings,* vol. XLI, no. 2 (May, 1951), pp. 315-320.

## Part Three: The Politics of Development

BOOKS

Almond, Gabriel A., and James S. Coleman, eds., *The Politics of the Developing Areas*. Princeton, Princeton University Press, 1960.

Baran, Paul, *The Political Economy of Growth*. New York, Monthly Review Press, 1957.

Black, Eugene R., *The Diplomacy of Economic Development and Other Papers*. New York, Atheneum, 1963.

Kautsky, John H., ed., *Political Change in Underdeveloped Countries*. New York, John Wiley and Sons, 1962.

Millikan, Max F., and Donald L. M. Blackmer, eds., *The Emerging Nations*. Boston, Little, Brown, and Co., 1961.

Pepelasis, Adamantios, Mears, Leon, and Irma Adelman, *Economic Development, Analysis and Case Studies*. New York, Harper and Brothers, 1961.

ARTICLES

Aubrey, Henry G., "The Role of the State in Economic Development." *American Economic Review, Papers and Proceedings*, vol. XLI, no. 2 (May 1951), pp. 266-273.

Baster, J., "A Second Look at Point Four." *American Economic Review, Papers and Proceedings*, vol. XLI, no. 2 (May 1951), pp. 399-406.

Lipset, Seymour Martin, "Some Social Requisites of Democracy: Economic Development and Political Legitimacy." *American Political Science Review*, vol. LIII, no. 1 (March 1959) pp. 69-105.

Pye, Lucian W., "The Non-Western Political Process." *Journal of Politics*, vol. 20, no. 3, (August 1958), pp. 468-486.